May It Fill
Your Soul

May It Fill Your Soul

Experiencing Bulgarian Music

Timothy Rice

The University of Chicago Press
Chicago and London

The University of Chicago Press, Chicago 60637
The University of Chicago Press, Ltd., London
© 1994 by The University of Chicago
All rights reserved. Published 1994
Printed in the United States of America

09 08 07 06 05 04 03 02 01 00   2 3 4 5 6

ISBN: 0-226-71121-8 (cloth)
ISBN: 0-226-71122-6 (paper)

Library of Congress Cataloging-in-Publication Data

Rice, Timothy, 1945–
    May it fill your soul : experiencing Bulgarian music / Timothy
Rice.
        p.   cm. — (Chicago studies in ethnomusicology)
    Includes bibliographical references, discography, and index.
    ISBN 0-226-71121-8. ISBN 0-226-71122-6 (pbk.)
    1. Folk music — Bulgaria — History and criticism. 2. Folk songs.
Bulgarian — Bulgaria — History and criticism. 3. Folk dancing.
Bulgarian. I. Series.
ML3602.R5   1994
781.62′91811—dc20   93-34083
                                                     CIP
                                                      MN

This book is printed on acid-free paper.

For
ANN
who could write another book full of stories

Contents

Part Three: Living the Tradition

Part Four: Changing the Tradition

Part Five: Continuing the Tradition

Illustrations

Figures

Musical Examples

A gallery of photographs follows page 166

Musical Excerpts on the Compact Disc

25   Instrumental tune and song played and sung simultaneously during the wedding processional to the bride's house, solo gaida played by Kostadin Varimezov, sung by Todora Varimezova, recorded by Tim Rice in 1979 (p. 156)

26   *Zlata dobra devoiko* (Zlata, Virtuous Maiden), wedding song sung by Todora Varimezova, recorded by Tim Rice in 1979 (p. 156)

27   *Temna mŭgla napadnala* (A Dark Fog has Fallen), wedding song sung by Todora Varimezova, recorded by Tim Rice in 1979 (p. 157)

28   Men's wedding *rŭchenitsa,* solo gaida played by Kostadin Varimezov, recorded by Tim Rice in 1979 (p. 159)

29   Women's wedding *rŭchenitsa,* solo gaida played by Kostadin Varimezov, recorded by Tim Rice in 1979 (p. 160)

30   *Ishala mashala, momina male* (Praise the Girl's Mother), wedding song sung by Todora Varimezova, recorded by Tim Rice in 1979 (p. 161)

31   *Reche mamo da me zheni* (Mother Decided I should Marry), a choral arrangement by Filip Kutev, sung by the chorus of the Bulgarian National Ensemble of Folk Song and Dance under his direction (p. 177). Balkanton BHA 125. Used by permission

32   *Trite pŭti,* played by Kostadin Varimezov accompanied by the orchestra of folk instruments at Radio Sofia (pp. 180, 201). Balkanton BHA 11283. Used by permission

33   *Buenek,* played by Kostadin Varimezov accompanied by the orchestra of folk instruments at Radio Sofia (pp. 195, 201). Balkanton BHA 1268. Used by permission

34   Motivic variation in *Pravo horo,* solo gaida played by Kostadin Varimezov, recorded by Tim Rice in 1979 (p. 196)

35   Variants in a variety of meters, solo gaida played by Kostadin Varimezov, recorded by Tim Rice in 1979 (p. 199)

36   *Daichovo horo,* played by Strandzhanskata Grupa (p. 211). Balkanton BHA 10160. Used by permission

37   *Lyulka se lyulya* (A Swing Is Swinging), arranged by
        Kosta Kolev and sung by the chorus and orchestra
        of folk instruments at Radio Sofia under his direc-
        tion (p. 215). Balkanton BHA 10822. Used by per-
        mission

38   *Dzhinovsko hortse* and *Dzhinovsko horo,* solo gaida
        played by Kostadin Varimezov, recorded by Tim
        Rice in 1979 (p. 218)

39   Wedding band from the village of Bistritsa, Sofia dis-
        trict, recorded by Tim Rice in 1969 (p. 241)

40   *Ivailovsko horo,* Ibryam Hapazov with Radio Sofia or-
        chestra (p. 241). Balkanton BHA 11330. Used by
        permission

41   "Mladeshki Dance," a Turkish/Gypsy style piece per-
        formed by Ivo Papazov and his wedding band (p.
        243). Hannibal Records HNCD 1363. Used by per-
        mission

42   *Rŭchenitsa* by the wedding band Shumentsi, at the
        Stambolovo Festival, recorded by Tim Rice in
        1988 (p. 254)

43   *Sindzhirliiska rŭchenitsa,* solo *kaval* played by Stoyan
        Velichkov, accompanied by electronic instruments
        played and programmed by Dimitŭr Penev in a
        style called *folklorna diskoteka* (p. 258). Balkanton
        BHA 12320. Used by permission

44   *Rŭchenitsa v slozhni gami* (*Rŭchenitsa* in Complex
        Scales), solo gaida played by Dimitŭr Todorov, ac-
        companied by Jimmy Vasilev, tŭpan, recorded by
        Tim Rice in 1988 (p. 265)

45   *Pravoslavensko horo,* solo gaida played by Maria Stoya-
        nova with the wedding band, Kanarite (p. 270).
        Balkanton BHA 11880. Used by permission

46   *Provikna se zmei iz gora* (A Dragon Cried Out in the
        Forest), sung by Tsvetanka Varimezova, accompa-
        nied by the orchestra of folk instruments at Radio
        Sofia (p. 279). Balkanton 12180. Used by per-
        mission

47   *Trite pŭti,* solo gaida played by Ivan Varimezov, ac-
        companied by the orchestra of folk instruments at
        Radio Sofia (p. 280). Balkanton 12180. Used by
        permission

Note on Transliteration

The Bulgarian language belongs to the family of Slavic languages and is written with thirty letters in a Cyrillic alphabet. At least two transliteration systems are commonly employed. One, used by Slavic linguists, requires a large number of diacritical marks and some letters (for example, *c* and *j*) whose pronunciation is not intuitively obvious to English speakers. The other system, used by the Library of Congress, contains a number of infelicities, including a diacritical ligature for certain characters. Neither system is, in my opinion, entirely satisfactory for the general audience to which this book is addressed. As a consequence, I have devised my own system of transliteration that, although it may annoy some specialists, should make it easy for nonspecialists to read and pronounce Bulgarian words correctly. It requires only one letter with a diacritical, *ŭ* for the Bulgarian letter ъ, which is pronounced like the *u* in but and is distinguished from *u*, which is pronounced like the *u* in yule and corresponds to the Bulgarian letter y. One letter of the Bulgarian alphabet, й, the structural equivalent of the English letter *j* and pronounced like *y*, is not represented in my system but may be inferred anytime the letter *i* occurs next to another vowel: *ai* in *gaida*, for example, represents ай not аи, that is, гайда. Diphthongs in Bulgarian, written ьо, я, ю, are rendered *yo, ya,* and *yu,* respectively. Where a Bulgarian name occurs frequently in English, such as Maria and Bulgaria, I have written them as such rather than Mariya or Bŭlgariya. Vowels are always long, as in Italian, for example, and only two sounds are significantly different from English: the rolled *r* and *h,* an aspirated sound between the English *h* and the German *ch.*

а = a in *f*ather
б = b in *b*oy
в = v in *v*alley
г = g in *g*iven
д = d in *d*ance
е = e in *e*xtra
ж = zh as z in a*z*ure
з = z in *z*oo
и = i in mach*i*ne
й = i in gra*i*n
к = k in *k*it
л = l in *l*amp
м = m in *m*it
н = n in *n*ice
о = o in *o*rder

п = p in *p*ig
р = r, lightly rolled
с = s in *s*aint
т = t in *t*able
у = u in congr*u*ent
ф = f in *f*lute
х = h, aspirated more softly than German a*ch*
ц = ts in bi*ts*
ч = ch in *ch*ange
ш = sh in *sh*all
щ = sht in *sht*etl
ъ = ŭ, as u in b*u*t
ь = y in *y*odel
ю = yu in *yu*le
я = ya in *ya*cht

The consonant cluster дж is written *dzh* and pronounced like the *j* in judge and jazz.

Acknowledgments

Writing, filled as it is with long, solitary hours processing words with or without a word processor, often seems a lonely, isolated, and isolating process. In reality, it is, like making music, a richly social experience, and I am pleased to have the opportunity to thank those who have contributed to the social construction of this book. My enthusiasm to include them in the process, however, must be balanced by the necessity to absolve them of any responsibility for errors of fact and interpretation that remain despite their best efforts to prevent them.

In a book based on field research, pride of place goes to those in the "field" who agreed to spend precious time—and in many cases material and emotional resources as well—on an initially uninvited guest with strange concerns and priorities rather different from their own. Theirs was the ultimate act of trust. My principal informants, Kostadin Varimezov and Todora Varimezova, are almost too close merely to thank. Because of Kostadin's initial willingness to teach me and then to come to Canada for an academic year to live and to teach, our lives became interwoven in unusual and, for both of us I think, beneficial ways that transcended the making and studying of music. Their and their children's (Ivan's, Todor's, and Stanka's) open-hearted friendship was a balm that transformed field*work* into pleasure, formality into intimacy. Their extended family, mentioned frequently in the following pages, were endlessly hospitable and I thank them all, but let me single out Ivan Varimezov, Kostadin's brother's son, and his wife Tsvetanka, who opened their home to me on numerous occasions. Other musicians and music professionals were also helpful; while I can't name them all, I am particularly indebted to the help and hospitality of Maria Stoyanova, Encho Pashov, Dimitŭr Todorov, Georgi Doichev, Neno Ivanov, Stoyan Velichkov, Jimmy Vasilev, Kosta Kolev, Lili Tabakova, and Rumyana Tsintsarska.

Work in Bulgaria was also aided, indeed indispensably so, by the expertise, contacts, and willingness to help of local researchers at the Bulgarian Academy of Sciences (BAN). First among these was Nikolai Kaufman, Bulgaria's most prolific musicologist, who acted as my 'scientific leader-by-the-hand' [*nauchen rŭkovoditel*] during my dissertation research in 1972–73. He introduced me to Kostadin Varimezov and extended many courtesies to me during my trips to Bulgaria. Vergilii Atanasov, in charge of the Archive at BAN's Institute for Music when I worked there in the early 1970s, extended the hand of friendship, as he did to so many visiting foreigners, at a time when it was perhaps dangerous to do so. Over the years, he repaired my tape recorder, responded honestly to my ideas, entertained me, with the help of his wife Nadya, in his home, and provided many of the photographs for this book—a rare friend indeed. A number of other scholars took turns, as they say, 'answering' for me during my relatively short trips to Bulgaria in the late 1980s: Tsenka Iordanova, Lyuben Botusharov, Todor Todorov, and Veselinka Andreeva. Words alone hardly suffice to express my gratitude for their conversation, help, and hospitality, thankless tasks even with glasnost.

While fieldwork was an obviously social process, writing itself became social when friends, students, and colleagues agreed to read the manuscript at early stages and provided helpful criticism of the way ideas and topics were organized and expressed. Donna Buchanan read the entire manuscript and provided detailed comments and suggestions. Her fine 1991 dissertation helped me to flesh out a number of points in earlier drafts. Mark Levy, Ellen Koskoff, and Ted Levin read portions of an earlier draft. I am particularly grateful to Philip Bohlman, a co-editor of this series, who read an early draft, provided helpful comments, and expedited its submission to the Press, whose anonymous readers also made useful suggestions. Roger Savage, a colleague at UCLA and a specialist in the philosophy and aesthetics of music, aided my understanding of phenomenological hermeneutics at a crucial period in the project, and allowed me to participate in his fascinating seminar on interpretation. A number of UCLA graduate students wrote helpful critiques, especially Sonia Tamar Seeman, Paulette Gershen, Michael Frishkopf, and Ken Sachs. Sonia Seeman acted as my research assistant during the final phases of the project, completing innumerable tasks—her Timfo Info bulletins saved me many hours in the library—and providing indispensable critical assessments of at least two drafts. Wanda Bryant, another UCLA graduate student, entered into the computer many of the musical and textual transcriptions and translations that eventually found their way into this book.

Institutional support played an important role in the project, and I gratefully acknowledge a number of small grants from both IREX (International Research and Exchanges Board) and the Academic Senate of UCLA, the former providing for travel to and expenses in Bulgaria and the latter providing research assistance from graduate students at UCLA.

A number of institutions and individuals gave permission to use their recordings and photographs. Kostadin and Todora Varimezov allowed me to reproduce recordings I made of their performances in 1978–79 on the accompanying CD, and let me copy a number of family photographs. The archive at the Bulgarian Ethnographic Museum gave permission to reproduce two of their historic photographs. I thank Vergilii Atanasov, who copied these for me and supplied a number of his own photographs as well, for his assistance. I am grateful to the music publishing house, Balkanton, and its general director, Georgi Vachev, for permission to reproduce a number of their recordings on the CD. Lauren Brody was especially helpful in expediting contact with Balkanton. Thanks also to Joe Boyd at Hannibal Records for allowing me to reproduce a few of his Bulgarian recordings on the CD, and to publish an advertisement for a group he produced, Balkana. Dan Beltran, a design student at UCLA, did the clever drawing of a gaida.

Finally and most profoundly, I thank my wife, Ann, who has contributed so much to this book—and in ways she would hardly have chosen: accompanying me on my first two trips to Bulgaria, providing moral support and patience during its writing and my absences in the field, and then reading the darn thing. If I were a poet. . .

Part One
Encountering the Tradition

What men or gods are these? What maidens loth?
What mad pursuit? What struggle to escape?
What pipes and timbrels? What wild ecstasy?

John Keats, "Ode on a Grecian Urn"

ONE

Dancing in the Scholar's World

My desire to write a book about musical experience flows from a set of personal circumstances that, while unique in detail, are probably widely shared by music scholars. At the heart of the problem lies a gap between the descriptive, scientific, language-encoded methods used to study music and the vivid, deeply moving, often unarticulated inner experiences we have performing or listening to it. Some lines of research, particularly those borrowing from structural linguistics, semiotics, and communications theory, have moved us closer to an understanding of musical experience.[1] These approaches include elicitation of insider (emic) verbal categories, the positing of underlying deep structures or homologies that inform musical and other modes of artistic production, and the hypothesis that music's iconicity with other cultural values and styles is the source of its power to move us profoundly.[2] While indebted in some ways to these advances, this book proposes and experiments with another way to move beyond the aporia I feel between musicology and musical experience. I begin by recasting the dilemma in slightly different terms.

The intellectual foundations of the antinomy between objectivity (musicology) and subjectivity (musical experience) have been undercut by philosophical and phenomenological hermeneutics, as developed in a stream of thought from Martin Heidegger to Hans-Georg Gadamer to Paul Ricoeur.[3] They have argued that there can be no objective position from which to view either nature or human affairs, because we are, before reason, born—or "thrown"—into a world that gives us the symbols through which we come to understand that world. Since we understand our world in terms of preexisting symbols (for

3

example, language) before we attempt to explain it, our explanations are always conditioned by preconceptions and pre-understandings (Gadamer 1986:236–44). Following this line of argument, the attempt to understand musical experience then becomes a reflexive process that begins with the self's encounter with musical symbols in the world. The self-conscious task of understanding music, of bringing that understanding to language, involves what Ricoeur (1981:164) calls a "hermeneutical arc" that—substitituting music for text—begins with pre-understanding, moves through explanation of the structure—or what he calls the "sense"—of music, to arrive at an interpretation and new understanding of the world referenced by music acting as a symbol. Hermeneutics thus helps to recast the problem of understanding the experience of music from a fruitless and methodologically unsound search for an unknowable, untalkable, subjective, inner quality in the self or the Other to an interpretation of the world of music by a self operating within finite but expandable "horizons."[4]

The hermeneutical suggestion that being thrown into a world of symbols precedes understanding and explanation certainly mirrors the history of my experience of Bulgarian music. I first encountered it as an imported symbol system—although I couldn't have called it that at the time—in the world of "international folk dancing," which flourished in colleges and clubs in the United States from the 1950s to the early 1970s and continues in somewhat attenuated form in the present. In these clubs, recordings of Bulgarian musicians, freed from any reference to a visual image of the musicians and their instruments or to Bulgarian dancers and their styles—or to their names, or to the places and contexts in which the music originally developed—were appropriated productively to create a unique social world within American culture. In this world we manipulated Bulgarian music, and particularly our dancing to it, as symbols that helped us establish new friendships, demonstrate our attractiveness and attractions to others, enjoy the physical and mental exertion of maintaining repeated aesthetic patterns in the body, and create a sense of small-scale community within the vastness of American society.

Few of us cared about or knew anything of either the culture that produced these recordings and dances or the structural principles underlying their forms, and yet we understood them at a nonlinguistic level well enough to make sense of their patterns (that is, we performed them) and used them to construct and reference meanings in our world, one rather different from the Bulgarian one in which they were created. In the process we learned new ways of, as Heidegger calls it, "being-in-the-world": how men can hold hands with men without inviting sexual innuendo, how to express personal joy or interest in others through whole-body involvement of a particular kind, and how status in a community can be manipulated by acquiring competence in its central tasks. In Ricoeur's terms, we appropriated Bulgarian music and dance while disappropriating our original selves.

This claim is probably at the core of the hermeneutic argument. While Enlightenment philosophy leaves us with a certain confidence in a rational and fixed ego analyzing the world while keeping it at a distance, hermeneutics suggests that the ego becomes a self in the encounter with the world, and that therefore the notion of the subject as constant and above the world, "as reigning over objectivity," is an illusion (Ricoeur 1981:190), one critiqued by Marxist and Freudian thought. It follows that, if such an independent ego existed, it would impose its interpretation on the world. In Ricoeur's view, on the other hand, the ego constructs itself as a self by being thrown into a world and "appropriation ceases to appear as a kind of possession. . . . It implies instead a moment of dispossession of the narcissistic *ego*," in which a new self emerges from a new understanding of texts, symbols, and symbolic action (ibid., 192–93).

In the late 1980s, a comparable kind of appropriation, blind (and deaf) to the original intent and context of the practice, occurred when Bulgarian music reached a much wider audience than folk dancers through the enormous popularity of a set of recordings of arranged Bulgarian choral music produced under the clever title, *Le Mystère des voix bulgares*.[5] Suddenly the general public, and even my students, who previously had been unable to remember whether I was interested in Bulgarian or Bavarian music, were accosting me for solutions to the "mystery." Through the marketing of "world beat" music, Bulgarian music became a part of the musical life of thousands of people in Western Europe, Japan, the United States, and elsewhere. Like the folk dancers, these new listeners may know little and care less about the meaning of this music in its homeland, understanding it largely through the lens (the earphones) of their previous encounters with music. But the horizons of their musical and intellectual world have been broadened slightly by their opening themselves to the sound of Bulgarian music.

Ethnomusicologists have usually been uncomfortable with these and other kinds of nonacademic appropriation, simultaneously failing to acknowledge the role of appropriation in scholarly understanding and feeling themselves intellectually and ethically superior to appropriations by ignorant and naive listeners, whether performance-oriented aficionados of folk dancing and Indian music in the 1960s, or greedy music-industry moguls and recording stars in the "ethno-pop" scene of the 1980s and 1990s.[6] While one of the definitions of appropriation (*Webster's New World Dictionary,* 1980) is "to take improperly, as without permission," other definitions are more benign, such as "to take for one's own . . . use" or "to set aside for a specific use"; precisely, I would argue, what ethnomusicologists do when they study another musical tradition or culture.[7]

Paul Ricoeur, in particular, has shown appropriation to be a central and inescapable feature of understanding in the humanities and social sciences. For Ricoeur (1981), appropriation is "understanding at and through distance," to "make one's own" that which was initially "alien." It is the process by which a scholar, or anyone thrown into a world, "struggle[s] against cultural distance and historical alienation." Since, in this starkly un-Romantic view, access to the inner experience of the Other is neither attainable nor sought after, one is left to interpret symbols in terms of the world or worlds they potentially reference, an understanding that is finite, changeable, multidimensional, forced to compete with other understandings, and limited by the expandable horizons of the individual.

When, as in ethnomusicological research, a new world of music is encountered, new understanding results when the horizons of the researcher's world are expanded to include at least some part of the world that the new music symbolically references.[8] From this perspective, the researcher seeks not so much to understand the inner experience of people from another culture, but rather the world suggested by music sounds, performances, and contexts. Because ethnomusicologists find themselves at some cultural and historical distance from the musics they study, appropriation is the dialectical counterpart to that distanciation. Even so-called "insider" ethnomusicologists, those born into the cultures they study, undergo a productive distanciation necessary to the explanation and critical understanding of their own cultures. As we shall see, productive distanciation is not only characteristic of outsiders and scholars; individuals operating within tradition continually appropriate their cultural practices, give them new meanings, and create their own sense of "being in the world."

I am now prepared to define musical experience as *the history of the individual's encounter with the world of musical symbols in which he finds himself.* That history consists not merely of the immediate, unanalyzed, sensate events that constitute a person's life but, more profoundly, of the dialectical movement between distanciation, which invites explanation, and appropriation, which suggests a new understanding.[9] To illustrate with my own initial experiences of Bulgarian music, they began with a performative act of nonverbal appropriation and under-standing of initially alien expressive forms—a process suggestive of what children must go through in encountering their world. As a musi-cian, I eventually distanced myself enough from the joys of dancing to explain the different Bulgarian dance meters in terms of 5/8, 7/8, and 11/8 time—for me, surprising new meters I had not encoun-tered before. This verbal, musicological explanation, which resulted in a new understanding of the structural principles at work in the music and dance, had not been necessary for the original performative ap-propriation of it, but it expanded the horizons of my understanding and helped me to make sense of the relationships between items within the repertoire and between this tradition and my own.

In semiotic terms, I was beginning to understand the code used to construct musical messages in Bulgarian style, to form a structural, syntactical explanation that, for all of its lack of reference to worlds beyond the music, influenced my experience of it. In hermeneutic terms, the world referenced by these music and dance symbols ex-panded from the narrow one of folk dancing to one that included my previous musical experiences. My expanded understanding of both the structural sense and potential reference of the music and dance altered and reconstituted my experience of them. As a result of this process of distanciation and appropriation, I was moved for the first time to wonder about the world that produced and exported these symbols to us. If this incident illustrates the first hermeneutical arc in my experience of Bulgarian music—from understanding to explana-tion to understanding, and from appropriation to distanciation to re-appropriation—then this book contains an account of other such moves as I conducted fieldwork in Bulgaria to broaden the horizons of my understanding of the world of Bulgarian music.

Although my own experience and Ricoeur's arguments highlight the extent to which understanding is a reflexive process ultimately re-leased as self-understanding, they do not lead to the solipsism that the self is the object of enquiry. Neither the self nor the Other is exclusively the object of understanding; rather interpretation seeks to expose the world or culture referenced by symbols and symbolic behaviors, a pro-cess necessarily finite, open-ended, and contestable.[10] This world is neither the inner life and intentions of a single producer nor a projec-tion of meaning by a particular observer, but a complex world of multi-ple meanings opened up by the symbols and symbolic behaviors and available for interpretation by all who have the opportunity to experi-ence them. It is an unavoidable ontological consequence of ethnomusi-cological fieldwork (and of the circulation of recordings far beyond the cultural boundaries within which they were originally produced) that the symbolic reference of music includes both the original world of the performance or recording, the world of the researcher or listener, and productively imagined worlds such as that of folk dancers. In all of these instances, since, as I suggested above, experience is the history of the individual's encounter with the world of symbols in which he finds himself, any effort to understand musical experience must bring both time and the individual to the center of the enquiry.

On Individuals

There are undoubtedly many ways to focus on musical experience as the relation between individuals and the worlds they encounter, but this book experiments with one way. I have made two individuals—Kostadin Varimezov (a historically important instrumentalist), and his wife, Todora Varimezova (a knowledgeable singer)—the center of the study. By following the history of their interaction with the world into which they were thrown, I hope to show (1) how they have defined themselves in interaction with that changing world; (2) the dramatic changes in that world over the seventy years or so of their lives; and (3) what aspects of that world—of that culture—are opened to our understanding by musical sounds, performances, and contexts acting as symbols.

Their lives, which have paralleled major developments in the recent history of Bulgaria and its music, provide the historical thread on which the narrative hangs. They have continuously constructed their lives and music to meet the changing demands of a rapidly moderniz-ing society. By focusing the study on them, I can report on how music, history, and social, economic, and ideological forces unite in everyday experience, and, in the process, create a picture of what it has meant to be a Bulgarian making music through the rapid changes of the last seventy years. I will show how music lives through the agency of, and is given meaning by, individuals operating in particular social, cultural, economic and historical contexts. In this goal I am guided by the view, articulated by many but perhaps most eloquently by John Blacking (1974), that music, song and dance are at the center of what it means to be human.

Another way of stating this study's three goals would be to say that I want to understand how music is individually created and experi-enced, how it is historically constructed, and how it is socially main-tained. These, in my view, are dialectically related formative processes at work in all musical cultures, and understanding them in particular situations has, I hope to show, the power to enhance ethnomusicological analysis and interpretation.[11] Although the subtitle of this book, "Experiencing Bulgarian Music," suggests an emphasis on the first question, that is, on the individual, to answer it requires recourse to the other two, and, in particular, to the dialectical relationships between the individual and the world or culture where actions and symbols have meanings that are socially and historically constructed and maintained. In fact, my definition of individual experience invoked both history and the social world—the history of the individual's encounter with the world of symbols—as necessary to its interpretation, showing in another way how completely these three questions are intertwined. This task returns us to a variant of my original predicament by asking how social life and inner experience can be dialectically pulled together. My decision to structure the book in this particular way is an experiment designed to illustrate a possible approach to ethnomusicological analysis and writing in terms of these three questions and their dialectical interactions.

On Dialogue in Monologic Form

In the wake of recent publications on ethnographic writing by James Clifford, Mary Louise Pratt, Stephen Tyler, Vincent Crapanzano and others,[12] it is less possible to write musical ethnography unselfconsciously and without embarrassment. Their critique flows out of a postcolonial guilt about the conditions of early, pre-1950s ethnography, a problem ethnomusicology shares insofar as the remnants of the colonial mentality push us to go elsewhere to find our objects of study. Both ethnomusicologists and anthropologists continue to participate in the structurally unequal relationship of powerful to poor, where issues of representation and narrative authority have political and ethical, as well as epistemological, dimensions (see, e.g., Keil 1979). These critics' arguments, simply put, seek to replace the omniscient monologue of the ethnographer with a more modest report that acknowledges the way ethnographic writing is situated in experience, interpretation, dialogue, and "polyphony" (Clifford 1988). The manner of writing and the construction of this text intersect with their concerns in a number of ways.

Particularly relevant here is their attempt to rehabilitate personal experience, especially in the form of interaction with others, as the locus for research. Mary Louise Pratt, in *Writing Culture* (1986), points out the tension in traditional ethnography between "personal narrative," which serves to situate the author in a particular place, time, and situation, and contains the self and its experience, and normative statements about tribal beliefs that claim some generalized, scientific authority from an Archimedean, above-the-fray, selfless point of view. Usually these two writing styles are clearly marked by grammatical and rhetorical differences: the personal narrative by the past tense, the use of the pronouns I/you/we, and reference to specific persons and particular events; the authoritative, analytic, scientific parts by the present tense, the use of the pronouns he/she/they, generalized descriptions, and reference to "tribal beliefs." According to Pratt, the personal narrative was used primarily to establish the ethnographer's authority to make scientific claims. Whereas earlier ethnographers were somewhat embarrassed by the subjective character of personal experience and narrative and tried to "kill [them] by science," (Malinowski quoted by Pratt), these critiques, tied to the hermeneutics of Gadamer, Ricoeur, and Clifford Geertz, weaken the ethnographer's claims to scientific authority and absolute truth modeled on the physical sciences, and affirm personal experience as the starting point for the interpretation of meaning.

Certainly personal experience is central to this book's narrative, not simply to establish the "I was there" of traditional ethnography, but as the place where understanding begins and in some sense remains located. However, I am not, nor are the aforementioned critics, content with a complete personalization of research, but seek understanding "in hermeneutic terms as a dialectic of experience and interpretation" (Clifford 1988:34). In this dialectic, Clifford's "unruly experience" is transformed into a "text" through a process by which "unwritten behavior, speech, beliefs, oral tradition, and ritual come to be marked as a corpus, a potentially meaningful ensemble separated out from an immediate discursive or performative situation" (38). Textualized events then become synecdoches for what we call culture. Citing Ricoeur, Clifford points out that such fragments of a world "must be conceptually and perceptually cut out of the flux of experience" (ibid.); in fact, according to Gadamer (1976), they only become experience when we remember them as significant, a distinction that could be made by either the producer of the behavior or its interpreters. Textualized behavior presents itself to experience in ways that limit the possibilities of interpretation and generate a hermeneutic arc between experience of the "text" and an interpretation that takes into account its "englobing reality" (Clifford 1988:38)—or what hermeneutic philosophers call a world, and anthropologists call a culture. The tactic of locating interpretation in the interaction between researcher and his "text" authorizes statements of meaning that are not limited to those given by so-called informants and yet have a provisional, nonexclusive claim to truth.

The textualization process, however, masks the dialogue or discourse in which the text was created in the first place.[13] Citing Emile Benveniste's *Problems in General Linguistics* (1971), Clifford (1988:39) defines discourse as "a mode of communication in which the presence of the speaking subject and of the immediate situation of communication are intrinsic." In many ethnographies, "as specific authors and actors are severed from their productions, a generalized 'author' must be invented to account for the world or context within which the texts are fictionally located" (39–40). These generalized authors are called The Nuer, The Balinese, and so on.

In this book I have tried to keep alive the sense of dialogue and discourse in which my knowledge of the tradition actually developed and in which Bulgarians' arguments about its meaning occur. Without resorting explicitly to the dialogue format, a possibility Clifford acknowledges, I do this in at least four ways. First, rarely do I refer to what Bulgarians believe about, or do with, music, preferring to locate statements of belief in particular individuals, who sometimes are talking to me, sometimes to each other. Second, since our dialogue occurred at a particular time, not in some abstract ethnographic present, I use the past tense more often than the present. Third, the primary way I indicate the authorial presence of those with whom I worked is with direct quotes, which are not separated from my text but integrated into it. Sometimes the dialogue is marked, as when someone says, "Tim, ..." or when I insert a question, "I asked Todora, ..." More frequently, the direct quotes are merged with my text, but they should always be read as the product of dialogue. Fourth and finally, I gave quite a bit of thought to how the quotes should be represented in the text. One common tactic, especially for longer quotes, is to separate them from the "author's" text by placing them in smaller, indented, or single-spaced type. While such a procedure is undoubtedly intended to draw attention to the difference between the author and the Other, perhaps in the process creating the possibility of another author, it often has the unintended effect of minimizing the importance of the quote—by visually presenting it in reduced form, almost like a footnote or addendum—and separating it from the author's text, where presumably the "real" analytic work is being done. Quotes often seem to exist merely to support the author's point or to bring some local color to the analysis. By embedding quotes directly in the text, I hope to suggest that parts of the text were created in dialogue, that somehow "we" are telling both "my" and "their" story, but in a way that is

very difficult to pull apart because of the dialogic nature of the interaction.

Of course, my own monologic authority is present in selecting the
quotes and creating them in English translation; I haven't overcome
this problem. But I hope a sense of the other as author and interpreter,
constructing meanings that are not wiped out by my representations
and interpretations, manages to surface even within the confines of
the monologic form.

If acknowledging the dialogic character of research helps fend off
the creation of both an omniscient ethnographer and a fictitious author called The Bulgarians, it also opens up the possibility of a polyphony of perspectives that displays culture "as an open-ended dialogue
of subcultures, of insiders and outsiders, of diverse factions" (Clifford
1988:46). My tactic of focusing on one or two individuals would seem
to limit the possibilities for polyphony, to privilege the discourse of
certain individuals and factions at the expense of others. This is partly
so and partly not so. Certainly the bulk of the story centers on one
tradition, the tradition of Kostadin and Todora, and their interpretation of it is given weight simply by the amount of time spent on it. But
as individuals they interpret not only their own work but that of others, and others have interpreted their work. To shine a light on their
views is to illuminate the experience and interpretation of others and
the dialogue between people and groups over the diverse meanings
they give to music. Thus the technique of focusing on my and the
Varimezovs' experience and interpretation of music leads to a modest
polyphony of different voices and beliefs. I have not tried to mark
these differences in any formal way, but I trust they will emerge clearly
in spite of that.

In the final analysis it is difficult to escape an account that typifies
the individuals involved. If I no longer take individual expression as
representative of Bulgarianness, it has been nearly impossible to avoid
generalizations to some subgroup within society based on gender, age,
residence, ethnicity, religion, education, and occupation. In that sense
the text perhaps occupies some middle ground between scientific,
modern ethnographies that purport to represent an external reality
through processes of generalization or abstraction and interpretive,
postmodern ones that seek to evoke experience and "local
knowledge."[14]

On Tradition

Tradition, which I invoke in a formulaic litany of titles to the major
parts of the book, is a vexing concept because it is constantly used

but annoyingly difficult to pin down. Many ethnomusicologists would probably prefer to avoid it as either so full or empty of meaning as to have no explanatory usefulness. In the Bulgarian case, however, tradition is an analytically apt concept, because notions of tradition and its authentic, truthful, and useful representation and practice were precisely what was at stake for many Bulgarians during the times I visited there between 1969 and 1989. They were asking in a variety of ways, What is the nature of our tradition and how should it be preserved and presented in a manner appropriate to our modern life? If Bulgarians weren't themselves arguing about tradition, then I might not use the concept, and the structure and approach of the book might be very different. But since they were self-consciously trying to define their own traditions, it is appropriate to use the concept as a structural pillar of the analysis and to try to define it.

I will define tradition in four senses, proceeding from the nonre-flective to the fully self-conscious. First, in some instances tradition must be constructed analytically by the researcher because it is beyond discourse in the culture itself; second, the word "tradition" sometimes labels a subset of the world or culture in which it is found, as, for example, musical tradition, political tradition, literary tradition; third, where it is explicitly invoked in "native" and scholarly discourse, it is a concept requiring both historical or cultural distanciation and reflection; and fourth, when made the object of reflection, tradition becomes a "text" for interpretation and appropriation.

Taking up the third sense, some ethnomusicologists call the object of their study "traditional music," name their journals and societies after it, and suggest, by my definition, that it stands at some distance from other kinds of usually unspecified, presumably closer, music, by inference perhaps "my," "contemporary," "modern," "Western," or "classical" music. Ironically, having jumped into some lively traditional (that is, historically or culturally distant) musical culture, the ethnomusicologist may find that no one speaks of tradition. Everything that one experiences seems contemporary, "ours"; the natives report, "it is what we do when we make music." Other cultures, including Bulgaria, on the other hand, possess a strong sense of the distant past being appropriated for contemporary use and a corresponding sense of discontinuity between past and present. In such cases, a native notion of tradition figures prominently and must be acknowledged by researchers. It is presumably this feeling of discontinuity and distance that gives rise to the self-reflexivity that, according to Anthony Giddens (1990), is one of the markers of a modern, as opposed to a traditional, period. As Gadamer (1986:xxi) says of the task of interpreting texts received from the past, "Tradition, part of whose nature is the handing-on of tradi-

tional materials, must have become questionable for an explicit consciousness of . . . appropriating tradition to have formed."

It is precisely in this sense that the litany of tradition appears in the
titles of the chapters. If Bulgarian or any other culture were viewed
exclusively in the ethnographic present, or if Bulgarians acted as if the
past were unknowable or irrelevant, then its traditions and the dynamics of appropriating and giving meaning to material from the past
might fade in comparison to the task of finding systematic relationships between extant bits of behavior. But the explicit and repeated
use of tradition as a central concept in this account is justified not so
much by virtue of its original distance from my experience, that is,
traditional from my American perspective, but because in the Communist period (1944–1989) Bulgarians made their pre-Communist past
an object of reflection, in the process distancing themselves from it
and making necessary its reappropriation and reinvention in terms
suitable for the new, "progressive" (where we might say modern)
times.[15]

If we periodize the history of Bulgarian village culture into a traditional period and a modern one, the irony remains that in the traditional period, defined in the modern period by reflection upon the
past, tradition as a global concept was probably not an object of reflection. In the chapters that follow, we will learn that Todora rejected
learning particular songs because she thought they were too difficult
or the meaning too distasteful, but the entire body of work, the corpus
of songs, was accepted as "true," as commenting on things that really
happened. Only occasionally did the tradition become questionable, as
for example when a Gypsy wanted Kostadin to become a professional
musician, an unthinkable occupation for a villager such as he, tied to
the land. This challenge to what we typically call tradition was rebuffed
not by citing tradition and its dictates—as Tevye does in *Fiddler on the
Roof*—but by invoking moral values: professional musicians in those
days were 'bums,' and Kostadin's father refused to allow him to become one. In what we call traditional society, tradition as a whole is
beyond discourse and appears only in fragmentary admonitions, occasional acts of defiance or rejection, and individual works and events.[16]

By contrast, the modern period of Bulgarian music, after the Communist revolution of 1944, was a period of intense reflexivity about
the past and about tradition. Having distanced themselves from the
supposed backwardness and degradation of the past by establishing
new goals for the spiritual and economic growth of man, the Communists called into question a whole tradition, a manner of making music,
an entire repertoire, its style and associated values. Tradition, brought

into consciousness, could now be acted on in any number of ways, including appropriation, rejection, dissolution, fragmentation, alteration, reconstruction, and criticism. The parts of the book on changing and continuing the tradition detail these acts, often performed by different people with different interests and perspectives on the tradition, each acting in what they perceived to be their own, or the country's, or even the tradition's interest.

The tradition's interest? This last claim, related to tradition in its fourth sense, as an object of reflection, suggests that one of the important consequences of bringing tradition to consciousness is that it takes on the appearance of objective existence, as if it were a being with a life and therefore demands of its own. In modern societies tradition becomes a text for interpretation, and its "readers" act as if it made claims on them, as if the "truth" of tradition were being served by the precise manner in which they appropriate it—thus the claim to authenticity. The conscious encounter with tradition creates a tension between the world it once referenced and the modern world it must be made to reference. In the later chapters, as we observe older musicians extol the tradition, composers arrange it, younger musicians struggle with its limitations, and Gypsies extend its expressive range, the tensions not only between the participants in the argument, but between them and the tradition, conceived as existent being, are given particular expression as human and musical experience. Some of these tensions surfaced in my first encounters with Bulgarian music in Bulgaria.

TWO

First Impressions

During my first trip to Bulgaria, in the summer of 1969, I visited Yambol, a southeastern provincial town in an area known to this day by its ancient name, Thrace (fig. 1; pl. 1). On Sunday, the day for weddings, my wife, Ann, and I drove out to one of the surrounding villages in hope of hearing some traditional wedding music. Just before noon we headed south along a road that, according to the map, had a good density of villages along it. We passed well-tended fields in one of the broadest plains in southern Bulgaria and finally stopped on the outskirts of one of the neatly kept villages.

As we walked toward the village square, I heard music coming from a small, nondescript, unmarked building. I peered into the dimly lit room through the open door and could just make out a restaurant's long banquet table. To my surprise and delight, at the back of the room a small band consisting only of 'traditional' [*bitov*] instruments—*gaida* (bagpipe), *kaval* (end-blown, bevel-edged flute), *gŭdulka* (bowed, pear-shaped fiddle), and *tŭpan* (cylindrical, double-headed bass drum, played with a large stick and thin wand)—performed for the assembled guests. I was thrilled to experience live the music I had, until then, only heard on recordings, and to realize that it existed not just in studio recordings, but in the lives of villagers as well.

We didn't have much time to listen, however, for just at that moment the band and the wedding guests began to leave the restaurant and cross the square, not to the church, but to the village *sŭvet*, or council, where the marriage would be consecrated in a civil ceremony, an example of the almost complete secularization of Bulgarian society since the Communist revolution of 1944. After a few moments, the bride

16

Figure 1. Map of Bulgarian Towns and Folklore Regions

and groom and their relatives and friends emerged from the sŭvet and processed around the square to the band's accompaniment. Members of the wedding party offered bystanders, including us, sips of *rakiya,* a strong grape brandywine, from a *bŭklitsa,* a small, decorated wooden cask used especially for weddings. When they learned we were Americans interested in music, they enthusiastically invited us to join the wedding party, and we spent the next 24 hours happily processing, eating, drinking, and dancing to the accompaniment of prodigious amounts of music-making. The musicians, their fingers flying with astonishing rapidity, played nonstop for as much as an hour as the wedding procession wound around the village. I could hardly imagine moving my fingers so fast for so long, let alone that any music should come out (CD #1).

Although we had planned to return to our hotel in Yambol by evening, everyone enjoined us to stay. The best was yet to come, they said. After the feasting, the evening dancing was particularly energetic. The leader of the line dance *(horo)* held a torch to light the yard, while others swung torches at our feet, forcing us to jump over them. Alcoholic visions of Greek and Roman bacchanalia danced in my head, but whatever the ancient and mysterious, pagan and Christian roots of the tradition, the experience on that night was mainly fun. Everyone was having a great time.

The culmination of the evening and the moment we had been waiting for came near midnight, when a group of young men, and a male "bride" in drag, arrived to reenact a bawdy version of the main events of the wedding in a very funny skit. Dressed in traditional costumes rather than the modern dress worn by the rest of us, the mock wedding party processed around the yard. The "groom" defended his "bride" from the lewd attention of the other boys, who grabbed at her breasts and reached under her skirt. Everyone laughed, but the grannies, dressed in black, were the best audience, cackling with delight at every word and action, and nearly falling off their chairs during the most obscene and uproarious bits.

At one point, as the groom swung his gun around to protect his bride, it accidentally went off. To his horror, and the delight of the crowd, the bride flopped to the ground, supposedly hit by the errant bullet. A "doctor" was called, and arrived complete with white coat, stethoscope, and black bag—a costuming contrast of ancient and modern that also touched off gales of laughter. After deliberating for quite a while and trying out various remedies that didn't work, the doctor suddenly had a brilliant idea. He reached into his bag, pulled out a giant cucumber, and performed some sort of operation under the bride's skirt. As the grannies doubled over with glee, the bride leapt to her feet, miraculously cured, and the mock wedding continued happily with the exchange of small gifts and jokes.

Back in Yambol the next day, our memories of the wonderful music and this ancient fertility ritual were interrupted by a knock at the door. Our presence was requested by the head of the Yambol district Committee for Culture. We had gone to see him the previous week to announce our visit and ask for his help in learning more about folk music in his district. He told us that not much was happening during the summertime, since all the professional musicians were playing at resorts on the Black Sea coast. He seemed at a loss when we tried to explain that we were also interested in more traditional aspects of musical life, and we finally thanked him for his time and left. At this second meeting we encountered a very stern, glum face as he ordered us to leave Yambol by noon the next day, saying in the dark, resonant voice some Bulgarian men have, "I thought I told you there was no folklore in the Yambol district."

This anecdote illustrates the contradictory joys and tensions, satisfactions and absurdities, of fieldwork in Bulgaria during the Communist period (1944 to 1989), and it introduces one of the important themes of this book: the conflict between tradition and modernity.[1] The latter took the form of the awesome power of Communist ideology and practice, personified in this case by the chief of culture for the district, a job with direct links to the Party's central committee. Tradition, in the form of rituals, instruments, songs, and virtuosic performance practices with deep roots in the past, was revivified weekly in weddings, one of the few traditional contexts to survive the communist transformation of society. Weddings continued to provide one of the main venues for the development of instrumental skills, patronage of musicians, and negotiation of musical aesthetic values. On the other hand, the Communists were deeply committed to changing, defining, and controlling all aspects of society and culture, including folklore and music. To achieve these goals, they assumed command of the presentation of culture to Bulgarians and the outside world, and, in the process, created professional cadres of organizers, arrangers, choreographers, and musicians to execute a centralized vision of Bulgarian culture, recast in a socialist mold. Caught between forces of tradition and modernity, individuals negotiated meanings and practices for themselves, simultaneously acknowledging the authority of the Party while maintaining, adjusting, and questioning their relationship to their heritage.

Individual appropriation of tradition was at issue as the culture boss and I clashed over differing expectations of how Bulgarian culture should be experienced. I found myself trapped between a love of the tradition, together with the naive assumption that I could experience it on my own terms, and the Communists' desire to control my, and indeed everyone's, access to it. I learned in a direct and unpleasant way of the limited powers of the individual in a Communist society, and confronted for the first time the official suspicion that in those days accompanied any American working in a Communist country. We were obviously being kept track of, the objects of more than idle curiosity. The studiers were clearly being studied, and that recognition was deeply troubling. Even as late as 1988, during the glasnost thaw, my videotapes of music performances were checked at an office in the Bulgarian Academy of Sciences called "national secrets" before I could take them out of the country.[2]

Other individuals at the wedding were caught in the same bind between freedom and control and between tradition and modernity. Some made the decision to welcome Americans into their midst, following a deeply ingrained tradition of hospitality, when prudence might have suggested that contact with vilified "American capitalists" should be avoided for fear of harassment or even worse reprisals. The bride and groom chose to marry in the sŭvet, not the church, because the religious aspect of tradition had become nearly untenable in an officially atheist state.[3] Some acted out a traditional, blatantly sexual skit, flouting the Communists' attempts to wipe out all that was 'dirty'

in Bulgarian village culture and replace it with a prettified image of a
clean and perfect communist society. The groom's family decided to
hire the local village players of traditional instruments rather than
town musicians, from Yambol or even farther away, who play modern,
manufactured instruments, particularly clarinets and accordions. How
individuals experience, manipulate and weave their way between the
opposing forces of tradition and modernity, freedom and control, cultural heritage and imported ideology is the subject of the second half
of this book.

My first encounters with Bulgarian tradition in the country itself
were largely haphazard and serendipitous. The metaphor of being
"thrown" into a world, with its suggestion of an awkward landing,
therefore seems appropriate. I begin by reflecting on these encounters
with Bulgaria, its people, its traditions, and its musical life during the
Communist period. Distancing myself from the immediate jumble of
those initial events, I organize them into three kinds of experiences:
encounters with history; with social, cultural, and economic support
systems; and with individuals.

Bulgaria's History in Music

History as Experience

How is history experienced? For those growing up in a tradition, history is the continuous appropriation of lived experience: the lifelong
involvement in and observation and interpretation of events as they
occur.[4] History, as an inheritance from the past, is encountered when
some constituents of everyday life—texts, monuments, art, performance styles, and everyday practices—are bracketed, fixed, or "textualized" in a way that makes them seem simultaneously near and distant, of our time and of another time.

When I arrived in Bulgaria, I found that one of the most obvious
reflections of its history was its architecture, where the past is jumbled
up, juxtaposed, and observable in the present. In the capital city, Sofia,
home to more than a million people, the headquarters of the Communist party and the huge central department store, both in an imposing
Stalinist-era style, flanked the sunken archaeological excavation of the
ancient Roman city, Serdica, built during Emperor Trajan's reign (98–
117 B.C.). In view up the street stood a Turkish mosque built during
the nearly five centuries of Ottoman domination. A few blocks down
Ruski Boulevard, the Austrian-style palace of the former Tsar of Bulgaria had been turned into the national art gallery and ethnographic
museum, and in a nearby park sat the fifth-century Byzantine Church

of Saint Sofia.[5] By the late 1980s, bright new signs for American- and Japanese-owned hotels illuminated dark city streets, suggesting the dawn of integration into the world capitalist system.

I wanted to experience the village as a symbol of an ancient, unchanged way of life, but it, too, contained many layers of historical reference. Ancient Thracian burial mounds in the midst of a wheat field, donkey-carts and horse-drawn plows, and Turkish-style houses with wooden balconies shared the landscape with the tractors, combines, and huge barns of the collective farms, and here and there a Russian-built Lada or occasionally a Mercedes sat parked beside a newly constructed and still unfinished brick house.

The history that can be seen in Bulgaria's architecture and material culture, can also be heard in its music. I went to Bulgaria interested in its 'folk music' [narodna muzika], the product of what I presumed to be an illiterate or semiliterate rural population. In the city I experienced transplanted versions of the village tradition when I watched Gypsy clarinetists and accordionists at hotel weddings and danced to homemade village instruments in restaurants with traditional decors. But I also bought records of Turkish music played by Bulgarian Turks, attended the opera and the symphony, heard English rock bands at stadium concerts, and saw Bulgarian popular singers and jazz musicians on television. The villages, it turned out, were no haven from this modern musical Babylon: all these styles could be heard there on the radio.

During my first trip in 1969, I made a pilgrimage of sorts to Dragalevtsi, a village close to Sofia and the subject of an early anthropological account of Bulgaria, Bulgarian Village by Irwin Sanders (1949). As I stepped off the bus into the village of my romantic dreams, a loudspeaker in the square, installed to broadcast the Party's propaganda, shattered my enchantment with a static-filled recording of a Shostakovich symphony. Walking around the dirt streets; looking at ox-drawn hay carts and square, two-story brick houses with yards filled with vegetables, out-buildings, and animals; and listening to Russian art music, I experienced vividly the complex intermingling of music and life in a society whose densely textured, condensed history continues to inform the present.[6] The coexistence of the ancient and the modern, the old and the new, somehow defined life and music in Bulgaria—perhaps as it does everywhere—in a way unique and vivid.

My encounters with contemporary Bulgarian music and architecture suggest that untangling their complexities must include identifying the historical conditions that spawned the varieties of expression one can observe in the present. This historically constructed jumble of sounds and cultural forms can be partially explained by a conventional chronological ordering of history, and of the texts, monuments, and styles ostensibly sedimented out of it and appropriated and used in the present. Bulgaria's political, cultural, and musical history, in outline, includes the following major events.

History as Chronology

Before the fifth century A.D., the Bulgarian lands contained indigenous populations in areas called Thrace, Macedonia, and Moesia by the Greeks and Romans who dominated the region. Some historians believe that the village mummers [*kukeri*] of today are relics of Thracian civilization (Crampton 1987). In the late fifth century, Slavic peoples from northeastern Europe settled the rural areas, obliterating for the most part these ancient cultures and probably bringing with them the striking leap of a 7th or octave at the end of drone-based polyphonic songs from the area around Sofia, which have their analogues in similar singing styles from the Briansk region of Russia (Svitova 1966).[7] In the seventh century, warriors of Turkic origin from Central Asia, called Bulgars, invaded the Balkans and competed with the Byzantine Empire for dominion over the land and its people. The ninth-century conversion of the Bulgarians to Christianity affected musical and ritual practice tied to important moments in the Christian calendar such as Christmas, Lent, and Easter.

In the fourteenth century, the Ottoman Turks fought their way through the Balkans, capturing Sofia in 1385 and the rest of the country by the end of the century. For nearly five hundred years, until 1878, Bulgarians languished under what they call the 'Turkish yoke,'[8] and Bulgarian historians assert that their culture was preserved primarily in villages. There the influence of the church, headed by Greeks and served by an uneducated, corrupt clergy, and of town culture, with its heterogeneous ethnic mix of Turks, Jews, Armenians, and Greeks, was minimal. As a consequence of this overly idealized view of urban-rural separation, some Bulgarian scholars have claimed that their folk tradition remained free of Turkish influence. Yet it is likely that the instrumental tradition, in particular, evidences that influence. Many of the instruments, such as tŭpan, *zurna* (oboe-type aerophone), *tambura* (long-necked, plucked lute), and kaval, are distributed primarily in West Asia and probably entered the Balkans with the Ottoman advance. Some aspects of the playing style—such as particular ornaments, the upward glissando, the augmented second, and certain microtonal inflections—may also have been brought into Bulgaria during the Ottoman period. Gypsies, who entered the Balkans in large numbers with the Turks, were probably responsible for bringing in these instruments and styles, some of which were then adopted by Bulgarian villagers.

After 1878, with a German aristocratic family providing the newly independent state's tsars, central European cultural influence predominated. Czech and Russian music teachers, instrument makers, and band and choral directors introduced instruments like clarinet, violin, trumpet, trombone, and accordion, as well as choral singing and ensemble playing in Western harmony (Krustev 1978). From their beginnings in military and town bands, Western instruments eventually moved into some villages and became part of the rural tradition.

After 1944, a Russian-backed Communist revolution introduced dramatic changes in village economy and national ideology, the musical effects of which included a decline in village musical life, a corresponding urbanization and professionalization of the tradition, the introduction of Soviet techniques for the choreography, arrangement, and presentation of the tradition, and centralized control of musical and cultural production. Finally, in the late 1970s or early '80s, the prestige of American and Japanese culture influenced the introduction of instruments like the electric guitar, electric bass guitar, synthesizer, and drum set, musical styles like jazz and rock, and the widespread use of private cassette recordings as a means of transmission.

This thumbnail sketch of the history of Bulgaria's folk music linked to social, cultural, and political change shows the extent to which any contemporary musical culture, or musical practice as culture, is an accretion of "capacities and habits" that must be part of the story of how and why people make the music they make.[9] I would argue, however, that these historically derived cultural and musical forms don't determine contemporary practice so much as provide its symbolic forms and possibilities, which individuals then select, assign meanings to, and manipulate. Rather than view historically constructed forms and practices as influencing the present, I prefer to observe individuals appropriating, understanding, and interpreting them in culture.

Similarly, while some ethnomusicologists regard culture as the ultimate determinant of music (see Nettl 1983:131–43, 234–44 for a useful review of these arguments), this mechanistic, causal metaphor would need to be extended to argue that culture, and therefore music, is "predetermined" by history. However, I suggest abandoning a deterministic, cause-and-effect metaphor in favor of sets of dialectical relationships between history, culture, the individual, and music. I view culture not so much as generating or "determining" musical practices, which then "reflect" cultural ones, but rather I interpret musical performances and styles as helping individuals construct notions of what social and cultural practices mean—and how those practices feel.

Maintaining Music in Society

While this brief history may partially describe how and when certain musical forms, instruments, contexts, and practices were introduced into Bulgarian culture, it doesn't explain how and why they were re-produced in particular historical periods. To understand this, I examine the maintenance of tradition in two distinct periods of Bulgarian history: the years from 1920 to 1944, when some 80 percent of the population lived in villages; and the postwar, Communist era from 1944 to 1989, when about 65 percent of the population lived in cities and towns.[10] I suggest that, in order to understand social maintenance of music in these periods, four social units need to be examined: the village, the state, the ethnic subgroup, and the family. Each of these social groups operated in different ways and with variable degrees of efficacy in each period. Furthermore, within and between these social units, ideologies and economic conditions operated to discourage some inherited cultural practices while maintaining and fostering others. I examine each of these units of social structure for how they provided a locus of support for music, the ways they were affected by ideology and economics, their relevance and limitations for a study of Bulgarian folk music, and the nature of my encounter with them.

The Village

If "folk music" is to be the subject of study, then the village, almost by definition, is the social unit that supports it and, by implication, generates one of its important textualized forms: commercial recordings of what purports to be traditional village music, including many songs linked to calendric and life-cycle rituals.[11] When I arrived in Bulgaria, however, I discovered that most traditional contexts had disappeared, partly as a result of the secularization of society and ideological attacks on Christianity. Even though many rituals were pre-Christian in origin and tied to animal and agricultural fertility, they had been linked for centuries to the Christian ritual cycle, as, for example, in the union of *koleda,* an animal fertility ritual involving the return or birth of the sun, with Christmas, the birth of Christ. Similarly, *Kukerovden* [Mummer's Day or Carnival], an agricultural fertility ritual around planting time, coincided with the beginning of Lent. Easter, an important occasion for dancing, fused the rebirth of the animal and plant world in spring with Jesus' resurrection. These elaborate ritual observances disappeared from most Bulgarian villages during the Communist era, partly because of their religious connotations, but also because they seemed superstitious in the face of modern agronomy. In addition, people lacked time for them due to Communist demands for more productivity. Some of the joy of life slipped away as villagers lost most of their lands and animals to collectivization in the 1950s. Even such simple, nonritual practices as a shepherd playing to amuse himself in the fields waned. As one told me, when I questioned why I never saw a shepherd playing a shepherd's flute [ovcharska svirka], "There is no life, little cousin."

In 1972, Bulgarian musicologists, with vast collecting experience in particular villages, listed on one hand for me a few villages "where they still perform the koleda ritual." With their help I was able to find, attend rehearsals of, and accompany a group of eight young 'carolers' [koledari]—plus a bagpiper and assorted ritual noisemakers (a 'cat' and a 'donkey')—from a village near Sofia as they went from house to house to awaken and wish each family good fortune in the coming year. After singing a song blessing the household or one of the family members celebrating a special event such as a marriage or birth, the carolers asked which was the eastern wall, and faced it as one of them recited a lengthy blessing, echoed periodically by the koledari's response, "Amin, Amin, Amin" (CD #2). Since the Orthodox Christian icon that traditionally adorned the eastern wall of the house was always missing, it was an empty gesture—except in one case where the wall had a calendar with a photo of a scantily clad woman on it, occasioning much hooting and giggling among the men in the room. Unfortunately, such delightful encounters of tradition and modernity were difficult to observe during the middle years of the Communist period.

If many prewar musical practices had died in the villages, important features of the tradition remained alive in the memories of the generations born before the Second World War, and much of what I and other scholars know of them was elicited as songs, music, and stories performed for a tape recorder. It was difficult, though not impossible, to observe them in practice—a matter of no little detective work at one extreme, or, conversely, of chance encounters. In 1988 a woman in one village suggested I come back for kukerovden, a ritual they had revived in her village after years of avoidance due to fear of sanctions from authorities ("they have stopped the fun," she said). Martha Forsyth, an avid collector of Bulgarian folk songs, told me she had heard from a Bulgarian folklorist about women who still performed harvest songs while haying in the Samokov district.[12] She made a special trip there to observe this singing in context only to find that, in fact, the women no longer sang as they harvested.[13] Thus, while songs, music, and dance linked to specific occasions were still alive in the memory of middle-aged and older people, were the historical source for contemporary *narodna muzika*, and were recorded and put on record, they nearly disappeared in everyday practice during the Communist period.

Because some sort of remembered or constructed notion of what village music was like in the pre-Communist period was crucial to its experience, presentation, and understanding in the Communist era, I describe in parts 2 and 3 the yearly cycle of music as it once existed: which families made music, the role of music in the economic life of the village, how it was valued, and how it was passed on from generation to generation—in other words, how it was socially maintained. But my encounter with Bulgarian music in the Communist period suggested to me that a musical ethnography of a village might not be a particularly rich study, and that a village with a rich musical life, if found, might have been an exception rather than the rule, and hardly representative of the situation in Bulgarian villages during the Communist period.[14]

Studying the village became less viable during this period because so many of them were destroyed by the policies of the state and the exigencies of modern economic life. Many small villages, such as the one Todora and Kostadin Varimezov grew up in, ceased to exist, except as repositories of memories and a place for holiday picnics. For me and many Bulgarian musicologists, placing music in a village cultural context was essentially a process of collection and reconstruction of traditional materials. Large villages, drained by rapid urbanization and industrialization, were hardly more interesting as sites for the study of the social maintenance of music. Except those that had become towns, suburbs of major cities, or were near factories, villages were practically empty of young people and families of working age. A few old people remained to do the work, and the results were disastrous, not only for music but for the success of the agricultural sector of the economy as well. In the late 1980s, there were no longer enough people to work the fields and bring in the crops, and so shortages for some foodstuffs existed where before there had been plenty.

The State

Although the state may have been largely irrelevant as a unit of social maintenance for village music before World War II, it emerged as perhaps the most potent force supporting it—and indeed all kinds of music—in the postwar period. While the Party's state-saturated economic, social, and cultural policies contributed to the death of older village traditions and practices, a complementary set of programs, including politically inspired state holidays and state-sponsored patronage of 'folk ensembles,' revived them in a new form suitable for a new society. State holidays, which required folkloric display as a symbolic statement of national identity and pride, and hence loyalty to the ruling Party, included May Day and the 9th of September, celebrating the establishment of Communist rule in 1944. On these holidays huge parades, *manifestatsias*, were held in Sofia and smaller versions in towns and villages. Displays of nationhood, particularly folk traditions, were part of these processions, as brightly costumed dancers joined the parade along with political banners and masses of workers (see pl. 2). The national holidays also took on special significance as moments for private celebration in place of traditional, but religiously implicated, Sunday fairs.

In addition to holidays where traditional costume, music and dance were used, along with many other artifacts, to symbolize national pride and political celebration, the state created contexts that had never existed before for the display of the folk arts as valuable symbolic cultural property. At the amateur level, state organs of culture formed village 'collectives' to perform and keep alive rituals, songs, and dances that otherwise might have disappeared completely from view. This movement, known as 'artistic amateurism' [*hudozhestvena samodeinost*, lit., 'artistic self-activity'], eventually organized regional, district, and national competitions of village ensembles and individual performers. The national festival, held every five years in the museum town of Koprivshtitsa, achieved an international reputation with folk dance mavens.

The purpose of festivals and competitions was to motivate participation, to give the performers an external goal and reason to participate, and to provide the participants with an extra few days off work. The collectives' concerts symbolically presented their own village traditions to themselves and fellow villagers, not as remnants of pagan or Christian superstitions, but as "artistic," beautiful, well-organized statements of local, regional and national identity and pride.

At the professional level, the state established in the early 1950s a National Ensemble of Folk Song and Dance, led by the composer, Filip Kutev, and an Ensemble for Folk Songs of the Bulgarian Radio (Radio Sofia).[15] These organizations presented the entire nation, urban and rural, (and indeed the world) its village traditions in a "progressive" manner consonant with its modernizing goals. By the mid-1980s nearly every large town in the country had its own professional ensemble, consisting of a core of paid, professional musicians, a choir direc-

tor, and perhaps a few soloists, a choreographer and composer, an artistic director and some administrators, and a number of amateur
singers and dancers.[16] This growth in professionalism led in turn to
the need to train those who would direct and play in these ensembles,
and by the 1970s two high schools of folk music and a High Musical-
Pedagogical Institute, a post-secondary conservatory, educated musicians and singers in village music traditions.

This new "tradition" produced another kind of recording encountered by American and European audiences: not memories of village
music but what Bulgarians call 'arranged folklore' [*obraboten folklor*].
The recently popular records of Bulgarian arrangements, *Le Mystère
des voix bulgares,* emerged from these institutions of state support for
folk music. Thus, although many traditional village contexts died after
World War II, its traditions lived during the Communist period as an
instrument of the state, resurrected from their death after collectivization of the land and secularization of the belief structure. Organized,
prettified, and cleaned up, village forms and practices were given back
to the people as a symbol of national pride, of the state's ability to
organize itself and its people, and of progress made by the Communist
party in creating an industrialized, educated society in which new values replaced old ones.

Changing the unit of analysis from the village to the state and studying how music lives in a large-scale contemporary society provides a
necessary adjunct to the village as a social unit supporting music. In
many socialist states, as well as in Western democracies, the support of
music was and is taken as seriously as in any self-indulgent monarchy
of the past. If the patronage of music was once a frivolous expression
of the selfish interests of a protected monarch distanced from and exploiting the masses, in the modern world governments of all kinds take
the task of supporting music seriously and deliberately. In particular,
the ideology and practice of East European socialist societies required
a concern for precisely those segments of society overlooked in aristocratic and bourgeois societies.[17] The betterment of the masses in every
aspect of life—economic conditions, health, education, and culture—
became the primary raison d'être of the state. The desire to engineer
the progress of man—Stalin called himself "the engineer of human
souls"—from his degradation under capitalism to his full flowering
under communism led socialist governments to scrutinize and control
nearly aspect of life, including the arts. Activity that might have been a
mere pastime and enthusiasm of an elite and its professionally retained
minions became the serious business of a state dedicated, at least in
theory, to the improvement of man. Such contexts where music and

art take on new and vital meaning are important units of analysis for ethnomusicologists interested in how music works in society.

While, from a historical point of view, "the tradition" was created in villages in a previous era, in the new era the tradition was substantially recreated. Through the agency of particular individuals, the state preserved, supported, used, consumed, and changed it—and from some points of view ruined it. But a musical tradition cannot be accounted for completely by reference to its contemporary supporting mechanisms. Music making has a history and is located in individuals and performance contexts not entirely under the control of the state. The interaction of music and folklore with the state and its mechanisms was not the only thing happening in a socialist society, even one as tightly controlled as Bulgaria's was during the forty-five years of Communist rule.

The Ethnic Group

The tradition central to this book is principally (and most Bulgarians would argue exclusively) a Bulgarian one that originated and was socially maintained in the Bulgarian village of the 1920s. In addition to ethnic Bulgarians, however, Gypsies (of whom some were nominal Christians, residing in the village, and others Muslims from outside the village) were important performers of instrumental music, particularly as paid professionals.[18] The unequal social and economic relations between these two ethnic groups were woven into the fabric of social maintenance and are crucial to an understanding of how music was made in the 1930s and 1940s (cf. Popov 1993).

In the postwar period, when the local interactions of village tradition become national in scope, the relationship of ethnic groups to the social maintenance of music became more vexed. In Europe in general, the governments of many nation-states tend to regard national boundaries and ethnic boundaries as coterminous, which leads to at least two predictable, and often tragic, consequences: neglect or mistreatment of ethnic minorities within national boundaries and tensions with neighbors over the issue of expanding current borders to include ethnic "brothers" presently outside the nation. Communist ideology added to the problem, which exploded in Yugoslavia and the former Soviet Union after 1989, by suppressing ethnic and even national aspirations when they came into conflict with the solidarity of the working classes necessary for world peace and an international socialist order.

Bulgaria's problems with the concept of ethnicity in the postwar period were both internal and external. Bulgarian historians and policy makers claimed periodically that the Slavic-speaking inhabitants of

northern Greece and the southern Yugoslav Republic of Macedonia
were ethnic Bulgarians, creating the fear in those countries that Bulgaria aspired to expand its border south to include northern Greece
and the city of Thessaloniki (which Bulgarians call Solun) and west
to include Macedonia. Internally, Bulgaria's cultural policy aimed at
obliterating ethnic differences by emphasizing national, rather than
ethnic, consciousness and, particularly in the 1980s, forcefully suppressing ethnic expression of any kind. Singled out for particularly
poor treatment were the Muslim minorities: Muslim Gypsies, Pomaks
(Bulgarians who converted to Islam during the Ottoman period), and
Turks, especially from 1984 to 1989.[19] Other groups, less stigmatized
by association with the hated Turkish Yoke, flourished in the professional and intellectual classes, including Jews, Armenians, Russians,
and Greeks.

While each group has its own traditions, the Gypsies played a particularly important role in the Bulgarian tradition, acting as professional
musicians to the dominant Bulgarian culture and participating in
many domains of musical life, including state-sponsored ensembles of
traditional instrumentalists, where their expressive, virtuosic playing
often set the standard for others to follow. But nowhere was their prestige and influence greater than at weddings, which, as a spontaneously
negotiated communal practice not strictly dictated by Party ideology
and aesthetics, flourished during the latter part of the socialist period
as an alternative to the state for social maintenance of music. The enormous amount of instrumental music and singing provided by professional musicians, many of whom were Gypsies, is a third source for
recordings of Bulgarian musicians that have reached the rest of Europe and America.[20]

Like the state, Gypsies and their relationship to Bulgarian tradition
formed an important social nexus in support of musical life in the postwar period. In a complexly textured way, their lively performances are
both central and peripheral to the Bulgarian tradition, and, while any
study of Bulgarian music has to take their enormous influence into
account, an exclusive focus on them would miss key elements at the
core of the village tradition. On the other hand, although it is rarely
discussed in the literature, a focus on one, ethnic Bulgarian, tradition
ignores the vibrant expressions of ethnic minorities within the national boundaries.

The Family

The fourth social unit supporting Bulgarian music is the family. In
villages before the war, music, song, and dance were first learned in

the family circle. Children watched their mothers and fathers, grandparents, aunts and uncles, and older siblings visit, dance, sing, and
play instruments during long autumn and winter evenings. Bulgarians
call this natural learning process the 'mother's school,' and music pro-
ficiency tended to be passed on in families, although certainly not rigidly ascribed to them.

After the war, especially within families of musicians participating in
state-sponsored professional, amateur, or wedding-music institutions,
a lively musical life continued, centered around holiday meals and get-
togethers. In these contexts, young people experienced music as an
intimate, family practice, and in some cases were inspired to take up
playing, singing, and dancing because they were activities that, as Bulgarians say, 'bring people together' and 'create fun.' In this way, the
family continued, in the Communist era, to spawn some of Bulgaria's
best young musicians.[21] If music was missing from family life, then it
was difficult, although not impossible, for children to develop a feeling
for the tradition. In some ways, the family remained the last village
institution where traditional values and practices were preserved; it
certainly was the last of these four social units that I encountered and
began to try to understand (see Katsarova 1952 for the classic study of
a Bulgarian musical family). For many Bulgarians outside the circle of
musicians supported by the state and the wedding scene, folk music
was encountered primarily as a product of the state in highly stylized
performances on stage, radio, and television, and, as one young urban-
ite said after witnessing a Varimezov family gathering full of music,
song, and dance, "I had no idea this still existed in Bulgaria."

As a social structure, the marriage exchange of a bride between two
families prompted, in both the pre- and postwar periods, the most
intense celebration, carried along by the most brilliant music-making
the groom's family could afford. Thus the family was also a patron of
professional music making, the most important one in the prewar period, but was surpassed by the state for much of the postwar period.
By the late 1980s, increased family wealth brought the state and the
family into an equilibrium that caught musicians in a battle between
competing patrons, economic incentives, and aesthetic demands.

From the foregoing discussion, it should be clear that a balanced discussion of the social maintenance of Bulgarian tradition cannot focus
on only one of the social units that supports music, but has to understand music in relation to the family, the ethnic group, the village, and
the state. To review the changing status of these social structures in the
pre- and postwar periods, the village declined in importance as the

state's role increased dramatically; the co-existence and economically structured relationships between ethnic groups became ideologically and politically charged; and the family retained its importance as a locus of learning and celebration and as an economic patron of musicians and musical life.

Individual Musical Experience

From some points of view, the historically constructed forms and socially maintained practices reviewed in this chapter can be seen as formative processes determining musical practice and culture in the ethnographic present. But a number of questions remain. Does history, society, or culture determine musical practice? Are historically constructed musical forms doomed to repeat themselves? By what mechanism do social units select or shape music? One way to answer these questions, and an alternative point of view, is to examine the human agent acting upon history in society to create cultural forms such as music. The individual inherits and appropriates musical practice, along with economic, ideological, and social practices, and then recreates, reconstructs, and reinterprets them in each moment of the present. The choices that he or she makes, the forms that tradition takes, and the interpretations of their meanings are self-interested, socially informed strategies at the intersection of the past with the present.

Can the individual, however, be a locus of study in a "social science"? How unique is the individual? To what extent does he or she occupy a social and historical position shared by others in the society? Like the old television detective series about New York, *The Naked City,* whose opening announced that there were eight million stories in the city, there are just about as many stories in Bulgaria. While Americans, influenced by an ideology of personal freedom and rights, tend to overestimate the autonomy of the individual, anthropologists, typically working with more homogeneous societies than our own, often emphasize the shared features of culture at the expense of intracultural variation.[22] Most contemporary societies, particularly where society is understood as the nation-state, occupy a middle ground between the extremes of American individualism and anthropological homogeneity, and are structured into groups according to class, occupation, gender, sexual orientation, race, ethnicity, and age.

From this sociological point of view, the individual shares culture rather fluidly with members of the various groups to which he or she belongs. Pierre Bourdieu (1977:86) writes, "Since the history of the individual is never anything other than a certain specification of the collective history of his group or class, each *individual system of dispositions* may be seen as a *structural variant* of all the other group or class habitus." (Disposition and habitus are neotheoreticisms he develops to account for the dynamics of practice, as opposed to the reified, static, givenness of the culture concept.) He continues, "In a class society, all the products of a given agent, by an essential *overdetermination,* speak inseparably and simultaneously of his class—or, more precisely, his position in the social structure." In this way, the individual can properly enter the domain of social science, not as a self or ego independent of history, society, and class, but as an agent living in a world of actions and symbols whose meanings can be interpreted from a variety of different social and historical positions.

From the previous review of the historical and social forces affecting Bulgarian music, individual musicians could be defined in terms of such group-identifying dichotomies as rural/urban, Bulgarian/Gypsy, professional/amateur, musical family/nonmusical family, man/woman, and old (raised before Communism)/young (raised during Communism). If they were truly independent, these six sociomusical factors would define 64 classes of socially positioned individuals whose culture (or world, or habitus) hypothetically differed, one from another. If even this oversimplified, hardly exhaustive, classification by dichotomy yields so many socially situated types of individuals, how should the individual be handled in a study that purports to be about Bulgarian music or the music of any complex society? Could there possibly be a "representative" individual? What would the individual represent?[23]

Given the complexity of Bulgaria's social structure, an individual could hardly represent the entire country. Since, however, individuals appropriate, activate, and manipulate the social and historical world of symbols—that is, traditions—and in the process give to culture and history whatever expressive force they have, some way must be found to introduce them into a study of music.

While innumerable strategies could be adopted,[24] the one I adopt here is to focus on two individuals, writing about them in relation to the particular, socially defined tradition they acquired, the social, ideological, and economic forces they encountered during their lives, and other individuals who challenged their experience from the perspective of the different histories and social positions within the larger society called Bulgaria. This particular choice suppresses certain issues and emphasizes others, but it should allow the many factors contributing to how and why Bulgarians make music to be identified, explained, and understood.

To claim that I selected the individuals who form the center of this study already suggests a kind of freedom that never exists in fieldwork. I was thrown into the world of Bulgarian music, and, through a series of distinctly social relations, came to know certain individuals better than others and to believe that I could tell an interesting story about Bulgarian music from their perspectives. How they entered this study was determined by the same model used to form it: a somewhat serendipitous combination of personal histories and values, both theirs and mine, with the social conditions of music making in Bulgaria at the time we met (cf. Rabinow 1977).

In the early 1970s, when I spent over a year in Bulgaria, it was possible to work only on ethnically Bulgarian traditions. Minorities, particularly Muslims like the Turks, Gypsies, and Pomaks, were problematic for Bulgarian cultural policy, and I was specifically forbidden to enter their villages or their sections of town, although local friends often took me there.[25] Since I already played clarinet, I wanted to learn to play a traditional wind instrument, the gaida or kaval,[26] and my 'academic leader' at the Bulgarian Academy of Sciences introduced me to the professional musicians at Radio Sofia's Ensemble for Folk Songs. It was here that I met the principal subject of this study.

The Radio orchestra rehearsed at that time in one of the innumerable, undistinguished, one-story, dirty-yellow buildings lining the streets of Sofia. I was thrilled to meet two of the best-known performers, the *gaidar* (bagpiper), Kostadin Varimezov, and the kaval player, Stoyan Velichkov. Arriving for work wearing suits and ties, carrying their instruments in briefcases, and yet somehow looking not quite like bureaucrats, they played in an orchestra of folk instruments, patterned after a Western orchestra, and consisting of one gaida, three kavals, six gŭdulkas, two tamburas, tŭpan, cello, and bass. After our introduction, they, along with Kosta Kolev, their director and a well-known accordionist and arranger, continued rehearsing a complicated arrangement of a folk song by one of Bulgaria's leading composers in the genre of 'arranged folklore.' When they finished playing through it, the orchestra turned toward me en masse, soliciting my opinion. At the time, involved as I was collecting remnants of village music, I didn't like the sound of such orchestras, and this arrangement used far too complex harmonies and counterpoints for my taste, destroying the integrity of the song and instrumental tunes it was based on. I shrugged my disapproval, and, to my surprise, the musicians all laughed and smiled in agreement. They didn't like it either. Much later I understood their response as another manifestation of the tension between tradition and modernity, but at the time our shared abhorrence of their music established an instant rapport.

While some in the orchestra were less than enthusiastic at the prospect of trying to teach a foreigner to play (and they had other fish to fry), Kostadin Varimezov (pl. 3), born in 1918 and raised in the village of Rosenovo in the foothills of the Strandzha Mountains east of Yambol, was the most receptive to the idea of helping me learn to play his instrument, the gaida. He was a short, stout, kindly but serious man, in his fifties at the time, and one of the oldest musicians in the ensemble. Like the others, he was extremely busy, but expressed his willingness to take on the extra duty of teaching me, saying, "I will teach you because I feel an obligation to my instrument." I later learned he was one of the few village musicians who took the idea of teaching seriously. Most had taught themselves to play, had no idea how to teach, and therefore had no interest in it. Kostadin agreed to meet me after rehearsals and at the Palace of Pioneers, a scouting-like organization, where I could join his group classes for young people. Occasionally I visited his home, a fifth-floor attic in the downtown area, to learn how he made reeds and goatskin bags for his and his students' instruments. I was impressed both by the quality of his musicianship and the seriousness with which he took his teaching and other obligations. I joked that one day perhaps he could visit me in America, a distant dream for Bulgarians living within the country's sealed borders.

My opportunity came in 1978, soon after I finished my doctoral dissertation. I invited Kostadin and his wife, Todora, to come to Toronto, he as visiting artist at the University of Toronto, where I was teaching. During the nine months of their stay, I continued my study of the gaida, recorded Kostadin's repertoire of instrumental tunes and elicited his life story, including how he learned the tradition and became a professional musician. Todora, whom I had met only briefly in Sofia, turned out to be a treasure trove of songs. Born in Rosenovo in 1923, she grew up with Kostadin, she the best singer and he the best instrumentalist of their generation in the village. I recorded her repertoire of 250 songs, together with extensive commentaries on their meaning in her life, first as a way to help her pass the time while in Toronto and then with increasing fascination as they opened up a new world for me. A tall woman, then 55 years of age, with light reddish hair and fair skin, she possessed a wonderful memory for people and events, a sensitive soul hurt by tensions in and around her, and a quick and ready laugh to deal with adversity. As in many traditional songs, Kostadin and Todora's love of music, song, and dance brought them together; they married and continued ever since to 'create fun' for themselves, their family, and friends. I don't believe it is a romantic exaggeration to say that we became like family during this period, the most intensely rewarding "fieldwork" experience I have had.

In subsequent trips to Bulgaria in 1986, 1988, and 1989, I met their large family, including a daughter, two sons and their spouses, five granddaughters, his three living brothers, her three sisters, and innumerable in-laws, cousins, nieces, and nephews. To my delight, they adopted me as one of their own, continually insisting that I was now part of their family. I met other professional and amateur musicians with connections to Kostadin and observed many music events to update my impressions in 1972 and '73. Thus a study that began with an individual quickly expanded to include the network of people with whom he interacted musically and socially throughout his life and, in the process, took on a more general significance.

Kostadin's musical career is representative of his social and historical position within Bulgarian tradition in ways that are particularly telling. During his life, he passed from one side to the other of three of the six dichotomies crucial to defining the sociomusical location of individuals in Bulgarian society. He grew up as a young, rural, amateur musician, and, through the agency of the state and the passage of time, was "reborn" as an older, urban, professional one—an excellent example of how the self changes as the symbolic and social world changes. His biography parallels the main transformations in Bulgarian society as a whole, and he in some sense represents both the older village tradition and the modern, state-supported professional one. Together, Kostadin and Todora represent both sides of a fourth dichotomy between male and female. Todora's view of the tradition contributes substantially to the first two parts of this book, and together Kostadin and Todora form the nucleus of an extended musical family that was an important locus for music making in the 1980s.

As for the other two dichotomies, they represent one side only: they are Bulgarian, not Gypsy, and they come from and perpetuate families with rich musical lives. In this book, we will come to know the other sides of these dichotomies mainly through Kostadin's and Todora's contact with them, and so in that sense they are more weakly represented. But by telling Kostadin's and Todora's life story and showing how it intersects with other lives and with competing or complementary interests and histories, I hope to generate an engaging ethnomusicological account of why and how Bulgarians make the music they do.

The story begins as Kostadin and Todora—and I through their stories—are thrown into the world of Bulgarian music in the 1920s.

Part Two
Acquiring the Tradition

Not to know what happened before one was born is always to be a child.

Cicero

THREE

Social Processes of Music Learning

I first saw Rosenovo, Kostadin's and Todora's native village, in 1986, seven years after learning its stories, songs, music, and dances in Toronto. They, their elder son Ivan, and I drove the length of Bulgaria together in Ivan's tiny Soviet-built Lada. Arriving first in Grudovo, a small town east of Yambol in the foothills of the Strandzha mountains, we spent a few nights with Todora's youngest sister, Irinka, and her husband, Kolyo. In the 1950s nearly everyone in Rosenovo had moved to Grudovo because the new government decreed that basic services like power, water, health care, and transportation would not extend to their own and other small, remote villages. One morning we left Grudovo behind, ascending on a gently curving asphalt road into the foothills of the Strandzha Mountains. It was a perfect warm summer day, the blue sky and green fields a picture of rural beauty and peace. Ivan talked about how important it was for him to return occasionally to this place where he was born and had lived until he was a teenager. His fond memories and nostalgic feelings made Rosenovo a peaceful and rejuvenating place, far from the pressures of Sofia and his job as a cinematographer. Kostadin and Todora shared many of those feelings and were anxious to show me the place where they learned the songs, dances, and tunes we had talked about for nine months in Toronto.

The Varimezovs' stories of Rosenovo begin before 1878, the year Bulgaria was created out of the Ottoman Empire by the Treaty of San Stefano.[1] Their ancestors had lived in a village named Kofchas, 40 kilometers south of Rosenovo in what is now Turkey, near the town of Kirklareli (the Bulgarians called it Lozengrad, 'Grapevine Town'; see fig. 2). In the Ottoman Empire, Turks, Greeks, and Slavs lived in close proximity and shared many elements of culture. At village fairs Bulgarians delighted in the Turkish-style wrestling and the *davul-zurna* (drum and oboe) tradition, while Bulgarian and Greek songs and dances of Thrace share many common elements.[2] In 1878, as word of the formation of a Bulgarian state reached Kofchas, the villagers realized the new borders would still place them in the Ottoman Empire, and so they packed up what they could and headed north to resettle in their new, independent homeland, Bulgaria. They founded the small village of Gergebunar, Turkish for "George's Well." After World War II, it was renamed Rosenovo for Petŭr Rosen, a Communist from the village.

The Varimezovs remember the Gergebunar of their youth in the 1920s and '30s as a small village divided into two neighborhoods with a total population of about 300 people in twelve or so extended families, each marked by an identifying last name. Its location in the hills, where water and arable land were scarce, limited its size; larger villages flourished in the plains, where better transportation and richer soil supported larger populations. Besides houses, the village included a church, a small office for the mayor, a general store, some taverns, a central square or 'dancing place' [*horishte*], and a school for the first four grades, which Kostadin and Todora attended. Beyond the center of the village, where the houses were clustered, each family worked small plots of private land to raise enough vegetables and fruits to feed themselves and tended its own animals, including a cow and goats for milk, chickens and a pig for meat, and horses for transportation. Communal grazing lands extended beyond the village and the fields around it to the forest's edge. Whatever wealth a family had was measured primarily by the number of sheep in their flock, whose sale provided an important source of income. A few families held no property except the houses they lived in, and worked in the fields and around the house for the landed villagers, who called them *ratai* ['workers' or 'servants'] and *Tsigani* [Gypsies]. These settled Gypsies, also called Bulgarian Gypsies, were nominally Christian and spoke Bulgarian. The villagers distinguished them from the Muslim, Turkish-speaking Gypsies who came to the village fairs as professional musicians. This system of private labor and the class/ethnicity hierarchy on which it was based continued to operate during the Communist period; in 1986 I saw some Gypsies making straw brooms for one of Kostadin's brothers, who lives in Grudovo.

Kostadin's father owned and managed a large flock of sheep quite successfully by village standards, a fact he attributed to his large family

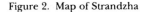
Figure 2. Map of Strandzha

of five sons, who were able to help him. Kostadin remembers his father as an extremely disciplined, hard-working man who once told him, "If I had nothing to do, I would grab the door and shake it back and forth." His father imparted that discipline to his sons. Kostadin's youngest brother, Stoyan, told me that their father expected them to rise early each morning, just as he did. Kostadin continued to rise at 5:30 or 6:00 each morning, even after a long night of playing, drinking, and socializing, an act he called "his discipline." His father's work habits resulted in the accumulation of many tools and a well-kept household. But apparently he was not generous with his wealth, and, when he refused the village joker's request to borrow a tool, the latter, noted for his wit in assigning nicknames, dubbed him "varimez," from the Turkish *var, yemez,* "he has, he doesn't give," which became the family name, Varimezov.[3]

Todora's grandfather built the first house in Gergebunar, a low, small, one-story, whitewashed building with slate tile roof that still stood in 1986, its modest condition reflecting the haste and poverty of the life being constructed in a new locale. Later a much more impressive family home was built with many rooms spread over two stories, the lower floor devoted to animals and workshops, and the second floor, with its long balcony, to living quarters (pl. 4). Todora's grandfather and father traded in sheep, buying them from the other villagers and selling them in Grudovo and Burgas. As Todora told me, "Grandpa was thought of as a merchant. He bought sheep from neighboring villages and had people who herded them. He paid them to herd them to Burgas," the largest town in Strandzha. As one of the wealthiest and most respected men in the village, her father acted occasionally as its mayor, under supervision from Grudovo.

In these circumstances and in this place, Todora and Kostadin were born into a disciplined world of hard, grinding work, but one also filled with frequent opportunities to sing, dance, and play musical instruments. In Gergebunar, they acquired the tradition they eventually imparted to their family, to much of the rest of Bulgaria, and to me.

Social Constraints on Music Learning

Music learning is a social process as well as a cognitive and psychomotor one, a matter of social maintenance as much as of "talent."[4] Who learns music and how they go about it is, in important ways, given to us by the world into which we are born. In some cultures, such as the Venda and Flathead, music learning is widespread; virtually everyone learns to sing or play or even compose as an integral part of social behavior.[5] In other cultures, the status of musician is ascribed to certain families (as for example, in North India), or, as in the West, is the rare achievement of only the most talented individuals.[6]

The Bulgarian case lies between these extremes.[7] In a Bulgarian village before World War II, not everyone sang or played an instrument (although nearly everyone danced), and people who sang and played did not occupy separate social statuses—except for Gypsies who played for weddings and fairs in towns and larger villages. Gergebunar was small enough that Gypsy professional musicians rarely came, according to the Varimezovs' account. The villagers provided their own music and song, and those who sang and played did so 'among other things' while eking out a living as subsistence farmers and shepherds like their neighbors.

Perhaps the most important social factor determining music acquisition was gender. Men were almost exclusively the instrumentalists, while women seemed to have known most of the songs.[8] The tradition was imparted differently to boys and girls, at least in part because of differing expectations about how boys and girls were to behave.[9] Virtually every boy had the opportunity to learn to play a simple instrument, like a shepherd's flute, while herding animals, but not all boys became proficient at it. And girls, who were learning skills necessary to women, like cooking, sewing, and embroidery, never had free hands to practice an instrument and were discouraged from taking up what was viewed as a male activity. On the other hand, while many girls were diligently taught songs by their mothers and acquired a large repertoire, not all did. Boys typically learned a few songs, usually casually in the company of friends and family, but rarely acquired a knowledge of the complete text.[10]

While not everyone in Gergebunar became equally proficient music makers, singing, playing music, and dancing were culturally valued behaviors, mainly because of their many functions.[11] During the courtship years, these activities, along with personal beauty and the ability to work hard, were evaluated by potential mates and in-laws as criteria for marriage. Many song texts imply that a girl made herself more attractive by singing and dancing well and a boy by playing an instrument. Singing and playing were also social skills that 'created fun' and 'brought people together.' Anyone capable of generating fun by initiating a song or playing for a dance was—and continued to be in the 1980s—an attractive, valued person. Playing and singing were also important pastimes, particularly as entertainment during work. Boys whiled away long hours herding animals by playing on small flutes they either carved themselves or bought for a few pennies (pennywhistles) at a fair. Girls sang as they weaved, fed animals in the stables, and worked in the fields; singing made the time go faster and lightened their work. Thus, music clearly had at least three social functions: it was a means of self-presentation and "decoration," social cohesion, and entertainment. But these functions for music were not sufficient to drive everyone equally to learn the tradition. While it seems that many young boys and girls learned parts of the tradition with varying success because of its obvious attractions, skill was distributed unequally, and some children never learned to sing or play.

Boys Learn to Play Instruments

Kostadin's memories of how he learned the tradition provide a basis
for generalizations about the social mechanisms of learning to play an
instrument in Bulgaria. Although his story is in some sense unique,
much of what happened to him is part of larger patterns affecting every male in this culture. The key factor determining success in music
seems to have been the family and the extent to which its members
were musical. Kostadin began to learn the tradition in his family,
a widespread and typical pattern for most of the accomplished musicians and singers in the country.[12] His father played the kaval, his
mother sang, and their music-making initially impelled young Kostadin toward music. "As a young family, my mother and father got
together with other young families and danced and sang and he
played kaval (pl. 5). It entered my head that this was pleasant. That
was the first spark. It is very important for the family to love fun.
There were families that gave out this sense of fun, both for themselves
and for other young people." By implication, and as Todora explains
later, some families lacked this tradition of music and fun, not because
of any ascribed, hereditary rule, but as a function of personality and
life experience.

The Struggle to Learn

Kostadin first played music as a boy while herding pigs. "My mother
bought me a *pishtalka* [double-reed pipe with six fingerholes made of
straw] at a village fair when I was in the second grade. Later my
brother Todor [born 1913] gave me a 'shepherd's flute' [*ovcharska
svirka*].[13] He played svirka and had a big influence on me." The name
of the first instrument boys play, shepherd's flute, indicates quite a bit
about its function. Related to the verb *svirya,* 'I play,' svirka might be
translated as 'plaything,' a kind of musical toy specifically played by
shepherds, who were typically boys, not girls. Its greatest virtue was its
low cost; it could be bought cheaply, along with other trinkets, by parents or older brothers at village fairs, and no one seemed to care
whether or not the boy eventually learned to play it. As Kostadin said,
"No music was taught. I played it for other kids while another kid
banged on some wood." Instrumental music was merely a pastime,
introducing a bit of fun into life, but valued neither as an art for its
own sake nor as a source of income.

   With these playthings, the children imitated adult musicians and entertained themselves outside the village. Adults were not interested in
the results and preferred that the music—actually the play—of children be kept as much as possible out of hearing range. Boys' musical

play was strictly for self-amusement and best not heard at all within the confines of the village by adult listeners. In 1972 I bought a similar "toy," a clay whistle-flute with eight fingerholes and two thumbholes [okarina], in a market in Sofia. As I stood on the sidewalk and tried to figure out how to play a tune on it, the merchant who sold it to me scolded, "Please go away and play somewhere else. You sound like a child."

The instrumental music produced by young children was thought of as functioning for the child's entertainment. Except for buying the instrument in the first place, adults didn't intervene to guide or to teach. In a sense the child-learner was actually banished from the village until and if he mastered the instrument well enough to play correctly. Only then was he welcome to play in the company of older youths and adults. Kostadin's first "teacher" was an older boy with whom he herded pigs. They sat together and "noodled" for hours, the older boy providing a slightly more advanced model to follow. This mode of learning might be called "peer learning" and has been frequently reported for children's music and the popular music tradition.[14]

In spite of his early exposure to the svirka and his father's kaval playing, Kostadin's first love was the gaida, constructed of a goatskin bag with wooden stocks tied into the neck and front-leg holes, and melody, drone, and blow pipes inserted into the stocks (fig. 3). Single reeds of cane placed at the top of the melody and drone pipes initiate the gaida's sound, a two-part combination of high-pitched melody and unchanging drone two octaves below. "I felt dragged to the sound of the drone. The bagpipers [gaidari; sg., gaidar] in those days used to put the drone pipe under one arm. It stuck out behind them. I used to follow along behind them during wedding processions or at fairs with my ear up against the drone." He still loves the drone sound. When I recorded him and asked him to select the microphone placement that created the best balance between melody and drone, he chose a powerful drone sound in the mix between melody and drone. Thus, his earliest musical experiences represent a combination of social and musical elements. On one hand, he was drawn to music as a pleasant activity experienced directly in the family circle, and playing svirka for his age mates replicated in the world of children the pleasant experience of adults. On the other hand, his first active commitment to music, his first love, was the result of a personal, aesthetic, mostly sensory, reaction to the drone of a bagpipe. This boy of seven had found his sound.

Simply obtaining an adequate instrument, however, proved to be a struggle. Whereas a svirka cost a penny, a gaida, with its rather intri-

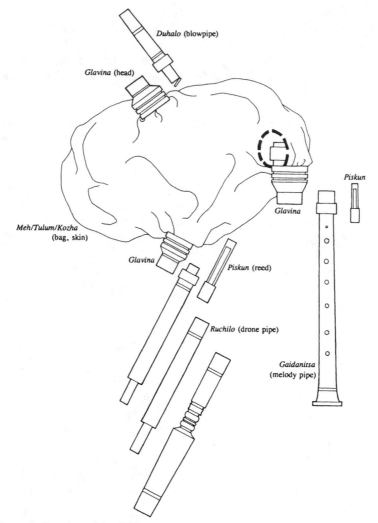

Figure 3. Drawing of the Gaida

cate parts made by a master craftsman [*maistor*], represented a substantial investment not to be taken lightly. His father, as his nickname, "Varimez," might suggest, opposed spending money for such frivolities. Young Kostadin found his mother more sympathetic. She gave him an old skin that had been used to store fresh cheese, and from it he fashioned a primitive bag [*tulum*] for a gaida. "Gaida and svirka were basic to our village. When we began to herd animals in grade school, we improvised various instruments. I tried to play this gaida with the cheese-skin bag with Stoyan [his youngest brother], who played tǔpan," but the results were unsatisfying.

In spite of his obvious love of the instrument, his family ignored his requests for a proper gaida. "I was mad at my mother and asked her to get me a gaida, but she refused. But my father's father, Dyado Todor, was there and said to her, 'Why don't you get the boy a gaida.' He understood that I was interested in it." So his mother, already sympathetic, used the intervention of her husband's father to buy Kostadin his first gaida against his own father's wishes. They obtained it through barter from an older boy, a neighbor named Yani Bogdanov (born 1912). Kostadin's oldest brother, Todor, acted as their family's shepherd. Yani loved to sing, played the gaida a bit, but was willing to part with his. As it turned out, this was no wonder. "I played this gaida only a year or so. I had so much trouble with it. The reeds were a real problem. At one point I actually was in tears from the frustration of trying to play it." So the search for an adequate instrument continued.

As Kostadin told these stories, the sense of struggle was almost palpable. He had developed a dedication to this instrument that was going to overcome all obstacles, including his father's indifference. "My father didn't pay much attention, so I turned my complaints to my mother." Eventually the combined pressure of his son and wife moved Kostadin's father to seek a good gaida from Gergebunar's best bagpiper, *Bai* Stoyan Dobrev ("Popeto").[15] *Bai* Stoyan, born in 1906, was a professional musician who came from the propertyless class of Bulgarian Gypsies in the village. He traveled to neighboring villages and towns, played in taverns and at fairs, and during the 1930s even traveled to England and France (Ognyanova and Bukureshtliev 1981:77). "He learned more technical stuff than the other gaida players in the village. He knew tunes from other villages and modern stuff, like Macedonian songs, which were like popular songs [*shlageri*] for us." Unfortunately, *Bai* Stoyan, with his sophisticated ways and need for money, was not about to give the young enthusiast a gaida or even to trade one for some service or goods in the traditional village manner. "*Bai* Stoyan wanted only money, and money in those days was hard to get. My father offered him 'doubloons' [*dubloni*, old Turkish gold coins], but he refused." Finally Dyado Todor volunteered to pay for half of it,[16] "my father sold a cart-load of firewood in Burgas to get the money," and the purchase was made.

With the acquisition of an adequate gaida, Kostadin's career and playing took off. "When people heard I had a new gaida, they invited me to play at an engagement party [*godezh*] that very evening where Ivan Kuchukov was playing. Even though I was about seven years younger, I played lighter, and people seemed to enjoy dancing to my gaida more." So the years spent playing svirka and acquiring a decent gaida had not been wasted. During that time Kostadin had learned the basic tunes of the repertoire with some sense of style and a certain speed and lightness that was highly valued by the listeners and dancers in the village. His dedication in seeking a good gaida had apparently been matched by extensive listening and practice. When he finally had an adequate instrument in his hands, he was ready to play it well.

Kostadin's Main Influences

How and from whom had he learned the tunes and ornamentation for his beloved gaida? Who were the main sources of his repertoire? The immediate and earliest sources for his repertoire can be divided into two categories: older gaida players and others who did not play the gaida but who had significant musical knowledge. According to Kostadin, over fifty men and boys could play the gaida in this one rather small village, an indication of how widespread the playing of traditional instruments was among village men at this time. For boys and men, playing an instrument was a basic part of their upbringing, a skill that they learned along with animal husbandry and later house building and horticulture.[17] In Gergebunar some of the village gaida players were members of Kostadin's immediate family. "One of my father's brothers played a bit on gaida but he wasn't well known. My mother's uncle played gaida, but I never heard him." Although family members played gaida, they were not the immediate sources for his playing. Rather, he learned from some of the better known gaida players of the village. Five older gaidari from Gergebunar influenced his style and repertoire: Dyado Todor (not his grandfather), Gotsata, Georgi Darakev, *Bai* Stoyan, and Ivan Kuchukov. An examination of his contact with them shows both how the tradition was learned and how knowledge of it was differentially distributed.

The oldest gaidar, Dyado Todor, "was from our neighborhood, the upper neighborhood. He was quite a bit older than the other gaida players [he guesses he was born in the 1870s]. He knew only a few tunes, but he played them very well. Most of his tunes came from songs." Kostadin also learned wedding dance tunes in a meter of 7, called *rŭchenitsa*s, from him. Although it is difficult to know what the criteria for "playing well" were at that time, from my conversations with Kostadin, I infer that Dyado Todor had good ornamental technique and a strong sense of rhythm; that older players may have had a smaller repertoire than became the norm in Kostadin's time; and that song tunes and wedding ritual dance tunes formed the core of the older instrumental repertoire in Gergebunar.

The second influential gaidar, Gotsata, "was born in 1891. He was from the lower neighborhood. He knew the instrumental tunes [*svirni*, sg., *svirnya*] that are played during wedding processionals and banquets." Unlike the metrical *rŭchenitsa*s, these *svirnya*s are slow, nonmetrical tunes. One of the implications of this statement is that not all the gaida players in those days knew all the possible tunes: the repertoire of the village was a composite of a number of individual repertoires, each slightly different from the others. Again, however, wedding tunes formed the core of the older gaida repertoire. Kostadin admired Gotsata's playing at a distance, both social and geographical, since Gotsata was older, not related, and lived in another neighborhood.

The third gaidar, Georgi Darakev, "was born in 1906. He learned tunes from Gotsata, and since our family were 'christeners' [*krŭstnitsi*, i.e., godparents] of his family, I learned many of Gotsata's tunes from him." Closeness, either in social or geographical space, greased the transmission of repertoire. Georgi was closer in age, residence, and social position than Gotsata, and thus became the source of his repertoire for Kostadin.

Kostadin's fourth and perhaps most important influence, *Bai* Stoyan Dobrev, also born in 1906, was more difficult to approach than the other musicians because he was from another social group, the landless "Bulgarian Gypsies," and was often away from the village, playing in taverns in Burgas and other towns. Kostadin learned an important aspect of playing technique from him through observation. "The older players curved the fingers of their top hand and stopped the holes of the melody pipe [*gaidanitsa*] with the tips of their fingers. The lower hand was flat and the middle joints covered the holes. *Bai* Stoyan used flat fingers on the top hand too, and I saw how he was able to create a nice effect by moving his first finger slightly in songs. So I changed my hand position to imitate him." This change of hand position allowed *Bai* Stoyan, and Kostadin after him, to create a pleasant finger vibrato of about a quarter tone, imitating vocal technique, on long held notes in nonmetrical tunes, rather than the rapid trill that results from raising and lowering a curved forefinger.[18]

This story illustrates a common fact about folk traditions: there are few if any rules and quite a bit of individual variation. In the 1960s and '70s I saw both curved and flat top hands, although a flat top hand is almost universal among better players, who consciously compare it to singers' vibrato and say that imitating singers is their goal.[19] Kostadin's modification of his top-hand position also shows how playing style was learned in this aural-visual-tactile tradition: he saw how a particular sound was produced, just as clearly as literate musicians see musical structures in notation. Kostadin surmised that *Bai* Stoyan learned this

manner of playing from outside the village, since the older players
Kostadin observed in the village used the curved top hand. The village
in the 1930s was not a closed system, but interacted with villages and
towns in the region through the agency of musicians who left the village and outside professionals who came in to play for fairs: Muslim
Gypsies who played zurna and tŭpan, an occasional accordion player,
and perhaps a 'song-singer' [*pesnopoets*], a person who sang and sold
sheets or little booklets of printed ballads [*pesnopoiki*].[20]

Kostadin's fifth and final model, Ivan Kuchukov, "was born in 1911.
He was closest to *Bai* Stoyan and learned a lot from him. I learned *Bai*
Stoyan's repertoire from Ivan because we were in-laws. He and my
older brother Todor married sisters." Again social and generational
closeness provided the conditions for learning this tradition. As Kostadin concluded, "I learned the old melodies from older gaida players
and then relearned them from the younger ones." He learned from
the older players by hearing them occasionally at weddings and fairs,
but he sat for long periods with the younger, socially closer players
from whom he imbibed the tradition on an ongoing, intensive basis.

Kostadin's recollections of the five most important sources of his
repertoire suggest four important lessons about how instrumentalists
acquired the tradition in the 1920s and '30s. First, knowledge of the
repertoire was scattered among different players; no single player
"knew it all," and the size of the repertoire varied from person to person and may have been smaller than Kostadin's came to be. Second,
song tunes were the basis of most instrumental repertoire, and, since
the gaida was the most important instrument at weddings—a common
expression was "a wedding without a gaida is not possible"—ritual
tunes for weddings formed the core of the gaida repertoire. Third,
there was no standard playing technique, and the flat upper hand,
which Kostadin uses, may have been a relatively recent introduction
from outside the village. Fourth, and finally, social closeness in terms
of age, neighborhood, social status or ethnicity, and family connections
provided the direct contacts necessary for learning the tradition.

Other Sources of Repertoire

Although instrumentalists provided the models for details of playing
technique, Kostadin learned much of the melodic content of the tradition from singers and dancers, who sang tunes on nonsense syllables
like "ta-da" to the would-be gaidar in a process I translate as 'to hum'
[*tŭninika*] but which resembles something closer to "scat" singing in
jazz. Many people who loved music and song but didn't play the gaida
helped Kostadin's development. While they couldn't directly produce
and model style and technique, they provided him with repertoire.

One important person was his mother. "I played a lot for my family. My mother didn't sing much, but she knew many songs and I learned a lot from her. In every house the women sang while weaving and embroidering. I remember we used to sit and she would sing and I'd play the gaida." So while elements of technique such as hand position and ornamentation were learned by observing other gaida players, key elements of the repertoire, particularly songs, the domain primarily of women but the core of the men's instrumental music, were learned within the family or from close family friends in social situations.

Kostadin also learned from some of the young men of the village who were older than he but who took him under their guidance when they realized how dedicated and skilled he seemed to be. "Stoyan Darakev, Georgi's brother, sang a lot. He used to take me to the tavern and have me sing Gotsata's tunes. He knew these tunes really well. I would play and he would say, 'Not like that, like this,' and he would sing it. He would say, 'Our Georgi can't learn these well. You will.'" Thus social recognition of his talent was important to his development, particularly the learning of repertoire, as nonmusicians helped him become a musician to take the place of older, less gifted players. The story also indicates that teaching, particularly of repertoire, occurred only after the boy acquired the skill to play stylistically correctly and learn tunes on his own during hours of practice outside the village.

"My brother Todor also taught me a lot. He would go to village fairs, hear other gaida players, and then whistle their tunes to me. I learned part of *Trite păti* [his favorite tune] this way. He would say, 'I heard this. I can't play it, but I'll whistle it for you.' One tune I learned this way was called *Odzhemarska*. I later played it so much at various fairs that it became associated with our village and then was called *Gergebunarsko* (ex. 3.1; CD #3). The naming of instrumental tunes was flexible and depended on context. Some tunes, for example, were simply named after a particular person whose favorite tune it was and who kept requesting it.

"A couple of friends of my brother were also helpful. Yani Bogdanov gave me my first gaida and knew many songs. Rale Birbuchkov [born 1910] liked me a lot. He sang me a lot of evening dance songs, the ones called *Buenek*. He was a fan of Gotsata and wanted me to play like him."

Kostadin cited a young musician's ability to get along with, respect, and gain the friendship of older people as a key social factor in becoming a good musician. Once the older men and boys recognized his talent, they were strongly encouraging and provided the social context in which he perfected his skills. "I went together with my [older] brother Todor and guys his age to nearby village fairs, maybe up to 20

Example 3.1. *Gergebunarsko horo*

kilometers away: Bukovo, Pŭnchevo, Drachevo, Grudovo (see fig. 2). They preferred me to Ivan Kuchukov, who was their age, because he drank a lot and also didn't play fast enough. We boys from Gergebunar were famous for our dancing. Two would lead the line at the front and two would take the end of the line and curl it in on *Vŭrtenata* [from *vŭrti,* 'to turn']. Traveling to fairs I had the opportunity to hear gaidari from other villages. I remember learning some tunes for wrestling from *Dyado* Dimo Pandata from Dyulevo."[21] Kostadin also acquired sufficient fame in the region to be invited to play for weddings in neighboring villages. "I remember playing my first wedding in Pŭnchevo when I was sixteen years old. I played for two days straight, and it was extremely tiring. My lips were killing me." Thus in 1934, at the age of sixteen, Kostadin completed his apprenticeship and became a respected and sought-after gaidar in the villages around Gergebunar. For the next few years, until the beginning of his military service, he led a typical young bachelor's life, traveling to fairs and playing for weddings and engagements, evening dance parties, while in the fields herding animals, and for the winter Carnival ritual, *kukerovden.*

Moving Beyond Gergebunar

In 1934 Kostadin received an invitation that illustrates the value system within which he acted and made music at that time, specifically the general attitude toward professional musicians. "I remember one time when I was sixteen we were in Burgas with my father to sell some wood. Popeto [*Bai* Stoyan Dobrev] said to my father, 'Give me this boy. I will teach him to play better.' But my father didn't want me to become a bum without a home, someone who goes wherever he wants, but doesn't come home." Such was the reputation of professional musicians in those days, and villagers could point to details of their lives as confirmation. In fact, Kostadin said, "*Bai* Stoyan eventually divorced his wife and left his four kids, married another woman and had three more." So Kostadin's potential for growth was restricted in this period by the opposition of his father, and the rest of the community, to the status of professional musician, a status further tainted by its association with Gypsies. The key values of this village culture were violated by professional musicians: they did not appear to work hard on a regular basis; they did not build up property to pass on to the next generation; and they were not at home to care for their family and provide hospitality to others. Musicians had no assets aside from their ability to play music, and instead of staying home to improve their property and build their wealth, they left home and family in search of payment for services. To a Bulgarian villager, this was no way to live. As Kostadin's father told him, "A musician cannot feed a household."[22] It would be twenty years before the social and economic conditions of music and their attendant values had changed enough for Kostadin to accept an invitation to become a professional musician.

The final stage of Kostadin's acquisition of the tradition began in 1939, during military service at the beginning of World War II, when his musical horizons expanded beyond the region around Grudovo and he was introduced to musicians, styles, and tunes from a wide area of Thrace. He was assigned to an army unit garrisoned near the town of Sliven and the Balkan Mountains forming the northern border of Thrace. There he formed his first trio with a kaval and a gŭdulka player, the latter nonexistent in the area around Gergebunar. They played together virtually every evening for dances after dinner and before lights out. From them he learned new repertoire, particularly Thracian *Trite pŭti* tunes in 2/4, 7/8 *rŭchenitsa*s, and *drobezhi*, the fast triplet variations that follow duple-meter song tunes illustrated by the last two phrases of example 3.1. He felt his growth as a musician was aided by this contact with Thracian musicians and by Gergebunar's location in a border area between Strandzha and Thrace where he was able to learn tunes in both traditions. For him, purity of regional style, valued by academics in the postwar period, was a handicap. A good musician should have mastered many different tunes and the styles implicit in them.

On the Social Processes of Music Learning

Reviewing Kostadin's personal history, five ideas about the social processes of music learning emerge.

First, instrumental music was primarily a pastime and pleasant social activity, at least for property-owning villagers. Aside from these functions, instrumental music lacked substantial economic value, and too great a concentration on it, as by professional musicians, was viewed negatively as a sign of profligacy.

Second, since music had little economic potential, there was a lack of adult involvement in the teaching process and little interest in the musical success or failure of young boys, at least until they demonstrated some musicality. In that context the potential musician had to learn the details of musical style more or less on his own through observation of sound and playing technique in a process that might be labeled peer-oriented visual-aural-tactile learning; the technique and the concepts generating musical performance were learned but not taught (Rice 1985).

Third, social closeness was an important factor in determining which members of the older generation were observed; relatives and friends from the neighborhood were more immediate sources than distant neighbors or players from other villages, and, as a consequence, the repertoires of individuals, even from the same village, differed.

Fourth, in addition to instrumentalists, nonmusicians were important in the learning process, for they provided and actively taught tunes by singing and whistling them. Older boys and men were crucial to learning repertoire, and an ability to get along with them and be recognized by them as talented was an important factor in musical success.

Fifth, what was actually learned and which instrument was chosen was at least partly the result of individual preference. Boys had a small range of choices, but within that range they were drawn for largely unexplainable aesthetic reasons to one instrument or another. Within the limits of the local tradition, their choices were not determined for them by family tradition or other forms of ascription.

These then were the social bases for learning the instrumental tradition. Every boy had the opportunity to learn, but success was not especially demanded or encouraged. Of those who did learn, some were better than others, their success a result of both musical and social skills. Music learning was embedded in a social structure and system of values in which every boy had potentially equal access to a wide range of skills and techniques, but in which, compared to hard work, hospitality, and caring for one's family, music was merely fun, a pastime, and a potentially dangerous diversion from a man's proper duties.

Girls Learn to Sing

Although boys were stimulated to learn instrumental music by the pleasant atmosphere at family gatherings and by the support of close relatives, much of the active learning started outside the village in the fields while herding animals and continued outside the home, with male friends in taverns, and at fairs. Girls, on the other hand, learned to sing around the hearth, literally at the knees of their mothers, grandmothers, aunts, older sisters and cousins (pl. 6). If a father or grandfather loved to sing, as they did in Todora's case, so much the better: "My first song, I think, was *Sŭbrali sŭ se sŭbrali*," a song whose title, appropriately enough, means 'they gathered together,' and which, in its melodic, rhythmic, and formal complexity, is far removed from stereotypes of simple songs appropriate for children (ex. 3.2; CD #4). "Our people sang it. But there wasn't just one [first song]. My aunt sang, my father sang, my mother sang in the house. Grandfather sang. I hummed along quietly with them. My two aunts came and they sang while spinning. They sang in the fields. How was I not going to sing?"

In contrast to Kostadin's story of indifference and even opposition to his learning gaida, Todora received encouragement and active teaching from a very young age. Whereas boys were cast out into the

Example 3.2. Todora's First Song: *Sŭbrali sŭ se sŭbrali*

"wilderness" to learn their instruments, girls were kept in the home and taught a desirable, publicly acceptable behavior at the same time that they were taught important female skills such as cooking, sewing, embroidering, and weaving. Singing, a desirable pastime for girls during endless hours of work, was a key element in making female friends, in self-presentation to boys in public, and in dealing with their structurally weak position in society.

Learning by Following

Todora called the traditional learning method 'following' [*sledvane*], which occurred before active teaching began and paralleled the boys' acquisition of basic style and technique before repertoire was taught. For example, the song Todora remembered learning first by following adult singers, *Sŭbrali sŭ se sŭbrali*, is nonmetrical, highly ornamented, and, by my standards, rather complex. By 'following' adults, she claimed to have learned this complicated song before what sound to me like simpler, metrical songs that children sang at school and during Lent. (In fact, in Bulgaria a distinction between adult and children's music is a difficult one to maintain.) I watched Todora exercise her following skills one evening at a party in her apartment in Sofia. One of the guests, Komna Stoyanova, a family friend and professional singer from Strandzha with a very loud voice, sang quite a few songs, and Todora, inspired by her singing, sang along with her loudly and enthusiastically, moved by the intensity and pleasure of the moment. After one particularly complicated, nonmetrical song, Todora's daughter, Stanka, said, "Mother, I didn't know you knew that song," to which Todora replied, "I don't. I have just always been good at following. That's how I learned so many songs. I followed a lot. Words and other things [for example, rhythm]. I never danced on the right side, always on the left," referring to the fact that the circle dance [*horo*] moves to the right and the person on the right would lead both the dance and the singing. "Even if I don't know anything, I can sing along. Not everyone was able to follow." Singing regularly with her mother was "how I learned to follow. She knew the songs and I followed her. Our neighbor said once, 'Dore [a short, affectionate form of Todora], I am amazed at you. You sing the song at once, even when you don't know it.' I would follow once and the second time I could sing it alone."

After beginning to sing in family settings, girls formed 'friendship pairs' [*drushki*] and sang and practiced together constantly from then on. Todora's best friend "lived near us and we sat together at working bees [*sedyankas*, lit. 'sitting parties']. At our house my mother would sing 'in front' [*napred*, meaning to lead both spatially and musically] and we after her in one voice. The next night at her house her mother

would sing first and we after her. And that's how we learned songs. We
didn't record anything" [a reference to her children's and my way of
learning songs]. Singing in pairs facilitated contact and sociability, and
a pair tended to sing together for a long time, causing some jealousy
when loyalties were perceived to change. "We knew who sang with
whom. If you sang with someone else, the other would say, 'Ah, you
are with her now!?' [laughs] I sang most with Milka Hristakeva. We
lived across [the road] from each other. We had sedyankas together.
Her mother sang well. My mother sang. We had big sedyankas in the
neighborhood." While friendships were a key to forming these singing
pairs, musical considerations, particularly blend, played a role in
choosing a singing partner. "We didn't sing with just anyone. We asked
who blended with whom. [I blended best] with Nanka Anastasia, even
though she was from another village. She was Kostadin's first
cousin."[23]

After the girls acquired a few songs by 'following' within family circles, they continued to learn and practice in public places, particularly
in school and at neighborhood and village dances. Although she can't
recall when she learned her first song, by the age of six she had already
learned quite a few. "In the first grade we made a dance at recess in
the school yard. In school, how we danced! I started [school] at six
years old, but I started to sing before that. Surely I was already singing
with mother at four years old. I remember my grandmother saying
once, 'This child will become a better singer than you.' My mother
said, 'Ah, I don't believe it' [laughs]. Because I was so little. I was a lot
younger than that when I learned the first songs. Surely I was around
five or six years old. It was easy for me. In the first grade we didn't
know just one. We knew a lot of songs already."

Soon youth and adult dances in the village square superseded home,
sedyankas, and school as places to practice and learn. At public dances,
older girls from other neighborhoods sang, providing a source of new
repertoire not heard in the family circle: "We also learned at dances,
everywhere I heard something. If there wasn't kaval or gaida [to accompany the dance], we sang all day. The whole day the horo was with
songs. We sang, sang, sang, and then repeated. The older women
would say, 'Ah, you've already started to repeat.' And we would search
for ones we hadn't sung."

Practice and Repetition

Like the boys who spent hours practicing in the fields outside the village, girls rehearsed songs many times over, both inside the family circle, where practice was a familial, social activity, and privately during
solitary work. For the processes of practicing and performing songs,

Todora used three verbs in conjunction with the object, song [*pesen*]:
(1) *tŭninika pesenta*, 'to hum or scat the song,' referred to performing a
vocal melody without words, to remember it or to teach it to another;
(2) *kazhi pesenta*, 'say the song,' although used to describe a sung performance, emphasized the text and the act of remembering the words;
and (3) *pee pesenta*, 'sing the song,' referred to a complete performance
and emphasized its melodic character, vocal style and overall quality.
"Simply when I heard a song and returned home, [I sang it] constantly
if it pleased me." Remembering a song was not, however, only a matter
of repetition. It was hard work, and there was a mysterious moment
when "all of a sudden it would disappear. The melody. I tried [to re-
member] and I couldn't. After two days or after one day it came to me
and I began [to sing it] constantly, wherever I went [*laughs*]. Only it.
With the horses. I cleaned the stables, filled the trough with chaff.
Because others couldn't hear, I could let out my voice [*laughs*]. Everywhere." Thus for girls learning began in the family, spread to nearby
relatives and friends, eventually reached the public spaces where
dances were held, and then became a matter of private repetition.

From Todora's stories, it sounds as though she never stopped singing. "I sang some songs a lot. Simply if something came to me, then I
would begin to sing the song at once. It didn't matter what I was doing.
When I was weaving, what songs I used to sing! Because I was alone.
I threw the shuttle and banged the pedals, threw and sang, threw and
sang." Her singing was obviously appreciated by others. "During the
winter, [I wove] in one house near us. They had a separate building
with an oven, a silo for wheat, and a room with a loom. There was only
one grandma and grandpa there. She worked and worked and then
came in, and I stopped. She said, 'Don't stop [singing]. I was tired of
standing outside and listening to you' [*laughs*]. At the loom I sang the
most. Whatever I thought of: harvest, dance, *sedyanka* [songs], that's
what I sang." All this singing implanted these songs firmly in her mind,
which is why she remembered them long after she left the village. Yet
she denied for herself the role of "singer," a modern role created for
professional, state-sponsored ensembles. "I am not a singer, but I sang
a lot at dances and at weddings. You have to sing a lot to remember
these songs. The ones who didn't sing [a lot] will have forgotten them."

Selecting and Rejecting Songs

Although songs were taught socially, not all of them were learned, and
individual taste shaped which songs were selected, practiced, and remembered. Thus, the size and content of each singer's repertoire differed substantially, just as the instrumental repertoire did among men.
Todora said she learned a song only if it pleased her. "Not all did."

She believed, for example, that she has a smaller repertoire than her mother: "Uf, Uf. She knew a lot of songs. I overlooked a lot of songs. Dropped them. I didn't pay attention to all the songs. For example, this summer [1988] a cousin came to visit. She is the daughter of my father's sister. Since childhood I hadn't seen her. When she came, do you know how many songs she 'said' from her mother, my aunt's songs. These were songs we used to sing with my aunt, my mother and I in the fields. We harvested with my aunt in the fields. How the three of us sang! She knew some songs from my aunt that I had skipped. I asked her, 'From where do you know these songs?' She said, 'From my mother.'" Todora estimated the size of her mother's repertoire at more than 400 songs and attributed its large size to the tradition of singing within the family. "My mother knew more than 400 songs, because I was able to list 408 [of my own] songs when we came to Sofia. My mother knew more, because grandfather knew songs and father knew songs. Father sang. Grandfather 'died' for songs."[24] In Todora's account, we have a clear example of selection operating at the individual level, rather than the community level suggested by some discussions of folk-music processes.[25]

What were the criteria for selection? Clearly one of the factors motivating the desire to learn a song was an aesthetic evaluation of text and melody, which could be separated analytically for this purpose. For example, Todora reported remembering a melody that pleased her, but forgetting the text, which presumably didn't, because, as she said, "When I heard some song, and the text pleased me, I would remember it from end to end." What pleased or displeased her about a text or melody? Since we were not able to find a vocabulary to discuss musical structure together,[26] it was difficult to speak with Todora about why certain melodies were pleasurable and thus memorable, but she readily acknowledged that some melodies were more pleasing than others. The pleasures of the text were easier for her to describe, however, because she could refer to their meaning or reference, rather than their structure, which was as difficult as musical structure for us to discuss. When I asked her what she liked in a text, she said, "Sometimes separate moments, sometimes the whole text, its contents, how it proceeds. It has a sense, it tells the truth. There is always something true in a song. [When something notable happens], afterward a song is made. Like films, that's the way they make them." For Todora, the "truth" of a song was contained in its relationship to previous experience and events, and Todora elected to learn those that answered to that experience and rejected those that did not. For instance, Todora tended to reject texts that told stories of overwhelming sadness and brutality, which she rarely experienced in her life and didn't want to experience in songs. As we shall see in more detail in part 3, the truth of the text was often emotional rather than reportorial or literal, and the way a song related "truthfully" to emotional experience was a key to its aesthetic pleasure and selection for inclusion in a singer's repertoire.

Differences in Singing Ability

How widespread was singing in those days and how did singing ability vary? Todora divided the population of potential village singers, that is, young girls, in Gergebunar into "three generations: the older, us, and the younger ones." As for the cohorts' size, "there were at least ten, maybe fifteen, in each generation." But singing ability and knowledge of songs were not distributed equally among the girls, and Todora rated only one or two in each generation as outstanding, herself among them. "Tim, do you know what kind of voice I had. If only you could have heard it. It was so strong, it was heard everywhere. It was as if it sprang out of me. And so melodious. There was a cousin across from us who sang well. There were several, three or four girls. The others sang, [*pause*] but differently. Of the singers, we were three then [who were particularly good]" out of a possible ten to fifteen in her generation. "Among the older girls, there was 'older sister' Stanka. She was my cousin. She sang very well."

To illustrate differential singing ability, Todora mentioned a wedding song with a narrow range (ex. 3.3; CD #5) that was particularly difficult to remember and sing correctly: "Some girls couldn't sing this," and she imitated them by singing on just one tone, sliding into and out of it grossly and failing to discriminate pitches clearly. "It was as if they were afraid of the song." Here the difficulty arose from the restricted range and the correspondingly undifferentiated tune. Todora's account suggests that musical ability was not distributed evenly in this society, some girls sang better than others, and discriminations were made about who sang well and who did not.

Todora's stories also suggest that some teaching, in the form of corrections to words and melody, occurred in family settings. She attributed her ability to sing these difficult songs to her mother's direct intervention. "Maybe it [ex. 3.3] was easy for me because my mother taught me. 'Not this way, that way. Not this way, that way.' So I knew it while others didn't." No attempt was made to enforce or teach the details of vocal production, tone quality or ornamental style; this was left to each individual to learn by imitation and practice as best she could. This recalls the boys' pattern, in which details of playing technique were learned alone, while older men and boys taught Kostadin some melodies by singing them to him.

Although Todora regarded herself as one of the best singers of her generation, she respected her mother's singing even more and found it difficult to imitate her perfectly. "Oh, my mother, how she sang this song [sings ex. 3.4, CD #6]. Her voice glided. It was light. I loved it, but it was difficult." She commented on how her mother's ornaments were more beautiful than her own. Interestingly, Todora's account lacked a culturally held notion of progress in this period. Unlike many younger singers and musicians of the postwar generation who claimed substantial progress in skill and complexity of repertoire compared to the older generation, Todora did not seem to view her generation as surpassing the previous one in skill or size of repertoire. Rather, modesty in the face of tradition and respect for the achievements of elders characterized her comments. As I will show in part 3, her attitudes toward music, song and dance performance were part of a general pattern of respect and 'shame' [*sram*] felt by youth toward their elders. As Todora put it, "We had shame in those days," and so her evaluation of performers centered on the achievements of the past rather than the progress of the present.

Todora attributed the differences in singing ability primarily to family background and the kinds of personalities engendered by them.

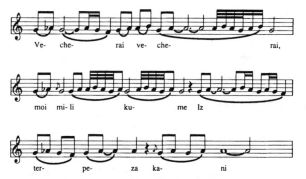

Example 3.3. Wedding Song with Narrow Range

Example 3.4. *Slŭntseto trepti zaoda* (The Sun Flickers and Sets)

Some families simply didn't sing. "I sat next to a girl in school. Her name was Ivanka. She didn't know one word of a song, and she was very bright. There just were no songs in their house. It was foreign to them. And some places everyone sang." So knowledge of songs and the desire to sing were not universally distributed at that time, and Todora viewed some families as distinctly more interested in music than others. Aside from Ivanka's family, where playing and singing seem to have been nonexistent, the skill and abundance of musicians and singers within families differed considerably. "Most [families] didn't have many, but there were other families with singers and musicians. Tuhichkovi, they were a large family. They had four or five children, and among them was a gaida." She named two other families with singers and musicians, which means that, including her and Kostadin's family, there were at least five of perhaps twelve families with a large coterie of singers and musicians. Along with her estimate of the number and quality of singers in her generation, her account suggests that extensive knowledge and skill at music and song were distributed among about a quarter to half of the village's population at that time.

The Social Basis of Girls' Song Learning

The social basis of girls' song learning in this tradition included the following eight features: (1) learning was encouraged by providing appropriate social settings, primarily within the family; (2) it began in the family and spread outward to neighbors, the whole village, and later to other villages; (3) it started at a very young age—four to six years old; (4) it was selective with respect to repertoire; (5) learning ability varied, and some were more successful at it than others; (6) active teaching, in the form of corrections of errors, was done, primarily by older women; (7) private repetition was crucial to absorbing the tradition; and (8) learning was linked to personal qualities such as sociability. This list summarizes the effort female adults and children devoted to learning the singing tradition in the prewar period, a process whose effectiveness depended on family circumstance, individual skill, and practice.

In this chapter, I examined the social parameters affecting how boys learned instrumental music and girls learned to sing. Singing and playing were important pastimes during gender-differentiated work, ways of making oneself attractive to others, and a means to bring family and friends together. For girls and women, singing was important enough that they spent a great deal of time passing it on within family circles. For boys and men, on the other hand, instrumental music was taught only after boys acquired on their own some basic musical skills and concepts, from how to produce a good sound to how to articulate a simple melody.

For Todora and Kostadin, the link between music making and sociability was an especially important part of their lives. People who did not sing or play music "were quieter, shier. And strangers didn't enter their house. My friend, Ivanka, they never had guests. It's not that they were bad people; they just didn't have contact with people. Ivanka's mother and father were very quiet, but not sociable, more independent, more closed." There was a dialectical relation between sociability and playing and singing. Music was sparked and aided in social settings, on the one hand, and sociable people often found themselves in situations where playing and singing were required. Musical skill, the opportunity to perform in public, and sociability reinforced each other. As Todora explained, "Songs help bring people together. I don't remember [Ivanka] coming to sitting bees [*sedyankas*] or corn-shucking bees [*medzhiyas*]."[27] Todora's family, on the other hand, and the one she created after marrying Kostadin, were the opposite. "My father was well known and people traveling from Bogdanovo to Grudovo would stop and spend the night. We were never without guests. Later after we [Kostadin and Todora] built our house near my mother and father's house, mother said, 'Eh, our guests came to you, just like to us. Rejoice that you have guests. If you don't have guests, it's not good'" [*laughs*]. Their hospitable reception of guests remained a constant in their lives, even after moving to the city. "Even now when we go back to Shishman [the street where they live in Sofia], we haven't even put our bags down and the bell rings."

In part 3, Living the Tradition, I examine in more detail the ideological and economic climate in which music and song were acquired. But in the next chapter, I focus on the cognitive processes involved in learning the instrumental tradition, using my own experience and observations, to expand my musical horizons and develop a more detailed understanding of this tradition.

FOUR

Cognitive Processes in Music Learning

Acquiring a musical tradition involves not only social processes but cognitive and physical ones as well. In this chapter, I examine how some would-be gaidari, including myself, acquired the intellectual and motor skills necessary to play in this tradition. To understand these processes in the instrumental tradition, I employ my own performance and the introspection that results from it to explain elements of musical cognition, and in the process suggest a way to mediate the insider/outsider or emic/etic dichotomy that has loomed so large in ethnomusicological theory.

The previous chapter reconstructed the social processes that supported learning to sing and to play instrumental music in a Bulgarian village in the 1920s and suggested that active teaching of playing technique and singing style was almost nonexistent: such details were learned but not taught. Girls learned song tunes and their style by 'following' older girls and women, and boys learned to play an instrument by listening to and watching older musicians and then retreating to the outskirts of the village to understand and apply what they had seen and heard. In the girls' case, the older women's willingness to sing with them for long hours implies both their interest in a certain kind of teaching and their high valuation of singing and of songs. Older boys and men, however, intervened to teach only after the youth had demonstrated a competence implying that some form of musical knowledge or understanding had already been imbibed. In effect, older men had no way to teach cognitive skills such as the relationship between fingerings and pitches, how tunes were articulated with ornamentation, and how melodic fragments or whole melodies could be remembered. Boys had to learn at least these rudiments on their own. Only after they demonstrated these skills would older men sit with them and teach them tunes by humming, whistling or playing. How young instrumentalists came to understand musical concepts—from melodic structures to complicated ornamental technique—is the subject of the first two sections of the chapter and is based on my observation of other musicians in various stages of the learning process and on my own attempts to learn to play gaida.

First Lessons

My desire to learn the playing tradition foundered on the simplest problem: how to acquire music lessons. When I first visited Bulgaria in 1969, I wanted to meet musicians, record their playing, buy instruments, and ultimately learn to play the music myself. The musicians were usually very friendly and, when I thought I had established good rapport with them, I asked them for "music lessons" in my halting Bulgarian. In spite of what I thought was a reasonably good relationship, my requests were typically greeted with indifference, ignored, or, in some rather indirect way, refused. I was puzzled. Had I misjudged their interest in me? Did I not know how to ask for lessons properly? What was the problem? Only much later did I realize that most of these musicians, like Kostadin, had never taken a music lesson themselves and had no idea how to give one. They could perhaps have corrected my playing if I already played something, but they had no idea how to teach me to play "from scratch." When, after more systematic study, I realized that the tradition was learned but not taught, I expressed my surprise to a highly skilled accordionist and arranger who had attended the conservatory in Sofia. He concurred, saying, "Not even fathers taught their sons to play these instruments." One of my many requests for help was finally answered affirmatively by Dimitŭr Grivnin, a fine gaida player from the Rhodope village of Shiroka Lŭka.[1] That lesson provided some of the best ethnographic evidence I have for how young boys acquired the cognitive categories necessary to play the instrumental music—and the gaida in particular.

When I arrived at *Bai* Dimitŭr's house for my first lesson, he was already playing, and his ten-year-old grandson was attempting to follow along as best he could. The lesson consisted of Grivnin playing at full speed without simplification, while his grandson played along simultaneously, in effect, 'following.' The grandson, however, could neither play the melody nor mimic in any precise way what his grandfather was doing. His playing resembled "noodling," that is, it consisted of disorganized fragments of sounds played with rapid finger movement, but he produced no discernible pattern. I infer that what he saw, heard, and understood was that his grandfather's music burbled with dense sounds and required rapid finger movements; he probably didn't understand the metrical, melodic, and ornamental structures of the music; and certainly, if he did understand these things, he wasn't able to coordinate his fingers to produce them.

Bai Dimitŭr invited me to join in the playing and soon the three of us were making a terrible racket. My tack at this point was to hold a drone and listen for the melody and rhythm, notice the fingerings he used to produce the melody, ignore the ornamentation and rapid finger movements, and find the tune on my instrument. After a few trials I managed to play a hesitant, clumsy version of the melody absolutely devoid of any ornamentation or much rhythm. Suddenly *Bai* Dimitŭr stopped, pointed at me, and shouted enthusiastically at his grandson, "*That* is what you should be playing. See what a good musician he is." "That" meant the melody, with its pitches and rhythms, but he had no word or more specific way of telling his grandson what to do or what the problem was.

Bai Dimitŭr's own playing I take as prima facie evidence that he possessed the cognitive categories, strategies, or schemata necessary to produce music, although these categories, in the case of older village musicians like himself, were tacit, nonverbal ones. They existed beyond verbalization in the domain Seeger called "music knowledge" and Bourdieu (1977) the "habitus" from which the strategies of practice emerge. The verbal knowledge about music captured in music terminology, theory, and notation allows the corresponding categories to be actively taught in a particular way. However, in aurally transmitted traditions without such terminology and theory, music knowledge and categories are acquired in a different way.

Although the older man was frustrated that his grandson couldn't produce a tune on the instrument, it was clear to me that the child had learned and understood something, and probably was closer to becoming a gaidar than I was. Although I had the cognitive categories necessary to abstract a tune out Grivnin's maze of amazing sound, it would be years before I had the cognitive equipment to play the ornamentation as well as his grandson surely came to play it. The boy, for example, occasionally produced sounds in patterns very close to or even exactly like his grandfather's ornaments, whereas I had no idea of how these ornaments worked and couldn't imagine my fingers moving fast enough to produce them. The boy understood, or was trying to understand, the total sound of the instrument, not just the melody and rhythm. What he saw were rapidly moving fingers; what he heard was a dense succession of sounds; and he tried to reproduce both. His mind and fingers had grasped, or were close to grasping, the essence of the ornamentation, but he had not yet integrated his aural and visual understanding of the total sound with whatever understanding of melody and rhythm he may have had. In succeeding days, I watched him walk through the streets of the village, fingers flying, bagpipe burbling, happily searching for the music in the gaida.[2]

At this point, I can only speculate about the cognitive processes involved in playing the gaida, and which of these *Bai* Dimitŭr's grandson may have possessed. My first hypothesis is that, at the age of ten, he may have lacked the cognitive categories necessary to understand and produce melodies. Since boys didn't sit at their mother's knee for long hours of following tunes, perhaps they developed the ability to apprehend and generate melodies, that is, this particular kind of "musical understanding," later than girls and mainly in the context of playing alone in the fields. In the absence of the sort of intimate and ongoing modeling of song melodies girls experienced, boys probably acquired the instrumental tradition on their own, in a less intensely directed fashion, and therefore at a later age than that at which girls came to understand the song tradition. On the other hand, if we recall that young girls of four or so were apparently learning complicated nonmetrical tunes, that Kostadin sat and listened to his mother sing, and that children were taught songs in school, perhaps *Bai* Dimitŭr's grandson—and other boys learning the tradition—had some ability to conceptualize sung melodies. Why then could he not play? Where was he cognitively?

If the boy could sing songs but not reproduce them on the gaida, there are at least four possible reasons. First, the ornamental richness of gaida playing may have obscured the relationship between played melodies and sung melodies. Since *Bai* Dimitŭr didn't hum or sing them to him, he wasn't taught the connection between sung and played melodies. Although older boys and men taught Kostadin by singing for him, they did so only after he had demonstrated his ability to make the connection himself.

Second, his particular stage of cognitive development may not have allowed generalization of the rules of melodic formation to a new case, that is, from song tunes to instrumental music.[3]

Third, perhaps different "cognitive schemata" are used in apprehension and production of music.[4] For example, he may have had aural schemata in place for understanding melodic form but lacked the finger schemata necessary to produce them on the gaida—and perhaps a feedback loop linking aural and finger schemata.[5]

Finally, he may have been at the very beginning of the learning process and, like children who bang out complicated chord clusters on the piano when left to their own devices, vainly hoped to make some sounds like those he heard from experienced musicians.

We needn't choose between these last four hypotheses; all could be true in some sense, but they illustrate a set of interesting questions and problems, all in principle testable, that more extended research and observation, perhaps of the sort done by psychologists, would be necessary to solve.

Kostadin Acquires the Concept of Melody

Kostadin's account of his own learning suggested that similar processes to those described were at work as he tried to learn the tradition. He remembered playing the instrument for three years, from about the age of eleven to fourteen, before learning his first 'melody' [*melodiya*] from an accordion player at a village fair. If he wasn't playing melodies during those three years, what was he doing? I surmise that he was (1) watching and trying to organize finger movements at the smallest level of detail, "noodling," learning to "finger" the instrument; and (2) playing short fragments of melody, built on ornamental 'licks' [*persenks*] that underlay instrumental improvisation.

As Kostadin tried to remember his learning process in the 1930s from the perspective of the 1970s, he used two words, *melodiya* and *persenk*, whose cognitive salience had shifted over the years. *Bai* Dimitŭr had no word for melody in 1969, and I doubt that Kostadin did either when he learned his first one in 1932. I surmise that he learned the concepts underlying well-formed, multimeasure melodies nonverbally in the 1930s and learned to apply the verbal category *melody* to that musical knowledge after the war, when he trained as a professional musician. He told me that, in the 1930s, *persenk* was the only word he and others in Gergebunar used to label a musical fragment. He recalled, for example, his oldest brother Todor saying, "Here's a nice *persenk* I heard from so-and-so," and then humming something. In the 1970s, Kostadin translated *persenk* as 'a thing,' a musical thing to be sure, but one whose exact structural dimensions he no longer could reconstruct, presumably because the new verbal category, melody, had displaced it. From our conversations I concluded that *persenk* had two possible meanings: it referred to a not quite fully formed melody, but rather a one- or two-measure melodic fragment; or it referred to a range of melodic expression from one-measure fragments to complete melodies.[6] Thus, when Kostadin said he learned his first melody after playing for three years, I assume that was the moment at which his nonverbal understanding of melodic fragments enlarged to include phrase-structuring principles such as cadences, which define the endings of extended melodic forms.

That instrumental performance in the 1920s and '30s was based on strung-together melodic fragments [*persenks*] with few if any cadences is illustrated in example 4.1, a 9/8 dance tune called *Testemelichka* performed in 1929 by a violin player from a village in the Kirklareli area, the Varimezovs' grandparents' original home.[7] Vasil Stoin, the most famous Bulgarian folk song collector, transcribed it in the field and included it in his collection of Thracian songs (Stoin 1939: #1681). The example illustrates what I suspect was a common instrumentalist's practice of the period, namely repeating one-measure melodic fragments without cadences followed by contrasting strings of repeated fragments. What Kostadin probably meant by "learning his first melody" was that he played one or more fragments and ended in a cadence on the tonic, the cadence in effect defining a melody as opposed to a 'lick,' fragment, or *persenk*.[8]

Kostadin, unaware of the transcription but knowing the material in local, aural tradition, used the last fragment of example 4.1 for a tune from a set of tunes he calls *Daichovo horo*. To construct a four-measure ABAC melody (ex. 4.2), he alternated the 1929 *persenk* with a new measure of melodic material and a cadential phrase. (Example 4.2 is written a fourth above example 4.1 and in 9/8 rather than 9/16.) I hypothesize that his growth in understanding at the age of fourteen, his cognitive shift from *persenk* to *melodiya*, occurred—possibly over a

Example 4.1. Tunes in 9/8 Built on One-Measure Motifs, from Stoin's Thracian Collection

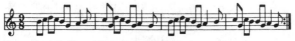

Example 4.2. Kostadin's *Daichovo* Melody

period of time—when the cognitive categories necessary to form melodies longer than one-measure fragments appeared; the intellectual connection between song melodies and instrumental tunes was made;[9] and his fingers gained enough motor control to articulate a melody with some stylistically appropriate ornamentation. When these understandings coalesced, he had the mental equipment to acquire a rich store of melodies and richer ornamental technique as he travelled throughout the region, meeting and hearing other musicians.

Acquisition of Cognitive Categories

From these interviews and observations, I suggest the following five principles for the acquisition of cognitive categories in this instrumental tradition.

1. Older musicians learned at least some aspects of ornamentation, which was so aurally striking and yet difficult for me to achieve, in combination with melody such that they couldn't pull them apart in order to, for example, teach them.

2. Older Bulgarian musicians took ornamentation for granted as a relatively unproblematic aspect of musical performance that followed upon careful listening, watching, and practice. Their technique, which to me seemed magically virtuosic and beyond my capacities, was, to them, a fairly straightforward skill to be acquired if one wished and had the time and patience, although some, like Kostadin, were recognized as being especially skilled at it. Many village men learned to play the gaida adequately from a stylistic point of view, but relatively few of them seem to have acquired the cognitive categories, or had an opportunity to play often enough, to develop an extensive repertoire.[10]

3. In the absence of verbal markers and descriptors of melodic form, the cognitive structuring, acquisition, and memory of a repertoire of melodies, which Western notation captures so clearly and makes so easy for musicians to think about and remember, was much more of a problem in this aural tradition. Composers in many European and American styles and traditions use notation to prescribe melodies but are content to leave style and ornamentation to an aural tradition, whereas, in the Bulgarian instrumental tradition of the 1930s, technique could be seen and imitated, but each new student had to generalize and learn on his own the abstract conceptions governing melodies

without verbal or visual aids. The difficulty of this task helps explain why Bulgarians so often cited to me the size of repertoire as one of the most important criteria of a good musician, in the process ignoring virtuosity and technical ability.

4. In at least some cases, musicians seem to have learned and understood the main features of style and ornamentation, located in the shortest spans of time, before or without grasping the principles necessary to remember and recreate melodies over longer spans of time.[11] These examples suggest that the concepts necessary to produce ornamentation and style, in the form of basic finger patterns and movements, were learned in many cases in advance of concepts necessary to produce melodies longer than a 'lick' [*persenk*], and that knowledge of repertoire separated good from bad musicians as much as virtuosity or technical facility. Kostadin, for example, joked with me about gaidari he had heard who very impressively 'blew up' the gaida, filling the bag with air, and began with an ornamental flourish [*razsvirvane*] before settling on the tonic pitch and beginning the tune proper (ex. 4.3). "From the *razsvirvane* you thought they were good musicians until they began to play"; then it turned out they didn't know many, or even any, tunes properly.

5. Better musicians, such as Kostadin, probably went through a long, complicated learning process in which they alternated back and forth between new understandings of fingering technique and increasing the density and subtlety of their ornamental style, on one hand, and adding new melodies, and perhaps new melodic understandings, to their repertoires on the other.

Since Kostadin and most musicians of his generation could describe little of the structure of either melody or ornamentation, I turn next to my own attempts to acquire aspects of the tradition for further evidence of the cognitive processes underlying the playing of music in this tradition.

Pre-understandings of the Tradition

If acquiring ornamental style seemed less problematic for village gaidari than understanding and remembering melodies, the opposite was true for me. With my Western musical training, I could easily explain,

Example 4.3. The *razsvirvane*

understand, and remember the typical four-measure tunes of the instrumental tradition, but the gaida's burbling ornamentation remained beyond my horizon of understanding. This was particularly frustrating, since ornamental style seemed to me, and probably to Bulgarians as well, crucial to defining the music as Bulgarian or Thracian. If I was going to understand Bulgarian music in general, and gaida playing in particular, I would have to learn more about how these ornaments were produced and what they represented in terms of musical experience.

The problem was that village musicians possessed little vocabulary to describe the structuring of either melody or ornamentation.[12] Whatever cognitive structures and conceptions the musicians acquired were nonverbal and expressed entirely in the music itself. To understand what concepts were necessary to play this music and how they were acquired, I could not turn to cognitive anthropology, the usual way to approach a so-called emic or insider understanding, because there was little speech about music to guide the enquiry. Even Kostadin, who, by the time I met him, had learned a Western musical vocabulary for melody, mode, and rhythm, could not teach or explain the ornamentation. It would have to come on its own, just as it did for boys in the village.

While I learned in the inverse order of the traditional manner—that is, melody and rhythm before ornamentation and style—I eventually moved beyond both Western concepts and the few words of explanation older musicians had for their music to a much more complete understanding of the tradition than I began with. That new understanding is neither an insider's (emic) nor an outsider's (etic). It is the provisional endpoint of a hermeneutic arc that allows me to explain the previously opaque nature of gaida ornamentation and to understand one way that it can be acquired and produced. Some positivist scholars might argue that my personal journey to such understanding, that is, my appropriation of the playing tradition, is irrelevant to an understanding of Bulgarian music cognition, but I believe the broadening of my cognitive and musical horizons in the direction of a "fusion of horizons" with those of Bulgarian musicians has important lessons to teach about music cognition, crossing musical barriers between cultures, and Bulgarian music itself.[13]

While there were good scholarly reasons to understand more about ornamentation, learning to play it became a kind of obligation when I studied it under Kostadin's tutelage. As I mentioned earlier, he was one of the few musicians of his generation who could give a music lesson. That's one of the primary reasons he was willing to work with me, and that's why I invited him to Toronto. When he arrived there in 1978, he said, "I don't want to waste my time here; I want to pass on the tradition to someone, and Tim, I think you have the best chance." What a burden! I wanted to learn to play but had no confidence I could. Bulgarian instrumental music seemed hopelessly fast and virtuosic. I had never played any instrument at that level of accomplishment before and yet foolishly wanted to try. Kostadin turned my selfish desire into a duty. Ironically, although no one cared much whether Kostadin learned, he cared that I learn, which set in motion my own struggle to play the gaida. Following Ricoeur (1981:190–193), I had to lose myself (and my self-consciousness) "in front of" the music in order to develop a new self capable of understanding and appropriating it.

Five Lessons

My learning began by applying and refining concepts from my training in Western music in order to explain what I heard and saw in Bulgarian music and dance. If we ask, for example, what do you understand when you play the gaida, or what do you have to learn in order to play it, the easiest answers, for those trained in Western music theory, concern meter, melody, and form. Rather than approach learning the tradition as a child might, imitating the style with its rapid notes and finger movements, I began as a musicologist, conceptualizing musical structures. At this first move toward explanation, I learned five important lessons, based on careful listening, transcriptions of performances, and an examination of the gaida itself.

The first lesson concerned meter and rhythm, probably because I encountered the music first as a dancer. I learned that each dance type, labeled with its own generic name, had a unique, repeating pattern of unequal-length "beats," which American dance teachers referred to as short (S) and long (L) beats, for example:

> *paidushko horo* (2 beats): S-L, S-L, S-L;
> *rŭchenitsa* (3 beats): S-S-L, S-S-L, S-S-L;
> *kopanitsa* (5 beats): S-S-L-S-S, S-S-L-S-S, S-S-L-S-S.

Only after I literally embodied these patterns did I realize that the unequal "beats" could be subdivided conceptually into equally spaced pulses and therefore "measured" and "explained," as in example 4.4. The dancers' short "beats" contained two pulses, while their long "beats" contained three pulses. The two unequal "beats" of *paidushko*

Example 4.4. Representations of Rhythm and Meter

could be explained as five equal pulses and transcribed in 5/8 time.[14]
This relationship of two to three was foreign to my previous experience of Western music, but I had already taken it into my body naturally and without recourse to the intellection associated with music theory: in hermeneutical terms, I understood the meters before I
explained them.

When I began to play the gaida, I learned that my explanation was
not arbitrary but expressed in the music itself. While dancers danced
to the unequal beats, gaidari and other instrumentalists often played
the equal-spaced pulses that underlay and "measured" the dancers'
recurring beat pattern. Musicians transformed the three-beat count of
the dancers into a musical meter of 7 pulses per measure by playing
equally spaced tones (ex. 4.5).

The second important lesson concerned modality on the gaida. The
tonic, two octaves above the drone and transcribed here on a', was the
middle pitch of the melody pipe. There were five notes above it and
five below it. The standard fingerings, shown in example 4.6, yield two
conjunct major pentachords around the tonic.

Most tunes were played in the pentachord above the tonic, and gaidari typically played four pentachordal types by altering the second
and third degrees above the tonic (ex. 4.7). The "standard" pentachord, the most easily played, was the familiar major pentachord. The
other pentachords would be called "minor" by Western music theory,
"phrygian" by Medieval music theory, and "hijaz" by Arabic and Turkish theory. The chromatic possibilities in this five-note range are
achieved by opening the 'flea hole' [*mormorka*], a tiny hole at the top of
the chanter (hole 7). Given any finger position, when hole 7 is uncov-
ered, the pitch goes up approximately a half step. Learners can hear
these modal possibilities, and while village gaidari didn't name them,
they could see them being consciously manipulated by the use of alternate fingerings. Thus, even when not labeled verbally, the outsider can
understand pentachordal differences as part of Bulgarian musicians'
motor and aural experience.

The third lesson was that the gaidari "changed keys," that is, they used a number of different pitches as tonal centers for their melodies. The gaida's drone pitch on A, two octaves below a', never changes, but other pitches on the chanter can be used as tonal centers, and Kostadin commonly played tunes that cadenced on a', b', g', and e'. Example 4.8 (CD #7) contains a sequence of tunes that Kostadin played in different keys and modes.[15]

The fourth lesson was that many gaida melodies, as Kostadin played them, consisted of short, one-measure motifs organized into four-measure phrases, which were then repeated, as in example 4.8. Kostadin turned a *persenk* or fragment into, in postwar terminology, a *kolyano* ('knee' or 'joint,' but 'phrase' in music theory) by inserting a cadence every two or four measures. He typically constructed such phrases by repeating the motif three times followed by a cadence or by alternating the motif with a half cadence and full cadence. Kostadin's gaida melodies, perhaps more than those for kaval and gŭdulka, depended on such repetition of short motives (see ex. 4.9).

The fifth lesson was that Kostadin and other Bulgarian musicians manufactured performances by stringing together a series of repeated four-measure melodies, some related and some contrasting (exx. 4.8, 4.9). In the postwar period, Bulgarian musicians like Kostadin consciously used variation for unity and tonal and modal contrast for vari-

Example 4.5. Rhythmic Treatment of 7/8 Meter

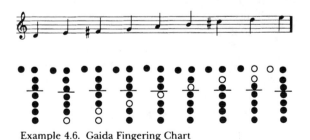

Example 4.6. Gaida Fingering Chart

Example 4.7. Pentachords on the Gaida

Example 4.8. Key and Mode Changes in *Pravo horo*

Example 4.9. Motivic Construction of Melodies in *Trite pŭti*

ety to create interesting, satisfying performances. How they learned to do this is examined in chapter 7.

These five "lessons" or explanations describe and make sense of the most important structural principles that Kostadin employed in his playing of dance tunes. I arrived at this understanding by applying, with only slight modifications, pre-understandings of music that were part of my world before I encountered Bulgarian music. Given the regularity with which musicians and dancers expressed these principles in their performances, it is reasonable to infer that, even if unverbalized, they, or something analogous to them, exist as "structuring structures" (Bourdieu 1977) in Bulgarian musicians' cognition.

The Mystery of Ornamentation

If the structural principles of gaida music are relatively straightforward, its rich ornamentation—and musicians' ability to play at enormous speeds—still seemed magical, and beyond my meager musical powers. My love of the music, and Kostadin's prodding, impelled me to enter this mystic land of virtuosity, a territory I had never before explored, but my initial efforts were pathetic and discouraging. While

I could explain many things by carefully listening, watching, and transcribing, I failed to grasp, and my notations failed to record, Kostadin's playing style. My preexisting Western concepts handled the rudiments of Bulgarian melody and rhythm adequately, but the manner of playing remained a mystery—*le mystère des doigts bulgares*. How could his, let alone my, fingers work so fast? Since this is a central feature of a gaidar's musical experience, I outline the various stages I went through to understand and be able to play the gaida's ornamentation. Perhaps the most profound discovery was that I learned to fuse my concepts of melody and ornamentation into a single concept expressed most vividly in the hands, not in musical notation—precisely the kind of integration I imagine young Bulgarian boys achieved when they learned this tradition.

Articulation and Accentuation

The most basic kind of gaida ornamentation results from the need to separate one melody note from another when the reed sits in the top of the melody pipe and air from the bag flows over it uninterruptedly. You cannot use your tongue to stop the sound, as you do on the clarinet or oboe. Kostadin showed me how to use a "closed fingering" technique (ex. 4.6), in which only one or two fingers are lifted off the gaida at a time to produce a tone. In consequence, a quick strike of the finger on the open hole separates two melodic tones with the briefest possible descent to a lower note that replaces and functions like the momentary silence created by tonguing the reed (ex. 4.10). Although barely audible, it contributes to the gaida's distinctive sound.

A tonguing effect can also be achieved between two different pitches in an analogous manner, so that a gaidar can choose conceptually and physically between a detached or a legato style. To play legato, he raises the finger over the new hole that will sound before he closes the hole that is currently sounding. In this case, the desire to play legato leads to a physical act that produces no sound between melody notes and a legato playing style. To play detached, the player closes the

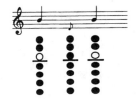

Example 4.10. Fingering for Repeated Notes

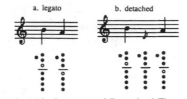

Example 4.11. Legato and Detached Fingering

sounding hole slightly before opening the next hole to omit a faint low-pitched sound that functions like tonguing. (This effect is called a "crossing noise" in Scottish bagpiping and is considered an undesirable error.) Since a sound emerges, this detached manner of playing can be captured in Western notation (ex. 4.11), but insofar as notation might try to describe conception and intention, the low sound has meaning in opposition to or paired with the absence of sounding articulation.

Before Kostadin showed me these techniques, I had no way of evaluating their importance by listening to recordings. Nor did I understand whether they were accidental or intended. With my new knowledge, I was able to play with adequate articulation of repeated and "tongued" notes and to choose between legato and detached articulation. In the postwar period, Kostadin had learned to teach this aspect of a tradition he had learned without being taught.

Articulation was one of the few ornamental details Kostadin could show me, and he often insisted I add articulation where it was missing. During this phase of his teaching, I learned that players consciously manipulated these barely audible sounds, which might be interpreted by a listener as accidental, haphazard, or meaningless, in three important ways.

First, they controlled the strength of the accent or articulation by choosing the ornamental pitch between melody notes and then preparing the closed fingering to get the result they wanted. In general, the lower the grace note is pitched, the stronger the effect of the accent. The most common choice is between e′ and d′, the latter creating a slightly stronger effect and often used at the beginning of measures or beats to create a heavy accent (ex. 4.12). When pitches above the tonal center, a′, are accented or separated, the notes chosen are also an index of regional or personal style. For example, to separate c♯″s, Kostadin preferred a relatively light feeling using b′; *Shop* bagpipers used e′, creating a much more staccato-like effect; and Georgi Doichev, a young professional gaidar from Thrace, used a′ because it fit into

Example 4.12. Choice of Accent Note in Mid-Range Melody

a. Thracian   b. *Shop*   c. Thracian
(Kostadin)   (Doichev)

Example 4.13. Separating c″

Example 4.14. Measure Played Detached and Legato

the A-major chord that often accompanied his playing in professional ensembles (ex. 4.13).

The second way gaidari manipulated accents for aesthetic effect was by choosing the style of articulation: Kostadin sometimes played a melodic motif legato and "tongued" it on the repeat for the sake of variety (ex. 4.14).

The third and most subtle way Kostadin manipulated accentuation was by lengthening the articulatory low tone. In principle, this note lasts a mere instant, but good players like Kostadin actually seemed to lengthen the note slightly when they wanted to create a particularly strong accent. This tiny detail, which I have not attempted to transcribe because it is simply too subtle, seems to be one of the most important devices that a player can use to play expressively on this continuously sounding, uniformly loud instrument. In example 4.15, Kostadin emphasized the first note in this way by lengthening slightly the d′, and in the second measure he accented e″ by lengthening slightly the grace notes on a′ and taking time away from the melodic pitches.

As I learned to play, Kostadin constantly corrected my articulation. Although nearly imperceptible to the listener, it is part of the performer's art par excellence, and Kostadin had learned how to teach it in the years after he became a professional musician. With his guidance I learned to play a phrase of music that could be transcribed with the articulation or accentuation added, as in example 4.15. Compared with my earlier melodic transcriptions, the considerable increase in

Example 4.15. Phrase with Strong Accents

detail indicates an increase in the number of concepts I used to explain and understand the music. Not only did I know they existed, I knew what they "meant" in terms of a players' intention. In that sense, by learning to play, I moved from hearing the music strictly as a "text" that in some ways eclipsed or hid its author's intention, to understanding the music as a discourse or dialogue between musicians. A dialogue contains an ostensive reference to the world around it, to the speaker's meaning, and the listener's understanding; the object of dialogue is to settle on these intended and understood references. A music lesson of the sort Kostadin was able to give in the postwar period provided just such a dialogic opportunity to learn about one aspect of a player's conscious intentions in performance and therefore part of the meaning of a performance. The understandings I achieved in this phase of my learning referenced part of a Bulgarian musician's expressive world.

High-Pitched Ornamentation

While Kostadin was satisfied when I learned to play the tunes and articulation notated here rhythmically and at a tempo fast enough for dancers, I was not. I heard many more sounds in his playing than in my own, and wanted desperately to make my gaida sound like his, with all its high-pitched ornamentation. He couldn't, however, explicitly teach this aspect of his performance, and I couldn't learn it. When I tried to add the high ornamentation, it invariably sounded gross and awkward, and Kostadin at one point said to me, "Tim, don't add the thumb [the finger that produces the highest pitch, e″]. When you play without it, it's fine. When you add it, you completely lose the style. You don't have 'gaida player's fingers'" [*gaidarski prŭsti*]. How depressing! He could not explain to me in words precisely how to play these high-pitched ornaments, and I could not figure them out for myself by watching and listening. I did not have the cognitive categories to organize them. Whereas notation had brought melody and rhythm to consciousness for Kostadin, it did not indicate ornamentation, and so these remained, for him, beyond verbal explanation. He tried to comfort me by saying, "Relax. It will come with more playing. Besides, when you play fast, the ornamentation disappears anyway." This was true. Careful listening taught me that his and other gaidari's ornamentation varied subtly from performance to performance, and decreased slightly in density as the tempos increased.

In retrospect, I realize his priorities as a teacher and player in the tradition conflicted with mine as an outsider trying to understand it. He valued good playing in the context of dancing; I appreciated it aurally as style and technique. To play for dancers, a musician created a strong, fast beat and varied the tempo at the command of the dancers. Style, technique, and sound changed to satisfy the demands of the context. Specifically, slow tempos were more richly ornamented than fast ones, and tempo was driven by the dancers rather than the musician. As an outsider, I wanted to produce a single sound—what I took to be the gaida's style—out of context and for its own sake. He, however, wanted me to be able to function as a musician who could play for dancing.

It was at this point in my learning that Kostadin and Todora left Toronto—and left me in the lurch. I now had to learn the gaida on my own, but, instead of operating like a Bulgarian child, I reverted to ethnomusicological technique: aural analysis and transcription. My first efforts yielded transcriptions like example 4.16. As can be seen in the transcriptions, I distinguished cognitively melody notes, "thumb blips" on e″, mordents, trills, and lower articulation notes. Physically, I produced each of these sounds, just as they are notated here: (1) I lifted the thumb to produce the e″; (2) I played the melodic pitch; (3) in the middle of it, I lifted the forefinger of the top hand to produce the mordent or trill; and so on. If I wanted to play at a good dance tempo of MM ♪ 480—and given that an ornament separated each eighth note—I would need to process nearly a thousand concepts per minute. Needless to say, my mind was very busy as I tried to play these concepts, and the results were tense and slow. Furthermore, the thumb blips were too long, too loud, and not precisely in the right place.

Careful transcription led to yet another problem. I realized that the ornamentation was even more complex than I had supposed; I began to hear that it was varied as well. To capture this new understanding, I altered my transcriptions to show the variation in the "thumb blips" (ex. 4.17). On c♯″, there were actually four possibilities, illustrated in example 4.18, and a similar set of four on b′.

Example 4.16. Conceptual Image of Tune Plus Ornamentation

Example 4.17. Variation in Ornamentation

Example 4.18. Variations in High-Pitched Accent on c♮‴

Were these conscious choices? How was the d″ produced? Did you sometimes lift the thumb to produce e″ and other times the forefinger to produce d″? Both in succession? How could you possibly raise first the thumb and then the forefinger in such a short space of time? I could barely get my thumb going. My conceptual and physical schemata would not allow me to play these ornamental variations. Now my musical exasperation was matched by curiosity. Where did those d‴'s come from? It was another *mystère des doigts bulgares*.

The solution came, as Kostadin predicted, with more playing—and taking literally one of his instructions that I had previously found cryptic and therefore ignored. During one of my many attempts to question him about the ornamentation, he said, "Tim, the key to the ornamentation is the *razsvirvane*," which translates roughly as 'playing around,' and refers, as I mentioned earlier, to a nonmetrical introduction ritually performed by gaidari when they begin to play: it warms up their fingers and they can make sure the instrument is in tune (ex. 4.3). In learning to play the *razsvirvane*, I discovered a new approach to fingering in the form of a new physical image or schema. Instead of lifting only the thumb to produce e″, two or three fingers are lifted off, depending on the next note: for example, when moving to c♯″, the top two fingers and thumb lift off the chanter simultaneously and then the thumb followed by the forefinger return to cover their holes, the latter "bouncing" once. The middle finger remains above the hole to sound c♯″.

Having understood the fingering of the *razsvirvane*, it suddenly dawned on me that this was, indeed, the solution to the mystery of 'gaida player's fingers.' If I shortened the e″ until it became an ornament to the other notes rather than part of the "melody" of the *razsvirvane*, and if I lifted other fingers simultaneously with my thumb, then I got exactly the sound I had previously heard but not understood. The *razsvirvane* transformed into melodic ornamentation is given in example 4.19.

Example 4.19. *Razsvirvane* as Melodic Ornamentation

I had made a distinction between accent and mordent and melody note, but now I realized that they should be integrated into a single concept located in a mental and physical image of how the hand worked to produce a complex of sounds. The transformation of my understanding of separate melodic and ornamental concepts into one image might be schematized in prose as follows:

original understanding:
e″ [where is d″?]
+ melody note (c♯″)
+ mordent on d″

operation:
rethink, explain, integrate, and transform into

new understanding:
hand gesture to produce c♯″ with all its ornaments.

This transformation in understanding unified at least four concepts into one, and simplified enormously the mental process of playing. Furthermore, it accounted for the existence of d″ as a feature of finger movement. Even more fundamentally, whereas my original ideas were determined by Western concepts represented in musical notation, my new understanding added the hand motions necessary to produce the sounds: physical behavior became part of the conceptual source generating musical ideas. In this process I returned after a long detour to the place where I suppose many Bulgarian players began, namely to a conceptual unity of melody and ornamentation, of melodic concepts and physical schemata.

Furthermore, I now understood and could explain the variation in Kostadin's playing. In terms of competence, a single concept (morpheme) governed it: the desire to play the most complex ornament (both e″ and d″ before c♯″). In performance, however, four variants (allophones) emerged, notated in example 4.18. The variants occurred as a function of tempo, unconscious accidents in performance, and conscious decisions to place a particularly heavy accent on a given tone. Kostadin had already told me, as he tried to urge me to play faster and not worry so much about ornamentation, "the ornamentation disappears" at fast tempos. As for the accidental variation from the most complex version, Kostadin's aesthetic statements provided a rationalization. He said the ornamentation is "like salt and pepper in a stew. If you put in too much, it spoils the taste." It should, in other words, be light and therefore sometimes omitted. Finally, the ornamentation was consciously varied with the occasional, selective addition of strong accents in some repetitions of tunes. Kostadin signaled their consciousness, their playfulness, by looking at me or whomever was sitting around him and making some obvious upper-body or head gesture as he applied the ornament. He clearly meant us to understand that something slightly out of the ordinary was occurring at that moment. It was a wink, not a blink, as Geertz might say (1973:7).

The effect of this conceptual shift from notated ideas to movement ideas astonished me. I went from tense, slow playing to relaxed, fast playing in the blink of a concept. Without further practice, I doubled my playing speed, relaxed my hands, and emitted more ornaments than ever before. I had found the elusive 'gaida player's fingers' and solved *le mystère des doigts bulgares*. I now understood that the myriad sounds I perceived as melody and ornamentation were, from a player's conceptual and physical point of view, unified into a single concept as ways of moving from tone to tone. Gaidari needed to think only of melody tones and, as they moved between them, their fingers produced ornamental tones. Conceptually and physically it became no more difficult for me to play with ornaments than without them. The ornaments were simply part of the physical motion of playing the melody, just as playing without ornaments had been.[16]

Having understood that a general principle, a single idea, led to observable variation in performance, I no longer had to copy exactly the details I heard in order to play. Rather this principle generated my own performances, which then varied both from Kostadin's recordings and from performance to performance, just the way Bulgarian musicians' performances did. I could now recreate the flexibility of tradition, not merely copy it. In terms of my self-understanding, this represents a "fusion of horizons" with those of Bulgarian musicians.

Reflecting this move, my playing was finally deemed at least adequate by a number of Bulgarian musicians. When I saw Kostadin in 1986 after learning these ornaments on my own, he no longer asked me to leave out the upper ornaments as he once had. His son, Ivan, noticed that the forefinger of my top hand, the key to the e″-d″ ornament, moved just like his father's, something I learned not by watching him but by reconceptualizing the way the hand must move. A younger gaidar, who also used Kostadin as a model, recognized the affinity between my and his ornamental style, saying to a colleague, "It's as if you are listening to Varimezov." While that was not literally true, by judging my performance adequate at some level, these Bulgarian musicians moved my performance within their horizons as well. At last, we could communicate musically, which was only possible when there had been a "fusion of horizons."[17]

Pulsation, Duration, and Tone Quality

With this new understanding, I was able to work on other physical movements and concepts that gaidari use to create the sound they want. These additional techniques create the effect of constant pulsation, even on held notes, and make the sound 'warmer' [*po-toplo*] and 'sweeter' [*po-sladko*].

First, all tones longer than the basic pulse rate, notated in these examples as an eighth note, are broken up with mordents and trills a half step above the melody, produced by raising the forefinger of the top hand and uncovering the *mormorka*. Unlike the other aspects of ornamentation discussed above, these mordents and trills are mandatory and always used; they help define the style. As Kostadin said, "music is too plain and unattractive without them. They warm the tone." The mordents and trills of this style are not identical to grace notes and their notation in Western music. In Western notation the melody note and its upper neighbor are given equal length (ex. 4.20a). In Bulgarian music, however, the upper neighbor is an instantaneous interruption of the melody note, dividing it into two or three pulses of equal duration. The aesthetic effect is to keep the music moving along at a constant rate of pulsation, notated as an eighth note (ex. 4.20b), while at the same time creating the rhythmic variety of a mixture of eighth, quarter, and dotted-quarter notes. A melody can, in effect, be heard in two ways: isorhythmically as a continuous stream of eighth note pulsations, and heterorhythmically as an alternation of three different note values (ex. 4.21).

The sound can also be 'sweetened' by using the thumb (e″) between melody notes in descending passages, a manner of performance I interpret as referencing the world of Gypsy, Turkish, and Balkan urban musical styles. In these traditions, pitches in a descending passage are often separated by the upper neighbor of the preceding note (ex. 4.22a); it is a characteristic feature of much instrumental music in Bul-

a. Western mordents, trills   b. Bulgarian mordents, trills

Example 4.20. Mordents and Trills

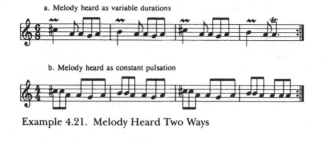

Example 4.21. Melody Heard Two Ways

Example 4.22. Ornamentation in Descending Passages

garia, particularly on clarinets and violins but also on kaval and gŭ-dulka.[18] Gaidari achieve something like this effect by separating pitches in a descending melody with e″ (ex. 4.22b), and the aesthetic effect links gaida style to that of other Bulgarian musicians and ultimately to Gypsy and Turkish styles of performance. Kostadin appreciated these styles; at one point he told me, "Gypsies always add something sweet to the music," in the form of additional ornamentation.

Reflections on Learning the Tradition

With a vastly expanded range of concepts to use in thinking about Bulgarian gaida playing, I can now explain the conceptual and physical schemata necessary to produce the "ornamental" sounds characteristic of gaida playing. By uniting my separate concepts of melody and ornamentation into a single conception centered on mental and physical images of hand motions, I came to understand and experience the unity of melody and ornamentation that I posited from my observations of Bulgarians' learning. Among the cognitive tools I acquired was the ability to think efficiently as I produced Bulgarian music at what I used to believe were incredible speeds.

Unlike a Bulgarian learner, my understanding passed through language and verbal cognitive categories in a mediation Ricoeur labels explanation. While I can't claim that my verbal explanation and its associated productive understanding are homologous with a Bulgarian gaidar's, especially one without my specific knowledge of Western music theory, my struggle to learn the tradition allowed me to experience the learning process in this aural-visual-tactile tradition from a new vantage point, similar but not identical to that of an insider. While

I might be tempted to infer that nonliterate Bulgarian musicians think about their music in the same way, this probably needs to be resisted. When Bulgarian gaidari play, however, my new understanding allows me to interpret which ornaments are intentional, which are the accidental results of tempo and technique, which are consciously varied and manipulated, and how they function aesthetically to 'sweeten' and 'warm' the sound. My interpretation of Bulgarian playing is a good example of Ricoeur's point that understanding is ultimately realized as self-understanding, in this case one that was objectified and tested in the crucible of performance and eventually judged at least marginally adequate by Bulgarian musicians and listeners.

Self-understanding of the type gained here does not operate within fixed horizons, however. I argue that, rather than imposing an interpretation on distant material, I expanded my horizons until at least a partial fusion of horizons occurred; the distant tradition was brought closer and made demands of its own on me, the interpreter. The tradition could not be learned and played in just any way but in particular ways, and my explanatory devices grew, adapted, and adjusted to account for new understandings.

My understanding of the variation in ornamentation, of how to move my hands to produce melody and ornamentation rapidly as an integrated whole, and of the formal properties of melodies are examples of the kinds of culturally and musically appropriate knowledge that I constructed in the attempt to play and reflect upon the tradition and to expand and fuse my own horizons with those of Bulgarian musicians. But there are still areas of the tradition—for example, sung pitch concepts and durations in nonmeasured melodies—that elude my understanding and explanation, where neither introspection nor verbally expressed native concepts have intersected to produce a new understanding. Todora, for example, clearly sings as if she understood something like the difference between the Western intervals of a major and minor second, but sometimes she sings an interval between these pitches. What is this interval, how is it manipulated, and what does it "mean"? Similarly Kostadin corrected my playing of nonmetric melodies by asking me to play certain tones longer or shorter. But, since there is no pulse or beat to measure time or the duration of a pitch in such tunes, how long should they be? At this level of performance, neither etic measurements nor emic verbal or musical categories have so far provided me with adequate explanatory devices. Some sort of culturally sensitive understanding, ultimately rooted in introspection and the expansion of my ability to perform the music, will be necessary to close this gap.

My attempts to learn to play the gaida led me to the edge of some seemingly unbridgeable chasms, some of which I crossed and others which I hope to bridge in the future. These gaps manifested themselves as an inability to use either my words (etic) or theirs (emic) to reach a level of understanding necessary for adequate performance. In practice, I reached a point and encountered a problem elucidated by hermeneutic philosophers like Heidegger, Gadamer, and Ricoeur. The emic/etic dichotomy, however, is rooted in an epistemology that assumes both an objective, outsider position (for example, a phonetics of language sounds) and an insider set of meanings (for example, a phonemics) that objective outsiders can elicit in language, arrange, and understand. Not only are words not an adequate tool for understanding nonverbal musical practice, but the objective position underlying the emic/etic distinction doesn't exist. Researchers always already live in a world of meanings, interpreting other's meanings not from a single, objective, etic position but from their own emic positions. Understanding another world of meanings and experience is not a matter of simply observing and arranging words into taxonomies and contrasting pairs, but of expanding the researchers' horizons to include interpretations and meanings that help to account for other's behaviors. Even when cultural insiders verify researchers' verbal, musical, or physical behaviors as appropriate or "true," these meaningful actions and interpretations remain the products of a self-understanding whose location is neither precisely emic nor etic, insider nor outsider. To the extent that research creates a productive understanding, researchers have appropriated aspects of the tradition into new selves whose horizons of understanding intersect in at least some ways with those of the people they study.

Part Three
Living the Tradition

As I listen to these songs, maybe you think this is simple stuff, but it's rich. When we forget these stories, they won't exist anymore. It will pass and depart. It must be written.

Kostadin Varimezov

We have not the real life of their being—the tree that bore them, the earth and elements, the climate that determined their substance, the seasonal changes that governed their growth. Nor does fate give us, with those works of art, their world, the spring and summer of the ethical life in which they bloomed and ripened, but only the veiled memory of this reality.

G. W. F. Hegel, on art preserved from a past world

FIVE

Five Perspectives on Musical Experience

My reconstruction of the way Kostadin and Todora and other Bulgarian villagers experienced music in the 1930s is largely an act of imagination and interpretation, both on my part and on theirs. This account is based on two kinds of evidence: recollections of the past collected in the present; and observations and interviews during the ethnographic present of my visits there from 1969 to 1989. The story told here about the musical life of Gergebunar refers both to the past, where questions of its "truthfulness" or "accuracy" can be raised, and to the present, where it represents the way a personal and cultural heritage is remembered, interpreted, and given meaning by two individuals, Kostadin and Todora. Understanding how they remembered the past is important because remembered history provides the measure of the truth of current events, as each new experience is evaluated for the way it resonates truthfully with past experience.

Part 3 points to both the past and present. At one level it can be read as a musical ethnography of the period before World War II, particularly the relationship between musical performance and the patterns of everyday life as elicited in interviews from Todora and Kostadin. At another level, it provides the background for interpreting their experience of music as reported in parts 4 and 5, which outline the dramatic changes in musical life under the Communists. Further complicating the issue of what the ensuing descriptions represent and their validity is the fact that I constructed them, adding yet another layer of interpretation and reference in the process.

This chapter approaches the question of experiencing music from five perspectives. The first section outlines the main features of the

91

economics and ideology of music, which provided the limiting conditions for musical practice in the 1930s and help to explain the social learning patterns discussed in chapter 3. The second section extends the previous chapter's discussion of cognition in music learning to more general problems of cognitive experience as inferred from musical, verbal, and physical behavior. The third section extends the discussion of musical aesthetics beyond the cognitive structuring of music to issues of performance practice, music's relation to dance, the structure and meaning of song texts, and their relation to melody. The fourth section examines Bulgarian metaphors for evidence of where and how music is experienced in the body. The fifth section interprets the meanings of song texts as an expression of women's experience and as an ideological expressive tool they employed from a structurally inferior social position.

The Economics and Ideology of Music in the 1930s

The imposition of Marxist ideology and its associated economic practice in Bulgaria after the Second World War provides a nearly unavoidable interpretive frame within which to analyze the social maintenance of musical practice in both the present and past. The Marxist-derived distinction between economic practice and ideology may be both a useful and appropriate heuristic device to explain the practice of music during the 1930s and the causes of musical change in the periods since. Analogous to the usual ethnomusicological claim that music should be studied not so much *in relation to* culture but *as* culture, musical practice is not simply determined by or related to economic and ideological practice but partakes of both. In many important respects, music is both economic and ideological practice. As ideological practice, music often serves or expresses the interest of one group or another in society and either generates, challenges, or assuages the tensions, inequalities, and power relationships between social groups. As economic practice, music is embedded in larger systems of production that define the economic value of music and therefore the amount of social energy devoted to its patronage, production, and maintenance.

During the Varimezovs' youth, nearly two thirds of all Bulgarians lived in rural areas, operating in a subsistence, family farming economy. In contrast to the large estates in Hungary and some other parts of Eastern Europe, Bulgarians' small land holdings were sufficient only to sustain a single, extended family. For Bulgarian peasant farmers, money was scarce and its accumulation almost impossible. On ei-

ther side of this economic median were urban dwellers, who participated in the capitalist money economy, and groups such as the Gypsies
and urban factory workers who eked out a shabby existence without
benefit of either property or much money. This split between an urban
money economy and a rural subsistence farming economy supported
two distinct but not mutually exclusive types of musical practice, one
based on money and the specialization of labor it makes possible and
the other a nonspecialized practice we label "amateur" only where the
possibility of payment exists.

From Kostadin and Todora's account, only the latter was possible in
the Gergebunar of their youth, at least for those of their class, who
owned land and sheep. As each family struggled to maintain and build
its real property in an economy with little money, professional music
making was not a realistic substitute for farming and raising sheep. On
the other hand, the village Gypsies, marginalized by their lack of access
to the land, were forced to work as laborers or to provide some service
or skill to land-holding villagers, who paid them with food or small
amounts of money. Music was one such skilled service, but, because
the local economy lacked the money necessary to support a specialist
musician, *Bai* Stoyan, Gergebunar's Gypsy gaidar, had to travel to
larger villages and the town of Burgas to support himself solely with
music. Devoting his life to music making, an opportunity provided by
entering the urban money economy, contributed to his skill. He turned
music into an economic practice in a way land-holding villagers could
not, and as a result become Gergebunar's best musician. As a professional, he played much more than his village counterparts and traveled more widely, which gave him the opportunity to hear and, as the
musicians' say, 'steal' technique and tunes from a wider range of musicians.

Kostadin and Todora's musical horizons were much narrower, since
they practiced music not as an occupation but, as they say, 'among
other things.' Beyond a division of labor between the sexes, family
farming allowed for few other specializations. Men tended the horses
and herd animals, plowed the fields, and built the houses, while
women cooked, made clothing, cared for the children and domestic
animals (a cow, a pig, chickens), and worked in the fields. Men's instrumental music and women's singing accompanied these activities and
enlivened the periods of respite between them, but were never the
object of true specialization.[1] What money was available in this "poor"
economy had to be used for necessities the villagers didn't make for
themselves such as salt, cooking oil, and metal utensils and tools. Most
of Gergebunar's musical instruments were primitive, homemade ap-

proximations of the good instruments made by master craftsmen in other villages and towns for professional musicians, like *Bai* Stoyan, with the money to buy them. For a villager in Gergebunar to spend what little money he could acquire selling wood or sheep on a professionally made instrument—remember Kostadin's father's reluctance to do so—or on a professional Gypsy musician for a wedding required a serious and difficult choice between a staple product for the home and something comparatively frivolous. For the villagers of Gergebunar, music was homemade, just as nearly every other item in the house was. To decide to become a professional musician was impossible. As Kostadin's father said when he refused to allow his son to follow *Bai* Stoyan, it was tantamount to becoming a bum.

If a village economy with little money or specialization of labor formed the context in which music was practiced, then Kostadin's father's statement shows how ideology as value system supported and reinforced both the economic system and musical practice. Many Balkan and Mediterranean societies share, with local variations, a value system discussed in terms of a contrast between honor and shame, in Bulgarian, respectively, *chest* and *sram*. Kostadin spoke of 'discipline' [*distsiplina*] rather than 'honor,' a value important to the Communists and an example of how a narrative about the past is colored by concepts learned at a later period.[2] *Sram* can be translated as shame, embarrassment, deference, or modesty. However they are put, discipline/ honor and shame/modesty acted as guiding and controlling principles for appropriate behavior in nearly every domain of life and seem to have been important determinants of musical practice in Gergebunar.

In a general sense, discipline and shame defined behaviors with respect to the inequalities and hierarchies of the society. One behaved 'with discipline' in order to maintain standing with one's equals and 'with shame' in dealings with one's superiors, defined usually by age and sex. Discipline and honor involved such simple things as getting up early in the morning, keeping one's word, working hard, and maintaining one's house and property in a neat, clean, productive condition. Shame or modesty was demonstrated by deference and obedience to one's elders, avoiding public displays of affection, and, for women, by acting demurely in the presence of men and remaining a virgin until marriage. A lapse in discipline or modesty was *sramno* ['shameful' or 'embarrassing'] and caused community comment and censure. Discipline and shame provided the ideological framework for how people worked, how they welcomed guests, how they behaved as men or women, how they treated their elders, and how they made music and danced. Many of these values and behaviors were still in force in the 1980s, talked about and performed every day.

The Ideology of Work and Hospitality

Bulgarians frequently and explicitly acknowledge the fundamental importance of a work ethic in their value system. In characterizing themselves to a foreigner, many people told me almost formulaically, "We Bulgarians are hardworking [*trudolyubivi*, lit. 'work-loving'] people." Kostadin's father thought it preferable to shake a door pointlessly than do nothing, and in this context music and singing were always secondary accompaniments to work, as, for example, when a boy herded sheep or a girl embroidered items for her trousseau. But to set aside time to make music for its own sake, as professional and amateur musicians do in many societies, was a waste of time, and a challenge to the disciplined work required of all.[3] Because resources were limited, villagers were suspicious and critical of anyone who accumulated too much property and wealth; they tended to assume that, since everyone worked hard, excessive wealth signaled something dishonest. In music, the development of a rich technique such as some Gypsies had may have been taken as a sign that essential duties were being neglected. Furthermore, excessive self-aggrandizement violated the code of discipline and shame.

Even the demands of subsistence farming and shepherding didn't consume every instant of time, however, and music was not limited to accompanying work. In addition to work, another form of obligatory social activity consisted of visits to family and friends. One of the greatest honors Bulgarians could do each other was to visit, 'to go as guests.' Reciprocally, the hosts had to maintain a well-kept house and have on hand the necessary food and drink 'to receive guests' in an honorable fashion, a demand that required a considerable amount of work before the guests even arrived. Bulgarians self-consciously acknowledged the culture-defining character of these visits, frequently telling me, "We Bulgarians are hospitable [*gostopriemlivi*, lit. 'guest-receiving'] people."

To have guests was, and continues to be, one of the greatest joys Bulgarians experience and one of their most serious obligations. Any perceived lapse in the treatment of guests was shameful and the subject of gossip. During my fieldwork I frequently observed how the potential to displease guests resulted in a great deal of concern before they arrived and in worries about ungrateful guests such as the one who, after being presented a lavish spread, complained that there was no green garlic, the simplest of foods. Music, song, and dance were important enhancements of these visits, but the value placed on work and socializing defined the contexts in which music could properly occur and, to some extent, its function. As many people said, "Music brings people together." The forms and performances of musical relaxation were always subordinated to the demands of discipline and shame to work and socialize in appropriate ways at appropriate times.

Since working hard and receiving guests were, in principle, behaviors required of all, everyone felt free to comment upon, gossip about, encourage, and censure actions in relation to these values. Breakdowns in discipline, such as spending too much time playing music with guests and not enough time working to maintain and improve the household's condition, were liable to rebuke in the strongest possible terms. This form of verbal social control and coercion operated between peers and through hierarchies of gender and age to reinforce and maintain the value system, its associated economic practice, and ultimately the hierarchies themselves.

The Ideology of Gender and Age

Bulgarian village society was based on patrilineal descent and patrilocal residence, which create extended, patriarchal families.[4] Before the state competed for children's loyalties with alternative educational and economic incentives, the oldest male and his wife commanded their sons and in-marrying wives and their grandchildren. In exchange for the nearly total obedience and respect the father demanded from his children in all matters, he accepted the responsibility of providing for his sons both before and after they married, in effect, for his entire life. The family was the nexus for exercising discipline and control over individuals, sometimes until late in their adult lives, when the father became infirm or died. The father's authority was not unique to him, but generalized in every elder-younger relationship, the older person claiming authority over the younger, who behaved 'with shame' toward his elders. The age-graded discipline and shame relationships within the family were transferred to all such relationships outside the family through the widespread use of kinship terms in place of names. Thus, it was—and still is—common for a young person to address the oldest generation of adults as 'grandpa' [*dyado*] or 'grandma' [*baba*], middle-aged men and women as 'uncle' [*chicho*] and 'aunt' [*lelya*], a slightly older person as 'older brother' [*batko*] or 'older sister' [*kaka*]. This fictive kinship symbolically recreated the village as an extended family and in practice reproduced on a wider social scale the age-based patterns of control typical of the patriarchal family.

In music, the deference to elders that shame required limited the possibilities for personal expression, improvisation, and change. While some African, Caribbean, and Latin American societies are rich in improvised, topical songs, older Bulgarians required young girls to sing the same set of songs year after year. Although Todora was capable of improvising new texts, shame prevented her from performing her inventions in public. While Gypsy professional musicians improvised to display skills and generate more repertoire for an audience able to pay for something special, villagers demanded their favorite tunes repeatedly and wanted their children to play them correctly, the way they remembered them. A young village musician intent on self-display with new techniques and tunes was quickly criticized for his lack of self-control, modesty, and shame.

The kinship structure and residence rules institutionalized a second hierarchy in Gergebunar, one between men and women. Men owned the property and controlled its descent through the male line, while women were exchanged between families, moving upon marriage from the consanguineal to the affinal family's residence and becoming in the process a kind of property themselves. Injunctions to discipline and shame required a girl to preserve her virginity, called 'maiden's honor' [*mominska chest*], before marriage in order to ensure her future husband's exclusive ownership of her sexuality. She had to behave modestly, with shame, in all relations with men, before and after marriage. Continuous work and service to the men in the family was her lot, particularly after marriage, and as a mother she sought to ensure the proper behavior of her daughters and daughters-in-law. This gender-based structural inequality effectively limited women's musical practice to singing, not because instrumental music was a prestigious male activity, but because it required free hands, which no 'disciplined' woman had time for. She was too busy cooking, making clothes, tending children, cleaning the house and yard, and working in the fields. In this context, women's songs and singing may well have functioned to lament their subordinate position in the social structure; this complex topic will be examined in more detail below.

So far I have made some generalized claims about how economic and ideological practice provided contexts within which music was socially maintained and circumscribed in a Bulgarian village in the 1930s. In this analysis musical performance is embedded in a dialectically intertwined economic practice and ideology, or value system, of discipline and shame. Both systems have the effect of limiting the possibilities for musical expression, of overdetermining them as it were. The lack of money and specialization of labor and the consequent moral impera-

tive to work hard and build real property meant that village musicians'
musical experience was restricted for the most part to the local area,
their instruments were often homemade, and their opportunities to
play and develop technique limited to work-related and other appropriate social activities. The value system, constructed to support economic practice, further limited women's musical expression to singing,
created a narrow range of appropriate personal expression, and kept
a tight rein on changes that young people might try to introduce. But
this normative account, in specifying the economic and ideological
ground for musical performance, suggests that music was overdetermined by other practices, describes only a part of music and its attendant experience, and lacks the ethnographic detail that might suggest
the ways musical practice constructed its own meaning in relation to
economics, ideology and itself. As Mark Slobin (1992:57) puts it, "The
space between the hegemonic drive and the individual's imagined
world . . . is a meeting-place of the overdetermined and the accidental.
The resulting union is unpredictable."

While viewing music as the overdetermined product of economic
and ideological practices yields some insights, here and in the next
chapter I try to overcome the limitations of that analysis by examining
musical experience in more detail and in relation to some of the issues
raised above: variability of musical cognition, variation and change in
performance, body metaphors as sites of aesthetic experience, song as
an expression of women's subordinate social position, and music in the
yearly ecological and economic cycle.

Nodes of Musical Cognition and Understanding

Within the constraints of economics and ideology, individual variation,
including occasional attempts to break the bonds of tradition, are facts
of musical life. People not only play music, they play with music. Trying to understand how gaida players learned the tradition led me to
consider the individual variation associated with musical cognition and
understanding: I had to understand more deeply than questions or
casual observation would allow the cognitive processes gaidari use to
generate their sound. To interpret music cognition, however, I had
go beyond verbal behaviors to physical and musical ones since older
Bulgarian musicians and villagers possessed few words to express the
full range of their musical experience.

From my observations of behavior, interviews, and introspection, I
conclude that Bulgarian musical understanding can be interpreted in
terms of six nodes around which these understandings cluster. These

nodes of understanding vary from individual to individual; and for an individual, they vary as the context shifts and the individual directs attention to different dimensions of music. By identifying six nodes of experience I hope to find an intermediate position between overgeneralization about Bulgarian musical thought and the reality that there may be eight million unique Bulgarian experiences.[5]

The first node of understanding is represented by people who observably failed to organize some aspect of musical structure.[6] Although I never heard so-called tone-deafness in Bulgaria, singing was not demanded of everyone. On the other hand, dancing was required on many occasions as an outward manifestation of happiness and social engagement; at weddings and other celebrations those present were expected and in some sense socially coerced to dance, to help make the 'fun.' Under those conditions, I frequently observed some people's inability to coordinate their movements with the music's beat. Three- and four-year-old children, for example, mimicked all the body shakes and movement styles of the dances—like *Bai* Dimitŭr's grandson, they seemed to understand "the dance ornaments"—but they usually couldn't dance on the beat. A few adults continued to dance in this disorganized fashion and were the objects of knowing winks and giggles from those observing the dance. In simply observing the performance of "beat deafness," we don't know whether the beat was heard and the performance disorganized (a comparable gap between cognition and performance might be true of tone deafness) or whether the beat remained unperceived and undifferentiated at the cognitive level. Other psychological tests or performances would have to be designed to ferret out the answer to that question. But as observable behaviors, Bulgarians and I tended to interpret such performances as less than fully competent, no matter the actual cause, and they form one node in the range of Bulgarian musical cognition.

I observed the second node of understanding in Bulgarians who correctly danced to musicians' duple and asymmetric meters. Such dancers expressed their understanding verbally when they heard a melody and labeled it, for example, *rŭchenitsa* and not, say, *paidushko*. They demonstrated their understanding physically when they danced correctly. While they couldn't explain the mathematical patterning of the beats as specified in music theory, it seems reasonable to infer that their cognition included: (1) an understanding based on differences between recurring patterns; (2) differences between short and long beats; (3) the ability to perceive or locate these beats or patterns in the music; and (4) the ability to control their bodies adequately to perform their understandings. Example 5.1, although it contains far too much

Example 5.1. A Dancer's Understanding of Meter

mathematical detail about relative lengths of beats, is one way to translate and explain this node of musical understanding and behavior, that is, the correct perception and performance of the metrical features of the music.

I inferred a third node of musical behavior in people who responded to different rhythmic treatments of a given meter.[7] The rhythmic character of instrumental music differs, depending on whether the musician is playing a song tune or a strictly instrumental tune. Song tunes contain relatively long notes or a mix of long and short notes. In Thrace and Strandzha, good dancers responded to this rhythmic treatment by dancing in a heavy, knee-bent manner with gliding movements that expressed or mirrored the rhythmic quality of the music. Instrumentalists typically alternated song tunes with sections in which the long notes were subdivided to create a more pulsating, motoric rhythmic effect. Musicians called these sections *drobezhi* or *sitnezhi* ['fine, tiny things'], a verbal indicator that they understood the difference between the rhythmic structure of song tunes and *drobezhi*. At least some dancers acted out physically their understanding of the rhythmic character of *drobezhi* by abandoning their relaxed, smooth movements in order to shake their upper body at close to the speed of the individual pulsations and to perform larger and more angular leg movements. From the verbal behavior of musicians and the physical behavior of dancers it seems reasonable to infer that they are able to make distinctions and differences not just at the level of meter but also of rhythm. Example 5.2 illustrates this node of conception and performance—this level of musical understanding—by specifying the actual durational values of melodic notes in a given meter. Although village musicians and dancers couldn't express the rhythmic relationships as precisely as notation does, some conveyed their understandings of the differences in rhythmic quality very clearly in the intensity and character of their bodily movements and in labels for sections of the music: *pesen* and *drobezh/sitnezh.*

At the fourth node, I observed some dancers who, through various physical and vocalized responses, seemed to recognize changes in melodic construction. The two main melodic qualities dancers responded to were mode changes and contrasts between stepwise, legato melodic

Example 5.2. A Dancer's Understanding of Rhythmic Duration

Example 5.3. Dancers' Understanding of Melodic Features

motion and disjunct, staccato melodic motion. These differences are illustrated in example 5.3, where the first melody is stepwise, relatively legato and in a minor tetrachord with subtonic, while the second melody is disjunct, staccato, and in a major pentachord. When musicians changed from the first type of melody to the second, the dancers often intensified their movements and shouted or whistled, thus expressing, I believe, their perception of these differences in melodic character. (Register changes—that is, moving the tonic up or down a fourth, fifth, or octave—also elicited similar responses and thus are probably a part of the dancers' cognitive repertoire.) Again, musical notation assigns a plethora of detail and meaning probably not consciously present in the dancers' cognitive schemata, and most traditional musicians like Kostadin apparently did not have labels for different modes,[8] but the dancers' expressive responses in sound and body motion suggest that they understood music well enough to make the kinds of melodic distinctions, contrasts, and differences that music theory labels with terms such as major/minor and conjunct/disjunct.

While I inferred the previous four nodes of understanding from dancers' physical behaviors, I posit at least two additional nodes primarily from musical behaviors: singers' singing and musicians' playing. I observed the former as a fifth node of understanding in people who recognized and remembered melodies and their structure and demonstrated their understanding by reproducing it through singing, whistling, or humming. Such behavior was obviously crucial to singers, but it was also important to gaidari when, as Kostadin reported, older men and boys who had this kind of understanding sang to him. He then translated their singing into the technique of the instrument. Singing entire melodies presumably requires a musical memory that grasps the formal properties of Bulgarian tunes, pitch relationships between tones, and patterns of repetition, contrast and return. Exam-

Example 5.4. A Singer's Understanding of Pitch and Form

ple 5.4 captures this productive but nonverbal understanding in a notation that records the motivic variations, cadences, and repeats typical
of most Bulgarian instrumental tunes.

I observed the sixth node of understanding in instrumentalists
whose knowledge included the finest level of ornamental detail, specifically the fingering gestures necessary to produce the melodies and
the ornamentation. (Singers demonstrated their knowledge of vocal
ornamentation [*izvivki*] in practice, but since I didn't learn the details
of singing, I am not able to comment in detail on what that understanding entails.) This level of understanding is implicitly expressed in
the playing and is represented in example 5.5, which includes a note
for every sound the gaida emitted. Kostadin wasn't able to describe or
explain certain details of the high-pitched ornamentation and, although I could notate them in detail, I wasn't always able to perform
them with the subtlety and nuance necessary to satisfy him. But during
the teaching process, I came to understand some of the meanings that
Kostadin attributed to the ornamental notes: the e″ functioned as an
accent, the e′ and d′ to separate and articulate notes, and the upper
neighbors to 'warm' the tone quality and keep the music pulsating.
This explanation of the "sense" of the ornamentation emerged during
the teaching process and would have been inaccessible to an analyst
who merely transcribed the ornamentation. It was when I reached this
sixth node of understanding that a fusion of horizons took place. For
the first five nodes, I interpreted Bulgarians' understandings in terms
of my own preexisting explanatory apparatus; at this node, I had to
develop new categories, first to explain gaida playing and then to understand it well enough to begin to perform it myself.

These nodes of behavior, and the understandings inferred from
them, rather than providing evidence of consistently employed rules,
seem to be something like strategies that are deployed in particular
contexts, vary as attention shifts, and in some circumstances even fail.
Occasionally, for example, I have found it difficult to perceive the meter of a performance, particularly one in an unusual meter; before an
understanding crystallized, my attempts to dance led to failure. In a
similar vein, Kostadin told me that people in his village had to hear a
particular instrumental tune for the dance *Trite pŭti* before they could
dance to it. They couldn't abstract the meter from every melody.

Example 5.5. A Gaidar's Understanding of Ornamentation

From introspection, it also seems likely that people listen to music in different ways at different times. For example, when I want to evaluate a player's technique or learn something new from him, I become attentive to the most refined ornamental details. When I want to learn a new tune, however, I attend only to the melody and then apply ornaments from my new-found understanding of the tradition. When dancing, I often concentrate on little more than the rhythmic values, while chatting in the line to friends. Occasionally a mode or rhythm change might jolt me into a renewed attentiveness to the music and I would change my dancing, along with others beside me, to correspond better to its character. Having observed such variability of behavior in others, I assume that their attention, like mine, also shifts between various nodes of musical thought and understanding, and that it is reasonable to infer and interpret their musical thinking from observation of a combination of physical, musical, and verbal behaviors in light of my own expanding understanding and appropriation of the tradition.

Aesthetics and Creativity in Performance

The most important structure of Bulgarian musical performance before World War II was the song, either sung or played. Kostadin, for example, told me, "The richness of Bulgarian instrumental music is thanks to the wealth of songs." The overall melodic and rhythmic features of a song's tune were known and relatively fixed by communal performance, either women singing in groups or an instrumentalist accompanying group singing. Older people used a strong notion of correctness, linked to a wide range of disciplined ways of doing things, to guide young people's learning. For example, Todora said her mother worked with her to sing correct versions of the tunes, and Kostadin, after he had acquired fundamental concepts of ornamentation and melody, was coached to play certain tunes "just as Gotsata did." The ideology of music making imparted by such teaching suggested to young people that there was a correct way to perform each song or song tune. In practice, the details of the melody varied from singer to singer, performance to performance, and verse to verse, because there was no extramusical way, such as notation, to fix them.

Although Todora's performances varied in detail from verse to verse in accord with her mood or with her desire to express the meaning of the words, she had in the past reserved such variation and personal expression for when she was working alone. When singing with others, she shaped her performance to theirs, following and, in effect, behaving modestly or with shame in relation to her older relatives and friends and even to her peers. In spite of her musical ability, Todora didn't want to stand out from the crowd; thus the demands of tradition, expressed in countless critical comments, limited her freedom to vary the song's structure to minor variations in melodic and rhythmic content performed mainly when no one else could hear her.

Instrumental Improvisation as Practice and Value

The men of Gergebunar probably sang more freely and with more ornamental license than women, due to their dominant social position and the fact that they were not constrained by the same requirements for modest behavior as women. But they were still constrained by an ideology of correct performance.[9] Male instrumentalists in turn were slightly freer than singers to vary song melodies, because they were not required to match them to a text. When accompanying singers in slow, nonmetrical songs, instrumentalists often shadowed the singing, playing a slightly delayed approximation of the melody. When Kostadin played an interlude to a sung melody, he often played a melodic variant that suggested the melody but didn't mimic it precisely. Nevertheless, some players challenged even this small amount of freedom. For example, the well-known kaval player, Stoyan Velichkov, knew how to sing a large repertoire of songs, advocated playing them exactly as they are sung, and criticized the vast majority of instrumentalists, like Kostadin, who don't play slow songs precisely and with the words in mind. Stoyan's aesthetic position, although partly a rationalization of textual knowledge he possesses that many of his colleagues lack, also illustrates the overall tendency of Bulgarians to limit individual variation by strongly expressing the value of doing things correctly.

In the 1930s, the primary form of instrumental and vocal performances seems to have been a simple, binary form consisting of either an alternation between two pairs of girls singing antiphonally, a singer and an instrumental interlude, or a musician playing a song tune followed by an interlude. In dance music, these types of alternations allowed for two different kinds of dance experience. When the girls sang, they danced quietly, conserving their energy and concentrating on their singing. When not singing, they were free to dance vigorously. As illustrated in example 5.6 (CD #8), the contrast between the longer rhythmic values of song tunes and the shorter, isorhythmic values of

Example 5.6. Song Tune and Interlude for *Kukersko horo*

their interludes inspires this kind of alternation between stately and energetic dancing.

This simple alternation of song tune and interlude, based on the dancers' desire to dance in contrasting ways, is the formal kernel from which three types of more extended instrumental forms grew. First, two or more song melodies could be combined into a suite of tunes. Kostadin remembers *Bai* Stoyan regularly playing two Easter dance songs together, separating each with the same interlude (ex. 5.7; CD #9).

A second extended form occurred when the dancers warmed up, got excited, and wanted to dance energetically for an extended period. Good musicians tried to match their lively movements with fast, motoric, largely improvised tunes or motives [*drobezhi* or *sitnezhi*]. Here the formal rigor of known song tunes and interludes was cast aside as the gaidar used motives based on ornamental technique or borrowed from songs to match the dancers' excitement. The length of phrases was not predetermined as it was in song, and the repetition or succession of musical ideas was unstructured and haphazard rather than molded by any formal principles. As Kostadin said, recalling those days before the war, "We played unconsciously, accidentally. Whatever came into our heads." Eventually these improvisations may have crystallized into more or less fixed tunes.

The social mechanism for the transformation of improvisations into tunes was probably the formation of small groups of two to four players, which may have become widespread for the first time in the

Example 5.7. *Bai* Stoyan's *Velikdensko horo* (Easter Dance)

1930s.[10] Such groups may have worked out fixed versions of individuals' improvisations in order to have more tunes to play together as a group. The fixed tunes, like the improvisations, were based on the repetition of short motives and consisted usually of four measures, repeated with or without variant endings.[11] Suites of tunes, each four measures long and played two or four times, became a hallmark of postwar recordings of instrumental music, but how important they were for Kostadin in the prewar period is a matter of conjecture. He recorded the piece notated in example 5.8 (CD #10) in the 1950s and again for me in the 1970s, and claimed that he had worked it out as a suite during the 1940s in Gergebunar before becoming a professional musician. It begins with a song tune, followed by two slightly more rhythmically active interludes. For a village dance he might have played these many times before launching into the improvised *drobezhi*.

Example 5.8. *Pravo strandzhansko horo* (continued on next page)

Example 5.8. *continued*

In the recording, the *drobezhi* follow immediately without repeating the song tune, and, instead of being improvised, they are played as fixed *kolena*. They preserve, however, the pattern of motivic construction, variation, and mode change characteristic of improvisations. Both the increasing cooperation of musicians in groups during the

1930s and the general values of discipline, control, and order contributed to the tendency of village musicians to fix improvisations as tunes.

Musicians also escaped the strictures of song-and-interlude form when performing instrumental, nonmetrical tunes called *svirni* ['instrumental tunes,' 'play things'; sg., *svirnya*]. Shepherds played 'shepherd's tunes' [*ovcharski svirni*] during the long hours herding sheep, and gaidari played a 'godfather's tune' [*kumova svirnya*] (CD #11) or a 'bride's tune' [*bulchenska svirnya*] during wedding processions.

Svirni resemble fragments of slow songs, but are collections of slow-song motives and phrases that musicians improvise on, playing minor variations or combining them in different orders, during long periods of playing. While a shepherd was free to combine tune fragments in any way he could—since no one was listening but the sheep—the gaidar was constrained by tradition to maintain the recognizability of his wedding tunes, because they signaled to the wedding party and other villagers important stages in the progressing ritual. Again we see music performance as a paradigm of cultural ideology. Men traveled outside the village where they had considerable freedom. Inside the village men had greater opportunities than women to express themselves, but were still constrained by discipline to behave appropriately.

This account suggests that instrumental improvisation may not have been valued for its own sake by Bulgarian villagers, but was mainly a strategy used by musicians to keep up with energetic dancers, to amuse themselves during long stretches of playing in the fields, or during ritual processions. According to Kostadin, listeners wanted to hear recognizable tunes, and musicians who strayed too long or too far from them didn't have to be told of the criticism and pressure to conform they would receive.[12]

Improvisation as valued musical practice seems to have been mainly the province of Gypsy musicians, who borrowed the improvised, nonmetrical *mane* from Turkish tradition. Kostadin learned a *mane* from *Bai* Stoyan, but, in line with his village practice and values, transformed its essentially improvisational character into a fixed composition. He preserved some of its 'oriental' quality—*orientalno*, as he calls it—including the augmented second, glissandi, melodic sequences, and timbral manipulations, but improvising in a *makam* [a 'Turkish melodic mode'] is foreign to him as musical practice, and not valued by the village culture. In his *mane* (CD #12), he borrowed the name and some features of style from Turkish and Gypsy culture, but fundamentally altered its conception and performance to fit it into the ideology and practice of Bulgarian village culture.

Singing as Aesthetic and Creative Practice

While Kostadin's approach to improvisation and variation was colored by his subsequent training as a professional musician, Todora's singing was much less influenced by modern professional practice. She acknowledged her essential freedom to vary a melody in certain contexts while being constrained in others. "Folk songs you can ornament and change as you want. If you change it, then you sing from the heart. It's not like you have learned it lifelessly, as if it's an obligation. Different people sing it different ways." These variations occurred, as she said, "according to your mood," primarily when she sang alone, for example, while weaving. "When I sang alone, I could put in more emphasized stuff from the heart."

When she recorded her songs for me, she achieved such emphasis in dance songs primarily by lengthening the duration of the tone associated with a particular word. But this freedom to express and manipulate the text was constrained by group performance in public. The *drushki* had to blend and negotiate in performance these textual emphases, and their performance was subject to public evaluation. If singers altered the melody too much, they could count on hearing about it from the 'aunts' and 'grannies' who were watching and listening.

Most song texts, like melodies, were known by a large number of women, and their precise form was negotiated in communal performance. Details varied and memories failed, but in group situations the correctness of a text could be argued about and agreement reached. The texts were constructed using the same formal principles outlined for Bosnian epic ballads by Albert Lord in *The Singer of Tales* (1960). The poetic form of a song text consists of a set of lines, all with the same number of syllables per line—in Bulgaria usually eight syllables, but also six, seven, or ten syllables (fig. 4). The lines are not required to rhyme and are not grouped into couplets or longer verse forms. The same kinds of repetition and formulas described by Lord are typical of Bulgarian song. Lord emphasizes the way poetic formulas, combined with syllabic poetic form, allow the singer of epic ballads to create long texts that might otherwise be nearly impossible to memorize. The same processes are at work in Bulgarian song, but their shorter narrative and lyrical texts are more fixed than Lord claims for Bosnian texts.

Significantly, not only are the Bosnian texts longer, they are sung solo by men. There, length of song, solo performance, and the relatively superior position of men conspire to create song performances of great variety, flexibility, and freedom. In Bulgaria, on the other

1	2	3	4	5	6	7	8
Vi-	di-	na-	ta	sta-	ra	mai-	ka
tya	si	na	Vi-	da	du-	ma-	she
Vi-	do	Vi-	do	ya-	vor	Vi-	do
sta-	ni	Vi-	do	pri-	me-	ni	se
pri-	me-	ni	ta	se	na-	re-	di
s nai	bash-	na-	ta	si	pri-	me-	na

Translation:

> Vida's old mother
> She said to Vida:
> "Vida, Vida, maple Vida,
> get up, Vida, and change,
> change, get dressed
> in your finest clothes."

Figure 4. Eight-Syllable Song Lines

hand, most song texts are shorter and sung by groups of women, their length, group singing, and women's subordinate position limiting the need and desire for variation in performance. Performed Bulgarian song texts, sung in public, vary through omission of details and of certain lines which are understood by implication—such as "Georgi said to his mother"—rather than through conscious improvisation as Lord suggests for Bosnian songs. However, given that the processes of text construction are the same, it is not surprising to learn that some singers, including Todora, were able to improvise texts.

While working alone, Todora cobbled together new texts if she didn't remember or like the original words or, if the song was too short, to lengthen the performance. "A song has no end. If a song pleased me—the melody—and I didn't remember the words, then I created the text by myself. And I sang. I could sing two songs, not just one [to a given melody]. If I remembered the melody of some song I heard at a village fair [*sŭbor*], I would create words, and there was no end [*laughs*]. I would near the end, near the end, near the end, and yet I couldn't completely finish. But I left it there [in the weaving room] because I would forget it later." Thus, while she worked at the loom, she sang endlessly, stringing themes and ideas together from many songs as it occurred to her at the time. But she never felt it appropriate to perform these improvised songs in public. Public songs had been created in the past and were known potentially by everyone. Her own songs, sometimes made in the company of a friend, were, from her point of view, a young girl's silliness, to be heard but not seen.

Although Todora could not describe the technical details of the text, such as their isosyllabic structure, her description of the creative process indicates that she understands composing song texts as a problem different from ordinary speech. "As I sang one thing [*pause*] I thought [*pause*] because you have to work on the text, how to say it so that you can tie it into the melody. You can't put in just anything. I sang *one* time, and as I stopped to rest, I thought [about what came next]." This reference to fitting the text to the melody refers to the process of making each line eight or ten syllables long. Although her descriptions suggest a somewhat laborious process, when I recorded her songs, parts of which she recited rather than singing the text, she was as facile as one of Lord's epic singers at creating and speaking texts in isosyllabic lines.

Clearly one of the factors motivating memory of either text or melody was aesthetic pleasure. What was pleasing about a text or melody? She described the pleasure of the text in terms of its meaning, rather than its structure, for which she had no vocabulary. When I asked her what she liked in a text, she said, "Sometimes separate moments, sometimes the whole text, its contents, how it proceeds. It has a sense, it tells the truth. There is always something true in a song. [When something notable happens], afterwards a song is made. Like films, that's the way they make them." The "truth" of a song is a function of its relationship to previous experience and events. That truth is often emotional rather than reportorial or literal, and the way a song relates truthfully to emotional experience is the key to its aesthetic pleasure.

Given the lack of musical vocabulary, it is not surprising that it was impossible to speak with Todora about why certain melodies are pleasurable and thus memorable, but she readily acknowledged that some melodies were more pleasing than others. Because she sometimes evaluated the words and music of a song differently, in the privacy of her work Todora felt free to pull apart text and tune and recombine them in ways that pleased her. "Sometimes the melody [pleased me] but not the words, and I began to put other words to it. But only I would sing it [with new words]. There were some songs with good words, but not very melodious, it seemed to me, and I looked for another tune [*pripev*], another melody. [*Sings a song about an army company commander.*] It's a good song because of the text. It's a true song about the liberation of Bulgaria. Dimo's Field is in Turkey. There was a big battle there. But the tune didn't please me so I thought up a new tune, but later forgot it." These new variants of songs were only for her own amusement. She sang them only "at home. At the *megdan* [village square where the dances were held] I wouldn't dare. I had shame."

Whereas tradition, in the form of an ideology of discipline and shame, dictated a particular combination of words and music so that the song could be shared, it effectively prevented young girls with shame from introducing new variants in public, even though some had the ability and freedom, in the privacy of their own homes, yards, and fields, to create new songs in any number of ways that pleased them. Todora's attitude toward, and practice of, self-control and creativity is a good example of how musical practice can be simultaneously constrained by and independent of the economic and ideological practices which bear on it.

Metaphors of Bodily Experience

As I tried to understand something of Bulgarian music learning, cognition, performance, and creativity, I relied heavily on observation, inference, and introspection, finding that in many instances villagers' verbalizations about their tradition stopped before my desire to understand and perform it did. Along the road to increased understanding, however, Kostadin, Todora, and other singers and musicians used a number of metaphors that located musical experience in various parts of the body. I've already mentioned three such locations: gaida player's fingers [*prŭsti*]; playing or singing from the heart [*sŭrtse*]; and the sense of taste [*vkus*], as in 'sweet playing' [*sladko svirene*]. Two other body metaphors can be added: the mind [*akŭl*] and the soul [*dusha*].

From my own experience with learning to play gaida, the fingers seem to be a locus of musical knowledge. In some sense it was my fingers that had to learn how to move from tone to tone with all the ornaments in between, and Kostadin attributed my inability to perform to my lack of gaida player's fingers. Once I learned how to move my hands in order to play, they seemed disembodied; as I played, I watched them move, heard the rich array of sounds, and wondered who was controlling them. The sense of my hands as possessing knowledge independent of my mind was quite vivid. When I pressed Kostadin on this, however, he was not willing to take the metaphor as literally as I did.

When I asked whether the fingers in some sense knew how to play or controlled the playing, he said, "No, of course the mind [*akŭl*] controls the fingers." For him, *gaidarski prŭsti* were the outward, visible manifestation of an understanding rooted in the mind. He inferred the understanding when he saw someone's fingers moving correctly and heard the right sounds. Indeed, I acquired "fingers" when my mind grasped how the hand must move in order to produce the sounds I was hearing. *Gaidarski prŭsti* is a metaphor that translates and projects the invisible act of understanding [*razbirane*] into the visible and audible world of playing [*svirene*].

Whereas the mind and fingers generate well-formed playing, the 'heart' is the metaphorical source of expressive playing, singing, and dancing. A good musician 'plays from the heart' [*sviri ot sŭrtse*]; a good singer 'sings from the heart' [*pee ot sŭrtse*]; a good dancer 'dances from the heart' [*igrae ot sŭrtse*]. Subtle variations in melody, ornamentation, and movement provide the main observable evidence that the performance comes from the heart. The variations occur as the musician appropriates and makes his own another's song or tune; adds his own ornamentation or subtle twists to the melody; and varies the melody, ornamentation, or movement subtly within a given performance. When listeners perceive these variations, they say the performance is not 'lifeless,' but full of the life a beating heart provides. The listener's experience of the liveliness and expressivity inherent in musical variation is captured and conveyed by a powerful reference to the source of human life, the heart.[13]

The metaphors of fingers, mind, and heart locate musical production in various parts of the body; two other metaphors speak to the corporeal sources of aesthetic pleasure and experience. One important set of metaphors link the aural sensation of good playing to the sense of taste. Kostadin and a younger gaidar, Georgi Doichev of the Bulgarian national ensemble, frequently described the pleasures of highly ornamented playing as 'sweet' [*sladko*] and 'rich' [*bogato*] and explicitly linked that taste to the sometimes barely audible tones surrounding the melody. For Kostadin, however, good playing was not too 'strong' [*sert*], with too many ornaments continuously and heavily played, but contained just the right amount of 'salt and pepper' sprinkled in the 'stew.' With these metaphors of taste, gaidari like Kostadin and Georgi Doichev translated their unique and detailed sensitivity to ornamentation into a more widely understood language of pleasure shared by nonmusicians, the taste of food.

The second metaphor of musical reception represents the apotheosis of aesthetic experience. When a performance of music, song, or dance is complete and satisfying in every respect, it 'fills your soul' [*napŭlni dusha ti*]. One day, as Todora and I listened to the radio in Sofia, we heard a performance on kaval by Nikola Ganchev of the Bulgarian national ensemble. Hoping that I had experienced the same sense of deep pleasure she had, Todora turned to me and said, "May it fill your soul" [*Da ti napŭlni dusha*]. This expression is used for a wide range of pleasurable social experiences, the most moving of which are transcendent. By invoking the soul as the seat of these experiences, Bulgarians link music, dance, song, drink, hospitality, and the other manifestations of social life to their most profound, deep-seated sense of identity as Slavs and as Orthodox Christians.

These metaphors of music as bodily experience cover a wide range of types of musical experience. Kostadin recognized the mind as the ultimate controller of form in performances. The fingers have to be trained to articulate the ornamental style and its relationship to melody and rhythm. The heart generates expressive playing through variation in ornamentation and melody. The sense of taste perceives the sweetness of the sound in the richness and quantity of the ornamentation. And the soul drinks in the meaning of the total experience as the perfect union of form, style, expression, and context.

Songs and Dances in a Woman's Experience

I began this chapter by examining the ways a culturally shared ideological and economic system constrained aspects of individuals' musical lives. In practice, the song tradition gained its coercive force when mothers, aunts, and older girls taught their daughters, nieces, and younger sisters their favorite songs, as well as ritually important ones, as part of a shared, social process. On the other hand, we have seen that Todora was not a passive recipient of tradition; rather, she rejected, selected, and manipulated songs that pleased or displeased her in ways having to do partly with their truth value in her life. The implications of this dialectic between the collective force of tradition and individual choice for the study of song repertoires in general are twofold. First, repertoires vary from individual to individual as each selects songs according to personal criteria and experience. Second, the meaning of a repertoire varies according to the person who performs or hears it: the songs in Todora's repertoire may have one meaning in relation to her life experience, another if found in a man's repertoire, and perhaps a third if found in a collection of Bulgarian songs. Old songs preserved as texts in the present are ripe for interpretation by whoever hears them or sees them, while at the moment of performance new meanings may be generated by ostensive reference to the performer, the audience, or the situation.[14] Songs, like any text or meaningful action, have an excess of meaning and the potential for widely varying interpretations.

Todora's account suggests that songs and singing were often performed by women for women, in circumstances with few or no men present. Whereas men sang in taverns and at family celebrations, singing was a continuous part of women's lives and work. One could predict that songs and singing had different meanings for women and men, and further that the meanings would be situated in the different experiences of men and women. In fact, many of Todora's songs seem to express a woman's experience more profoundly than a man's. They seem to be about women, and not just by and for women. For Todora, her songs are ordinary, 'truthful' [*verno*] descriptive statements of events, attitudes, or problems, but the interpretation of those attitudes and problems, and the precise nature of the truth of song texts, is still difficult for the ethnomusicologist.

The first major collection of Bulgarian folk songs, by the Miladinovi Brothers (1942 [1861]:iii), begins with the line, "Most of the songs were heard from women." They tend to know the most songs and are willing to sing them for collectors. In contrast, in my experience, men were often reluctant singers, willing to sing only when "in the mood"— which usually meant during an extended bout of drinking and socializing with male friends, or with me. Most Bulgarian professional folklorists, whether academics, media workers, or organizers of amateur performances, judged women to sing better than men, because women typically know more songs, ornament the songs more precisely and richly than men, and are more willing to sing for the tape recorder.

Although the willingness of women to sing for collectors could be considered an artifact of that nontraditional situation rather than part of the tradition, a review of the most important traditional contexts reveals that women were the main singers in the past as well. They sang all the dance and calendrical ritual songs except *koleda* [winter carolling] songs, while men mainly sang table songs at home and in the tavern during long winter evenings. The lion's share of the singing was the province of women, and this must have implications for the meanings of many of the songs.

Women as the Source of Songs

Much Bulgarian literature on song texts interprets them as expressions of Bulgarian nationality and customs, a common tack in the history of European folk-song scholarship, and construes their meanings and references in relation to a general notion of Bulgarianness rather than to the experience of one or another sex. My first inkling that relations between the sexes was at issue in these songs, and that an interpretation from a girl's or woman's perspective might be especially productive occurred when I reflected on a text I recorded from some young girls in the Velingrad region of the country in 1972 (CD #13):

Deli na Vaida govori:	Deli [a boy] said to Vaida [a girl]:
Vaide le pŭrvi merakyo,	"Vaida, my first love,

Vsyakate vecher ke doida	Each evening I will come [to your house]
I taya vecher ke doida.	And this evening I will come.
Da ne si, Vaide, legnalo	May you not have lain down, Vaida,
legnalo krotko zaspalo.	lain down and gently fallen asleep.
Kosite ke te otrezha,	I will cut off your hair [to your ears],
rukite do ramenata,	your arms to your shoulders,
krakite do kolenata.	and your legs to your knees."

The song rehearses a common Bulgarian song theme: lovers meeting secretly in the night without their parents' knowledge. The boy will make a slight noise, a prearranged signal, so as not to awaken her parents, and she must be attentive to hear it in order to sneak out of the house for a rendezvous. As a report of the threats girls received, the song might be true; as a girl's fear of mistreatment, the song might be true; but I doubt that the fear and the threats were matched by action. The question remains, why do Bulgarians sing songs like this? In fact, Bulgarians do not sing songs like this; Bulgarian women sing songs like this. The song may or may not express a literal truth, but it surely expresses an emotional and psychological one. Especially in the past, women feared men, girls feared boys, and women sang about that fear in their songs. These songs are not only sung by women; they are about women and articulate a female view of the world as well as female feelings about it. Perhaps because of the subordinate position of women, however, their feelings are rarely expressed directly; they must be inferred and interpreted in the rather bland, descriptive language of the texts.

The first and most dramatic confirmation of this hypothesis came from Todora when I asked her the obligatory ethnomusicological question, where do these songs come from. I fully expected the answer, "they are traditional" or "they have always been sung this way." Instead, Todora said, "Some sharp-witted woman made them up." In her view, women created them to express women's points of view. We know that men known as *pesnopoitsi* ['song singers'] made up melodramatic ballads and sang them at fairs; from Todora's perspective the truth of her songs lies in their being created by women for women to crystallize common elements of women's experience. As I examined the songs in Todora's repertoire, this presumption was born out.

Love and marriage, the central focus of a young Bulgarian girl's life, created the most intense emotions. In general, Bulgarian songs deal with these emotions in third-person narratives like the one above, rather than directly in the first person. Many of Todora's songs portray girls as helpless victims of those around them, rather than complain about the singers' personal condition. In a sense, the songs gain their power by generalizing a girl's individual circumstance to a social condition shared by all girls. According to the songs, a girl was potentially the victim of her parents, who might marry her to a boy she did not love; of her in-laws, who might mistreat her; and of her husband or an unwanted suitor, who might beat, 'steal,' or even rape her. Stealing refers to a practice, at least threatened in Todora's youth, in which a boy and his friends would kidnap a reluctant girl (or one whose family was opposed their marriage) and take her to a secret location for a few days. Having been shamed in truth or by implication, she had little choice but to marry the boy when they returned her to the village. Many songs capture the truth of the fear girls felt as they observed the power men and older people had over them.

Todora explained the pressure that girls felt to behave modestly, because any casual, overt, public expression of interest in a boy might get them married to someone they did not care for. "In those days there was shame. If you had a [boy]friend, it wasn't like now, to go with him, to meet him constantly." There were really only two possibilities for meeting in public: "He could only come to take your bouquet [or] to hold your hand and dance next to you." These signs were unambiguously interpreted as indicating mutual interest, but within the realm of modesty. "Everyone knew who [was interested] in whom. 'Did you know that he goes with that girl?' 'Did you know that he will be engaged to so-and-so?' Before us there was even more discipline. There was even more shame."

Because parents ultimately controlled young lovers' fates, even song performances were not protected places for the direct expression of their mutual interest, and Todora rejected my suggestion that they helped in the expression of feelings which were not appropriately expressed in speech. "No. We could express our feelings in this way and that. We spoke to each other, but we watched out not to be too insistent so that people wouldn't talk." Once talk started, the parents might act peremptorily to save the girl's reputation, "because everyone talks. It was a small village. You would hardly see the boy and your parents would take him" [that is, they would engage the girl to him].

The consequences of marriage to the wrong person could be disastrous. "There wasn't divorce. There wasn't anything. Maybe the songs came from women's grievances. There wasn't much freedom, and they made songs." This statement confirms my hypothesis that the songs refer to women's feelings, particularly their fears and misfortunes in relation to a social system in which they were virtually powerless. The songs were not used to express their feelings directly, which was not appropriate in public either in speech or song, but rather to console themselves during times of stress.

Todora acknowledged the relationship between crying and singing and the therapeutic role of the latter, telling two stories to illustrate it. "There is a connection [between crying and singing]. We were harvesting in the field somewhere around lunchtime. It was really roasting and we were hurrying, hurrying, harvesting, harvesting. My aunt, my father's sister, began to cry [*laughs*] as a joke. Her mother said, 'Stop that wailing. Start singing'" [*laughs*]. This whistle-while-you-work therapy for physical exhaustion complements a similar approach to emotional battering, relayed in a mother-in-law story Todora said was an exception to the good treatment she received from Kostadin's mother. "I should tell you how my mother-in-law once saddled me with some task. Kostadin wasn't there one Easter, and she ordered me around in an insulting way. I went to the barn and cried and, when I got back to the house, I began to cry. She wasn't a bad person and was getting dressed for the dance. She called out, 'Hurry up, bride, let's go out' [*laughs*]. And so my anger passed and did not show, and I began to sing. Instead of crying, I began to sing" [*laughs*].

Singing was a therapeutic act especially for young girls and brides in rather hopeless situations. When they could not control the situation, when they were forced to work hard or were mistreated in some other way, they could either cry or sing. The appropriate, "disciplined" public response was to sing; it either banished the "blues" or it covered them, replacing them with an appropriately controlled, disciplined, public act.[15]

In these stories we see women acting to preserve and enforce the ideology of disciplined work and shame since, particularly for married women, it was in their interest to do so. An obedient, hard-working, modest daughter or daughter-in-law was a sign of a woman's success within the system.[16] So from the girls' point of view, they often suffered mistreatment at the hands of older relatives and in-laws, who demanded disciplined work and modest behavior from the girls and brides—and the song texts reflect this. But the ultimate source of power in this patriarchal society was men, and songs imply that an important aspect of girls' and women's fear centered on their mistreatment at the hands of men. Some of the songs mention beatings directly, and, when I asked whether such things happened, Todora said she nearly married into a family notorious—and according to her an exception in their village—for its mistreatment of women. By examining this personal experience in detail, we can understand better the truth of these songs in Todora's experience in particular and in women's experience in general. We also learn how parental control, shame, and young people's wishes intertwined in Kostadin and Todora's own courtship.

Todora's Experience of Threatening Men

One day when Todora was about fourteen, an older boy named Dimo (a pseudonym) took her bouquet, a common sign boys used to show their affection. "Until then I hadn't paid any attention to him. I jumped up to try and grab it back and yelled, 'Give me my bouquet, *Bai* Dimo. Give it to me, *Bai* Dimo.' His cousin turned around and said, 'We are not going to take you as a bride' [*laughs*]. And I was ashamed that she spoke to me that way." However, the idea was implanted in Todora's mind, and she began to take an interest in Dimo, watching him as he herded cows and pigs past her house and at village dances. Her parents, knowing the reputation of his family for wife beating, refused to let her see him. "At every dance I cried. When I returned home, mother began, 'Again he joined [the dance] next to you. How is it possible?' He was from a family that beat their women. They didn't allow the women to speak."

In spite of her parents' opposition, Todora and Dimo tried to find ways to see each other and even talked of eloping. "We could go from the well to the road without them seeing. But at *sedyanka*s, if my mother was there, he didn't dare come and sit next to me." Here Dimo behaved with shame in the presence of an older woman. "However, we spoke together: how could it [marriage, elopement] happen, what would happen."

Most songs, conveying the young people's point of view, speak only of the love of the boy and girl, and treat the parents as interfering and selfish when they come between the lovers, for whom everything is perfect. Such scenarios may sometimes be true, when love is nipped unfairly in the bud, but, in Todora's case, her family seems to have had her best interests at heart. They continued to intervene strongly in the course of this affair, which progressed in a manner reminiscent of the story of Cyrano de Bergerac.

Eventually Dimo left the village to serve in the army, together with his age mate, Kostadin. Dimo's letters to Todora had to pass through the post office, where Todora's father, as mayor of the village, could see them. "The first two letters [from Dimo] he showed to me and then ripped them in two." Since she and Kostadin were "cousins" and good friends—"We knew each other's secrets"—she wrote to him, explaining the problem. "So [Dimo] wrote the letter and Kostadin addressed it and signed the letter. I wrote letters and addressed them to Kostadin. And in the end everything got mixed up" [*laughs*].

Eventually Kostadin took the initiative and wrote to Todora, saying that his family had suggested the two of them marry and writing, "Why should you go there [to Dimo's]. You see what sort of people his brothers are."

Unfortunately, Todora read his letter to some of her girlfriends as they were traveling in a cart to a fair in Drachevo. One of them, Dimo's cousin, told him of the letter "and he got fired up. They [his friends and relatives] wanted to steal me from the fair. Not to steal me, but to elope with them to their place. He said, 'Either give me the letter or we will take you, steal you this evening.'" Later that night Kostadin and Dimo fought "and for a long time Kostadin and I didn't talk. He got mad at me, because I had given away the letter." Eventually he asked her for an explanation and she told him what had happened, that she had given the letter to Dimo to ward off his threat to steal her. He understood, and "we started to see each other more often."

Among the few respectable places where young people could see each other were dances in the village square and communal working bees [*sedenki, medzhii*]. The songs indicate that these were important occasions for courtship, when affection could be shown by joining in the line next to a favorite friend and where fights sometimes broke out between rivals.

On one such occasion, Todora was the victim of the violence her family predicted from Dimo. She and Kostadin "were invited to a *medzhiya*. Kostadin played gaida and his brother, Stamat, the kaval. At one point Kostadin put his gaida aside and joined the dance next to me. Later the boys did a dance while Stamat played. Three of us girls joined the dance. I joined next to Kostadin. Dimo was there. He saw Kostadin join near me the first time, and I near him the second time. Tim, I was wearing long braids. As we were dancing around, Dimo grabbed my braids and dragged me down to the ground and ran out." That ended whatever lingering interest Todora might have had in him, and soon she and Kostadin became engaged.

The engagement struck Dimo's relatives "like thunder from a clear sky," but rather than accept it they renewed their efforts to steal Todora. At a village fair Dimo and his relatives tried to provoke a scandal by joining the line next to Todora.

"When you were engaged, it wasn't appropriate for a strange boy to dance next to you. That was the rule. And I wondered what to do, to let go, not to let go." Stamat, Kostadin's brother, joined the line between her and Dimo and argued with him as Todora dropped from the line. "We started a new *horo* and this Dimo came and joined next to me. I let go, but he wouldn't let go of me. Kostadin said, 'Let go of Todora, let go of Todora. What's the matter, Dimo?' And his relatives surrounded Kostadin and Stamat and began to quarrel." Kostadin's older brothers and uncles came to their rescue and they escaped a beating, but this was just Dimo's first attempt to prevent their marriage. "Simply, they sought at every moment to be able to get me alone in some house."

Dimo's male and female cousins tried to trick Todora into visiting them when he was there. She would then have been taken away from the village for a few days and forced by shame to marry him. "They abduct the girl somewhere and for two, three days, one week they can't find her. They made love. If they took her, yes. They would be a whole company, not just one or two. And after that, whether you want to or not, you will agree [to marry the abductor]. It's not like now. If you didn't return for a month, they wouldn't refuse you."

Although Todora managed to avoid this fate, it had happened to her aunt. Todora's grandmother had objected to her daughter marrying outside the village, and so her boyfriend "stole" her as a way to force her parents' hand. However, the grandmother sent the police after her, and they brought her back to the village. Having been shamed, she could find no other suitor and eventually married an old widower. "Such things happened. My aunt suffered a lot, the dear. And so I was afraid. I knew what happened to my aunt."

Dimo's desperate efforts to abort Kostadin's and Todora's marriage continued to the wedding day. Their engagement had been controversial even within Todora's family because they were considered cousins (fig. 5). They had acted toward each other as relatives rather than potential lovers when growing up, and so Todora's father objected to their engagement. Finally, a priest in Grudovo, asked to evaluate their relationship, ruled that they were distantly enough related to be married in the eyes of the church. But Dimo and his family seized on this problem and convinced the village priest that they were related. "When it came time to go out and go to the church, they said the priest was not there. 'The priest has run away. The priest has run away.' [Dimo's people] dragged him off and had gone as far as Drachevo before our people caught up to him and brought him back. We were at church and the priest had run away [*laughs*]. They waited right to the wedding to make us miserable. And the priest ate and drank all week [before the wedding] at our house" [*laughs*].

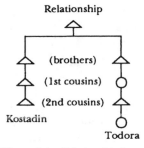

Figure 5. Genealogical Chart of the Relationship between Kostadin and Todora

Why Bulgarians Sing

Boys like Dimo, and the public evidence of beaten women, must have left girls in fear of what might await them in marriage, and the songs testify to that fear. Many songs deal with snakes or dragons, phallic symbols, emblematic of the girls' fear of their unknown fate, both sexual and general, at the hands of their future husbands. As Todora said, "We have a lot of songs about dragons. They are about fear." She agreed that the dragons were symbolic stand-ins for bachelors. "In the songs the dragons turn into bachelors, fall in love with a girl, take her away and then turn back into dragons. The legend is that the dragons turned into young, handsome boys and fell in love with the prettiest girls." Thus, Todora's family was not willing to allow her to marry into a family with a reputation for wife-beating. It was precisely this fear that resulted in women's songs and explains women as the source of songs. Conversely the lack of fear among men accounts, in her view, for why men do not have their own songs. "Men were not afraid. Men are men. That's why they don't have songs. Girls make songs, and they make them about men [*laughs*]. Men don't make songs. They make them less often. There were a few dirty, joking songs."

These statements and stories confirm a gender-based analysis of Todora's repertoire that interprets it—and the impulse to create and sing songs—as rooted in women's fear, unhappiness, exhaustion, and exploitation at the hands of men or of women acting on behalf of men. By the same logic, men did not have their own songs because they did not need them; they had nothing to fear, at least from women. In fact, men did sing, and their favorite songs—narratives of banditry and resistance during Turkish times—could be interpreted as being about what they feared: Turks, war, highwaymen, and the unknown beyond the safe confines of the village.

If we ask, as Anthony Seeger (1987) does for the Suya, why Bulgarians sing, or why they sang in the 1930s, the deep answer, beyond the obvious social one that it "brings people together," is fear. Bulgarian women sang because they were exploited by men. They sang about their fears, their exhaustion, and the tragedies of their lives, many induced by men, and singing was therapeutic. Whereas Bulgarian women sang soberly to express their feelings, Bulgarian men sang mainly when drinking. Since song expressed fear, it would have been inappropriate for men to sing "naturally." But protected by family groupings or among friends gathered *na moabet* ['in conversation'], with the help of drink, male pretensions to fearlessness were relaxed.[17] Even in the 1980s, when men were sober, they often sang as if they were drunk, making it clear that their guard was momentarily down. Their status as staunch defenders of the family was not permanently compromised. Thus the question of why Bulgarian men sing can be answered only by explaining why they often refused to sing, and why they sang the way they did when they did.

Todora's Repertoire

When I examined the 250 songs Todora recorded for me for evidence of gender perspectives in the texts, it was clear that there are both men's and women's songs, but only 38 seem to be from a strictly male perspective.[18] In these songs, men's activities are the subject; men act and think and feel. Nine of the songs are about *haiduks*, men who went into the forest to fight against the Turks; 16 concern going into the army, watching flocks, accidents involving guns, robberies on the road; and 13 are love songs expressing the boy's point of view. Perhaps a man's repertoire would contain more songs from a male perspective, but Todora's repertoire is strongly female in character. An additional 20 songs deal with male themes like those mentioned above, but as told to females, particularly the boy's mother or lover, as if the significant thing about his fighting, wrestling, loving, sickness, or death was the way it affected women. If these are counted as men's songs, more than a third of them deal with the impact of men's behavior on women. They may be just as easily interpreted as part of the women's repertoire and expressive of women's feelings about the troubles their men encounter.

The remaining 142 songs—excluding ritual songs and a few instrumental dance songs with only one verse of text—are about women and, if Todora is to be believed, by women as well. Half the songs about girls present essentially negative, fearful themes, listed here in the order of frequency:

1. being threatened, stolen, or even killed by Turks—and occasionally Bulgarian boys (17 songs);
2. family or future in-laws interfering to prevent a match (17 songs);
3. a girl's shame, fear, illness or death (16 songs);
4. losing a lover to another girl or by his separation or death (8 songs);
5. getting married to a bad or ugly person, often in a far-away village (7 songs);
6. girl's hard work and criticism for laziness (6 songs).

These 71 songs present a very negative image of a girl's fate, which, according to the songs, was too often determined by others: Turkish or Bulgarian boys who stole them; parents who denied their true love and married them to undesirable boys in undesirable places; a lover who rejected them. If girls are not done in by others' actions, then fate, in the form of hard work, illness, and even death, may overtake them.

The other half of girls' songs are more positive and playful, showing girls to be smarter than boys, many of whom have bad characters. The main themes, in order frequency, are:

1. a girl and boy love each other and perhaps marry (18 songs);
2. girls outsmart, tease, and win competitions with, and even kill boys (17 songs);
3. a girl rejects an unwanted suitor, usually for another boy (12 songs);
4. a girl rejects a boy for unfaithfulness, drunkenness, or bad character (10 songs);
5. pretty girls are more desirable than rich ones, a defense against the usual motivation of arranged marriages (6 songs);
6. girls are praised (5 songs);
7. girls are heroines in fights against Turks and bandits (3 songs).

In these 71 songs the girls are in control, overcoming the fates portrayed in the previous group of songs. They both reflect reality, in the sense that girls had some ability to fend off unwanted suitors and to tease them unmercifully, and construct an imagined world in which girls are masters of their fate rather than hapless victims of a patriarchal social structure.

To conclude, the contrasting images of girls and boys in Todora's songs are quite striking and provide further evidence for an interpretation that views them as women's expression. Men and boys, except when performing heroic deeds against the Turks, are a largely feckless, drunken lot who cannot be trusted and who have to resort to stealing the girls of their choice. Mothers, brides, and girls, on the other hand, when not victimized by men, are clever, beautiful, and occasionally even heroic. In between these two extremes, a few boys and girls find love and happiness with each other. Is it any wonder that girls and women sang these songs with alacrity, while men had to be "in the mood"?

In this chapter, I have described the experience of Bulgarian music from five perspectives, examining (1) how ideology and economics constrained experience; (2) how various nodes of understanding and cognition could be inferred from physical and nonverbal behavior; (3) how variation in performance was created and valued; (4) how metaphors link musical experience to other kinds of shared human experiences located in the body; and (5) how songs gain meaning from the truthful way their texts represent the psychological reality of girls. These perspectives illuminate the question of how Bulgarian music was experienced in the 1930s and how it might be conceptualized and interpreted by people coming to the tradition from different social and historical perspectives: insiders and outsiders; men and women; children and adults; musicians and dancers. The next chapter examines a sixth perspective: how music was experienced in time, specifically during the course of a year.

SIX

Music, Song, and Dance as Seasonal Experience

The economic, cognitive, aesthetic, and emotional experience of music, song, and dance typically played itself out during the course of a year, changing from season to season as work and ritual activity changed.[1] Living in a Bulgarian village in the 1930s demanded hard, but not unremitting, work that varied with the rhythm of the seasons: long hours of hoeing and harvesting under the hot sun of spring and summer, less physically demanding food preparation, preservation, and storage warmed by fires in the fall, and some respite during the cold, short days and long nights of winter. The rhythm of music and dance flowed from this seasonal work rhythm—in this sense, partly determined by ecological and economic conditions—and each season was marked by particular musical and ritual practices.

In the distant, imaginary past, Bulgarians may have believed that these practices not merely marked and celebrated but actually generated the fertility necessary to a successful year. For example, during the winter, at *koleda* (Christmas) and *kukerovden* (pre-Lenten carnival), male carolers went from house to house on luck visits that assured the fertility of plants and animals and thus the success of the coming seasons of work. In the Lenten period before Easter, dance was avoided, ostensibly to mourn the crucifixion of Christ. But peasants may have feared that if Mother Earth were trod on violently in the dances she might fail to germinate—or, metaphorically, give birth to—the crops on which these dancers depended. In the summer, if there was no rain, then rain-begging songs [*peperuda*, lit., 'butterfly'] might help. If the work became too heavy, then a harvest song lightened the burden, and work could continue with renewed vigor. Once there was enough food for all there was time for love and its consummation and celebration in the wedding. By the 1930s, during Kostadin and Todora's youth, belief in the efficacy of these rituals, as compared to fertilizer, was probably not as strong as they had been in the distant, imagined past, and yet no year went by without their celebration.

As Todora and Kostadin described the calendric song and ritual cycle they practiced in the 1930s, I began to understand that it also provided the temporal frame for reflections on the relationship between men and women, boys and girls, and a varied set of contexts for interactions between them. Since weddings in the late fall and winter were culminations not only of the yearly agricultural cycle but of the trajectory of courtship, many of the songs throughout the year helped young people, especially girls, express their fears and understanding of what would befall them when their childhood ended in marriage and they moved away from their mother's house to an uncertain future with a 'foreign mother,' as mothers-in-law are called in some songs, and a 'snake,' as some songs refer to men, both of whom might mistreat them.

In this chapter, I describe the seasonal cycle of songs, music and dances as remembered by Kostadin and Todora, with particular attention to the meaning it had in their own lives as they came together and married. I focus on how the seasons were marked musically and how the songs measured the progress through the seasons of work and love. I interpret the song, music, and dance cycle both as a response to the changing patterns of work, that is, as a kind of economic practice, and as a courtship cycle, initiated by boys and continued by the girls with comments on the various stages of love and marriage.

Koleda

The songs of *koleda,* the Christmas or New Year's caroling ritual, are marked in at least three ways: these are the only songs sung exclusively by men or boys; most *koleda* songs are in an asymmetrical meter such as 5/8 or 7/8 time, unlike the majority of ordinary 2/4 dance songs; and they constitute a *set* of songs, each addressed to a person who occupies a specific social role such as head of the house, a newborn child, a young girl of marriageable age, a new bride, and so on. Even though it was a boys' ritual, Todora remembered fifteen *koleda* songs: two sung at every house, two for the master of the house, six to a young girl, one to a new bride, one to a new mother, one to a boy, one to the host couple, and one is incomplete.

During *koleda,* which lasted from one to three nights starting on Christmas Eve, the 'carolers' [*koledari*] exchanged their songs and blessings and wishes of good luck for loaves of bread and gifts of freshly slaughtered pork, some of which they ate during ritual meals and some of which they gave away to poor people such as the village Gypsies. As Kostadin said, "There are people who don't have pigs at *koleda*. [The *koledari*] collect pork and give it at auction for one *lev*, for example [that is, cheaply]. This they do with the excess over what they can eat during the days of *koleda*."

As they approached each house, a good deal of noise was made to wake up the family, particularly if it was late at night and they had gone to sleep. "There is a 'donkey,' a person who carries the bread in a bag and makes sounds like a donkey. Another carries the meat they are given and meows like a cat." Two songs were sung at each house: one outside the door explaining that 'good guests' had arrived to ensure that all the animals they own—sheep, horses, pigs—will have particularly handsome offspring; the other as they left the house assuring them that God is now with them, and they will have health and their animals and crops enormous fertility in the coming year.

Inside the house, the *koledari* asked the master to whom he would like them to sing. According to Kostadin, he most often requested a song for himself, to ensure the fertility and continued growth of his holdings. They responded with a song such as the one in example 6.1 (CD #14) about a rich man whose hard work, good fortune in having nine sons, and charity to the poor made him so. Kostadin said his father often attributed their family's relative prosperity to his having five sons whose work made the family prosperous. In singing the song, they wished that the luck and qualities of the man in the song would become the lot of the head of the house.

Example 6.1. *Koleda* Song for a Rich Man

Prochul se e tezhŭk bolyarin,   An influential rich man was very
                                                                  famous,

stani nine gospodine,   *stand up for our lord,*
tezhŭk bolyarin, bash chorbad-   influential rich man, a head
   zhiya.   'soup maker.'

Ta ot shto stana tolkoz bolyarin,

tolkoz bolyarin, bash chorbadzhiya?
—Dade mi gospod dor devet
sina,
ta im napravih devet orala,
ta im kupih po chif bivoli,

ta razorahme pole shiroko,

ta go zasyahme s byala pchenitsa,

byala pchenitsa s zhŭlta klasitsa.
Dade go gospod, dade ta stana
ta napŭlnihme vsichki hambari,

i razdavahme na siratsi,

na siromasi i na siratsi,
i na bolyarin skŭpo davahme.
Ot tova stanah tolkoz bolyarin,

tolkoz bolyarin, bash chorbadzhiya.

And from what had he become
such a rich man,
such a rich man, such a head
'soup maker?'
"God gave me nine sons,

and I made them nine plows,
and I bought them each a pair of
oxen,
and we plowed a broad wide
field,
and we seeded it with white
wheat,
white wheat with yellow seeds.
God gave and it happened
that we filled up all of the gran-
aries,
and we gave away to the orphans,
to the poor and the orphans,
and to the rich we gave dearly.
From this I became such a rich
man,
such a rich man, a head 'soup
maker.'"

While songs like this might have been the most important ritually, since they assured the whole family's wealth and happiness, according to Todora it was "most pleasant for boys to sing to the girls at *koleda*." Many of their songs were love songs aimed at young girls and containing cute repartee and interaction between boy and girl, as in the following song, in which a girl complains that she has a snake lying near her right breast. None of her relatives wants to solve the problem, but her boyfriend was eager to help, resulting in some predictable sexual horseplay.

Mela moma ravni dvori,

ei koledo moi kolade,
ta izmela paun pero,

paun pero paunovo.

Che go slozhi v dyasna pazova,

che se shetna kŭm maika si:

A girl was sweeping her flat
yards
hey koledo my koleda
and she swept up a peacock's
feather
a peacock's feather, the feather of
a peacock.
And she put it near her right
breast
and she went over to her
mother:

—Ei ti male, mila male, / "Hey you, dear mother,
zmiya mi lyaga v dyasna pazova. / a snake is lying near my right breast.

Segni, male, izvadi ya. / Please pull it out, mother."
Otgovarya mila maika: / Her dear mother answered:
—Ei ti tebe, milo dusche, / "Hey you, dear little soul,
bez tebe si pominuvam. / I cannot get along without you.
Bez desnitsa chas ne moga. / I cannot get along without my right hand."

Tya se shetna kŭm brata si: / She went over to her brother:
—Ei ti tebe, mili bratko, / "Hey you, dear brother,
zmiya mi lezhi v dyasna pazova. / a snake is lying near my right breast.

Segni, batko, izvadi ya. / Please take it out, dear older brother."

Otgovarya mili bratets: / Her dear brother answered:
—Ei ti tebe, mila sestro, / "Hey you, dear sister,
bez tebe si pominuvam. / I cannot get along without you.
Bez desnitsa chas ne moga. / I cannot get along without my right hand."

Tya se shetna kol lyube si: / She went over to her lover:

—Ei te tebe, pŭrvo lyube, / "Hey you, first love,
Zmiya mi leti v dyasna pasova. / a snake is lying near my right breast.

Segni, lyube, izvadi ya. / Please pull it out, my love."
Otgovarya pŭrvo lyube: / Her first love answered:
—Bŭrzo, bŭrzo, pŭrvo lyube, / "Quickly, quickly, my first love,
bŭrzo, bŭrzo, da izvadim. / quickly, quickly, let's take it out,
Da izvadim lyuta zmiya, / let's take out the hot snake,
lyuta zmiya ot dyasna pasova. / the hot snake from your right breast."

Brŭkna lyube da izvadi, / Her lover quickly tried to take out,

da izvadi lyuta zmiya. / to take out the hot snake.
Ne izvadi lyuta zmiya, / He did not pull out a hot snake,
nai izvadi paun pero, / but he pulled out a peacock's feather,

paun pero paunovo. / a peacock's feather, the feather of a peacock.

Dvama si se prigŭrnaya, / The two of them embraced each other,

prigŭrnaya, tselunaya. / they embraced and kissed each other.

This is the first instance of a pattern in which the seasonal cycle of work and ritual is wedded to a cycle of courtship and marriage. At

koleda, and later at *kukerovden,* the pre-Lenten Carnival, the boys symbolically inseminate plants and animals, which women and girls then
symbolically gestate and birth during long hours of work in the fields.
During the same rituals, in songs like the one above, boys and girls
begin a symbolic cycle of courtship that culminates the next winter
in marriage.

Winter Dance Songs

January, according to Kostadin, was called 'drunkard's month,' a cold
and snowy time, the ground frozen, the days short, the nights long,
and, except for some animal care, not much to do. This left plenty
of time for socializing in people's homes, including eating, drinking,
talking, singing, and dancing indoors around a table. Because of the
restricted space, they danced in a closed circle, boys and girls interspersed and holding hands, and this afforded them one of the few
opportunities to express their affection for one another.

According to Todora, winter dance songs and the dances they accompanied were always a bit faster than those in the summertime, perhaps to keep warm. A small circle of dancers danced to the left and
right very quickly and energetically; the stamping of their feet on the
floor boards of the house created an especially satisfying, resonate
sound, missing in outdoor dances in the village square. Todora said,
"There were large rooms in the houses with boards on the floor. And
when you danced it sounded 'boom, boom' and it gave you even more
spirit to dance."

Musically, the dynamic quality of these songs springs from the nearly
monorhythmic character of the word-rhythms. Each word is one beat
long, with, in some cases, a two-beat duration at the end of the song.
The motoric rhythms of the winter songs made for a bouncy, dynamic
style of indoor dancing in small circles. This analysis was confirmed by
Todora, who said about one such song (ex. 6.2; CD #15), "It's a lively

Example 6.2. Monorhythmic Winter Dance Song

song, danceable [*tropliva*, lit. 'stampable'], so we danced it a lot." When I asked her what in the song made it "lively," she responded, "it's light" and began singing the tune using the syllables *da, da, da,* emphasizing the monorhythmic quality of the words and eliding the eighth notes in the melody. So winter (and fall) indoor dance songs, although in duple meter like their spring and summer counterparts, are marked by the uniform word rhythm, which is experienced as lively dance tunes that generate enthusiastic dancing.

I experienced this house-dancing energy one time in Boston, where Todora and Kostadin had gone in December of 1978 to give a workshop. Late in the evening, after a long tiring day, a number of us gathered at someone's home, giddy from exhaustion. Kostadin played a piece called *Boninata* in 7/8 time (ex. 6.3; CD #16). The dance is symmetrical with four steps to the right, then three sets of three quick steps in place. The pattern is then repeated to the left. As the circle moves to the left and right, the joined hands swing down energetically; for the quick steps in place, the hands are held in a tense **W** form and shaken vigorously in rhythm. Based on what I had observed of Todora's dance style, a few of us began the dance in a lazy fashion at a slow tempo. As Kostadin continued playing, the tempo increased, and our dancing became more energetic. When we tired, we danced less energetically, only to speed up again with renewed energy. In one transcendent moment it seemed to me we began to fly, as if our feet were not touching the ground, or, if they were, then they were propelling us to and fro with only the slightest effort. Finally Kostadin stopped playing and we collapsed, savoring an unforgettable and sadly unrepeatable moment. Todora, who had been watching us, came over to me and said, "Tim, you are always asking how it was in the old days. That's how it was!"

Todora's repertoire included 47 songs in duple meter which she identified as appropriate for or typical of winter, presumably because

Example 6.3. *Boninata*

of their motoric rhythmic character. About half of the songs are unmarked textually as winter songs; it was simply customary to sing them
at that time. The other half are connected to winter in at least one of
two senses. First, 8 of the songs mention winter weather, work, or other
activities: 'a dark fog,' 'awful killing winter,' 'a field full of roots' during
winter plowing, the hungry winter after a poor harvest, winter pastur-
age in foreign places, and such subtle things as sleeping inside instead
of outside (especially true of men), cold water, and going after dark to
the well. In addition to references to wintry physical conditions, a
dozen or so of these winter dance songs refer to dark, "wintry" emotions and various kinds of bad luck, bad dreams, sickness, imprisonment, and death. In this respect they are much different from the
more cheerful summer dance songs.

For Bulgarians, winter was a time of death, because they believed
many elderly people died then. Old people looked forward to spring
as a sign that they would live through another year. The text below is
the saddest, most negative song in Todora's repertoire, and, because
it is about the death of a Todora, our Todora said, "I hated this song."

Todora dvori izmela
i vodata si donela,
ta che na dvori izlyala,
na dvori na dolni vrati,
maitsi si son da kazuva:
—Male le, mila male le,
ya snoshti legnah ta zaspah.

Na sone losh sŭn sŭnuvah
che dovel teino dulgeri,

dulgeri, mladi maistori,

che sa gradishta gradili.
Na gradishta pelgore,

na peloreto siv sokol.
Todorinata mashteya,
tya na Todora dumashe:
—Shterko Todoro, Todoro,
na zlo e, shterko, na zlo e,
na zlo e ne e na dobro.
Gradishtata sa grobitsa,
pelgoreto sa nosila,
siv sokol, byala Todora.

Todora swept her yards
and she brought water,
she moistened the yards,
the yards at the back door,
and told her mother a dream.
"Mother, dear mother,
last night I lay down and began
   to sleep.
I dreamed a bad dream
that father brought some
   builders,
some builders, some young
   craftsmen,
and they built some buildings.
In the building were some
   windows,
in the window was a gray hawk."
Todora's stepmother,
she said to Todora:
"My daughter Todora, Todora
it is bad, my daughter, it is bad
it is bad, it is not good.
Those buildings are graves,
the windows are pallets,
the gray hawk is white Todora."

Winter songs like this one expressed poetically the negative aspects of winter, its emotional and physical coldness. Winter was symbolic of all that is dark in human emotions. But in the memory of Todora and Kostadin, winter was also a merry time of lively indoor dancing, long nights of partying, cavorting happily in the snow and mud, and rest from a long, hard summer of work. In a sense dance and song expressed opposite sides of the emotional and physical reality of winter. Winter was dark, cold, and trying, and this was expressed in the songs. But those same wintry conditions spawned, where possible, gaiety, merrymaking, and drunkenness as a defense, expressed mainly through dancing. Winter contained both happiness and sadness in its essence as did a song-dance event. The brisk motoric rhythms of winter dance songs generated a lively, stamping, laughing dance despite the often sad commentary on the harshness of winter contained in their texts. In this tradition, music, dance, and emotion were not matched but juxtaposed, as if the best defense were a good offense. Both happiness and sadness were part of everyday experience, and this experience was replicated in winter dance events.

Kukerovden

Winter symbolically came to an end on *kukerovden* (kuker's day), a carnival-like ritual insemination of the earth by male masqueraders designed to insure the fertility of the season's crops. Like *koleda,* it was performed by males, this time not with songs, but with instrumental music on the gaida, whose drone pipe and goatskin are interpreted by some Bulgarians as male sexual symbols.[2] The men dressed up in animal skins, attached belts of bells (seeds/balls), and wore tall, pointed hats (seeds/phalluses). They went from house to house bouncing up and down to jingle their bells, accompanied by a processional tune on the gaida that alternated nonmetrical and metrical sections (CD #17). At each house, they placed the master in a cart and led him around the yard, ritually seeding it. Afterward, they danced a simple *rŭchenitsa* in 7/8 with four steps forward and four steps back, at the end bowing from the waist, and casting their tall, pointed hats/seeds/phalluses on the earth. Finally the family and the *kukeri* joined together in a *horo* to celebrate the ritual insemination.

Bulgarians, by symbolically and ritually having men inseminate animals and plants at *koleda* and *kukerovden* respectively, mapped human sexuality onto the agricultural cycle. At that point men's symbolic participation in the agricultural cycle ceased and women took up the symbolic gestation of the crops through harvest and rain-begging songs, mirroring the sexual roles in human and animal reproduction.

Lenten Games: Na Filek

Just as a pregnant woman must exercise caution, so Mother Earth must be treated with care during her gestation period, a pagan explanation of the quiet, meditative Lenten season. During this season of forty days, dancing and merrymaking were prohibited and meatless fasting mandated. However, young boys and girls were permitted to play games or 'go *na filek*,' a practice Bulgarian folklorists say was especially well developed in Strandzha.[3] Many of the games were songs accompanied by rhythmic motion that might, in other circumstances, be called a dance but, because of the prohibition against dancing, were called 'games' [*igra*]. Todora remembers eight of them, in many of which there was as much or more physical contact between boys and girls as at a *horo*.

In one of the games, very much like the English "London Bridge Is Falling Down" (ex. 6.4; CD #18), girls and boys ran through an arch formed by one pair, who brought their arms down at the end of the song to capture someone in the line. The pushing and shoving and touching that occurred was a source of great fun for young people otherwise forbidden to have much contact.

Example 6.4. *Na filek* Game Resembling "London Bridge Is Falling Down"

—Kalyo portalyo,
otvori porti.
Gosti ke doidat,
Tsaryom Kostadin
s negova voiska.
—Minete, minete,
edno ostavete.

"Kalyo, door keeper,
open up the doors.
Guests will be coming,
King Constantine
with his army."
"Pass through, pass through,
but leave one behind."

One of the most enjoyable *na filek* activities was swinging from tall trees. The boys made swings and swung the girls, in the process lifting them up onto the swing, pushing them, and perhaps stealing a kiss. While some girls screamed with fright as the boys tried to scare them by swinging them higher and higher, Todora remembered loving it and demanding that the boys swing her ever higher. "The swing hung in a big tree. You can't imagine how scary it was. There were two boys in front with ropes and they swung us really high. They didn't care that we might fall. But I wasn't afraid. I would cry out, 'Eeee-hu,' so that they would hear and know I wasn't afraid. It was fun. If you asked them to stop, they wouldn't until you said the name of the boy you liked." Example 6.5 is the song *Lyulka se lyulya*, "A Swing Is Swinging" (CD #19). Although Lent was ostensibly a period of quiet reflection with no dancing or celebration, boys and girls conspired in their song-games to continue their courtships and teasing about love.

Example 6.5. Lenten Swinging Song

Lyulka, lyulka se lyulya, *devoiko*,	A swing, a swing is swinging, *maiden*,
lyulka, lyulka se lyulya.	a swing, a swing is swinging.
Ta koi, ta koi se lyulye?	And who, and who is swinging?
Yana, Yana, se lyulye.	Yana, Yana is swinging.
Ta koi, ta koi se lyulye?	And who, and who is swinging?
Ivan, Ivan e lyulye.	Ivan, Ivan is swinging.
Dvash e, dvash e zalyulye.	Two times, two times he swings her.
Trish e, trish e tseluvne.	The third time, the third time he kisses her.

Easter

Easter, a three-day festival of dancing, singing, eating, and drinking, celebrated the end of the Lenten fast, Christ's resurrection, and the arrival of spring. Todora said, "Easter was a big deal. Tremendous preparation. Everything was washed. The house was cleaned for a month, until the Sunday before Easter. And then for a week, at least from Thursday on, you could only move around the house, but you couldn't sit to sew or spin yarn [that is, work was forbidden]. This was a great holiday. The birth of Christ. A great day. The old people mispronounced it *Veliden,* but it was *Velikden* ['great day'] [*laughs*]. There was a special bread [*pogach*] with a red egg in the center, with a little bit of dough surrounding the egg. This was placed on the *sofra* [small round table with three legs] with a fine wool covering. And for three days constantly, eating . . . and then to the dance for three days, each day with a different outfit. Today with a green dress, tomorrow with red, the next day with another color. Everyone has a best friend and they will dress the same."

The clothing and rituals of Easter actually gave form to the Easter dance. In Todora's and Kostadin's day, the focal point of the Easter costume was the shiny new patent-leather Easter shoes. The Easter ritual game, in which two people struck each other's dyed Easter egg to see whose would break first, littered the village square with the brightly colored, broken shells. The beauty on the ground—the new shiny shoes and pretty eggshells—generated a movement unique to these dances: as the dancers stepped in place, they lowered their heads and rotated them from side to side to survey the beautiful new shoes and eggshells littering the village square. These head movements were unique to and defined the dances of Easter.[4]

The set of twelve Easter songs in Todora's repertoire are all in 7/8 time, subdivided either 3 + 2 + 2 or 2 + 2 + 3, a meter that sets them apart from the duple meter dance songs of the other seasons (ex. 6.6; CD #20).

The dancing began as soon as church let out on Sunday and continued for three days. Kostadin complained, "You began to hate the dance," but Todora would have none of that: "How could you hate the

Example 6.6. Easter Dance Song

dance. We waited for the dawn, and we ran to dance. In fact, it happened after noon. First, the smallest children went out to the dance square. Then bigger and bigger, and the biggest and the most important came out last. And we began. And people arranged themselves in the dance by groups and so did the public. This neighborhood over here, that one over there. And then they begin to see one another, to change places. It was nice."

As Todora described it, the form of the *horo* clearly reproduced the age and gender hierarchies of the village, with men dancing near the front of the line and women farther down. Within each gender group people of about the same age tended to dance together, arranged in order from oldest to youngest. Todora said, "On Easter a little child would lead the *horo*, then the singers. The older women were lower in the line than the men, and we girls had to be even lower still" (pl. 7).

The dance was a place where hierarchies of age and gender were simultaneously presented and negotiated; the rules of everyday interaction could be broken in the hurly-burly of the dance. "I and another girl, Kostadin's cousin—Nanka she was called—we and a couple of boys would join the line where they danced the craziest. They laughed at us and scolded us, 'Does it suit you to go there and dance with the old people?' I was silent, but Nanka called out, 'It suits us. It suits us.' Easter was fun." Easter dances, like all dances, provided a context where relationships could be tested, one could imagine oneself an older person, and where the gender separation and age-based hierarchies of everyday life could be briefly challenged.

As for the music, Todora said, "singing and the gaida, that was our music. And kaval if someone had one. But during our time there was only the gaida. And the tŭpan. And when we began to sing for the dance, again Easter songs. In our time we wanted to sing some other dance songs which resembled Easter songs. But the older people didn't allow us to sing songs other than Easter songs. Only on the third day. After [we sang], the gaida would play other things: *Trite pŭti, Paidushko, Boninata, Pravo horo.*" As in so many other domains, older people controlled younger people at the *horo*, demanding that style and repertoire be replicated appropriately and rather exactly in each new performance.

The texts of Todora's Easter songs are much happier than the winter songs and thus match the hopeful mood of the season. As Todora put it, the main theme of Easter songs was "love. But fun." Easter, a time of joy, included love songs in which the trials and tribulation of Turkish rule were overcome—perhaps an analogy to Christ's overcoming death. Even songs of death, which are so bleak in the winter dance

songs, take on a loving, positive character at Easter. Only one of Todora's songs mentions Easter directly, and it is about love and marriage; even the mother-in-law, vilified at other times of the year, is a
positive character in Easter songs.

As Todora explained, songs are assigned to the seasons more by
their musical qualities than their textual ones. When I asked what defines an Easter song, she laughed and admitted, "I have no idea. An
Easter song is an Easter song. We didn't ask why. We didn't pay attention to whether there was a connection or not to Easter. In no song do
they speak of Easter. They are chosen by the melodies. These [melo-
dies] are Easter, others *koleda,* others fall, others *sedyanka.* The harvest
songs speak of harvest. Easter and koleda songs could only be sung at
those times. The other dance songs could be sung other times, but still
there were summer, spring, and winter songs."

My analysis suggests that the melodies associated with particular rituals and seasons are more clearly marked by rhythmic characteristics
than by tonal ones. Textual content is most variable, although there
are suggestions of the seasons in some of the texts. In explaining the
inconsistencies and apparent lack of meaning in some of the songs,
Todora said, "Who looked for meaning in these songs. We just wanted
more words so we wouldn't have to repeat ourselves."

Spring Dances

Todora identified 21 songs in her repertoire as spring dance songs,
and two-thirds made some obvious reference to spring-like conditions:
dewy evenings, blossoming cherry and apple trees, new gardens, newborn lambs, cutting hay, and bouquets of flowers and herbs. Spring
songs are in duple meter, but, because they were danced outdoors, the
rhythmic character differs substantially from winter dance songs and
resembles the summer dance songs that follow.

Dances at Summer Fairs

Summer was a time of intense work in the fields. Even the long days
did not define the outer limits of work. Harvesting certain crops, like
tobacco, began before dawn, while harvesting wheat might continue
into the darkness. The drudgery was broken up only by an occasional
fair, held on the saint's day of a village's church. Even then, according
to Todora, people couldn't attend if they had too much work. Most
people were not content to go only to their own village fair, but walked
or rode in carts for miles to neighboring villages. A fair was an occasion

to visit and make friends, buy trinkets for the children, perhaps see a wrestling match, and above all to dance and sing, pretexts for boys and girls to get together.

Todora's summer (and spring) dance songs are in duple meter, but are distinguished rhythmically from their winter counterparts. Instead of the motoric, monorhythms of winter songs, summer dance songs usually have two words in the middle of phrases held out for two beats, creating a smoother effect and leading to slower tempos and less energetic dancing. These factors in turn sustained longer outdoor dance lines of hundreds of people, led by a leader in a broken circle formation rather than the small closed circles of indoor winter dances.

The slow tempos of summer dance songs also generated more subdivisions of the main beat, and the result overall is much more rhythmic variety in summer dance songs than in winter songs. Comparing winter and summer dance songs, Todora said the summer songs "are slower, not so 'emphasized' [natŭrteno], 'rhythmic' [ritmichno]" as the winter songs. To make her point, she sang a summer dance-song melody on the syllables *da, da* with the long notes emphasized (ex. 6.7; CD #21). "How can you stamp to that? You can't ever stamp to that." If winter dances are remembered for the mud outdoors, the resonate floor boards indoors and the energetic dancing, summer dances are remembered for the dust and heat and the long dance lines: "Oh what a long *horo* this song [ex. 6.7] made."[5]

All dance songs were sung antiphonally by four singers in two groups of two at the front of the line, although they often followed a male leader of the line. The girls who knew the song best sang first and the other two answered them. If the length of the *horo* made it too difficult for people at the end to hear the singing, Todora said "the pairs of singers would be separated, one at the beginning, and then the others in the middle somewhere. The second group repeated the words. Whoever knew the words better sang first." I asked, "Were you in the first group?" She answered, "Always." Kostadin chimed in, "My computer."

MM♩ = 132

1 Is- ka- la   Yan- ka da   i- de

6 na Gyu- na-   li- ya na   zbo- ra

Example 6.7. Summer Dance Song

As for content, half of her summer dance songs mention going to the dance or fair; most of these mention the theme of love and what can happen at the fair, especially boys and girls spotting each other and falling in love. Often the songs portray fairs as unstable moments of danger or change, when relationships might end because of jealousy, gossip, or finding a new lover. Lies were told that broke up relationships, both in songs and in real life. "The village was small and word traveled fast. Engagements were called off because people saw one of the engaged talking with someone else. There was morality in those days. If your aunt tells your mother you were with so-and-so, your mother will believe her and not you, unless you have someone to verify you weren't there."

While love conquers all in most of the summer dance songs, fully one-third deal with negative themes of death, sickness, stealing/rape, divorce, and beatings. These themes are treated lightheartedly in the text to example 6.7, in which a Turk takes a liking to a girl, but she objects to his offers by insulting him and his religion, a gesture Bulgarians find humorous.

Iskala Yanka da ide	Yanka wanted to go
na Gyunaliya, na zbora,	to Gyunaliya, to the fair,
na Gyunaliiski panayir.	to the Gyunaliya fair.
Maika i ne e puskashe	Her mother didn't allow her
a brat i ne e racheshe.	and her brother didn't want her to go.
Yankina maika dumashe:	Yanka's mother said:
—Tuk sedi Yanke, ne hodi	"Stay here, Yanka, don't go
na Gyunaliya, na zbora,	to Gyunaliya, to the fair,
che ti se kani, Yanke le,	because you have been invited, Yanka,
Gyunaliiskite seimeni,	by the Gyunaliya detachment,
seimeni, seimen bashiya.	the detachment, the head of the detachment.
Kanyat se da te otkradnat,	They invited you to steal you,
bela hanŭmka da stanesh.	to make you into a white Turkish girl."
Yanka maika si ne slusha.	Yanka did not listen to her mother.
Tya stana ta se primeni,	She got up and changed,
primeni, ta se naredi.	changed and fixed herself up.
Na panayire otide,	She went to the fair,
na Gyunaliiski panayir.	to the Gyunaliya fair.
Zaigra kakto igrashe,	She began to dance, and danced again,

i zapya kakto peeshe.

Sobash iz horo hodeshe

i si na Yanka dumashe:
—Yanke le, byala bŭlgarko,
ti ne ti, Yanke, prilyaga
na horo, Yanke, da peesh,
da peesh, Yanke, da igrash.
Nai ti, Yanke, prilyaga
byala hanŭmka da stanesh,

na visok chardak da sedish,
byala koprina da predesh,
zhŭlti altŭni da nizhesh.

Yanka na Sobash dumashe:
—Mi stavam belka ni stavam,

yako ti, Sobash, napravish
v Stambolo turska dzhamiya
i karash teinom svinete
vŭv tazi turska dzhamiya.
I az stavam byala hanŭmka.

she began to sing, and sang
  again.
The commander walked around
  the dance
and said to Yanka:
"Yanka, beautiful Bulgarian girl,
it doesn't suit you, Yanka,
at the dance, Yanka, to sing,
to sing, Yanka, and to dance.
It most suits you, Yanka,
to become a beautiful Turkish
  girl,
to sit on a high balcony,
to embroider with white silk,
to string golden necklaces of
  gold coins."
Yanka said to the commander:
"It could happen, it could
  happen
if you, commander, go
to Istanbul, to a Turkish mosque
and drive my father's pigs
into the Turkish mosque.
Then I will become a white Turkish girl."

Harvest Songs

Field work also provided an occasion for singing, as the women hoed weeds, harvested the wheat with a short sickle bent over at the waist, or rested in the shade of a tree at noon. Unlike the strongly rhythmic work songs of the African-American tradition, Bulgarian harvest songs [zhŭtvarski pesni] are nonmetrical and distinguished textually from other nonmetrical songs by reference to field work and harvesting in most cases.

Todora divided her repertoire of 13 harvest songs into four groups: songs sung at noon during the hottest part of the day; songs sung at dusk as the day cools and the end of work was approaching; songs sung on the way home to the village; and those sung at any time. Although songs sung on the way to the fields exist in Bulgarian collections, Todora joked that she and her friends were usually too sleepy to sing so early in the morning. Most of the songs, after mentioning the harvest or work context, go on to treat themes common to Bulgarian songs in general: love, violence, and fear. Only one of the songs, sung at noon, focuses exclusively on work: the tools used, working in a bent-over position, and the rows of harvesters moving through the fields (ex. 6.8; CD #22).

Example 6.8. Harvest Song

—Stoyane, Stoyane,
mladi postadzhiyo,
ne shiri postata,

ne shiri, ne dŭlzhi,
che pladnina stana,
stana i zamina.
Sŭrpa syanka stori,
sŭrpa i palamarka.
Robi popadaya,
robi i robini.

Stoyan otgovarya:
—Zhenete, zhenete,
i ne stoite pravi.
Posta da izkarame

do krai, do sam kraya.

"Stoyan, Stoyan,
young harvest leader,
don't spread out the section of
    the field,
don't widen it, don't lengthen it,
because noon is approaching,
is approaching and will pass.
The scythe is making shade,
the scythe and the swaphook.
The bondsmen are tired,
the bondsmen and the bonds-
    women."

Stoyan answered:
"Harvest, harvest,
and don't stand up straight.
We will finish the section of the
    field
to the end, to the very end."

Although harvest songs were only sung in the fields, many other kinds of songs, particularly nonmetrical *sedyanka* and table songs [*pesni na trapeza*], were sung as well. Singing functioned psychologically to help pass the time, lighten the burden of work, and relieve the fear women felt working alone in the fields far away from the village. "Because we were afraid to be in the fields during the war, we sang all day. I mean all day. We didn't stop. The most different songs. We were far away, four or five kilometers up in the forest—'pop songs' [*shlageri*], 'city songs' [*gradski pesni*], whatever we knew. Simply to make company, noise, so that we wouldn't hear other stuff [*laughs*]."

In the unstable period after the war, when the men had returned, women still worked alone in the fields. "One day we were harvesting and singing near the sheepfold. We had made a cradle for Vanyo [her first son] and the daughter of my eldest sister-in-law was watching him. At one moment she cried out, 'Bride! Bride!' And when we asked 'What?' and turned around, there was a man behind us. He was running for the border. We froze in fear. He said, 'Good day. Good day. You are working and singing.' He began to ask what village was where: Pŭnchevo, Grudovo. We told him where to go through the forest. After that we couldn't work. We were shaking all over. And we gathered up our baggage and returned to the village, washed up." This anecdote provides further evidence of the connection between singing and fear and of women's use of singing to fight off negative emotions destructive of disciplined work and deportment.

Autumn Sedyankas

The fall season was marked musically by communal working bees [medzhii], held in homes and yards to help the family shuck corn and process other harvested foodstuffs, and by sedyankas, at which the girls gathered to embroider, knit, and sew. In both cases, singing helped the work pass more easily and pleasantly; the girls sang together two by two, and boys came to play music, dance, and socialize with the girls. Often the work was done outside around a bonfire, a fact referenced in the songs in lines translated as "A sedyanka was lit." Sometimes just two or three girls, close friends, got together; at other times, the whole neighborhood was invited, and a large group of boys and girls gathered to work, sing, and later dance. Kostadin and Todora remember these fall sedyankas and medzhii as times of play between boys and girls and in some ways preparatory for the weddings to come, whether immediately in the winter time after work was done, the fields harvested, and food and wine prepared, or in the future as these youths matured and selected a mate.

Todora's sedyanka song repertoire has three parts, the largest consisting of 36 nonmetrical songs sung during handwork, the sedyanka songs proper. They also sang short, joking songs in which a particular boy's name was linked in the text to a girl's name. Todora said, however, referring to one of them, "This is not a song; it is a nadpyavane ['singing competition']." The third part of the repertoire consists of fall dance songs, sung at the end of the evening, after work was done.

Only five of the sedyanka songs actually mention the sedyanka. The song in example 6.9 (CD #23) describes explicitly what happened at a sedyanka, a place where relationships were negotiated and put on view.

In this song two boys try to sit next to the same girl, and the argument continues as they leave to return home. Previously we learned of a similar incident involving Todora, Kostadin, and Dimo, and Todora spoke in a general way about others as well. "Oh, God. If a bachelor came from another village, you should see what would happen. They would follow him and if there wasn't some more serious person from our village with him, they would beat him. Our village wasn't so much like this. We didn't have such fights. But over in Yanka Rupkina's village [one of Bulgaria's most famous folk singers, born in Pŭnchevo], there it was awful." Kostadin added, "Scoundrels."

Example 6.9. Nonmetrical *Sedyanka* Song

Stŭknala Rada sedyanka,	Rada kindled a sitting bee,
stŭknala, pishman stanala.	kindled one, but was sorry she did it.
Zashto be, Rade, sedyanka,	Why was there a sitting bee, Rada,
zashto be i za kakvo be?	why and for what reason?
Ta se sŭrviya, sŭrviya,	Because there came from all directions
vsichki beglichki ovchari,	all of the Beg's shepherds,
i sa sednali, sednali,	and they sat down, sat down,
do vsyaka moma i momche.	next to each girl a boy.
Do byala Rada dvamina,	By white Rada there were a pair of them,
dvamina, dor dva drugari,	a pair of them, two comrades,
Ivan i Stoyan dvamata.	Ivan and Stoyan, the two of them.
Ivan do Rada sedeshe,	Ivan sat next to Rada
i si na Rada dumashe:	and to Rada he said:
—Popridai, Rade, napridai	"Spin, Rada, spin up
kŭdelya ta si opredai,	the wool into yarn,
vretenoto se napredai	spin the spindle

i haide da te zaveda,
che shte kramula da stane,

kramula, Rade, za tebe.
I prela Rada, oprela,

kŭdelya ta si oprela,
vretenoto se naprela,
stanala da se otide.
Ivan da si ya zavede
i Stoyan trŭgna podire,
i do Radine stignali.
Stoyan si Ivan nastigna,
nastigna i go ulovi.
Rada se nazad obŭrna,

i si na Stoyan dumashe:
—Stoyane, holŭm Stoyane,
ti ne razbra li, Stoyane,

che tebe nyama da vzema?
Az shte si vzeme Ivane,
che Ivane mi e likata,
likata i prilikata.

and let us take you home,
because there is going to be an argument,
an argument about you, Rada."
And Rada spun and finished spinning
the wool into yarn,
spun the spindle,
and got up to leave.
Ivan was leading her
and Stoyan set out after them,
and they went to Rada's place.
Stoyan caught up to Ivan,
he caught up and grabbed him.
Rada turned around and looked back
and said to Stoyan:
"Stoyan, my friend Stoyan,
have you not understood, Stoyan,
that I am not going to take you?
I am going to take Ivan
because Ivan suits me,
he suits me and agrees with me."

The themes of the nonmetrical *sedyanka* songs can be divided into two parts: 8 songs deal with travel outside the village, banditry, and fights with the Turks; the remaining 28 treat love, engagement, and marriage. The former might more properly be called table songs, and were also sung by men in taverns and at home with guests. The emphasis in the latter group on engagement and marriage is appropriate, since the fall season immediately precedes the weddings of winter. "Engagements start in autumn. They don't wait a year. They wait two, three, six months. We [Kostadin and I] were engaged six months. Simply to get ready. We got married young so we had to hurry to get the gifts ready. Whoever is ready wouldn't have to wait so long."

As a group these songs tell the longest, most interesting stories in Todora's repertoire. They are filled with the tensions that accompanied life in the period of Turkish rule and the transitions from childhood to adulthood. In particular, marriage is often characterized negatively, particularly from the girls' point of view. While every girl wants to fall in love and get married, unhappy years often follow the carefree days of childhood. This song warns against getting married too early.

—Ne bŭrzai, Rade, ne bŭrzai.

Mŭninka da se oglavish
pŭk pomŭninka ozhenish.
Shte doide esen, Rade le,
esen, eseni sedenki.
Momi sedyanki shte stŭknat,
Shte stŭknat, Rade, shte viknat.

Pŭk ti v kŭshti da sedish,
polyulechitsa shte lyulesh,
polyulechitsa, nanchitsa.
I shte se rechesh, Rade le:
—Stori me, bozhe, prestori
dvash malka pa trish leftera,

da si se moma naodi,
mominska premyana da nosya.

"Do not hurry, Rada, do not
    hurry.
You're too little to get engaged
and even littler to get married.
For the fall will come, Rada,
the fall and the fall sitting bees.
The girls will kindle sitting bees,
they will kindle them, Rada, and
    they will sing.
But you will sit in your house,
you will rock a cradle,
a cradle with a child.
And you will say, Rada:
'Make me, God, transform me
two times younger and three
    times unmarried,
to be a young girl,
and girl's clothes to wear.'"

The most dramatic symbolic statement of how bad a marriage can be is expressed in the following song in which a man becomes ugly to his wife, ostensibly because of sickness and wounds, but surely these are symbols for any kind of relationship turned sour.

—Stanche le, momne, *mari*, der-
    venko,
dervenko, dervenska shterko,
se stana devet godini
kato te mama mari ozheni,
ozheni ta te zadomi.

Ni marama si oprala,

ni kosata si oprela.
Zashto si tŭzhna i kahŭrna?
Stanka maika si dumashe:
—Male le, mila male le,
zashto me pitash male le?
Ti ne vidish li, male le,
kolko mi e tezhko i grozno?
Se stana devet godini
kato se, male, ozhenih,
i moito pŭrvo lyubove.
Dva pŭti go sipka sipalo,
treti pŭt s mechka borilo

"Stanche, girl, *mari*, from
    Derven,
Derven, Derven's daughter,
nine years have passed
since your mother married you,
married you and placed you in a
    home.
You have neither washed your
    headkerchief
nor braided your hair.
Why are you sad and worried?"
Stanka said to her mother:
"Mother, dear mother,
why do you ask, mother?
Don't you see, mother,
how sad and awful it is for me?
All these nine years have passed
since I married, mother,
my first love.
Two times he has had small pox,
the third time he has wrestled
    with a bear

ta mu e nosa ozyalo	which ate up his nose
ta go e obezo brazila.	and mutilated him.
Ta ne moga, male, da sedna,	I cannot sit, mother,
da sedna da go pogledna.	sit and look at him.
Kamoli ya da se setya	How could I even think
marama da si opera	to wash my headkerchief
i kosite da si opleta?	and to braid my hair?
Cherno mi, male, grozno mi.	He is black and ugly to me,
	mother.
Ni mozha veke da zhive,	I cannot live any longer,
da zhive i da go gledam,	I cannot live and look at him,
kolko e grozen v litseto.	his face is so ugly."

Although I interpret songs like this symbolically as an expression of women's experience of entrapment in unhappy marriages, Todora always takes them literally. "This is a true song, you should know. Surely. It can't be that it isn't true. I figure something like this must have happened and they sang about it. I don't know the story. Maybe my mother or grandmother did, but I didn't think to ask. I liked the melody and I sang it a lot. I would sing it quietly to myself. Because of the text you couldn't sing it at table. I would sing it as I washed dishes or spun wool."

Much of the tension expressed in *sedyanka* songs resulted from interference by parents and in-laws who tried to prevent true love from fulfilling itself or who engaged their daughters to ugly or lazy suitors. Some songs deal with the guilt and fear associated with the young people trying to arrange their own marriages. "In the old days, of course, the adults, the parents, arranged marriages. For two young people to arrange their own marriage was not considered appropriate. The parents could refuse, and the father might then go out and arrange a different marriage for someone that the girl didn't love. It was very bad if the boy's parents didn't want the marriage because the girl went to live with them, and if she wasn't wanted or liked by them, they could make life very miserable for her." It is in the *sedyanka* and winter dance songs that girls' fearfulness of men and marriage is most clearly expressed.

The length of nonmetrical *sedyanka* songs stands in contrast to the short *nadpyavane*s, which are six to eleven lines long and in a variety of meters: 2/4, 5/8, 7/8, and 9/8. The texts all contain a boy's and a girl's name, which are changed each time the song is sung. In keeping with the playful nature of *sedyanka*s, in which love is being negotiated and displayed and engagement and marriage being talked about, the texts of these songs usually mention other playful acts, such as the exchange of water and flowers between boys and girls wishing to contact each other and display their affection. A boy often tried to meet and talk to a girl as she gathered water at the well, out of earshot of her parents. There he would ask her for a sip of water or for her bouquet. If she agreed, it was a sign that she liked him. Kostadin, for example, said he could see Todora's house from his and often watched to see when she went to the well so he could meet her there.

The song in example 6.10 (CD #24) is characteristic of this set of songs, and makes an analogy between burning up from thirst and from love, which a girl and the water she has collected from the well will quench. The girls repeated the song many times, pairing boy's and girl's names, either to comment on the obvious, speculate on hidden romances, or embarrass friends who didn't like each other. One can only imagine the joking and laughter that must have accompanied these songs. "At *sedyankas* we sang this [ex. 6.10] and changed the names. We knew who was going with whom, but sometimes we put people together on purpose who did not want to be together. You know what would happen. They would curse, get angry, throw things at us" [*laughs*].

Example 6.10. Sedyanka *Nadpyavane*

Voda teche (2) po beli kamenye	(2) Water flowed by the white rocks.
Ta koi ticha voda da nalee?	And who ran to fill up water?
Stanka ticha voda da nalee.	Stanka ran to fill up water.
Ta koi ticha voda da napiva?	And who ran to drink the water?
Ivan ticha voda da napiva.	Ivan ran to drink the water.
Toi da reche izgoryah za voda,	He said that he burned up for water,
pak toi reche izgoryah za Stanka.	and he said he burned up for Stanka.

After singing this song, Todora talked about courtship, and she and Kostadin joked with me about their own youth, a conversation that shows something of the warmth and humor in their relationship.

> *Todora:* Everyone wanted to get married. That's why they did it at fifteen years old. As soon as you started to work. At once. At 17, 18 and older, at 20, 21. As they say, "To each according to his fate."
>
> *Kostadin:* Todora was very hardworking and they sought her out.
>
> *Todora:* Yes, that's why his mother and father took me. Don't think they took me for my beauty. Only for work.
>
> *Kostadin: Ey,* and for beauty, don't you think. You are beautiful.
>
> *Todora:* There were more beautiful than I, *de.*[6]
>
> *Kostadin:* Who, *be?*
>
> *Todora:* Well, the daughter of our godmother, Minda, your lover. He deceived them all, Tim. The whole village were his girlfriends.
>
> *Kostadin:* She deceived them all?
>
> *Todora [shouts]:* You! You! He was a swaggering bachelor, bold, handsome, dapper. He was well-dressed, well-built. But he was a relative, and I never looked at him as a bachelor. But when he went with one, another said, "Your older brother Diko [short for Kostadin] went with whomever." Another evening with another. At the well. That was our meeting place.

The final group of songs in Todora's *sedyanka* repertoire consists of 8 fall dance songs, three of which mention fall or related activities such as working bees and engagements. The remaining 5 songs contain consistent joking banter between a boy and a girl, reflecting and contributing to the playfulness of the *sedyanka*. In their monorhythmic character, these fall dance songs resemble winter dance songs, which were notable for their vigorous stamping.

Kostadin and Todora also spoke about some of the physical contact these fall and winter dances allowed. In principle, the dances were done in a closed circle, either with the boys forming one half and the girls the other or boys and girls interspersed. But the perfection of the circle was often broken when an enthusiastic dancer led a charge of other dancers into the center of the circle to stamp vigorously. When the dancing was particularly energetic, the dancers raised their joined arms into a W position and shook them strongly. Kostadin laughed and said, "The boys would dance across the circle and try to touch the girls' breasts with their arms." Todora, not to be outdone, responded immediately, "Yes, Tim, and we girls danced across the circle like this." She then bent over, danced forward with her arms held down and moving in such a way as to threaten to come up between the boys' legs, and collapsed into uncontrollable giggles.

The contrast between the playfulness and tensions of love and marriage was a striking feature of this season of the year. While the dance songs, *nadpyavane,* and descriptions of tomfoolery at *sedyanka*s suggest the giddiness of young love, the *sedyanka* songs themselves warn of the dire consequences of poor marriage choices and how parents and in-laws can block the course of true love.

Weddings

With the success of the harvest and the completion of the work associated with it, the wedding season—"with sweet wine and new wheat"—began, lasting from fall through the winter to Lent. Fall was the favorite season, and in Gergebunar Kostadin said two to six weddings were celebrated each year. Weddings, the only Bulgarian life cycle ritual with music, were placed at the end of the calendric cycle, which provided the means to continue the life cycle as harvest fruits provided the substance of both ordinary and ritual life.

A wedding affected the participants in different ways. It marked the bride's passage from her maternal home to a new life as an adult, more exactly 'a bride' [*bulka*] in the home of her husband's father. Her parents grieved for the loss of a daughter, while the groom's parents rejoiced at receiving a new worker and childbearer. While the bride was the focus of ritual acts, the groom's concerns were not given much independent expression in these songs, as if he were a mere agent of his family. Both families forged a new affinal bond and become in-laws. All these feelings, passages, and relations were celebrated and symbolically expressed in the four-day wedding celebration and its songs, music, and dances.

Friday

In Kostadin and Todora's day, the wedding began on Friday with the gathering of two groups of four girls, called *shaferki,* in both the boy's and the girl's house. Their first task was a symbolic exchange of gifts. When the groom's *shaferki* arrived at his house, they carried a dish with some raw beans, yeast for bread, and a bouquet of whatever greenery or flowers were in season (basil, cherries, boxwood) tied to a red thread with some coins that had holes punched in them. The mother of the groom put all these gifts into a beautiful kerchief together with some wheat, candies, and the bride's slippers.

The groom's *shaferki*, the leader of whom was usually a close relative, went with this package and a specially decorated wooden decanter of wine [*bŭklitsa*] to the home of the bride, who was hidden from view, to present the gifts, the leader saying, "Good day. Health from my aunts and uncles. Here is a small modest gift." The bride's mother accepted the gift, opened the package, and gave the bouquets to the bride's *shaferki*. Toasts were exchanged, and the bride's mother presented the groom's emissaries with a somewhat larger kerchief, containing bouquets for his *shaferki*, candies and wheat, his embroidered wedding shirt, colorful knitted socks, and an embroidered handkerchief to wear on his belt. The groom's *shaferki* then returned to his house and distributed the bride's family's gifts and greetings of health.

The next stage of the ritual, the preparation and baking of ritual bread with the yeast and flour that had been exchanged, I interpret as insuring the fertility of the new couple through a magical act of the union of yeast and flour (insemination), the swelling/rising of the bread (pregnancy), and the singing of specific songs.[7]

In each house the four *shaferki* sat on the floor, two by two, on either side of a large sifter and next to a huge bowl of flour. The closest relation among the girls, called *zamesarka* ('the one who begins to mix [the dough]'), led the singing accompanied by the girl next to her; the two on the opposite side responded antiphonally [*otpyavat*]. While one group sang, the others shook the sifter, these roles passing back and forth between the two pairs of girls. As they sang, people in the wedding party threw coins into the sifter, an act of good luck and a tip for the singers, who continued to collect them as they sang throughout the wedding. Todora said, "They hurry, especially at the boy's house, to finish first. He will then command in the family. They continue singing, repeating the songs, until the work is done."

Three songs for each house were traditionally specified at this point: two were the same at both houses, and one was unique to each house. The first song compared the wedding to a muddy, swollen river sweeping away the unsuspecting, unprepared bride, an expression of her reluctance to leave the home of her family.

Vardar mŭten priteche, *Vardaro,*	The muddy Vardar river flows, *Vardaro,*
ta devoika podnese.	and carries away a young girl.
Devoika se moleshe:	The girl begged:
—Pusni mene, Vardaro,	"Release me, Vardar river,

az sŭm malka, glupava.
Ne sŭm dari sgotvila
da daruvam svatove,
i svatove, kumove,
i mladi go devero.

I am little and stupid.
I have not prepared gifts
to give to the in-laws,
to the in-laws, godparents,
and to the young best man."

The second song refers to the many ruses young lovers created in order to see each other. In this song they "protect" an apple tree, a ridiculous excuse made even more humorous since the tree hardly has any fruit on it. The third song at the groom's house talks about the preparations of the family for their new bride, which often meant building new quarters for the couple to live in. The third song at the bride's house has three friends discussing whom they will marry. The bride's lover is compared to a dragon—a phallic symbol—who is coming tomorrow to get her.

Sednali sa dve momi, tri druzhki,
vezok veza, drebni sŭlzi ronyat,

i se pitat koya kogo lyubi.

Pŭrva kazhe: —Ya chobana
lyube.
Vtora kazhe: —Ya selara lyube.

Treta kazhe: —Ya zmeyute
lyube.
Toi mi idva vecher po sred
noshti.
Krotko tropa i krotichko vliza

da go nyakoi ne chue, ne useti.

Tazi vecher zmeyu ke mi doide,

ke mi doide, mene ke me vzeme.

There sat two girls, three friends,
embroidering embroideries and
crying tiny tears,
and they asked each other who
loved whom.
The first said: "I love a
shepherd."
The second one said: "I love a villager."
The third said: "I love a huge
dragon.
He comes to me in the evening,
in the middle of the night.
He lightly knocks and he lightly
enters
so that no one will hear him, so
that no one will know.
This evening the dragon will
come,
he will come and he will take me
away."

Having made the dough, the *zamesarka* then began to knead it, followed in turn by the other girls. After the dough was set aside to rise, they went in pairs around the village inviting guests to the wedding. When they returned, they made the dough into loaves, singing the same songs as before. Two of the loaves were highly decorated and carried in the wedding procession by the *zamesarka,* while the others were given to wedding guests as gifts.

Saturday

On Saturday evening the bride and groom were ritually prepared for the wedding. Around four or five o'clock in the afternoon, the *shaferki* assembled and, with a *bŭklitsa* of wine, circled the village inviting the closest relatives to a party. In both homes a wedding banner [*firuglitsa*] was constructed by tying a handkerchief, together with an apple and flowers at the top, to a newly cut branch of the *shipka* tree.[8] At the bride's house, the central act of preparation was the braiding of her hair, accompanied by the *shaferki* singing a song which compared her braided hair to a grapevine and mentioned the exchange of bouquets that mark the wedding vows. The groom's preparation consisted of a ritual shaving. The *shaferki* held the four corners of a kerchief placed over his head, together with a candle, while singing the three songs from the previous day. During the singing, a gaidar played a special tune for the occasion, unrelated in key and melody to the girl's singing. The raucous cacophony of unmatched song and tune created an uncoordinated polyphony typical of the wedding called *gyurultiya*, 'joyous noise,' a desirable aesthetic and social effect at a wedding or dance.

Sunday

On Sunday morning the *shaferki* went around the village inviting the guests, who assembled, depending on the closeness of their relationships, at the homes of the bride, groom, and godparents. Writ large, the day consisted of the taking of the bride by the groom's family. It began with a long procession from the groom's family's house to the home of the godparents, whom they added to the wedding party. They proceeded to the bride's house, where she was brought out and presented to them. The union was then consecrated in church before the procession returned home with their new bride and ritually inserted her into the new family. Eating, drinking, music, and dancing, which had been going on all day, reached their apex at a celebration that lasted long into the night.

Special songs and instrumental tunes marked every moment of the ritual transfer of the bride from her natal house to her new in-law's home. As the groom's party set out, the gaidar led the way with a special nonmetrical tune [*svirnya*] for the godfather. Behind him followed the groom's oldest brother or a close cousin, who carried the wedding banner; the groom and his parents; and the *shaferki*, who sang a song asking if the bride was beautiful and healthy. In the song she is neither too pale ('white') nor too ruddy ('red'), but perfectly healthy ('pink-cheeked') with a fine figure. Behind the *shaferki* came the rest of the family's friends and relatives, delighting in the *gyurultiya* created by the simultaneous playing and singing.

After the greetings and toasts at the godparents' home, the godparents, their relatives, and close friends joined the wedding processional as it set out for the bride's house. The gaidar performed a special *svirnya*, 'Going for the Bride,' and the *shaferki* simultaneously sang a song rehearsing the unity of the groom's family with the godparents and their family, the wedding agreement, and the upcoming greeting at the bride's house with a ritual hand washing (CD #25).

Meanwhile the bride, sequestered in a room of her house, awaited her fate, dressed in her bridal clothes. Her *shaferki* sang a number of songs, including example 6.11 (CD #26), which speaks of how she must prepare the yard and wedding table for the coming of the in-laws, godparents, and best man, implying by pointed omission of the groom that she is marrying a family by arrangement rather than a young man.

Example 6.11. Song for the Bride

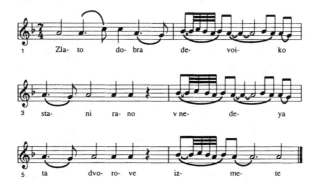

Zlato, dobra devoiko,	Zlata, virtuous maiden,
stani rano v nedelya,	get up early on Sunday,
ta dvorove izmete,	and sweep the yard,
i stolove naredi,	and arrange the chairs,
kye ke doidat svatove,	because the in-laws are coming,
em svatove, kumove,	the in-laws and the godparents,
i mladi go devero.	and the young best man.

As the noisy procession of the groom's and godparents' families approached the bride's house, her *shaferki* left the room where she was hiding to greet the guests with singing and dancing. Led by an older, close female relative of the bride, they sang and danced a simple *rŭchenitsa* in a line, taking four steps forward and four steps back.

The song tells of the many gifts brought by the new in-laws. As the groom's wedding party passed by the dancers, grain was thrown, people shouted, "*A bre*, in-laws, are you here?" the gaida played, the groom's *shaferki* sang their own song, and "everything was mixed up" in celebratory cacophony. As the song texts report, "A wedding is raised up."

The best man knocked at the gate of the bride's house. The bride's *shaferki* sang a song demanding that the best man pay for the new bride. Amid much joking the groom's party entered the bride's yard; at one wedding I attended each of the groom's guests gave a small gift of money for the couple as they did so. Once inside the bride's yard, the groom's and godparents' families sat at long wedding tables in the bride's yard and were treated to food and drink.

At this point the bride's *shaferki* returned to the secluded bride, where they sang a song (ex. 6.12; CD #27) comparing the wedding party and the bride's sadness at the prospect of leaving her family to a thick fog settling over her yard. The joy of the groom's family and the beauty of the bride become a bright sun, and the hope is expressed that the noisy wedding celebration, referenced by the line, 'a good horse neighs', will lift the sadness from the hearts of the bride and her family.

Example 6.12. A Song about the Wedding

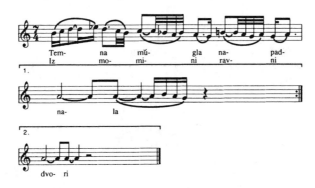

Temna mŭgla napadnala	A thick fog has fallen
iz momini ravni dvori.	over the girl's flat yard.
Yasno slŭntse e ogryalo	A bright sun has risen
iz momkovi ravni dvori.	over the boy's flat yard.
Vrano konche iztsvililo	A good horse neighs
ot momkovi ravni dvori.	in the boy's flat yard.
Temna mŭgla razdignalo	A thick fog lifts
ot momini ravni dvori.	from the girl's flat yard.

The last song sung to the bride before the next stage of the wedding enumerated the relatives who would accompany her to church and was altered to suit the particular circumstances. If a relative was missing, particularly if there had been a death in the family, Todora said, "we all cried. It was very moving. And even now I am crying," as tears came to her eyes and her voice choked slightly. "It's because I live through it now just like then."

The godmother then knocked on the door of the room where the bride was hiding. Inside, the bride's *shaferki* and other friends and relatives put up a modest resistance, asking who this was and where she came from. Finally the godmother and the groom's sister were invited in. The latter carried a bag full of wedding shoes for the bride and *shaferki*. As they tried them on, they complained that the shoes were too big, so the groom's sister stuffed them with money, another playful way to collect money for the couple. The bride stood on a stool and, as she was veiled, her *shaferki* sang a touching song comparing a girl to a grapevine that will be torn up and taken away from the family by the in-laws.

Kolko ti pŭti	How many times
ya tebe rekoh,	did I tell you,
momina male:	mother of the bride:
—Ne sadi loza,	"Do not seed grapes,
ne hrani moma.	do not feed a girl.
Dokyet svatove,	There will come eventually in-laws,
dokyet kumove.	there will come godparents.
Skŭrshikyet loza,	They will rip up the grapevine,
vzemekyet moma,	they will take the girl,
momina male.	girl's mother."

A second song compared unfavorably the girl's kind treatment by her own mother ('a summer dew') with what she could expect under the supposed tyranny ('a winter frost') of her mother-in-law ('foreign mother'). A third song reiterated the theme of harsh treatment in the new home ('they will give me, mother, two heavy large pails') and promised that she will always think of her mother.

During the veiling, the bride's male relatives placed a small round table and a few three-legged stools in the yard and sat down with the groom to offer him their version of hospitality. Placing bread, wine, stew, and salt on the table, they dipped some of the bread in the stew and salted it as heavily as possible. They offered it to the groom, but as he reached for it they drew it back, saying it needed more salt. On the third offer, they gave it to him, along with a sip of wine. With much joking, this was repeated three times, the salt a reminder that the "sweet" bride was given away with some reluctance. As the groom stood up, he kicked over the stool. If it landed on the seat, their first child would be a boy; if on its side, a girl.

The bride now prepared, her father led her out of the house, to be seen in her wedding finery for the first time by all the guests. The gaida played a special tune, "Leading Out the Bride" [*Izvezhdane na bulkata*], while her *shaferki* sang a song asking her to come back and care for her mother. Just as they finished the song, the groom's *shaferki* rushed up, pushed the bride's *shaferki* out of the way, and sang the song, "Let's Go, Let's Go, Maiden" in which the bride complains that she is not ready, but the best man assures her that their yard will be as pleasant as her own ("planted with sweet basil and with savoury").

As the procession set out for the church, the gaidar broke into a joyous "men's *rŭchenitsa*," marked by the use of a major pentachord, wide melodic leaps, and a high tessitura (ex. 6.13; CD #28). The first dance of the wedding Sunday, its exuberant melodic character signaled the groom's family's happiness at taking the bride, and the young people in the wedding party used it as an excuse to do an energetic dance, running forward and back, into and away from the main procession, which proceeded slowly. The groom's *shaferki* continued "Let's Go, Let's Go, Maiden," all the way to the church, repeating it as many times as necessary. As the wedding party neared the church— Todora remembers a particular large tree marking the spot—the *shaferki* began to sing "The Morning Star Shines," about the beauty of the bride and the transition from her house to the groom's.

While the exchange of the bride between families occurred in the *gyurultiya* at the bride's house, they consecrated their union in a church ceremony in which the priest exchanged gold crowns placed on their heads three times and led them by the hand three times around the altar in a kind of sacred *horo*. In one playful moment, after the exchange of crowns, the newlyweds tried to step on each other's toes;

Example 6.13. Men's *Rŭchenitsa*

Todora said, "whoever does will command in the future." As they emerged from church, the *shaferki* broke into a song, "Two Young People Are Married," which referred to the exchange of crowns and commented on the beauty of the boy and girl. Kostadin played 'the best,' 'the liveliest' men's *rŭchenitsa* he knew, and the procession set out for the groom's house, the proud godmother showering them with wheat.

As the procession approached the groom's house, the *shaferki* sang "Come Out into the Yard, You Boy's Mother" to announce the coming of a beautiful bride, 'thin and pink-cheeked,' with many gifts for her new in-laws. The groom's parents came out of the house to greet the new couple at the threshold, the bride's mother-in-law carrying a sifter from which she threw wheat and some candies. Her father-in-law carried a beautiful cup filled with wine, which he offered three times, first to the bride and then the groom. He then passed the cup between their heads to the godfather who, after drinking from it, tossed the remainder over his shoulder onto the ground. The mother-in-law wiped the brows of first the bride and then the groom. On each side of them, two close female relatives held candles with flowers tied on with red thread. As the welcoming foursome danced gently in place, the gaidar played a "women's *rŭchenitsa*" (ex. 6.14; CD #29) differing from the men's in its minor mode, stepwise melodies, medium tessitura, and slower tempo.

The bride's mother-in-law then entered the house and, on the threshold with the couple still outside, administered a mock test of the bride's competence, good upbringing, and ability to work. She gave the bride the sifter, which she dutifully shook, showing that she could

Example 6.14. Women's *Rŭchenitsa*

cook. Proffered water, she wiped both sides of the threshold, showing she could clean. Handed a bundle of red and white thread, she wrapped them around her fingers, showing she could weave. Having passed the test, she at last entered her new home.

A wedding banquet followed, highlighted by the exchange of gifts between the bride and the guests and exuberant dancing. The godparents were expected to give the most lavish gifts, and so the exchange began with the groom's *shaferki* singing three songs to them. The first song, which Todora couldn't interpret, seems to foretell good luck and riches for the bride. The second song praises the godfather for the gifts he has given and the protection he will provide, using the same imagery of wind, frost, and fog used in earlier songs. Todora said she did not understand the text of the third song, apparently a magical one about protection and fertility, whose sense she had lost by the time she sang it for me. After the songs, the godfather announced his gifts— in those days a sheep or goat and perhaps a barrel of wine, in the 1970s and '80s new, manufactured furniture for the house—and the banquet continued long into the night.

Monday

On the Monday following the wedding, yet another banquet, called 'sweet brandy' or 'women's wedding,' was held. All the women who received gifts at the wedding—mainly those from the families of the groom, bride, and godparents—gathered to celebrate the bride's virginity and praise her mother for protecting her honor. Each guest brought wine, *pogacha*, and *banitsa*, a common dish made from dough rolled into the thinnest possible sheets, which are then buttered, layered, and filled with a mixture of feta cheese, eggs and milk. Although everyone makes it, it requires great skill and is more frequently the focus of comments and comparisons than other dishes.[9] At the banquet, the women sang table songs with wedding themes, but the highlight was the dancing of a 'led *ruchenitsa*' [*vodena ruchenitsa*] in which the leader took the line in a serpentine pattern as the dancers ran in rhythm (short-short-long) while singing a song praising the girl's mother for raising a virgin ("she did not shame her mother") who is pretty and hard-working (ex. 6.15; CD·#30).

Todora said that, while in the old days they tested the bride's virginity by examining the wedding sheets, "in our time they didn't do it as much. We had respect for the girl's mother and wouldn't do something to shame her." Toward sunset, the girl's mother and her family were sent off to their homes and, as they left, the boy and girl raced to the house. According to Todora, "whoever arrives first will command in life."

Example 6.15. Song in Praise of the Bride's Mother

Ishala mashala, momina male,
dobro si, dobro si chedo gledala.

Maika si, maika si ne posramila.

Na snaga, na snaga s tŭnka i
visoka.
Na litse, na litse bela i chervena.

I mnogo, i mnogo dari zgotvila

da dari, da dari svekŭr svekŭrva,

da dari, da dari zŭlva i etŭrva.

Ishala mashala,[10] girl's mother,
well, well you have raised your
child.

Her mother, her mother she did
not shame.

Her figure, her figure is tall and
thin.
Her face, her face is white and
red.

And many, many gifts she had
prepared

to give, to give to her father- and
mother-in-law,

to give, to give to her sisters-in-
law.

Review of the Year

In this chapter, I have organized and interpreted Kostadin's and Todora's repertoire, collected long after they left the village, into a music
cycle that interweaves the life cycle of courtship into the calendrical
cycle of work and ritual. *Koleda,* ostensibly about agricultural, animal,
and human fertility, contained songs sung by boys to girls and initiated
courtship in much the way Dimo did by taking Todora's bouquet. In
winter, lively indoor dancing provided an opportunity to become ac-
quainted, even as emotionally dark song texts matched winter's gloom.
After the ritual insemination of the earth on *kukerovden,* courtship continued in a series of playful games, *na filek.* In Easter and spring songs,
winter doubts were cast aside, and true love conquered all. During
summer, relationships established in the village were challenged at distant, dangerous fairs by rivals who stole or seduced girls and ended
village courtships. At fall *sedyankas,* the disputes were settled, boys and
girls made their decisions, paired up, and endured teasing and warn-

ings about the impending marriage and loss of childhood innocence. The courtship and the seasonal cycle ended with the wedding, where the fruits of animals and the harvest were shared in a celebration of a marriage that would continue the cycle of human reproduction and the ability of the village to sustain itself economically.

During much of the year, the songs were primarily sung by and referred to the feelings of young girls, who held the structurally weakest position in negotiations involving not just boys and possible husbands, but parents, future in-laws, and unknown strangers. While many complex events occurred during the year, this analysis of the seasonal cycle focused on the changing patterns of courtship, viewed primarily from the point of view of girls' experience as it was expressed in their singing. Men and boys surely had different experiences and views, as did older married people, but singing and song were the domains par excellence for girls to voice their fears and rail against the tyranny of men and of tradition.

Reflections on the Social Maintenance of Music

In part 3, I examined music in relation to economics, ideology, aesthetics, cognition, bodily experience, seasonal work and ritual, and women's experiences during Kostadin and Todora's youth in the 1930s. In this period music was for them less an economic practice than a pastime whose character was partially determined by a moneyless, unspecialized subsistence farming economy. Since pastimes fit into the cycle of work, the rhythm of music, dance and song was governed by the changing seasons and their associated patterns of work, ritual, and socializing. But music was more than simply an overdetermined aspect of the superstructure, as Marxist theory might suggest: it also played an active role in the ideology which dialectically sustained the economy.

In learning and performing the tradition in accordance with the expectations of their parents and grandparents, Kostadin, Todora, and other young people behaved with the discipline and shame required of everyone to make the social and economic system work. They danced in appropriate places in the line and with vigorous or modest movements, determined by age and sex, Todora kept her individually created texts largely to herself, Kostadin tried to learn tunes just as the older gaidari had played them, and they both participated actively in the patterns of socializing and hospitality that greased the wheels of disciplined social interaction. In all these ways, music was not simply determined by ideology, but a part of ideology. Its practice was a visible and audible sign of adherence to the basic tenets of an ideology expressed in the form of gossip and criticism when breached and in countless other daily acts of observance.

Although economic, ideological, and musical practice worked dialectically to reinforce one another and their associated patterns of age- and gender-based hierarchies, song and dance were also arenas in which those at the bottom of the hierarchical ladder, especially women and the young, expressed their feelings and contested and negotiated their inferior status. The song repertoire and the act of singing, in particular, was the domain where women vented their feelings in the face of harsh demands on them to work hard and loyally for their families, their husbands, and their husband's families. At the dance, girls danced next to boys, boys broke the rules for decorous behavior with respect to girls, and both sexes engaged in normally forbidden sexual horseplay and lighthearted challenges to the solidarity of older age groups.

While musical practice and aesthetic experience were partly influenced by the constraints of discipline and honor and the life experiences of women and men in general, some aspects of songs, tunes, and instrumental suites had a life of their own and were recreated in performance with reference to their historical integrity as inherited forms. As individual choices were made about which songs, tunes or texts to remember and precisely how to perform them, the singers, dancers, and musicians may have felt a sense of momentary freedom and release from the social pressures to conform.

As an example of an analysis of music as culture or, in my terms, the social maintenance of music, these perspectives on the musical life of Gergebunar in the 1930s suggest five hypotheses about the relation of music and culture.

1. In probably every culture some aspects of musical practice can be said to be "determined" by other aspects of culture. In this case, I factored out economics as one such part of culture and tried to show its influence on music.

2. If music is regarded as a "practice" rather than a product, then it should be possible to show in what ways musical practice is not simply determined by other practices but identical to them. In this case, I viewed music not so much as an economic practice but as an ideological one, and tried to show how music contributed to the maintenance of certain social values and hierarchies in this culture.

3. Although music, song, and dance may be partially determined by some aspects of culture and identical with others, it may be realistic and not contradictory to view them also as practices with the power to

challenge or express alternatives to those same values and hierarchies, allied not with the culture as a whole but with groups in culture with well-defined interests. In the Bulgarian case, I interpreted song in particular as useful psychologically to women in their structurally weak position vis-à-vis men.

4. Aspects of musical practice should vary with individual experience and be used to express that experience. In Todora's case, for example, her song preferences, choices, and omissions were partly a result of her personal experience: her dislike of a song about death with her name in it; a memory of her grandfather's favorite song; or an unpleasant incident that she would rather forget.

5. Finally, music, as a highly abstract, modeled practice with its own interior order and history, probably contains elements which resist social and cultural determination at a given moment and thus in some sense have an independent life of their own. In this case, aspects of form, metrical and modal structures, and ornamentation live a playful life as much in reference to themselves and previous experience of them as to the strictures and influences of other cultural and social practices.

This analysis posits five kinds of relationships between music and culture (determination, identity, group interest, individual experience, and independence) and hypothesizes that they will be found in virtually every culture ethnomusicologists study. Our task then becomes the elucidation of these relationships in particular cases. The apparent contradictions between determination and independence, or group interest and individual experience, are resolved when we realize that music is a multifaceted practice whose myriad elements can variously be determined by, identical with, or independent of other cultural, group, or individual practices. However, we still face the task of specifying how those relationships work in each particular case.

1. The Thracian Plain. (Photo by Timothy Rice)

2. Costumed Dancers at a May Day Parade. (Photo by Timothy Rice)

3. Kostadin with Gaida.
(Photo by Vergilii Atanasov)

4. Todora's family home in
Gergebunar. (Photo by
Timothy Rice)

5. Family Wedding, Kostadin's Father and Mother in Front Row. (Family photograph)

6. Todora with 'Aunts' in Gergebunar. (Photo by Timothy Rice)

7. Girls' *Horo* in the Rhodopes with Gaidari in the Center of the Circle, 1892. (Courtesy of The Ethographic Institute and Museum, Bulgarian Academy of Sciences)

8. Kostadin Playing for a Horo in Grudovo. (Family photograph)

9. Bistrishka Chetvorka in 1936
   (Courtesy of The Ethographic
   Institute and Museum,
   Bulgarian Academy
   of Sciences)

10. Kostadin Soloing in the 1950s with the Radio Sofia Folk Orchestra.
    Isuyatko Blagoev in front row at left. (Family photograph)

11. Strandzhanskata Grupa at its Founding in 1957. (Family photograph)

12. Kostadin with his Pioneer Students in 1971. (Family photograph)

13. Kostadin with a Beginning Student in 1992. (Photo by Vergilii Atanasov)

14. Ivan, Tsvetanka, and Radka Varimezovi. (Photo by Timothy Rice)

15. Poster of Balkana.

16. Kostadin, His brother Stamat, and Kolyo Cherpenkov Enjoying Themselves around a Table in Rosenovo, 1988.
(Photo by Timothy Rice)

17. Kolyo Cherpenkov Playing Okarina for the 'Long Table' at the 'Grudovo Meeting'.
(Photo by Timothy Rice)

18. Strandzhanskata Grupa in 1986. (Photo by Vergilii Atanasov)

19. Kostadin and Tim Play *Trite Pŭti* at Kostadin's Seventieth-Birthday Concert. (Family photograph)

20. Varimezov Family Gathering in Their Attic in Sofia: *(clockwise from left)* Kostadin, Ivan, Neno Ivanonov, his wife Stefka, Todora, Stanka, Todor, Stanka's husband Petŭr, Todor's wife Mimi, Ivan's wife Ivanka. (Photo by Timothy Rice)

Part Four
Changing the Tradition

One sheep said to another: "Who is that?" The other sheep answered: "That's our new shepherd. We used to have a different one, but now he plays for Radio Sofia."

> Stoyan Velichkov, kaval player with Radio Sofia

From shepherds we made orchestral musicians.

> Kosta Kolev, former conductor with Radio Sofia

SEVEN

The New Society and Its Music

Why do musical traditions change? A fundamental tenet of ethnomusicology holds that they change because culture changes. Observing culture and music change in tandem is one of the easiest ways to show their relationship and interdependence.[1] As a general kind of "ethnomusicological law," however, it operates somewhat like a prediction that a rock thrown at a window will cause it to break. While it may be of little interest to science to predict or describe the precise pattern of the breakage, ethnomusicologists want to know what in music changes and how it changes when culture changes. In the absence of influential general theories, each case has to be considered as unique.

The story of musical change in Bulgaria is embedded in a context in which new economic and ideological practices were imposed on traditional ones, in a manner somewhat different from but analogous to the colonial imposition of capitalism and Christianity on native populations in Africa, the Americas, the Pacific, and parts of Asia.[2] The process of musical, economic, and ideological change is characterized by tension and struggle, acquiescence and resistance, progress and loss. The precise mix of abandonment, syncretism, and accretion of traditions can no more be predicted than the patterns in a shattered piece of glass, but the story of the change is bound to be a dramatic one, filled with individual protagonists and antagonists, each trying to appropriate and experience music and the new life in truthful and meaningful ways.

In this chapter I examine how the changes instituted by the new Communist government affected life in Gergebunar, created new institutions and contexts for music while destroying old ones, and confronted traditional values with new ones.

The New Society Comes to Gergebunar

In Bulgaria after 9 September 1944, a Marxist theory of change became a matter of state policy. It posited a dialectical relationship between the economic structure or "base" of society on one hand and the ideological, political, legal, religious, artistic, and philosophical "superstructure," on the other. As a corollary of this principle, "If the base changes or is eliminated, then . . . its superstructure changes or is eliminated; if a new base arises, then . . . a superstructure arises corresponding to it."[3] If music is taken as a part of the superstructure, then we have in these two principles a theory of the interrelationship between music and economics and a theory of why music changes that embeds cultural change in economic change.[4]

Ironically, the history of Stalinist regimes in Eastern Europe, where ideological change wrought economic change, gives the lie to any theory of ideology as a passive rather than active agent in change. Furthermore, in state socialism, as in advanced capitalism, it is very hard to maintain the distinction between base and superstructure as anything other than a heuristic device. As we saw in part 3, the practice of music is shaped by both economic and ideological factors. Before 1944, villagers' music making generated more symbolic than real capital in a subsistence economy; at the same time, its practice supported, and in one way expressed, an ideology necessary to sustain the economic system.[5] After 1944 the conscious use of music as an ideological tool by the Communists contributed to a major change in the economic status of music and musicians. Music making, formerly a moneyless pastime for landholding villagers, became a source of wages, a job, and a commodity with monetary value. Under Communism a fiddler could feed a household, and musicians became one kind of specialized laborer in the building of communism and communist ideology.

Perhaps the most profound social and economic transformation in Bulgaria following the imposition of Marxist-Leninist ideology was the abolition of private property and its reconstitution as ostensibly collectively owned 'people's' [*narodno*] property. In theory, this property was to be taken from capitalists, who exploited the labor of propertyless workers, and returned to the latter, who now had a collective interest in it. In Bulgaria, however, most land and property were taken from subsistence farmers, for whom work itself and the life and social relations it sustained were the primary values. The Communists proletarianized the peasants, transforming them into workers and exploiting their labor for the state's (and the Communists') benefit. The collective farmers' wages ensured their dependence on the state and erased the old distinction between a monied, specialized-labor economy in the towns and cities and a moneyless, nonspecialized economy in the villages. After 1944, every activity, even music, potentially had a price, since villagers could no longer sustain themselves through honorable and reciprocal work and hospitality. Instead of work, there were jobs. Instead of shame in relation to a patriarchal grandfather, there was obedience to the state's economic and political apparatus. The state transformed local face-to-face values into national, distant, and somewhat abstract values.

Marxist-Leninist ideology also contained notions of "progress" and "improvement" of man's condition and devotion to abstract and selfless goals, such as "building communism," that were largely absent from village ideology. If it was once sufficient for Kostadin and his father to improve their own condition, "to have but not to give" as the joking critique implied by their name suggests, under Communism each person was expected to contribute to the economic and spiritual growth of the entire society. The party mandated industrialization as the means to the end of economic growth, and education for spiritual growth. A "new man" would be created to build the new society, and all the educational and informational organs of the state served this purpose.

With the coming to power of the Communist party on the 9th of September, 1944, life in Gergebunar irrevocably and profoundly changed as the Party began to institute its ideological, social, and economic programs, including the collectivization of most private lands, farm equipment, and animals, an act that more than any other destroyed the traditional bases of village musical life. Kostadin's son Ivan, who lived in Gergebunar throughout the early years of Communism, remembered the anguish of Todora's father when his horses were taken from him and herded into the common barns of the collective farm, a trauma, Ivan believes, that hastened his grandfather's death. Demoralized at the loss of their property, some villagers were no longer "in the mood" to sing, play, and dance. For many villagers, communism ended the life that sustained the traditions they cherished.

Even had people wanted to continue traditional practices, the crude antireligious stance of petty officials, influenced by Marxist dogma, led them to ban some of the rituals forming the basis of musical life, particularly ones closely tied to religion, or "superstition," such as *koleda* and *kukerovden*. A Bulgarian musicologist told me he attended in 1956 probably the last "real" performance of *nestinarstvo*, a firewalking ritual honoring Saints Constantine and Elena and practiced only in the villages of Kosti and Bulgari in Strandzha.[6] Although a number of Bulgarian folklorists and a few tourists had gathered to witness it, a local Communist official stopped the performance, arguing that it cast Bulgaria in a backward, superstitious light, especially in front of the visiting foreigners. Even though, by 1973, I witnessed firewalking resurrected for presentation to tourists at hotels, these early acts of banishment and disapproval, coupled with the introduction of a new ideology hostile to many of the supposedly backward elements of village life, seem to have very quickly wiped out calendrical rituals in many villages.

Collectivization of the land started in 1948 in the large villages of the plains, with their huge wheat fields, but took until 1960 to institute throughout the country. As a small, isolated village in the hills, Gergebunar, which changed its name to Rosenovo to honor a Communist from the village named Petŭr Rosen, did not feel collectivization's effects until its relatively insignificant lands were taken in 1956. Consequently, many of its traditions were preserved until that late date. But other aspects of the Communists' modernization program—their determination to provide education, health care, roads and transportation, and services such as electricity and running water to the rural population—had equally dramatic effects on village life.

The government decided it could afford to bring modern services only to the largest, most accessible villages; small, isolated ones such as Rosenovo would be left in their backward state, labeled 'villages with waning functions.' Young families all over the country, realizing the future lay in cities, towns, and large villages, left their homes for the new life being created there and to work in the factories, offices, and shops of the new society. During the 1950s nearly every family left Rosenovo and moved down the hill to Grudovo, which had been designated as one such village center, destined to become a small town. Kostadin and Todora tore down the house they had recently constructed for their new family and moved it brick by brick to Grudovo, reconstructing it in a new part of town known as the "Rosenovo quarter"; the destruction, relocation, and reconstruction of their house is an apt metaphor for the social, cultural, and musical processes at work on a grander scale throughout the country.

Advanced education, once the nearly exclusive province of the urban bourgeoisie, also became a powerful force in the countryside and contributed to the demise of traditional practice. Whereas Kostadin and Todora attended four grades of school in their village and learned the rudiments of reading, writing, and arithmetic, the Communists encouraged a higher level of education for all and established more widely distributed schools. Bright young villagers like Todora and Kostadin—although they were now too old—could attend not just grammar school but junior high and high school as well. During my trips to Bulgaria, I saw more shepherds reading newspapers in the fields than playing flutes.

Todora's younger sister Irinka benefited from this policy, attending the middle school in Drachevo, then the new *gimnaziya* [high school] in Grudovo, and later a teachers' institute in Burgas. Her pilgrimage to larger, more distant towns in search of education functions as another metaphor for villagers' widening horizons under the Communists. Instead of farming and raising sheep as her family had for generations, Irinka became a teacher and her husband Kolyo the principal of a school for 'slowly developing' children. The price for the music tradition—she spent too much time in school to learn her mother's and sisters' songs, and he, in spite of a love of music, can play only a few tunes on an okarina—is difficult to measure against the Communists' forced progress. Commenting on this Todora said, "Petrana [her sister, three years younger] remembers a lot of songs. But Irinka, the poor dear, doesn't know anything. How she wants to. She says, 'Why didn't you teach me?' But she was always in school. She didn't live as a child among us. She's always saying, 'Why didn't I learn to sing?'" She need look no further than the Communists' dedication to education and literacy, which resulted in a specialization of knowledge that reduced the percentage of the village population with an active, performing knowledge of music and song.

The mere presence of schools did not guarantee that village children would be sent there, however. Kostadin's father, for example, strongly opposed education, just as he had opposed getting Kostadin a gaida and for very nearly the same reasons. As Todora told it, "When [his sons] wanted to study, [Kostadin's father] didn't allow it. He said, 'Educated children don't look after their father.'" He understood that education was largely unnecessary to sustain village life as he knew it and realized that it was a path to independence from the strictures of the patriarchal family. Perhaps it would lead to a new life in faraway towns where children might neglect their parents. While Irinka was able to prevail on her family to allow her to study, Kostadin's father was more stubborn. Todora said, "Stoyan, the youngest [brother], . . . he wanted to study along with my sister Irinka. There is five days' difference in their ages. He wanted to study with her. How he cried, how he cried to study, but his father didn't allow it." He worked instead on the collective farm in Grudovo, but as an adult fulfilled his ambition, taking advantage of the Communists' emphasis on education. To-dora continued, "After many years he finished junior high school when Ivan [her eldest son] was a pupil. Irinka, my sister, was [Stoyan's] teacher. After the 9th of September they gave such opportunities to become literate. They trained many illiterate people. He was supposed to study with [Irinka], but later she became his teacher" [*laughs*].

The new village also created new opportunities for work. Kostadin's father had been a member of the Communist party for years before they gained power in 1944, and so when Kostadin returned to the village from the war, the Communists, observing the traditional honor code's patriarchal hierarchies, asked his father if Kostadin would serve in the 'people's militia.' His father agreed, and for a short time Kostadin acted as a local militiaman, riding a horse and wearing a pistol as he patrolled Grudovo and its environs. He quickly realized, however, that he had no stomach for this kind of work. Often extremely upset by the demands of his job, he resigned and began to work for the new 'forestry collective,' ridding the forests of wild boars so that trees could be felled safely. Kostadin and Todora's quiet life, with its singing and playing for guests and at weddings, although transplanted to Grudovo, might have continued to this day, but for the intervention of fate in what was, to them, a most surprising way (pl. 8).

The State and Its New Music Institutions

In distant Sofia, the capital of Bulgaria, the Party and its organs of propaganda began to move into all aspects of the nation's life, including education and culture. Radio in particular and later television became organs of Party propaganda, and the state record company, Balkanton, linked to the radio, became the sole source for recorded music, its productions adhering to the Party line. The first Bulgarian Communist Party leader, Georgi Dimitrov, believed that support of music and the performing arts would "help to raise the cultural level of our people; of our youth—as a mighty factor in the construction of a new socialist society in our country" (quoted in Krustev 1978:183). He urged composers to use Soviet models and, in 1947, issued the following decree: "By researching and adapting our rich folk music and by making use of the achievements of the world's musical culture, especially that of the Slavs, [composers] are to express in the new musical works both the heroic struggle of our people against fascism before September 9, 1944, and also its all-round development in the present period" (ibid., 186).

To ensure adherence to these dictates, Party officials were assigned

permanently to all existing institutions, including symphony orchestras and opera companies, to guide their work. From the musicians'
point of view, many of the appointments were Party hacks, uneducated
and unqualified for their work except by virtue of family or political
connections. I was told one joke that circulated among musicians about
the supposedly uncultured ignoramuses appointed to handle cultural
affairs. "The Party appointed a simple villager to head the opera company, and after observing rehearsals for a few days he called a meeting
of the entire company. [Continuing in village dialect, an index of his
lack of education], 'I have observed three problems which must be
corrected immediately. First, where is this Figaro? All I hear is "Figaro
here, Figaro there." Bring him to me so I can keep an eye on him.
Second, why is this big fat guy playing the piccolo and this little slip of
a fellow playing tuba? It's inefficient. They must switch instruments
immediately. Third, I hear talk of the soprano *partia* ['part'], the alto
partia, and the tenor *partia*. In Bulgaria there is only one *Partia* [Party]
and only one will sing!'" The joke elegantly captures the new reality
facing workers in all domains: the Party and its state security apparatus
observed their every action; Party "leaders" assigned to every organization sometimes made arbitrary, nonsensical decisions; and a single
Party line existed in all matters, even, or especially, matters of culture.

In addition to Party control of existing urban, elite institutions, the
state also created and mobilized new agencies to meet the demands of
the "new society." One of the first of the new institutions to propagan-
dize villagers about the new life was called "Theater for the Village"
[*Teatŭr za seloto*], formed, according to Lyuben Tachev, in 1947.[7] "It was
a very fine group. There were two ensembles, one for drama and one
for music and dance performances, a total of 70 or 80 people. We carried all of our own equipment, including lights and a stage and curtains. We put on a good show. We would travel around one district for
twenty days and then have ten days off. Dayan Matein [founder of the
Bistrishka Chetvorka (pl. 9), the first group of traditional instruments
in the 1930s] was in the group, as was Kiril Dukov, the father of Atanas
Vŭlchev [Bulgaria's most famous gŭdulka player]. We performed Soviet and Hungarian dances, but mainly the repertoire was Bulgarian.
The goal of the ensemble was propaganda for the new life in Bulgaria.
The ensemble ended in 1957 or '58. There was a war between the
national theater and the local theaters. After this theater passed
through, the local theater wouldn't have an audience. The local people
didn't have the stages and technical facilities that the national theater
had."

Given the personnel of the group, it seems likely that it reproduced the musical style and aesthetics of the prewar period, probably with new song words added to glorify the new life.[8] Folk musicians organized the music themselves, and their playing probably consisted of unisons and parallel thirds with simple chordal accompaniment on tambura, accordion, and perhaps bass. The demise of this approach to modernized folk music was hastened by a completely new agenda, under the control of the urban elite rather than the musicians themselves, for presenting folk music as an aspect of state propaganda. The central figure in this new movement was the composer Filip Kutev; the key event, the formation of the National Ensemble of Folk Song and Dance under his direction in 1951.

The Kutev ensemble introduced to Bulgaria the aesthetic perspective of the large Soviet folkloric companies such as the Moiseev ballet and the Piatnitsky chorus. Unlike the "Theater for the Village," which utilized established professional musicians from the Sofia area, Kutev held national auditions to find the best village dancers, singers, and musicians from around the country, and he and his assistants collected dances, songs, instrumental tunes, as well as rituals and costumes, both in villages and from the new members of the company. While Bulgaria possessed trained composers, such as Kutev, to arrange folk songs and instrumental music, there were no comparable choreographers, and so a number of dance specialists were sent to the Soviet Union to train, at least briefly, in their methods.[9] Kutev and his choreographers then set about arranging and choreographing the tradition in a way that would change it profoundly.

Simply put, the aesthetics of the stage and of classically trained musicians dominated the performances of the ensembles. Retaining certain important elements of folk tradition but ripping them out of their original contexts and tearing apart their formal structures, choreographers, composers, and conductors recombined them into a performance style supposedly sensible to an urban, educated audience. The retained traditional elements included the vocal production, tone quality, and ornamentation of village singers, unaltered folk song tunes and parts of texts, instruments such as the gaida and kaval, village dance tunes and steps, traditional costumes, and the idea that music occurred in specific contexts such as a Sunday dance in the village square, a wedding, *koleda*, a *sedyanka*, and so forth. These elements functioned as signs or tokens of the rootedness of these new performances in the aesthetic traditions of an idealized, 'pure' or 'clean' [*chist*] rural past, untainted by urban, bourgeois developments and free of Turkish or other foreign influences. Village traditions, while useful symbolically as statements of Bulgarian nationality, were a little too 'muddy' [*mŭtno*]—a metaphor used by the kaval player Stoyan Velich-kov—to be attractive to the relatively sophisticated audiences of the Bulgarian capital, who, like urbanites the world over, often have little patience for traditions they consider beneath them, ones they have transcended by moving to the city. Kutev's ensemble attempted to clean up and 'perfume' [*parfyumira*] these traditions to attract an increasingly educated audience while remaining true to elements of the original tradition.[10]

Kutev's most famous contribution, aside from the overall direction of the ensemble, consisted of choral arrangements of village tunes. His singers knew how to sing in unison, and some from the southwestern region of the country had sung with drone-based harmonies.[11] He began by teaching them simple choral arrangements with little more than a drone accompaniment. Gradually his arrangements became more complex, with harmony at the third, homophonic textures, and some imitative counterpoint in a typically three-part texture with the introduction of an occasional fourth part (ex. 7.1; CD #31). The most important principle, and one that distinguishes his arrangements from many treatments of folk song by classical composers, was that the song melody was always heard in its entirety and then repeated in full, retaining the strophic structure of ordinary village singing. The song tunes never collapsed into melodic motives to be "developed" in the manner of classical composition. Motives might be used as counter-melodies or in brief points of imitation, but the tune proceeded unbroken through a number of varied repetitions.

Kutev's art, based on theme and variation in harmonic and contrapuntal treatment, eschewed many of the devices available to him as a trained composer. At their best, the resulting arrangements are simple gems meant to speak—to sing, really—in two directions at the same time: their changing harmonies and textures appealing to a sophisticated, urban audience; their texts and melodies, the latter heard over and over again in the traditional strophic manner, attracting a rural one.[12]

Instrumental music was treated in somewhat the same way: entire tunes, rather than motives, were arranged in a theme-and-variations format involving an orchestra of folk instruments constructed on the Western model. A choir of six gŭdulkas became the violin section, and three tamburas and a cello and bass, constructed in the form of overgrown gŭdulkas, filled out the newly composed harmonies.[13] Three kavals and two gaidas formed a woodwind section, with a single tŭpan as percussion. The resulting orchestral coloring of traditional tunes, ornamentation, and style turned soloistic and small-group village mu-

Example 7.1. Beginning of Kutev Choral Arrangement

sic into a symphonic form in the same way Kutev's song arrangements created choral music out of a solo and duet tradition.

If the union of classical aesthetics with village music and song was a syncretic process that maintained something of the latter's formal and stylistic integrity, village dance disintegrated in the hands of choreographers. With the exception of *rŭchenitsa*s, which are danced solo, in pairs, and in a variety of other formations, the basic form of Bulgarian traditional dance is the circle, closed or broken. While a wonderful form for creating group solidarity and interaction, it is a poor form for stage presentation, since the audience continually views the dancers' backsides. The Bulgarian choreographic solution broke the circle into lines and reconstituted them into squares, matrices, phalanxes, and other geometric shapes, continuously changing to amuse a passive audience. Individual simultaneous improvisation in the line, a hallmark of village dance, was eliminated in favor of choreographed variations performed sequentially in unison by the entire company. Traditional dance patterns, rarely more than three or four measures long, were not treated consistently as formal units, but were broken up into dance motives and recombined into new, choreographed sequences. From a structural point of view, it may be fair to say that village dance was altered more profoundly by the changes imposed by the educated elite than was music and song. This may be splitting hairs, however, since all these traditional forms changed profoundly in the Communist period.

The Kutev ensemble was an enormous success and quickly became the model for new ensembles all over the country. At the professional level, full-fledged music, song, and dance ensembles included the National Ensemble for Macedonian Songs and Dances (Blagoevgrad)—founded in 1954 and later called the Pirin Ensemble—and similar ensembles in Smolyan in the Rhodopes and Plovdiv in Thrace. Amateur ensembles patterned after Kutev started up in many of the major towns, including Pleven, Stara Zagora, Tolbuhin, Yambol, and Burgas (EBMK 1967: 116).

Although the Kutev ensemble set the stylistic standard for the new music of Communist Bulgaria, Radio Sofia played a crucial role in its dissemination, forming its own rival professional ensemble of singers and musicians. Its core included players from the prewar Ugŭrchinska Grupa ['Group from (the town of) Ugŭrchin'], whose leader, Tsvyatko Blagoev, played kaval, gaida, and clarinet. Because these and other Western Bulgarian musicians were local, they dominated concert and radio programming before the war; but the Thracian musicians Kutev chose for his ensemble, including the brilliant kaval player Nikola Ganchev, used richer ornamental techniques than their Western counterparts. For the Varimezovs' future, Kutev's most important decision was to select *Bai* Stoyan Dobrev, Kostadin's most important model, as the gaida player for his ensemble. The directors of the radio ensemble immediately made the invidious comparison between *Bai* Stoyan's brilliant Thracian technique and Blagoev's simpler West Bulgarian style and asked *Bai* Stoyan whether he knew other gaidari who played like he did. He answered by giving them the name of Kostadin Varimezov from his village of Rosenovo.

Kostadin was stunned by the Radio's invitation to come to Sofia for an audition and unsure how to respond. He had three young children and his father's dictum, "a musician cannot feed a household," to think about. He was inclined not to accept, but his friends and family encouraged him, saying it would bring honor to their village, and so he decided to try.

The audition consisted of a number of tests including playing some of his own repertoire and playing back tunes that were played to him by Blagoev. The directors were impressed, and selected him as the new gaidar for the radio ensemble, moving Blagoev to kaval, the original instrument on which he established his reputation (pl. 10; CD #32). Kostadin remembers, "After the audition, one of the directors told me, 'You played his tunes better than he did'"—and after only one hearing![14]

Thus did Kostadin become part of a new manner of making music that blanketed the country in the 1950s and '60s, including the radio airwaves, phonograph recordings, and concert performances. Bulgarian village music and dance, at least in their arranged and choreographed versions, became a more central part of the urban soundscape than they had been before the war at the same time that their importance diminished in everyday village life. The state's appropriation of village music for nation building paralleled its arrogation of villagers for industrial and urban work. The future of both music and life in general was in the towns and cities. The villages and their musical practices withered as their residents and traditions reappeared in new, urban garb.

Why did the Bulgarian state under Communism support art and particularly folk art so strongly? There seem to be two fundamental reasons. As one Bulgarian intellectual told me, "Both ideology and nationalism contribute." Continuing with the second reason, she said, "The function of folklore is to defend Bulgarian culture against the Turks and Greeks." This line of argument perpetuates a nationalistic view of folklore that flourished in Europe in the nineteenth century. Bulgarians view their cultural history as having been dampened by Ottoman Turkish political and Greek religious domination, which cut them off from major developments in Western Europe for nearly 500 years. Although they have no Western European cultural models from this period, as one classically trained musician told me, "the intellectuals know their history really well and tell it. They are proud of both their intellectual and national history. They believe they could have participated in the Renaissance, but didn't" because of the Ottoman occupation.

Since for much of its history Bulgaria's urban artistic forms partook of an Ottoman, rather than Western European, cosmopolitanism, Bulgarian intellectuals have, since the late nineteenth century, viewed folklore as the main repository of national culture during the Ottoman period, and endowed it with an ideological value far in excess of the aesthetic value they give it. The Communists adopted the strategy of allying themselves with and emphasizing Bulgaria's national aspirations as a way of bolstering popular support, their overweening concern with the defense of Bulgarian culture a way of co-opting an emotional issue for their own benefit. They must have hoped that something like the following syllogism would work in their behalf: I love my country and its culture; the Communists support this culture; therefore I will love and support the Communists. Thus nationalism was subsumed by political opportunism if not ideology and led in this way to the support of folklore.

While most Bulgarian intellectuals I questioned were at a loss to explain why political ideology caused the state to support folklore so strongly, I would cite at least three reasons. First, the fundamental new direction taken by the Communist managers of art entailed a complex of reciprocal actions, possibly not even articulated as theory, designed to overcome the class divisions within the country centered on an urban-rural split. On one hand, classical art would be made to speak not just to an aristocratic or bourgeois audience but to the masses, including villagers; no longer could the former speak only to themselves. If villagers were unprepared to appreciate this music, then they had to be brought out of their 'feudal' condition—listening to 'simple,' 'muddy' music—and brought into the light of the twentieth century. The class divisions of the pre-Communist period, expressed in rather separate musical traditions in towns and villages, would be overcome by, among other things, having the urban elite take the songs of the peasants, 'arrange/improve' [obrabotva] them, and have them sung back to them in a new, improved, 'progressive' form.[15] On the other hand, village art, taken as a symbol of the nation, could no longer be rejected by sophisticated urbanites; villagers would now sing their songs to this elite in a new form more palatable to them over the radio and in concert. Whereas in the pre-Communist period, educated city dwellers could identify exclusively with the aristocratic and bourgeois art of Western Europe, this class was now subjected to a barrage of national music arranged according to Soviet models. In this two-part syncretic process involving two musics (folk and classical) and two classes (rural and urban), class divisions could in principle be overcome and a new society created. If music alone could not create such a fusion, it would at least not be allowed to impede progress. Class divisions were to be overcome in all domains of life, including music.

The second aspect of ideology that resulted in the support of art in general and folk art in particular had to do with education. Socialist ideology required support of 'spiritual development' [*dushevno razvitie*]. The Communists dedicated themselves to raising the educational and cultural level of the entire population, that is, of all classes. The 'new man' would be better able to 'build communism' if he could be educated to the needs and goals of the Party. As an actor told me, "Culture is important so people will listen." It was a way to disguise and make more palatable a political message. The growth in cultural and educational institutions was one of the most far-reaching and indisputable achievements of the Communist period. As one intellectual told me, "Before the war there was one opera and one philharmonic in Sofia and now there are two philharmonics in Sofia and thirteen in the towns. Now there are seven large and five small opera theaters in the country. In bourgeois Bulgaria they used to say, 'A fiddler cannot feed a household,' but in Socialist Bulgaria it happens. The government has created a stable cultural stratum and is interested in the growth of all kinds of music. Ideology leads to this growth in culture." As one cultural worker told me, "From cultural growth will come economic growth." They believed that an educated, cultured, urbanized, industrial work force would create the Bulgaria of the future. As one intellectual said, the Communist government felt a "moral engagement to educate," especially given Marx's insight that ideology blinds people to the real conditions in which they work. An educated populace would be able to understand their condition and act, together with the Party, for the benefit of the working classes. State support of folk arts, the repository of the country's culture, in a supposedly improved form suitable for the 'new man' formed an important part of that education.

The third way political ideology affected culture was in its emphasis on the decorative. The new society would be a prettier, happier place than the old one, and the creation of professional folk ensembles to present beautiful, 'clean,' disciplined performances of folk music and dance became an important part of the program of the Party. Evaluating folk ensembles' treatment of music, one intellectual told me, "This folklore has a decorative function. It is not living folk art. Many are for it and many are against it, but the ensembles kept alive and even caused to be reborn an interest in folklore. Thanks to these ensembles the people have seen what was their true folklore. The ensembles dug up and put on the stage old material, like rituals, that had died out in most places. If there weren't these ensembles, then no one would know these *horo*s, these rituals, these costumes."

We return here to the theme of the national heritage, but the issue becomes its manner or style of presentation. In this case notions of 'true folklore,' an idealized image of what the tradition was like at some unspecified moment in the past, are constructed and presented 'beautifully' [krasivo] in the present. In the view of one intellectual, the early work of these ensembles made a strong, positive impression. According to her, 'arranged folklore' as performed by the ensembles "is an invented genre. In the 1950s it was necessary. It was very interesting and well-received. It was new and it created pride that our folklore could be put so successfully on the stage. It was refreshing. The best musicians, singers, and dancers were chosen, and there was prestige associated with their performances." She went on to cite the link between education and arranged folklore. "It also represented the end of closed Bulgarian culture. People had heard other music, so a fuller sound was necessary in our music. The success in America [of the Kutev Ensemble in 1963] was important. It was ours. It was pretty and youthful."

For the Party the argument again seems to have been, "we are giving you something Bulgarian that is beautiful. Believe in us, follow us, and everything in your life will be beautiful." The slogan of the Party might as well have been "beauty, cleanliness, and discipline are next to Communism." The beauty of folklore was part of a widespread propaganda campaign, a campaign in ideas and in action, to create the image of a beautiful new society under the leadership of the Communist party.

Command and Control of Music

The state's goals for folk music arrangements in the Communist era were certainly lofty ones: to improve the aesthetic appreciation of the rural audience; to sensitize the urban audience to its national patrimony; and, by creating a shared aesthetic experience, to fuse the two classes into a "new society" capable of "building communism." Explaining the first goal, Kosta Kolev, a director of the folk orchestra at Radio Sofia during Kostadin's tenure, said, "We wanted to make folklore grow to serve contemporary life. We tried to create music that would raise the taste of the people. These arrangements were a step toward art, so that [village] people could eventually listen to Bach, Mozart, and Shostakovich."[16] Goals such as these transcended mere entertainment: they served the educational and social goals of the Party, they privileged urban over rural practice as more 'artistic' [hudozhestveno], and they contained a fundamental optimism that the Party could remold people and their tastes to conform to their intellectual, social, and political goals. Folk music in its 'muddy' condition had nothing to do with those goals; in fact, it symbolized the backwardness they were determined to eradicate. Only in the hands of 'folk/people's artists' [*narodni artisti*] playing artistic arrangements could folk music have value for the new state.

The transformation of shepherds into artists and orchestral musicians took place in the context of the Communists' command and control of the political and economic system and of all elements of the country's social, educational, and cultural institutions. In the ideological domain there was, in a way, less conflict with old village values than in the economic one. While some Bulgarian scholars write as if the patriarchal family became a thing of the past under Communism, patriarchal values and behavior patterns remained strong throughout the Communist period and were extended to and used by the state. The Communist party simply replaced the father as the locus of authority, as in the slogan on many a roadside sign: "BKP [Bulgarian Communist Party]—Leader, Organizer." The system, like an extended family, worked as long as citizens were obedient, disciplined, and under control. Since these qualities were inculcated in Bulgarians from their youth, it is not difficult to understand why strong political resistance in Bulgaria during this period was as rare as well-stocked stores. In any case, arranged music during the Communist era functioned as an icon of the Communists' passion for command and control, a value transposed from the village patriarchal family onto the national level.

My wife Ann often ran afoul of the Bulgarian passion for parental control. Like most American parents, we were anxious to encourage our son Colin's developing skills and independence: he was left alone to play in his crib; as soon as he could crawl, he was on the floor; as soon as he could walk, he was toddling along cart paths, climbing on chairs, and exploring chicken coops. Ann, however, endured severe criticism for her "irresponsibility" in matters of child-raising.

Bulgarian infants were often heavily swaddled in the belief that their legs would grow straight, but it also reduced movement to a minimum. Older infants were not allowed to crawl on the floor, and even toddlers were held for hours in an adult's lap rather than allowed to fall or crawl on the floor and get dirty. These child-raising behaviors illustrated the truth of the popular wedding song in which a bride bids farewell to her mother, who "held her nine months near her heart and three years in her arms." While the practical reasons for this are understandable—a village house and yard are dirtier and more dangerous than an American apartment or suburban yard—the psychological causes and effects are equally powerful. Bulgarian children are typically raised for obedience, not independence. Parents control them from the earliest age and expect and get a disciplined response. Conveniently, the state also gets a disciplined citizenry, little inclined to opposition.

In the context of a centralized, state-managed economy and bureaucracy, it is easy to understand why government control of the arts was so natural. The controllers, in this case an intelligentsia of classically trained composers and conductors, saw themselves acting *in loco parentis,* ensuring the continuation of the tradition in their terms, as they understood it. They expected, and for many years got, a disciplined acquiescence from musicians because they held the economic and ideological reins, just as parents did within the family.

The traditional and modern practices of discipline and control manifested themselves iconically in music in the astonishing precision of contemporary Bulgarian playing. In an ensemble, musicians attempted to play each melody and ornament in the strictest rhythmic and tonal unison—and at enormous speeds. Bulgarian unison playing is in sharp contrast to the heterophonic style of, for example, Greek folk music ensembles. Suspicious that Bulgarian musicians' practice of tight unisons might be an artifact of orchestral training and the influence of notation, I asked Stoyan Velichkov whether it had always been so. He responded, "When you play alone, you can do whatever you want. But we always played together. There is a group [being played] on the Radio now from Koprivshtitsa [an amateur group successful at the national competition], and they play differently, but they are weak musicians. Better musicians always played together. I remember when *Bai* Stoyan Popeto, Mehmedaliya, Shahpas [famous Gypsy gaidari], Dragan Karapchanski [famous kaval player] got together at fairs. They wouldn't have seen each other for years, but they would say, '*Haide,* let's play something,' and they would play exactly together." Similarly, in matters of playing style, musicians cooperated to produce perfect unison, eliminating personal display.[17]

Musicians and singers under the state's direction were willing to change, negotiate, and blend, to create a harmonious whole for its benefit, just as they used to work for the family's benefit. Thus the notion of disciplined behavior with respect to a central authority was an element of both the old and new ideologies, and their coincidence, instead of changing traditional practice, undoubtedly reinforced and strengthened tendencies already in the culture to avoid excessive self-display. Whatever had been free, soloistic, and individual in traditional practice became rigidly formal, manufactured by a disciplined work force of trained musicians performing in the tightest possible coordination under the direction of a conductor functioning as shop steward. The performances expressed some nostalgia for the past at the same time that they demonstrated the ability of the individual to subject himself to centralized direction in the service of higher goals.

With these goals in mind, the composers "commanded" the musicians and controlled their output. They even directed and influenced the means of production and distribution: the ensembles, the radio, and the record company. Like Bulgaria's fledgling industries, the communications media gave consumers an annual quota of goods designed with the state's, rather than the public's, needs in mind. Predictably, they couldn't regulate its reception, as we will see in the next chapter.

A New Life in Sofia

What Kostadin and Todora—and presumably other musicians, singers, and dancers making the physical, spiritual, and musical pilgrimage from villager to urban professional—remember most vividly about the next few years is not their artistic transformation or the beautiful new society but the personal hardship they endured, as they and thousands of Bulgarians left their villages and their land for a new life in cities and towns. Sofia was not prepared for the massive influx of new residents, and housing was a major problem. The new Communist-run institutions, including professional music ensembles, promised to provide their employees with housing as well as jobs, but in the early years they were unable to deliver on their promises. Kostadin and many other musicians ended up living in a distant suburb in very modest circumstances. Todora remembered the first place they lived as little more than a one-room hut. Lacking enough room for the whole family, they decided to leave 12-year-old Ivan, their eldest child, in Grudovo with his grandparents. More than thirty years later Todora remembered the heartbreak of separation and his feelings of rejection: "He cried, 'Why is there room for the others but not for me?'" Her younger children, Stanka and Todor, were equally unhappy, crying at the isolation of their cabin and the absence of friends. The tension took its toll on Todora; sometime during the first year she lost her voice and didn't recover it again for two or three years.

With three children and a husband working as a professional musician, Todora had no opportunity to become a professional singer even though she apparently had the ability. Komna Stoyanova, a fine singer who came to Sofia at about the same time from the neighboring village of Drachevo, said, "If she had decided to, she could have become a famous singer. She knows lots of songs, she had a good voice, and there was dialect in her songs." This last comment refers to the radio's requirement that singers preserve the individuality of village dialect in their songs rather than using the literary language.

Unlike many professional singers who had learned where their voices sound best, Todora had no pretensions. She had a wide range and was willing to sing wherever the instruments were playing or other singers are singing. One professional musician, the gŭdulka player Neno Ivanov, said of Todora, "I can't begin playing for any other singer who can sing along as easily as Todora. It's amazing. She joins in at once." As Todora puts it, "When I have a voice, I don't search. They play and I begin to sing. Maybe it's high, maybe it's low. But I will find the scale [gama]." She learned this word from Kostadin, who learned it during his training in the radio ensemble. "I haven't studied music, but I feel it. But I don't have any pretensions [to be a singer]. I sing at the table. We got together with Bai Stoyan [Dobrev] in that shack we lived in. I didn't have a voice. I don't know what came out. I think I sang 'Young Stoyan became Ill' [Razbolyal se mlad Stoyan]. Bai Stoyan said, 'Say, Kostadin, what are you doing? Why are you holding this woman? She sings better than our singers.' Kostadin said, 'She sings better than ours, not just yours'" [laughs]. Todora, however, was totally preoccupied with raising her children and taking a job as a professional singer was not a reasonable option.

Eventually the radio found them the humblest of apartments in the attic of an old building on a street near the center of Sofia, where they live as of this writing. Todora was paid as a cleaning lady in the building, which housed some offices of the radio, so she could both work and care for her children. Life began to look up for her, Ivan joined them, and her voice returned. "When we came to Sofia, for two years I didn't have a voice. But when I began to work [in their building], I became more relaxed. I was young and, as I washed dishes, I sang." Even in Sofia she received recognition for her singing, as she had in the village. "The cashiers down below, they were like fathers, like brothers, that's how they respected me." One day she heard noises outside her apartment door and heard someone shout, "'Listen to Todora upstairs, what a concert she is giving [laughs].' I opened the door and asked, 'What are you doing? Why are you looking for me?' They said, 'We're not looking for you. We are listening.'" But this recognition and a growing understanding of the new role of professional singer and musician did not tempt her to try it. "In general, I didn't think about becoming a singer, because I had three children. Where was I going to leave them? He to a concert, I to a concert. That's why

I worked five years in the building, to be at home. So [the children] would get accustomed to it, because they were afraid."

As the children grew older, more confident, and increasingly absorbed in their school work, Todora sought work outside the home and found a job as a receptionist at the entrance to Radio Sofia, where she asked people for their passes to enter the building. Her native wit and extraordinary memory were turned not to song texts and tunes but to faces and names. "When I went to work at the entrance of Radio Sofia, I knew after two weeks everyone's number and face. When they arrived, I would say, 'Comrade Petkov, Comrade Dimitrov.'" They responded in surprise, "'Ah *be*, Todora, what are you doing? How do you know it's me?' It was amazing to them. They hadn't had such a person." Todora was simply doing what came naturally to so many of the villagers who moved into the cities in those years: translating and continuing village skills at face-to-face interaction into an alienating urban context.

She was soon offered a more interesting job, which caused her some pain as she confronted the gap between her poor village education and her obvious intelligence. "Later I was invited to join a section where they cut out and sorted articles from newspapers. But [the supervisor] didn't know I had only a fourth-grade education. It wasn't comfortable. There were people there with university educations. And I cried. Oh how I cried. I was ashamed to tell her. One day she was alone; the others had gone to the library and I went to her and began to cry. She said, 'Why are you crying, little chick?' 'I am crying because you want to hire me, but I don't have an education.' 'Don't cry,' she says, 'let's enroll you to finish junior high school.' 'How am I going to do that with three children. Tell me how?' I cried a lot."

Despite these crises in the early years in Sofia, Todora worked successfully for the radio, eventually winning many prizes as a xerox operator, until her retirement at the age of 55. Her story is one example of the psychological and artistic price paid by untold thousands of people who moved to the cities in search of the new life promised by the Communists.

Kostadin Changes

Although the governing Communist party developed an ideology that required state support of the arts, the particular form of support had to be negotiated on the ground, between people with different backgrounds, understandings, and interests. While the ideologies of political parties with a monopoly on power can be regarded as monolithic, hegemonic, and determining, they still had to be imposed by real people, who made decisions in their own or the state's interests, on real people with often opposing values and views.

In the case of 'folk music' [narodna muzika] or, to use the more politically loaded translation of the same term, 'people's music,' the battle was joined between composers like Kutev, trained in the methods of classical music, and village musicians like Kostadin, whom the former tried to mold into a new shape capable of playing the new kind of music appropriate for the new society.

Classically trained composers, acting as the directors of ensembles and the arrangers of music for radio, television, and recordings, controlled the professional folk music scene. As Kiril Dzhenev, for many years the artistic director of Ensemble Trakiya and one of Filip Kutev's first choreographers, told me in 1988, "Classical musicians command our folk culture." Their aesthetic values became the state's aesthetic values. The village musicians hired to play in the newly formed ensembles had to bend to their will.

One of the ways the composers and arrangers exercised control was through the exclusive use of written notation. Ensemble musicians and singers had to learn to read musical notation in order to play their compositions and arrangements, and guest soloists for the Radio, identified by collectors who held auditions in the villages, could play and record only after having a composer arrange their pieces for orchestral accompaniment. In orchestras and choruses musicians were no longer in control of their product. An arranger created parts for them and a conductor organized them into a cohesive whole, just as they lost their land to collective farms and Party bosses assumed a 'leading and guiding' role in their lives. But in order to achieve this control, the bosses had to recreate these musicians in their own image, and the first task was to teach them to read music.

Kostadin came to Sofia at the age of thirty-six, a mature village musician with a large repertoire, excellent technique, and vast experience playing for dances, weddings, and holidays. For him there were massive accommodations involved in learning to play in this new way, but according to his own and others' testimony he made the adjustment rather well. The woman who taught him notation, Lili Tabakova, a short, lively woman in her 60s when I interviewed her in 1988, remembered him. She was a music teacher specializing in solfège and music pedagogy at a "children's musical school" when Kostadin arrived in Sofia in 1954. Kosta Kolev, the director of the orchestra at Radio Sofia, and Dimitŭr Dinev, the head of folk music for the Radio, invited her to teach the musicians solfège and notation. As she remembered, "Dimitŭr Dinev decided that everyone should learn notation, and he set up classes two times a week. They had a heavy schedule of learning and recording four or five new songs a week. There were big demands to learn new repertoire. They couldn't just play what they already knew. Many of the musicians objected to learning notation. They said, 'Why do I need notation? I can find the tune on the string.' But notation allowed their repertoires to grow. They were very talented musicians. Some members of the older generation of singers in the Filip Kutev ensemble still can't read notes."

According to Kostadin, some of the older musicians didn't learn either. And how was Kostadin? Tabakova said, "He was very responsive and obliging. He was naturally intelligent and had a nimble mind. He was attentive in class and he worked hard to perfect himself. Now these musicians are able to teach, they are well-prepared musicians, and they can read anything." Kostadin was clearly one of those musicians who made the most of the training offered him. He was talented, disciplined, and, as a Party member, receptive to the new conditions being created for folk music. "He was a hereditary musician. His knowledge of music was unconscious, but he was a natural talent. With this as a basis, you can make a professional musician."

Tabakova saw the main function of notation as a storage medium for repertoire, simply enhancing the musicians' talent. Ignoring its function as a medium of control and its potential to change the playing style, she said, "From these music lessons [with me] he learned only a little. He is only literate in notation. This has not spoiled his performing style. It has only widened his horizons. As a gaidar he has not stopped in his growth. He continues to grow, continues to learn new repertoire, continues to teach his repertoire to the young."

While Kostadin's performing style may not have been "spoiled," he changed it in at least five ways: he began to play without a drone; he altered his treatment of the pitch and intonation of the gaidanitsa; he changed his approach to ornamentation; he developed an understanding of musical form; and he learned to compose, rather than improvise, new tunes. Nearly every village musician brought to Sofia made these or similar kinds of accommodations to the new demands of ensemble playing.

Playing without a Drone

Traditionally the gaida played two parts, melody and drone. As one Rhodope gaidar is reported to have said, "A gaida without a drone is nothing" (Levy 1985:282). But because the gaida's drone clashed with the arranged, constantly moving harmonies of folk orchestras, Kostadin learned to play the gaida with dronepipe stopped. He accepted the necessity of this, but, as we will see below, made adjustments in intonation for the two styles of playing: solo with drone and in an ensemble without drone.

New Approaches to Pitch and Timbre

The Thracian or Strandzha gaida was a relatively high-pitched instrument of indeterminate or relative pitch, and Kostadin remembered preferring lower-pitched instruments within the acceptable range of his day, which I have not attempted to reconstruct.[18] The new orchestras, on the other hand, used Western absolute pitch, and all instruments had to be built to approximate the tempered scale. The directors decided the new tonal center of Bulgarian music would be the pitch class A with the gaida's tonal center tuned to a'. Since the Thracian gaida was pitched somewhat higher—Kostadin believed it may have been around c"—two "standard" gaidanitsas were created in response to the new pitch level. One was raised in pitch to d" as the drone pitch and tonal center, with a conveniently playable a' on the second note from the bottom. Although slightly higher than the traditional Thracian gaida, it preserved a sound approximating the timbre and tessitura of the prewar gaida. The problem with this instrument was that it played most conveniently from d" whereas the best key for kaval and gŭdulka was a'. To play together in a', the gaidar had to play in the instrument's lower register, which required a difficult half-holing technique called kŭrma to play some of the modes, and whose intonation and timbre weren't as clear as in the upper register. To play in d" on the other hand, kaval players had to play uncomfortably high or low on their instruments. To solve this problem, a second gaidanitsa was created with a much lower tonic on a', making it much easier for the gaida to play with the other instruments. Conveniently, its softer, less shrill sound also blended better with the other instruments in an orchestral texture. Thus the new "orchestral gaida" in this period included a lower, more muffled sound.

Along with the transformation from relative to fixed pitch, the gaidanitsa's intonation was altered to approximate the tempered scale. According to Kostadin, gaidari always strived to play a perfect fifth above the tonic and a perfect fourth below it, but the other notes were variably configured, depending on the idiosyncrasies of individual makers and capricious reeds.[19] In ensembles, however, they had to play in tune with an orchestra built on the tempered scale, and there were a number of problems. The fourth above the a' tonic, d", was flat and remained so even after modifications; on long notes Kostadin's solution was to squeeze the bag harder, increasing the air pressure on the reed and raising the pitch. Otherwise, he constantly ornamented d″ with e″ to disguise its flatness. Kostadin maintained a dual aesthetic for the intonation of c♯″. When he played with drone, he pitched the major third slightly lower than the tempered interval he played with orchestra, a flattening he achieved by adjusting the overall pitch of the instrument until the third came into the old-fashioned, prewar tuning.

The most dramatic alteration from traditional tuning occurred on the f′, a third below the tonic. Kostadin said that in the prewar period this note had been a neutral interval (I'll call it f[neut.]) between f♮ and f♯, and the players used it to play two modes Kostadin has learned to label 'hijaz' (e f[neut.] g♯ a b) and 'phrygian' [*frigiiski*] (e f[neut.] g a b) pentachords.[20] In the postwar period the hole was adjusted to produce f♯; f♮ then had to be produced by half-holing [*kŭrma*], by uncovering the *mormorka* when playing the e′ fingering, or by putting a bit of tape over the top half of the hole in suites of tunes that required it. Strandzha tunes in the Phrygian scale formerly played on e′ (e f[neut.] g a b) were now more conveniently played on f♯′ (f♯ g a b c♯), which became a new tonal center for tunes on the instrument.

A New Aesthetic of Ornamentation

His orchestral experience also caused him to alter his approach to ornamentation. "When I arrived in Sofia, my playing was piled high with ornaments." After playing with the orchestra, he came to feel that the gaida's ornaments did not blend well with the other instruments and so cut back on his ornamentation in order to fit into the new orchestral sound. (A comparable change for singers was a new awareness of dynamics as an expressive device.) Although younger gaidari sometimes criticized his playing for its lack of ornamentation, he consciously altered his village playing style in order to blend and fit in with the orchestra. When playing solos, his style is richly ornamented, a "disciplined" contrast between public/group and private/solo performance paralleling Todora's "shame," described in chapter 3, at singing her private song creations at village dances.

A New Consciousness of Form

With musical notation and the orchestral training that required exact repeats, Kostadin became, as he says, "conscious" of musical form, in contrast to what was formerly unconscious and "accidental," "whatever came into my head." If in the old days variation was improvised and forgotten at the instant of performance, notation helped him create and manipulate variation and store the result in notation as well as memory. He conceded that notation created for him the idea of fixed melodic structures to be played identically each time, effectively wiping out the freedom and variation characteristic of village tradition.

Furthermore, the formal demands of a recorded performance were much different from playing for village dances. A dance could last for an hour or more, for example, when a procession was moving through the village or as members of the wedding party took their turn leading the "Bride's Dance" [*Bulchensko horo*]. The musicians strung together as many tunes as they knew, beginning with a ritually appropriate or requested tune and continuing with "whatever came into their heads" until the procession or the dancers stopped. Each performance was uniquely formed by the context, specifically the listeners' and dancers' responses combined with his own inventiveness and memory at that moment. At the Radio he was introduced to three new ideas: (1) a "composition" was a fixed set of instrumental tunes [*kolena;* sg., *kolyano*]; (2) tunes contained fixed four- or eight-measure phrases; and (3) each tune was played an even number of times (two or four). These regularized formal principles, called "*kolyano* form" by Bulgarian musicologists, became a hallmark of the new instrumental style, and Kostadin and other professional instrumentalists absorbed them as the norms of instrumental style.

While this form, as one aspect of performance, was not foreign to the tradition, there was much more freedom and variety in village playing. Some tunes, such as song tunes and their interludes, were played in relatively fixed, repeated forms, but the *drobezhi* [improvised tunes in constant motoric rhythm] were less constrained by formal conventions. They could be any number of measures long and would not necessarily be repeated. Lyuben Tachev recalled, "I don't know about Varimezov, but I talked to Atanas Vŭlchev [Bulgaria's finest gŭdulka player]. He grew up in a folk music family. He protested against the strict 4-measure phrases. Musicians would also play 7-, 8-, 9-, and 10-measure phrases. They might strive for 4-measure phrases but on repeats they would add measures. They couldn't repeat exactly what they had played a second time. In those days [before the war] you couldn't play without improvising."

Stoyan Velichkov also believed that older playing styles had fewer repeats and were more continuous. I observed this less regular, more improvisational approach among some nonprofessional musicians from the provinces, and Petko Radev, the most famous clarinet player of the 1960s and 1970s, told me of working with one such musician he invited to record for the Radio when he directed an orchestra there. The musician, a villager who didn't read notation, found it impossible to repeat what he had just played, so working out an arrangement with him was impossible, and the recording was canceled.

Thus, the formal structure so characteristic of instrumental music in the Communist period was the creation of composers and arrangers who demanded fixed, written-out forms. Kostadin, by learning notation and the new aesthetics of fixed repetition and perfection of form, became a composer himself. He told me that to prepare his village repertoire for recording he sat for hours in his attic apartment in Sofia working out the "best" versions of tunes. For unconscious variation, he substituted conscious composition, choosing from among the many variants that came to him the one that pleased him the most, which he then wrote down, practiced, remembered, reproduced at will, and taught to me and others as the "correct" version of the tune.

Kostadin's Compositional Techniques

In addition to playing the arrangements presented to him as a soloist in the orchestra, Kostadin was motivated to prepare his village repertoire for the Radio's recording program for two reasons. First, he earned money paid to him as an honorarium for the recordings. Second, he saw his recordings as a way to preserve for posterity traditional tunes that otherwise would surely have been lost. Kostadin made 84 recordings as a soloist for the radio,[21] each carefully prepared from his village repertoire together with some new *kolena* he composed to flesh them out. Of these, only six were recorded without accompaniment or with the tŭpan in the traditional village manner. The rest were accompanied by the radio orchestra or with a small group of instrumentalists he founded called Strandzhanskata Grupa ['The Group from Strandzha']. The bulk of his recordings consisted of dance tunes he had learned in Gergebunar, crystallized into suites of short, four-measure tunes, each repeated. They include the wedding *rŭchenitsa*s and some of the most frequently played *pravo horo*s from his youth, for example, *Gergebunarsko horo* and *Megdansko* ['village square'] *horo*. He also recorded favorite slow-song tunes, and instrumental *svirni* for wrestling, *kukerovden*, and wedding processionals for the bride and godfather. Through Kostadin's recordings, Gergebunar's local tradition, itself an amalgam of Kostadin's travels around Thrace and experiences with Gypsies such as *Bai* Stoyan, became, in a somewhat altered form and through recordings and radio broadcasts, part of Bulgaria's national heritage, copied by young musicians learning the tradition in many parts of the country.[22]

Kostadin claimed that many of the compositional techniques he employed had been developed unconsciously 'by the people' [*ot naroda*].

He only became conscious of them in Sofia, when he learned notation and some of its associated music theory. Among the techniques he consciously used—and believed to be traditional—were song borrowing, variation, melodic transposition, and metrical transposition.

SONG BORROWING

Kostadin's "compositions" usually begin with songs, which he and many musicians regarded as the primary source of instrumental melody in this tradition. As he put it, "Our instrumental music is as rich as it is thanks to songs." In most cases, he took a song tune from Todora's repertoire, composed a thematically related interlude [*pripev, otsvir*], and added instrumental *kolena,* either traditional or of his composition, the latter indistinguishable, according to Kosta Kolev, from traditional ones. His *Buenek* provides a good example of a composition that integrates some new tunes with traditional ones (ex. 7.2; CD #33). He borrowed three of Todora's winter dance songs, added interludes to them, and strung them together into a suite of tunes, fleshed out and extended at the end with his own newly composed tunes. As for the compositional principles and their aesthetics, he commented astutely on them. "When you play a song on an instrument, it lacks words," and so the melodies have to be dressed up a bit with added notes and more rhythmic variety. "The interludes," he continued, "should have some [melodic] connection to the song" and be more lively rhythmically.

VARIATION

Kostadin's variation technique can be illustrated by looking at a set of closely related *kolena* from a number of different *pravo horos* he "composed." Before coming to Sofia, he surely mixed these variants together haphazardly as he improvised *drobezhi* for dancers. During the act of composition, Kostadin fixed their form and position in a number of different compositions. The unifying motif in all the variants is an ascending scalar run from a' to e":

Kostadin used this motif to construct slightly different *kolena* in many different *pravo horos.* Perhaps the classic statement occurs in a performance he calls *Pravo strandzhansko horo* (ex. 5.8; CD #10), in which the motif forms the first and third measures of a four-measure *kolyano* (ex. 7.3). The last half of the motif also recurs as the first half of the second and fourth measures, giving the *kolyano* a great deal of internal coherence and economy (listen to CD #34 for exx. 7.3–7.7).

This motif appears three times in example 7.4, *Megdansko horo*. Each

Example 7.2. Kostadin's "Composition": *Buenek*

Example 7.3. *Pravo strandzhansko kolyano*

Example 7.4. *Megdansko horo kolena*

Example 7.5. *Yazmensko horo kolyano*

kolyano uses the same cadential idea, and deploys full and half-motif in subtly different ways.

In *Yazmensko horo* (ex. 7.5) the motif appears only in the first measure. In the third measure, where we might expect a repeat of the motif based on the previous models, he altered it slightly, and, in the seventh measure, substituted another idea for it, lengthening a four-measure *kolyano* into an eight-measure one.

In a variation on this technique in *Esekiisko horo* (ex. 7.6) the motif disappears in the first measure only to reappear in the fifth, making a four-measure *kolyano* into an eight-measure one.

In *Pravo horo* (ex. 7.7) the motif appears as a kind of "first ending."

This analysis shows how Kostadin and other instrumentalists use a very small amount of musical material over and over in different combinations to create variety within a highly unified style. It is these subtle one-measure variations within a composed *kolyano* that contribute to the impression that the player is "playing from the heart" even when playing a tune fixed in notation. In principle, Kostadin and other good musicians can continue the variation process indefinitely, spinning out countless "new" variants of existing material. These variation techniques are suggestive of Lord's notion of formula transformed from oral poetry into instrumental improvisational practice

Example 7.6. *Esekiisko horo kolyano*

Example 7.7. *Pravo horo kolyano*

and, after professional musicians learned notation, into compositional practice as well.

MELODIC TRANSPOSITION

A third compositional technique Kostadin learned to employ consciously, and which existed in the tradition unconsciously in the past, was transposition of a tune from one tonal level to another. In *Yazmensko horo* (ex. 7.8), for example, Kostadin transposed a melody on a' to g', altering the cadence only slightly.

METRICAL TRANSPOSITION

The fourth compositional technique that Kostadin acknowledged consciously is what might be called "metrical transposition," that is, changing the meter of an existing tune to create a new tune in a new meter. He called it "his secret," but admitted that many other instrumentalists also use it. One of the easiest and most common transpositions occurs between 6/8 *pravo horo*s and 7/8 *rŭchenitsa*s (ex. 7.9); in principle any 6/8 tune can be lengthened to an effective 7/8 tune, most typically by doubling the length of the first beat.

Metrical transposition served Kostadin well when, after coming to Sofia, he had to learn a national repertoire to add to his local, Strandzha tunes. These included the lively *Shop* dance tunes from the Sofia region in meters he had not played as a youth: 7/8 = 3 + 2 + 2 (*Chetvorno*), 11/8 (*Kopanitsa*), 12/8 (*Petrunino*), and 15/8 (*Buchimish*). To solo in these meters, he had to create his own tunes; to do so, he metrically

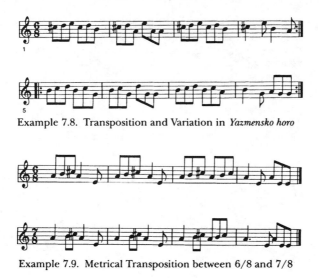

Example 7.8. Transposition and Variation in *Yazmensko horo*

Example 7.9. Metrical Transposition between 6/8 and 7/8

transformed tunes he knew in 7/8 and 9/8 into the longer meters of *Shop* music. For example, in many *Shop* suites, he played a set of related tunes emphasizing g′ before cadencing on a′ (ex. 7.10; CD #35). While they are not precise melodic variants, they have a very similar feel on the instrument and show another way metric transposition works.

Continuity and Change

Unlike Lili Tabakova, who saw little effect from notation, Lyuben Tachev emphasized changes in approach when talking about how Kostadin and the other musicians who came to Sofia in the 1950s were affected by their new situation. "Don't forget that [these musicians] turned away from the natural village style. The composers, the directors, and the technical demands of Radio Sofia put a stamp on them"; for effect he made a fist and hit himself on the forehead to show the mental quality of this influence. "The difference is they now understand dynamics and phrasing. Kosta Kolev [the Radio folk orchestra director] is the biggest part of this history. He created these musicians. He educated them. He was the only one of the composers and directors at Radio Sofia who came from the folk tradition. He was from a very poor family. He is the closest to the folk tradition. All the musicians will tell you that. They have to tell you that."[23]

Kosta Kolev, the arranger most respected by professional musicians, conducted the radio orchestra during its early years and created many arrangements for it, "the best ones" many musicians told me. A thin,

Example 7.10. Metric Transposition of Tunes

spry, distinguished-looking man in his 70s when I interviewed him in 1988, he was one of the few composers who grew up close to folk music. "I was a self-taught musician until I entered the conservatory. I finished in 1961. I played svirka, flute, trumpet, harmonium, and accordion." He played wedding music for many years, but, unlike most such musicians, taught himself musical notation. "I listened to the radio and transcribed tunes. In our village there was only one radio and I would go as a guest to their house especially so I could listen and transcribe tunes in order to play them."

As an accordion player, Kolev developed a rudimentary feeling for harmony. "I harmonized melodies before I knew about harmony. I taught myself about transposing instruments. The entrance exam at the conservatory was really easy for me. I finished it so quickly the other students thought I had failed and given up, that I couldn't do it." In a sense he shared the developmental history of many of the musicians he conducted, and his arrangements are uniformly respected by them, although Kostadin told me that Kutev criticized Kolev's arrangement of his *Trite pŭti* (CD #32) as too simple and merely "convenient for playing."

Kosta Kolev stressed the continuities between older and newer forms of playing, and claimed that the suite form based on *sitnezhi* and *kolena* was an old form. The changes of mode and key in Kostadin's recordings are also traditional. "They come from a feeling for the dance," as a way to stimulate dancers to change their level of movement, described in chapter 5.

Regarding his role in the composition and arrangement of Kostadin's and other instrumentalists' tunes, Kolev told me, "I changed some melodies. I put in new melodies, and I changed the order of tunes to create variety." In *Buenek* (ex. 7.2; CD #33), for example, he suggested beginning with the interlude rather than the song tune, which was the traditional practice in Gergebunar. With Kostadin, Kolev seems to have restricted himself mainly to changing the order of tunes, since Kostadin came to him with a rich supply of traditional melodies. "He was a good, mature musician. Kostadin is more conservative [than some of the younger musicians]. He plays what he played as a child. He came with a rich repertoire. His new tunes are almost authentic. It doesn't show that they are created. That is his strength." As for his own approach, Kolev echoed Kutev's aesthetic: "I always try to preserve the original form [of the tune]. I put in very complex harmonies but not to destroy the original."

With some of the younger musicians like Stoyan Velichkov, who came to the Radio orchestra with a less developed traditional dance repertoire, he worked to create new tunes in the 'folk spirit' [*narodna dusha*]. Stoyan "tries to create new melodies," but then gives them to Kolev, who composes additional tunes to fill out the suite. Evaluating Kolev's contributions, Stoyan told me: "They were so natural I felt as if I had composed them myself."

Thus Kosta Kolev—and presumably other composers—contributed mightily to the final form of many of the best-known recordings of Bulgarian dance melodies, not just by surrounding them with harmonies and counterpoints, but by composing new tunes and ordering the ones the musicians gave him.

In this chapter I described how the Communist party and the state imposed first ideological, then economic, then musical change on Bulgaria's prewar practices. The exact flow of events and the precise nature of the changes were not predictable by theory, however. Much depended on influential individuals and how they interpreted and acted on these changes. While it may seem contradictory that a Communist ruling class should want to preserve bourgeois performance practices and aesthetics, that is precisely what happened, both in Bulgaria and in the Soviet Union (Schwarz 1972:11–13). The Party's ideological agenda was enacted by a ruling intelligentsia who understood and interpreted it through categories and values they brought with them to the new society. In some sense, the horizons of revolutionaries and Western-educated intellectuals fused to create a sensible world with roots in bourgeois tradition. Even within a totalitarian state, however, the imposition of this newly imagined world was no simple matter. It was achieved in the dramatic encounter between individuals, who brought different horizons of understanding to bear on the problem.

Kostadin, for example, brought the understandings of a simple villager. As a disciplined person and, under the influence of this father, a Party member, he was willing to cooperate musically in the building of Communism. He expanded his horizons to include an understanding of musical notation, and understood that his traditions would be best preserved in the new society if he recorded them for posterity. In many ways, his was the ideal, unproblematic response of a disciplined citizen in the new society.

There were subtle differences in musicians' response to state control, however. While professional musicians were glad to accept the economic largesse of the Communist state, not all of them accepted the challenge and responsibility of preparing their repertoire for arrangement and recording as Kostadin did or composing new tunes 'in the folk spirit' as Stoyan Velichkov did. *Bai* Stoyan Dobrev, for example, failed to understand—or at least to act on—the socially constructive nature of the state's recordings and remained selfishly opposed to sharing his repertoire with the state and therefore with other musicians. Kostadin said that, when *Bai* Stoyan knew other gaidari were watching, he would turn his back on them to hide his technique and prevent them from 'stealing' it. Todora commented, "He was different [from Kostadin]. He didn't allow anyone else to play his melodies. He didn't want others to hear and to copy his repertoire. That's why he doesn't have recordings. It's not like that. Why? Let it be preserved.

Later he recorded one *horo*. He gathered them [melodies] all together, it became very long and they don't broadcast it."

In his refusal to record, *Bai* Stoyan failed to change with the times and to realize that recordings would compete with live performances as a source of income and fame. He retained the attitude of a prewar professional musician, whereas Kostadin, who had not been one, quickly accepted his role as one of public service and thought of himself as having an obligation to share his repertoire with others as part of the newly articulated ideology of a national folklore heritage.

In *Bai* Stoyan's resistance to recording, we have the first example of the confrontation between the older values of village and Gypsy musicians and the new values being practiced and inculcated by the state. Although Kostadin and Todora were largely in sympathy with many of these new values, they too felt the tensions between older and newer values and practices. While they responded with a sense of obligation to the Party's call for discipline in the building of a new society, the aesthetic practice of arrangements—used to image iconically in sound the discipline and control of the state—and the corresponding economic and aesthetic dictates of composers often tried their patience and contravened Kostadin's and other musicians' understanding of how their tradition should be performed and presented.

EIGHT

Reception and Teaching of the New Tradition

How did individual musicians deal with the state's hegemony in musical taste and production during the Communist era? In the face of totalitarian power and a restricted range of options, musicians and listeners managed to carve out aesthetic niches for themselves that built on their own previous values and maintained a modest sense of dignity and choice. Composers reasserted Western European ideals against any hint of Turkish decadence and at the same time lined their pockets with fees for their arrangements. Village musicians who turned professional struggled to maintain some sense of connection to their understanding of how *narodna muzika* worked among the people and played so effectively on their emotions. And some people turned their backs on—and closed their ears to—people's music, preferring a host of competing styles, ranging from popular, classical, and Gypsy music produced in the country to jazz, rock, and national music from other countries. Having examined the workings of the state's command and control in the previous chapter, I now examine the reception of the new tradition by Kostadin, Todora, their children and grandchildren, his students, and their colleagues and friends, and the concerted and conscious effort to teach it.

Reception of the New Tradition

Ordinary People and Villagers

The anecdotes and stories of people rejecting the composers' arrangements of *narodna muzika* are legion. Kutev's choreographer, Kiril Dzhenev, told me about a man coming up after an early concert in the

1950s and saying, "You sang really well. Now sing us a real folk song." One musician active in the 1950s told me of a saying that circulated in those days about 'arranged folklore' that illustrates the antipathy many people felt toward it: "A wine that has passed through Vinprom [the state winery] and a folk song that has passed through Filip Kutev— screw 'em!" Homemade wine is to manufactured wine as a village song is to an arranged song. An arranged song is unnatural and manufactured, and Filip Kutev, like the state winery, was an organ of the state. As such, people expected them to do their work less well than an individual or private concern would. So, while Filip Kutev held a revered position in the official history of Bulgarian folk music during the Communist period, the changes he initiated had many detractors, some of whom expressed themselves in the earthiest terms. While the state had good intentions to produce a new high-quality life, in fact what it produced was often shoddy or not what the people wanted, whether in wine, income, housing, jobs, or music.

In addition to the added harmonies, which displeased many village listeners, the truncated song texts, shortened for radio broadcast and records, annoyed them as well. As Todora said, "They cut out stuff. And the most interesting part of songs can't be said, that is, you start at the beginning, but the most interesting is later on. They give three or four couplets. Sometimes you can't understand what it is about. They just get started and there is nothing." From the point of view of the villagers, who know the tradition the best, the shortening of songs to fit producers' concepts of the limited attention spans of modern, urban audiences was one of the most profound alterations of the tradition. Whereas at a *sedyanka*, dance, or at home around a table, a song could "have no end," as Todora once said, radio producers assumed that their audience needed constant musical variety and was not interested in the texts. While this may have been true of the new audience of urban dwellers, the villagers were bored by precisely the absence of the content they remembered was there. In this case, as in so many others, the aesthetics of the literate and their assumptions about the worth of folk song won out over the values of the villagers.

The musicians heard the criticisms of their work as well; even the simplest arrangements offended most villagers. One of Kostadin's relatives complained to him of the orchestral accompaniments: "It's as if someone grabbed you and pinched you continuously." Kostadin continued, "People say they like my playing, but don't like the instruments that howl around me." For the villagers' taste, there were, as the Emperor supposedly said of one of Mozart's compositions, too many notes.

Thus while the genre of arranged folklore proliferated and monop-
olized the media, it was neither well nor widely loved. City dwellers
rejected it as symbolic of the rural past they and their families had
abandoned. Todora told me, "I was at the beauty parlor the other day,
and, when folk music came on the radio, someone said, 'Turn that
stuff off.'" And Kostadin frequently said, "People don't like folk music
anymore." Yet, when we traveled together in the countryside, he was
obviously well known and people enjoyed his playing. In spite of years
of trying to change the taste of both rural and urban audiences, in the
1970s and 1980s many people resisted the state's approach to folk music, mediated by classically trained composers and their values. In both
economics and music, the state took away from the people something
they valued dearly (folklore and land), and gave them back what they
did not want: jobs in collective farms and factories, and arrangements
of folk music.[1]

Just as the Party tried to obliterate the traditional aspirations of the
peasantry in favor of an urban, industrialized, proletarian vision of a
new society, so they tried to cover village aesthetic traditions with a
veneer, ironically enough, of Western aristocratic, bourgeois values. In
music and social life, a battle of sorts was joined; people did not simply
throw off centuries of tradition for a new one imposed from the political and ideological center. In every domain of life, people made accommodations and adjusted behavior patterns—but not without hard feelings. In the professional music ensembles, as in most cases of politics
and economics, the literate elite—the composers—won the battle to
impose their vision on society, but not without resistance from the
peasantry, in this case the shepherds turned professional musicians.

Reception by the Musicians

Kostadin and the other professional musicians, although thoroughly
co-opted by the composers, had little choice but to cooperate in order
to keep their jobs; nonetheless, they evaluated, criticized, and compared composers' work to their own notions of tradition. Both singers
and instrumentalists frankly expressed their disdain for most composers' work and their preference for traditional ways of singing and playing. Unfortunately, their sinecures as professional musicians depended
on the composers' decision to create large choruses and orchestras. So
while they complained about aesthetic issues, their participation was
assured, because these large organizations provided their livelihood as
professional musicians.

One arranger, Lyuben Tachev, who grew up, like Kosta Kolev, playing accordion, was adamant that Bulgarians didn't like arranged folk

music: "Even the composers don't listen to their own work after it is recorded." His cynicism about composers began when he was a student at the conservatory. A thin, intense man of medium height whose youthful appearance belied his years, he trained at the Sofia Conservatory in the 1950s. As a village musician, he was struck by how few of his fellow students, who would later become influential folk music arrangers for the Radio and various ensembles, were from villages, and what little connection to folk music they seemed to have. "I was the only player [*svirach*], and there were two singers from Thrace, Pavlina and Paraskeva Popova, who sang. We were the only ones and Todor Prashanov.[2] At parties and things I would play and they would sing, but we were the only ones who actually played any folk music. No one else would even whistle a folk song at a table," one of the traditional occasions for singing and dancing.

From Tachev's point of view, it was little wonder that musicians and villagers failed to appreciate arrangements by composers, who lacked a feeling for the tradition that might inform their work. In fact, musicians distinguished between composers and conductors who seemed close to the folk spirit and those who did not, respecting the former and denigrating the latter. In one telling gesture, a musician in the Kutev ensemble pointed to his heart as he complained that its director in 1988, Stefan Dragostinov, a stern-looking, red-bearded, thirtyish man, was not close enough to the people's spirit. He was rehearsing one of his choral arrangements in ten-part harmony the day I visited. Expectably, the performers' taste ran to the simplest arrangements. Kostadin believed that composers created complicated arrangements in conscious imitation of European classical music. "They [the composers] would say we musicians are 'conservators,'" that these new times demand new music. He once asked Nikolai Kaufman, a composer and Bulgaria's most prolific collector of and writer on musical folklore in the last forty years, why the Turks and Arabs don't use arrangements but the Bulgarians do. He remembered Kaufman answering, "We are further ahead. We learned this from France." While Kaufman may not have said precisely that, Kostadin got the message that these arrangements were a symbolic acting out of progress and a turn toward European civilization and away from a rural past under Turkish domination.

The musicians' favorite arranger was Kosta Kolev, not just because he was their director for many years, but because his arrangements are, according to Kostadin, "light. Filip Kutev criticized [Kolev's arrangement of Kostadin's] *Trite pŭti* because there were no subtleties in it. But then musicians say, 'If you want to spoil a song, give it to Kutev.'

Composers write for each other [rather than for the people], so they will notice the details in it."

Kostadin's main criticism of arrangements centered around his view that they were "heavy and not good for dancing. The tempo is too slow. You can't dance to it. It's only for listening, but people might want to dance to it." When dance songs were arranged, the composer usually provided the interlude [*pripev*], but often, Kostadin said, it "isn't lively [*igriva*] and doesn't contrast with the song," as it would if a musician provided it. Kostadin seemed to believe that an audience might actually use his records and broadcasts as if he were there to play for them in person. Composers, on the other hand, wrote what he called "listening music" cut off from the tradition and how people once used it. In fact, I never saw anyone dance to a record in Bulgaria, whether because the recordings were "undanceable," as Kostadin suggested, or because the relationship between live music and dancing was too complete and ingrained for such a response to a tape recorder or radio to occur to anyone.

When these arrangements found their way onto music stands at rehearsals, the negotiation between village musicians and composers continued. In 1988, at one Radio orchestra rehearsal that I attended, a composed melody contained a couple of odd melodic leaps clearly outside the typical parameters of the tradition. Presumably the composer was "playing" with those leaps rather consciously, but in rehearsal Stoyan Velichkov, with the assent of the conductor, effectively deselected them, and smoothed out the melody in the direction of traditional patterns that were easier for him to play. As he put it, "Why put your hands in the fire when you can use tongs?" If selection is one of the features of the folk music process, then it continued even in this environment of composed, written music, as musicians steeped in village traditions put the brakes on what they viewed as composers' ill-conceived attempts to move it forward.

The musicians' selection and deselection of particular innovations was governed both by their knowledge of tradition and by the dynamics of respect. Since the musicians didn't have much respect for the composers' knowledge of folk music, particularly in comparison to their own, they felt free to alter the latter's melodies whenever they strayed too far from tradition. Later in the same rehearsal Stoyan praised an arrangement with good, solid tunes from the tradition rather than from a composers' musings: "This is real. This is from the mud."

The musicians also knew that the performances would be totally unsatisfactory without their input, although they felt helpless in the face of composers' control. Kostadin remembered that Stoyan once suggested in a rehearsal that they play the tunes as written, totally eliminating the style and ornamentation, in effect everything that made the performance adequately Bulgarian. The antagonism was strong, but the musicians mainly lost in their confrontation with composers. Only at the most subtle, but perhaps most important level—the details of melodic construction and ornamentation—did musicians maintain both the tradition and their sense of self-esteem in the face of composers' command and control.

Reception by Intellectuals

How did these arrangements, disliked by the peasants and musicians who provided the source material for them, fare among the intellectuals who were to be part of the new audience for folk music? Even worse. Folk music, as practiced rather than as a glorified, idealized remnant of the national past studied in school, was simply too déclassé for a modernizing urban elite. Except for the small circle of directors, conductors, composers, scholars, organizers, and propagandists working directly with, and profiting from, the tradition, few intellectuals developed an interest in folk music. Even those in positions of power, who controlled the Party's interests in other domains, and who might have been expected to understand the state's goals for folk music and its new role in culture, often let their bourgeois values undermine their cultural ideology, and failed to support folk music and its display.

Lyuben Botusharov, who served as director of the Pazardzhik ensemble of folk song and dance before becoming a musicologist in Sofia, experienced the antipathy of many in the intellectual establishment toward folk music. He told me of the time the local chief of culture for the Pazardzhik district heard him play a Beethoven sonata in a concert and said, "Why do you bother with this simple folklore? Why don't we make you the director of the operetta?" Botusharov refused, arguing that, in fact, it was the other way around. All you did for the operetta was stand there and wave your arms around, while with folklore there were many interesting problems of collection and presentation. When it came time to argue with the culture chief for funds for the ensemble, however, the man said, "All right, folklore is simple stuff, but since Botusharov plays the piano, we'll give them the money he wants [for the ensemble]."

These examples of the uneven reception of arranged folk music during the Communist period demonstrate that political ideology, Western aesthetics, nationalism, modernism, traditional values, and personal interest clashed in virtually every transaction and had to be negotiated by those present. It is not obvious that political ideology and state hegemony were absolutely dominant in every case. Ordinary relations of personal power, long-established taste, and the prevailing political climate interacted in complex ways to determine musical practice in any particular case. Furthermore, the stories show clearly that, if we want to understand how culture, history, economics, or ideology determine or influence music, we will have to examine how these grand categories are translated into practice through the agency and action of individuals, who, even in a totalitarian environment such as Bulgaria's during the Communist period, had some room to choose.

Kostadin Forms Strandzhanskata Grupa

While musicians could do little but complain about composers' artistic distortion and economic manipulation of the tradition, Kostadin managed to sidestep their aesthetic control, at least in part, by forming a small ensemble patterned after his experiences in the army and after the war as a wedding musician. Unhappy with the "heaviness" of the Radio orchestra, he felt he could express himself better in a small group. With the directors' blessings, he turned first to his colleagues in the Radio orchestra, particularly the kaval player, Stoyan Velichkov, from the village of Zidarovo in Strandzha (see fig. 2). Together, they created Strandzhanskata Grupa ['The Group from Strandzha']—a small ensemble of gaida, kaval, gŭdulka, tambura, and tŭpan—to play an amalgam of Kostadin's and Stoyan's Strandzha repertoire. In a sense, he and the others in the group constructed a performance style true to their understanding of both tradition and the demands of the new society.

Stoyan remembered how they created their pieces: "Varimezov and I, while we drank half a kilo of *rakiya* at their place up in the attic, we created four *horo*s in one sitting. He knows a lot of melodies. I know a lot of melodies and we get together, 'Here you play, here I will play. Here the gŭdulka and so on.' The two of us make them, we get the others together and that is what we record." Seeking other musicians, they first turned to the famous gŭdulka player, Mincho Nedyalkov, widely respected as the best player of the period. Stoyan recalled, "Kostadin had the opinion we should take him, because he was the best gŭdulka player. He said, 'He is from Thrace. He knows our tunes.' We got together for a rehearsal and what happened? After two or three hours rehearsal, he can't remember anything." Nedyalkov was one of those musicians who couldn't alter his approach to the tradition; he never learned notation well and never became conscious enough of formal principles to remember new tunes. As Stoyan put it, "While you play, at the moment he plays," that is, he followed others extremely well, as Todora could, "but he is hardened, constipated. Whatever nature gave him, he can't take in anymore."

Realizing that Nedyalkov wouldn't work out, they turned to Neno Ivanov, whom Stoyan had met and played with for three years in the army. From Gara Drafal near Razgrad in north Bulgaria, he was a younger, less-experienced performer and knew Thracian material less well than Nedyalkov, but as Stoyan remembers, "He was more musical. He remembers quickly and copes at once." Neno, recalling those early days of Strandzhanskata Grupa remembered Stoyan telling him, "You are like a blotter. Whatever you hear, you remember at once and begin to play." Neno then brought into the group his friend from his early days in Sofia, the tambura player Iordan Tsvetkov. The group was completed with the addition of Ognyan ("Jimmy") Vasilev, the tŭpan player with both the Kutev and Radio ensembles (pl. 11; CD #36).

The group was an immediate success. Kostadin recalled modestly, "We received many [favorable] letters," but his younger brother Stoyan Varimezov put it more poetically: "Strandzhanskata Grupa was the sun that rose over Bulgarian folk music." He was referring to the quality of their playing; the fact that they played Strandzha and Thracian melodies rather than Western Bulgarian ones; and the contrast with the Radio orchestra and other large ensembles. Kostadin was much happier playing in the group than in the orchestra, which he felt always weighed down his playing, and he used it for 53 radio recordings, most containing melodies from Rosenovo and some of which were later released on Balkanton Records.[3]

With Strandzhankata Grupa, Kostadin also influenced matters of presentation and style; playing with them, he was not as helpless as in the orchestra. Kostadin objected to many of the long-playing records of the period, which featured songs on one side and instrumentals on the other. When the group made such a record with the singer Dimka Vladimirova,[4] Kostadin suggested they intersperse Dimka's songs and their group's dances on both sides: "That way people could use the record and dance to it or sit and listen," with a flow of music and song much like an informal evening party. The Balkanton producers agreed, and so the overall form of that particular production resulted from the aesthetics of a village musician, an unusual instance where village sensibilities were taken seriously and changed a format haphazardly imposed by urban producers and composers.

Strandzhanskata Grupa's fame spread far beyond Bulgaria's borders, providing both the standard Bulgarian sound many foreigners danced to and imitated and an opportunity for the group to travel throughout Europe, the Middle East, and North Africa. After recording, concertizing, touring, and playing weddings for over a decade, the group eventually broke up, mainly because of conflicts and jealousies between Kostadin and Stoyan. Stoyan formed his own group, the Trakiiska Troika [Thracian Trio] with Mihail Marinov, gŭdulka, and Rumen Sirakov, tambura, both from the Radio orchestra; that group continued the small group tradition at Radio Sofia, where it often accompanied singers. Strandzhanskata Grupa remained, however, one of Kostadin's most important contributions to the tradition in the changed social and political environment. It kept alive an aesthetic and practice—small group performance—at a time when they were in danger of being completely overwhelmed by the composers' orchestras, choruses, and dance ensembles.

Todora Confronts New Values

The discussion so far has highlighted problems between the composers and others—ordinary peasants, musicians, intellectuals—over largely aesthetic issues. But conflicts based on ethics and economics also developed between professional musicians and villagers, the 'pure source' [*chist izvor*] from whom many of them took their repertoire. The composers needed repertoire to arrange, and the younger singers and musicians, those who lacked their own repertoire, needed songs to sing and tunes to play. Both groups turned to the older singers, musicians, and dancers—the 'shepherds'—like Kostadin and Todora, who came to Sofia with a traditional repertoire.

While Todora's education in the village had not prepared her well for the new demands of urban life, her extraordinary knowledge of village songs was appreciated by professional singers and ensemble directors, who used her as a 'wellspring' [*izvor*]. Although Todora gladly gave her songs to these singers and the choir directors, she confronted two problems: some of the performances and treatments of her songs were not adequate, and the singers and composers often took personal credit and money for her songs, failing to acknowledge or pay her as their source.

As for the quality of performance, she explained, "the national ensemble had good singers: Vŭlkana Stoyanova, Iordanka Ilieva. They were the most famous, and truly they sang very well." However many of the singers recruited by the Radio ensemble were younger women in their late teens and twenties who had not grown up in the tradition.

They were selected for their pleasant voices rather than for their knowledge of the repertoire. "The Radio didn't have [singers like the Kutev ensemble]. Very weak singers. They were being formed at the time. But like me, that's how much they were soloists."

Kostadin let it be known that Todora was a good source for repertoire and many turned to her for help, although some of the singers were not very successful in learning her songs. "I gave *Mrŭknova se mrŭk po pole pada* [It Became Foggy, a Fog Fell on the Field] to [one singer] and she, the poor thing, struggled so to learn it [*laughs*]. It was foreign to her. She was from the Ihtiman region [West Bulgaria]. The recordings did not come out well. I said, said, said the song to her, and her head began to ache as she tried to sing it. I will never forget it. It's not at all hard, but she sang it woodenly, ta, ta, ta, without ornaments [*izvivki*] [*laughs*]." Todora gave some songs to the arrangers for the Radio choir to turn into choral arrangements, but was often not happy with the results. "I gave *Mete moma dvorove, zŭn zŭn Gankino le* [A Girl Swept the Yards, *zun zun Gankino le*] to the Radio ensemble and they sang it *zon zon* [*imitates singing in a very wooden, artificially resonant manner and laughs*]. It was so [*pause*] I couldn't listen." In both these cases, she experienced first hand the distortions of professional singers and choirs as they transformed their inadequate understanding of local traditions into a national sound.

Todora was also hurt by the ethical issue of credit for performance, part of a problem caused by the collision of village and literate traditions. In Gergebunar, songs were not private property; everyone knew them—or in principle could know them—since they were performed and potentially learned at public events like village dances. In any case, since no money was involved, the issue of ownership was moot.[5] Songs were freely and gladly passed between family and friends, who were proud to acknowledge the sources of their songs: my mother, my aunt, my girlfriend from Drachevo. In the new postwar society, however, copyright—or 'author's rights' [*aftorsko pravo*] as it is called in Bulgaria—reared its ugly head because the radio and Balkanton were willing to pay fees to the performers, conductors, or arrangers involved in the recordings. Todora and others, who served as the *izvor* or 'source,' were lost in the shuffle, reduced to invisibility by the intellectuals' self-serving understanding of folklore as anonymous art. Conveniently, the performer and arranger claimed 'author's rights' for songs learned not from anonymous tradition but from living singers and musicians.

This became a serious problem for Todora as more and better singers from Thrace and Strandzha joined the Radio choir and sought her out as a source. To accommodate the new singers, "they cut some [of the older ones]. They had an audition and they let many of them go and took better ones." The best of these singers, in addition to their work in the choir, were given the opportunity to record solo songs accompanied by the Radio orchestra; broadcasts and records of their performances made them individually famous, including, from Strandzha, Komna Stoyanova, Kalinka Zgurova, and Yanka Rupkina. All were much younger than Todora and turned to her for song repertoire. Todora explained their lack of repertoire: Komna Stoyanova "was young; she hadn't sung at the *horo*, as I had. Still she had some idea of it. She had sung at *sedyanka*s. She was a year older than our Irinka [her sister]. She came as a girl here."

Todora respected Komna because at concerts she publicly credited Todora as the source of some of her songs. "I gave Komna three songs for one broadcast. However, Komna is very modest. She didn't record them for the radio, only for a one-time-only broadcast on television. She had a lot of songs, and she collects them in villages, and she makes up her own words where they don't please her. I asked her once [about a song Todora thought was made up]. She said, 'Older sister Todora, a person can't hide anything from you'" [*laughs*].

Other singers were less considerate. "I gave *Mete moma dvorove* [A Girl Swept Her Yards] to [another singer]. She lived with us with her husband when we were first in Sofia. We learned songs. We were young then. She sang it at a concert and earned an encore. As we left, her husband said, 'Where did you learn that song? You sang it very well.' And she said, 'I don't know where I learned this song. I don't know.' Fine. I didn't say anything, but after that I didn't give her another song. One month hadn't passed and she forgot from whom she had learned this song. She wasn't willing to recognize those she learned from. She had a few of her own songs, but she left the village as a child. What songs would she have."

Other singers gave credit publicly and freely but took the author's rights and the money. Speaking of another singer, Todora said, "All her songs are from other singers. I gave her about ten songs. She told me the other day, 'Since you are here, I will sing your song, *Nikolcho duma mama si* [Nikolcho Said to His Mother], *Podi mi mamo, oglavi me* [Dress Me, Mother], *Dŭrgana odi za oda* [Dŭrgana Went for Water]. On television when they ask her where she has gotten the songs, she says, 'From this baba, from that, and from older sister Todora Varimezova.' Her husband is a composer and made an arrangement. He took the melody of a slow song and stuck it between *Dŭrgana odi za oda* but kept the same words [of Dŭrgana]. Sometimes she put her own name on, 'Text and music by [the singer],' but. . ."

This singer's simple act of public recognition was enough for Todora, even when her identity as the proximate source of a song was buried by an ideology of folklore as coming from "the people"; by writing a song down, composers and arrangers felt comfortable taking credit for it in the phrase, "text and music by ... ." In another case, Todora gave the *na filek* swinging song, *Lyulka se lyulya* [A Swing Is Swinging] to the Radio choir (ex. 8.1; CD #37).[6] The record jacket notes and the published arrangement (Stoikov and Spasova 1989:60–69) credit Kosta Kolev as the composer, saying it is a "folk text." Clearly neither the tune nor the words belong to Todora; they are part of a Strandzha regional tradition. But that tradition, at the moment of sharing and for some time after, was not anonymous. There were known sources. That Todora as oral source was forgotten by the literate tradition illustrates the power of writing, and specifically music writing, in a literate society. In this case, the musically illiterate village musicians were taken advantage of by their literate colleagues, the composers and arrangers, who controlled the recordings. In the new system, the village musicians, their knowledge, and their aesthetics no longer had any rights; they were mere workers in a musical factory run by the composers and arrangers who took the profits.

Teaching the Tradition

During the years when the state enjoyed unchallenged control over music institutions, they grew in importance, strength, and size, and a movement called "artistic amateurism" played a key role in that growth. Every village and many urban organizations such as factories, unions, colleges, and the Pioneers, a patriotic youth organization with cultural and athletic programs somewhat equivalent to American Boy and Girl Scouts, organized collectives for the artistic presentation of folklore, drama, and other arts in a manner appropriate to the new state. In villages, Party cultural workers encouraged older people to preserve song, dances, music, and ritual by joining the ensembles, and in both towns and villages the amateur collectives became important venues for young people to socialize and learn aspects of the tradition. Although the family remained an important institution for sparking interest in folk music, the village ensembles' rehearsals and staged performances replaced dances in the village square and the *sedyanka* as places where that interest was cultivated and nurtured. With their suc-

The middle verses have been omitted here. The song ends with a point of imitation and modulation to a new key:

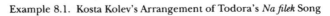

Example 8.1. Kosta Kolev's Arrangement of Todora's *Na filek* Song

cess, the amateur ensemble became important both as a source of income for professional musicians—Kostadin and Strandzhanskata Grupa received honoraria to play for one such ensemble—and as an incubator for a new generation of musicians and dancers.

To supply the growing number of amateur and professional ensembles with skilled, competent performers and directors, the state founded, in the 1960s and '70s, two high schools and a Higher Institute for Music Education (*VMPI*) devoted to folk music. According to Lili Tabakova, "The musicians coming out of these schools are all well-prepared musicians. They can read anything. But they are still small in number compared to the majority [in local ensembles] who are still amateurs," by which she means lacking extensive formal education in music, since most of them play for money at weddings.

Thus the state's interest in folk music as a symbol of national identity and its successful management of the new society created the need for a new type of musician, one capable of teaching the tradition as well as learning it. The state needed them to teach both amateurs, who put into practice the new ideology, and future professionals, who would one day take jobs in the newly created professional music establishment.[7] The musicians' response to the new challenge of teaching and the effectiveness of the teaching in passing on the tradition was predictably variable, even within Kostadin's and Todora's family.

Kostadin as Teacher

Kostadin, who taught gaida at the Palace of the Pioneers in Sofia for many years, proved to be one of the most successful and influential teachers of his generation of professional musicians, the one that moved from the village to the city (pl. 12). For musicians like Kostadin, teaching the tradition in formal settings like schools proved to be problematic, because none of them had been taught. They had learned the tradition by dint of their own effort and had no models for the teaching process. Many simply refused. Musicians who had played professionally before the war, like *Bai* Stoyan Dobrev, grew up in an environment where they hid their technique from enquiring youngsters, who, they feared, might eventually steal not only their music but their patrons as well. Others tried to teach, but had either no patience for children or no ability to analyze what they were doing and break it down into its component parts.

Kostadin, with characteristic discipline, gave a great deal of thought to the issue of how to teach. An important element in his success was the Western notational system that he learned after coming to Sofia. The notation abstracted out a fixed melody and formal structure, and imaged visually a profound simplification of the complex mix of mel-

ody, ornamentation, and variation that characterized traditional playing. Rather than teach melody and ornamentation as a unit, as he had
learned it, notation helped him conceive of melody as independent of
ornamentation, and he first taught the rudiments of gaida playing—
fingering and separating notes—by means of simple melodies which
he notated for his students. He quickly realized that if students had
early success playing simple melodies, they might be motivated to continue. If, on the other hand, they struggled for years, as he had, to
penetrate conceptually the complexities of the music, many would
quit. As he told Donna Buchanan (1991:305), most of his students were
"far from folklore." Most had, in fact, been pushed by their parents to
take music lessons—in order to feed a household—and were not
strongly self-motivated.

Kostadin also realized that his melodies, which had developed in
complexity over the years, had to be simplified for beginners, so he
created a primer of four tunes, which he called 'little horos' [sg., *hortse*],
and which would be easy for them to grasp both conceptually and
physically. In *Dzhinovsko hortse*, for example, which was usually the first
tune he taught, he altered the *Dzhinovsko horo* he recorded by changing
the mode from minor, which requires a more difficult "cross fingering," to major (ex. 8.2; CD #38). He eliminated a small variant in the
third measure of the first tune and reduced the number of *kolyano*s
from eight to three. The result, a pleasant but simple exercise, introduces the five easiest notes to play on the instrument. The other 'little
horos' introduced students to other notes on the gaida and some common asymmetric meters such as 7/8 and 9/8. He felt that, when students experienced success at playing simple tunes, he could 'light a
fire' under them, and they would feel motivated to continue.

One classically trained musician who had seen Kostadin teach told
me, "Nothing was arbitrary: 'Do this because I tell you.'" He explained

Example 8.2. *Dzhinovsko hortse*

everything." Her characterization certainly corresponded to my experience. He carefully thought through most issues confronting a music teacher and had reasons for why he did things the way he did. A simple example was his insistence that students play with the left hand above the right. Either way is acceptable on the gaida; for example, Nikola Atanasov, his successor at Radio Sofia, plays with his right hand above his left. Kostadin, however, taught the left-over-right technique not because he played that way, but so that, if a student eventually took up a Western wind instrument, his hands would be accustomed to the proper orientation.

Another key to his success was his extraordinary patience with young people. He seemed genuinely to love watching them progress. He was especially sympathetic to slow learners (like me), devoted hours to helping them, and claimed they often surpassed those who were initially quick. Although he retired from the Radio orchestra in 1978, he continued to teach at many cultural centers [chitalishtes, lit., 'reading rooms'] in the Sofia area.

Both Kostadin's recordings and his teaching flowed from two motivations: a sense of obligation to the tradition and a need for extra income. His combined income from teaching, the Radio ensemble, the amateur ensemble, weddings, and domestic and international tours gave him a handsome income by the Bulgarian standards of the period; he used it to buy a small piece of land in a village north of Sofia and build a cottage there for his family. While most ensemble musicians preferred to play at weddings rather than teach, Kostadin took seriously the state's injunction to elevate folklore and keep it alive in new circumstances. As a result, he had far-reaching influence on players of the next generation. As Lili Tabakova put it, "He has had a pedagogical gift with dozens of students. It's too bad that there weren't more like him to fill up the schools. The influence of Varimezov through records and radio is very wide. He has created one or two generations of people who have taken his skill." Kostadin, by his count, had about twenty former students who played professionally in important ensembles around the country, including the Filip Kutev and Pirin ensembles. Where he could not have direct contact with students—those from outside Sofia, for example—they grew up listening to his records and learned his repertoire and technique.

But his influence on succeeding generations was challenged, first by the exigencies of modern urban life, in which village traditions were often sneered at and ignored, and later, by the folk music schools and the popularity of wedding music, which drew the younger generation of gaidari in a new direction. Kostadin's attempt to pass on his tradi-

tion to a number of young people provides a variety of individual perspectives on how the new tradition was incorporated meaningfully into
people's lives.

Teaching His Sons

Among Kostadin's first students were his sons, Ivan and Todor, who
joined children's ensembles organized by the Pioneers. Todora recalls,
"Toshko played gaida with an orchestra of fifty accordions. They went
around the country a whole year. He played a lot, but in seventh grade
[his classmates] began to laugh at him and he quit"; and so did Ivan.
In the village, they probably would have continued their father's tradition, playing occasionally as amateur musicians for family gatherings
and perhaps even an occasional wedding. In Sofia, however, distracted
by a plethora of competing activities and teased unmercifully by their
friends for playing a primitive village instrument, they eventually were
shamed by their peers into giving it up. Although neither became
highly proficient players, both continued the tradition in their own
ways.

Todor, the younger son, is a sturdily built, intense man who worked
for the national railroad. "I don't have as many memories of the village
as Ivan has. I started gaida when I was about 11 years old and continued to the end of the eighth grade [at age 14], but then I stopped. I
was ashamed to play this village instrument and, besides, sports were
more interesting to me. I chose my high school mainly because it had
a good sports program. Now I am really sorry I don't play. I can't
whistle a tune and then find it on the gaida the way Ivan can, and,
although I can sing along, I can't remember the words the way Yani
[his cousin, Kostadin's brother's son] can. I can play one or two tunes,
but I can't create fun or start a party the way Ivan can. It's expected
of me because my father can play, and people say, 'Come on, Toshko,
play something,' but I can't."

Ivan, Kostadin's elder son, is tall and thin. A cinematographer, he
lived the alternately disciplined and crazy life of an artist. He worked
very hard and seemed to value exhausting himself both in work and in
play. More relaxed than his brother, he had a more passionate, 'artistic'
relationship to the tradition. Having grown up to the age of 12 in Rosenovo, his vivid memories of life and music in the village caused him,
as he said, to 'grieve' for the loss of the tradition. After quitting the
gaida as a child, he rediscovered it in adulthood as a source of pleasure
and connectedness to tradition. Whenever he could, he spent days at
the family cottage outside Sofia playing gaida. Most meaningful for
him were not the virtuosic instrumental tunes of his father, but the

songs of his mother. "I don't want to be a professional musician. I play for my own satisfaction. I am unhappy with my playing only because it doesn't express everything I know can be expressed."

Family gatherings, where Rosenovo's songs and dances "keep the family together," were particularly important to Ivan, and he tried to make them continue as long and as intensely as possible. At one such gathering near Sofia, when some relatives were packing up to go back to Burgas, he lamented, "I very much want to go back, I always want to go back." The poignancy of going back not only to Burgas but to a past when close family ties and frequent music making were the norm was a constant theme of his life and work. He had, he said, "lit a fire" under many a producer and director to make documentary films about historical figures and events.

Teaching his Daughter and Granddaughters

Stanka, Kostadin and Todora's only daughter, loved to dance and follow along as Todora sang, but she never learned to sing on her own. A tall, attractive, sturdy woman, she neither grew up in a village environment that encouraged singing nor did Todora sing much with her when she was a child. Upset by the trials of the move to Sofia, Todora said, "When Stanka came to Sofia in the first grade, it wasn't time for singing." So although Todora gave part of her repertoire to professional singers a little younger than herself, she didn't pass it on directly within her family, as had been the pattern from time immemorial. Stanka and her sisters-in-law occasionally wrote down the words of Todora's songs, but they didn't learn them, so in family celebrations they struggled to sing along as best they could. As Todora described it, "On New Year's Day we sing *koleda* songs and the kids record them.[8] Our children will remember these traditions, but their children won't. They won't remember the texts. They look at me [that is, follow] or write them in a notebook. For them it's foreign."

Kostadin and Todora's five granddaughters had the same opportunities to learn the tradition their parents had: from Kostadin and Todora in the family setting and from organizations like the Pioneers and *chitalishte*s that paid musicians and choreographers to teach the tradition. One new development of the Communist era was a more liberal attitude toward women's roles in society: women had to work outside the home, often at the most physically demanding jobs. In this context it became possible for girls to learn musical instruments, and Kostadin taught Todor's daughters, Blagovesta and Miglena, to play gaida—an unthinkable activity for girls in his youth. Todor said, "There is music in them. But again they stopped from shame, especially for girls. Both dance. Miglena was very agile, full of movement, and a lead dancer. She was also good at sports like me. But she contracted a kidney disease and had to stop. Blagovesta continues to dance, first in a ensemble at the Palace of Pioneers and now in the ensemble of the transport workers. She may try for the ensemble of the 'Student Home' when she goes to university, but they have a very high standard. She can still play the gaida." Thus the changed social circumstances gave Kostadin and Todora granddaughters who played gaida, at least rudimentarily, but who could not sing songs, a complete reversal of village practice.

For the Varimezovs, it seems that, despite their strong hold on the tradition and determination to continue to practice it, their family's experience of urbanization effectively undermined the age-old process of passing the tradition directly from generation to generation within the family. Todora's distress over the move from village to city prevented her from teaching songs to her daughter. But even had she tried, her sons' experience suggests that Stanka might not have learned them well. An appropriate context was simply missing. Although Kostadin tried to teach his sons and even his granddaughters to play gaida, they all rejected the instrument in the face of peer pressure. As Todora put it, "They are growing up in a time that takes offense at folk things." Their children's friends came from urban families who had no experience of village traditions. Todora said, "Dore [Ivan's eldest daughter] has a friend whose parents are both doctors. She doesn't come from a family like ours."

When we attended the annual family reunion in Grudovo in 1988, Todora commented on the dancing, "It was just like the old days. Only the children were missing" from the dance line. In the old days the children "got smaller and smaller toward the end. The youngest were at the end." The reunion was being filmed for a documentary about Kostadin, and its artistic director, a gentle, bearded bear of a man, noticed that some of the children even ran away when he and others on the film crew suggested they join in the dancing. He thought they should try to include this in the film, with the children turning into birds and symbolically flying away from the traditions of their parents and grandparents.

Teaching His Nephew, Ivan

Ironically, while Kostadin was ostensibly preserving the tradition by recording it in Sofia, it was withering on the vine of family tradition, an exotic plant transplanted into a hostile urban environment. He had to return to Grudovo and its more hospitable village-like setting to find a suitable heir to his tradition, turning his attention eventually to his nephew, Ivan Varimezov, the son of his youngest brother Stoyan. As Stoyan recalled, "There was no way for Ivan not to become a gaidar. His uncle visited here a lot and he was around this music a lot. One time Kostadin said, 'Let's see what we can do with this boy.' And he made him a gaidanitsa and began showing him things. Between visits Stamat [another of Kostadin's brothers] and I would help him" by singing and whistling tunes. Although Stoyan doesn't play gaida, he said, "I still correct his playing," mainly by recalling how Kostadin played the tune. Stamat, however, played gaida and helped with fingering. Ivan recalled, "They would slap my fingers, 'Not that one, this one.' My uncle, Stamat, was a good gaida player and he understood these things." Stoyan continued, "Then Kostadin would return and correct things and set him on a new course."

With that kind of intensive and expert care, support, and attention—the sort that was typical of learning in the old days, after a boy had demonstrated some interest and ability—Ivan indeed became a fine gaida player. Since he started around the age of seven or eight, he didn't remember a time when he couldn't play the gaida, and he recalled nothing of his own learning process. "You'll have to ask Kostadin about that." As a youth he won many awards, including a competition for gifted young artists whose prize was a trip to Cuba for an international festival. Unlike his city cousins, Ivan continued to play the gaida and eventually became a professional musician himself. It was only by leaving Sofia and returning to the village that Kostadin was able to pass on his tradition within the family circle.

Teaching Outside the Family

Not every child in the city was dissuaded from playing gaida as were Kostadin's sons. One of his best students was Dimitŭr Georgiev Todorov, a handsome, articulate young man born in Sofia in 1963. He said, "As a child I was afraid of the gaida when I saw it on television," but his fear eventually turned into fascination. "I tried to touch it on the screen because I was afraid. I took a pillow and put it under my arm and pretended it was a gaida." In the city, where there was no family tradition of music making, the media proved crucial in sparking an interest in folk music. Even there, however, family connections continued to be important. When Dimitŭr was ten years old, "a cousin of my father knew Varimezov, and he suggested I register at the Palace of Pioneers where he was teaching."

Dimitŭr remembered his first lesson. "I was so thin that Varimezov asked, 'Will he be able to blow up the gaida?' He put me on his knee as if I were his grandchild and beat rhythms on the table to see if I was musical," that is, if he could repeat them. "He was surprised and pleased. He put my fingers on the gaidanitsa. That was my first lesson" (pl. 13). He obviously learned very quickly. "In one year I learned many *horo*s. In the second year I was in the orchestra, and a year later I was a soloist. He sent me in 1975 and 1976 to a competition for young musicians in Chirpan. He was very sure of me. I played in a group with boys five years older than I. I took first prize the first year for my age, and I took first the second year for older boys." After these successes he took a leading role in the amateur music movement. "For the next two years I was concertmaster of the Palace's ensemble. In 1977 I earned a medal called 'Little Star–Morning Star' for active work with the ensemble. In 1978 they sent me to Cuba to a festival for youth. I was the only one who represented Bulgaria in the area of folklore. After that I played in restaurants and in many amateur ensembles [for which the musicians got paid] and at weddings. I played with my wife's father, who plays accordion. In 1984 there was a competition for the Kutev Ensemble and I was taken from among nine or ten people. You could play what you wanted and I played a slow song and *Yazmensko horo* [one of Kostadin's pieces]. They also gave me some sight-reading."

In spite of this success in folk music, Dimitŭr wondered how much it was appreciated in Bulgaria in the 1980s. "They didn't teach young people enough about folklore. My classmates laughed at me, but I told them it was my advantage over them." Indeed it was, since it meant he had a well-paying job in music, a skill that provided extra income, and the opportunity to travel outside the country, a rare privilege for Bulgarians during the Communist era. "On the radio in Greece today you hear only Greek music, in Yugoslavia only Yugoslav music, but here you hear everything. But I was breast-fed on folk music. I carry it in my blood. I play with *merak* ['enthusiasm']."

Teaching at the High School for Folk Music

Most professional musicians in the generation after Kostadin studied music at the high school level, and many finished the VMPI. Dimitŭr was an exception in not having attended these schools, but only the "conservatory of Varimezov." Situated as they were in villages and towns far from Sofia, Kostadin and the other major ensemble musicians did not teach there, but only visited occasionally as consultants. To understand better the nature of the new formal training, I visited the high school in Kotel in 1988 to assess Kostadin's influence and the impact of modern life there.

The music high school at Kotel was located in a beautiful but somewhat isolated mountain town on the southern slopes of the eastern Balkan range, surrounded by thick forests of small trees, the sort celebrated in song for hiding *haiduks*, the Bulgarian fighters against the Turks during the Ottoman period. Historically a center for small merchants and craftsmen, Kotel was home to many of the intellectuals who inspired the nineteenth-century Bulgarian national renaissance. The other high school, at Shiroka Lŭka, was located in a beautiful village in a deep valley in the central Rhodope Mountains that preserved many outstanding examples of eighteenth- and nineteenth-century house architecture. Selecting such isolated, historically important places for folk music schools stated symbolically that folk music represented a part of Bulgaria's history and cultural heritage, but it also had the effect of isolating students from the mainstream of contemporary life, a forced monastic retreat into the past. Ivan Varimezov, who went to Kotel, complained, for example, that there was no record store in the town, so students couldn't buy and listen to recordings of the musical models they eventually hoped to imitate.

Established in 1967, Kotel High School for Folk Music's new building had been completed in 1985, the handsome facilities evoking nineteenth-century Bulgarian town architecture. Sitting on the slopes of the mountains above the town, the school's clock tower was visible from the streets below. Georgi Penev, the school's director, was a short, handsome man in his thirties who used to play kaval. Asked to list the goals of his school, he thought of three: the preservation, popularization, and collection of folklore, the last done in classes that required students to collect repertoire from village singers and musicians for their own personal use. He said the school emphasized authentic folklore and taught students about each folkloric region of the country and the rituals that go with music. Finding it difficult to include ensemble music in his justification, he said, "arranged folklore is on the side, but it is practical." Indeed it was, because, as he acknowledged, the majority of students went on to the VMPI in Plovdiv, where they trained as performers in ensembles, teachers in school and amateur groups, and arts administrators. If they didn't go on to the Institute, the school helped them find jobs with amateur ensembles.

In 1988 there were 185 pupils specializing on the following instruments: kaval (25), gaida (22), gŭdulka (41), and tambura (41), as well as 58 singers, of whom 10 were boys. The balance among instruments reflected the structure of an ensemble orchestra, which typically had more gŭdulkas than any other instrument, and the purpose of the school to train young people for future jobs. Penev said they used to teach tŭpan, but no longer, the omission indicating the marginal position of this instrument in the culture, and of the Gypsies who are its best players. The model for education was a Western conservatory approach, modified so the content emphasized Bulgarian folk music. Each week the students had two hours of private lessons, two hours of chamber music in small ensembles, and four hours of orchestra or chorus—all of the ensembles made up of folk instruments. They took solfège, harmony, counterpoint, arranging, composition, acoustics, two years of Western music history, one year of Bulgarian music history, and four years of Bulgarian folk music.

Although the school was in theory devoted to all the country's regional styles, in practice, as Penev acknowledged, "the basis [of instrumental instruction] is the Thracian style." The best professional musicians and teachers played in that style, and, no matter what region they eventually worked in, they taught and played Thracian style, rather than the local style. However, in addition, students at Kotel were obligated "to learn their own local style and at least understand the other styles" in addition to the dominant Thracian style. Thus the school worked within an ideological framework that valued and demanded the preservation of 'authentic folklore,' and this was reflected in Penev's statement of goals and in peripheral aspects of the training such as courses in folklore and the requirement to learn the student's own regional style. But, in practice, they were preparing the students to work as professional musicians in ensembles of 'arranged folklore' where the Thracian style predominated.[9]

In 1988, twenty-nine gaida students took the exam to enter Kotel, according to Kolyo Sofinkov, an athletic-looking man in his thirties and one of the school's gaida instructors. They spent a week at the school learning and practicing solfège and then took the exam, which consisted of playing two previously prepared pieces, an exam in solfège, and an ear test. For the latter, the instructors created twenty or so four-measure *kolyano*s in various meters. After the applicants drew a number, the instructors played the melody twice and the students had to play or sing it back. The competition was stiff, and the range of ability wide. Sofinkov reported that one boy played everything in 2/4 time even if it was in 5/8, or 7/8. At least five others could only remember one or two of the measures played to them. Using a point system to rate performance on the three exams, the examiners rated those who scored above a certain level as good enough to enter, and put them on a list that was sent to the education ministry in Sofia, which ultimately decided how many to admit. Of the twenty-nine, ten were selected, and three were admitted. All were from eastern Bulgaria—Thrace and Dobrudzha—and all from towns rather than villages. In

1988 Kotel admitted only twenty-six new students, down from the usual forty to fifty, the cut-back a signal of diminishing support for folklore and culture as the state faced increasing economic problems.

That most students came from towns rather than villages represented a form of "secondary urbanization" of the tradition.[10] In the first stage of urbanization, village musicians like Kostadin and innumerable others moved to towns and villages to participate in the new professional ensembles located there. Secondarily, they influenced and taught a new generation of urban youth, many of their parents from villages. In this way, the town and the city become sources for new developments in a previously rural tradition. During the Communist era, folk music teaching flourished in towns rather than villages because that was where the best-organized schools and ensembles were and where the best older village musicians went to play as professional musicians.

I interviewed two of the three new gaida students, Dimitŭr Todorov Sherletov, age 14 (born 1974), from Varna; and Petko Kirov Stoyanov, the same age, from Yambol. Both claimed their interest in folk music and gaida came not from family, as was traditional, but from hearing it on radio, records, and cassettes, more or less the same story Kostadin's student, Dimitŭr, told. Thus the media provided not just a new method for learning music, but a new kind of family whose prestige and presence in the home provided a new social setting for exposure to music. It replaced mother, father, siblings, uncles, and aunts as a source of inspiration and the sounds to be imitated.

With teaching institutions at Kotel, Shiroka Lŭka, and Plovdiv, the state found a practical way to continue, on its own aesthetic and ideological terms, a tradition that its social and economic policies threatened. They produced what they believed to be an "improved" breed of musician, "better" in many ways than older village musicians, many of whom still had difficulty reading music. They could write down the songs they collected, compose new tunes, even provide their own arrangements. The state developed new musical workers perfectly matched to its goals, capable not only of playing but of valuing the 'clean,' 'sweet' music and dance it wanted. While the older musicians struggled with the composers over the latter's distortion of tradition, many younger musicians and choreographers trained at Kotel and the other schools embraced the new aesthetics unquestioningly. While they quibbled over the effectiveness of particular arrangements, they rarely challenged the need for them, and often professed themselves to be especially sensitive and skilled at producing just the right kinds of arrangements. The antagonism between urban composers and village musicians was resolved by their synthesis, at these schools, into musician-composers with academic knowledge of both traditions. Having embodied the state's values, they no longer criticized arrangements on principle, as the older generation did, but struggled with such issues as how to make arrangements even better, particularly in the face of the increasing popularity of rival forms of music.

Kiril Dzhenev, former director of the prestigious Trakiya Ensemble and a man with vast experience dating back to the early Kutev years, was in a good position to evaluate and provide some perspective on the new generation of musicians and dancers. Advanced students and recent graduates of the Plovdiv VMPI for folk music routinely trained by performing, choreographing, and composing for his ensemble. He seemed to be of two minds in our interview. One of his mandates is "to work with the Institute. We give them the chance to work here in the ensemble in the morning and then in the afternoon they study. They are then ready to go out and work professionally in other national ensembles and in amateur ensembles. Our graduates now work in all but one of the national ensembles, and I think it's safe to say the level has risen dramatically in their [the ensembles'] work in the last few years. The students are good, and I use them as a musician would a keyboard. We improvise."

In spite of this improvement, Dzhenev still compared the students invidiously to the first generation of dancers who came directly from the villages. He remembered the village dancers from whom he and Kutev collected material, the best of them joining the ensemble and serving as models for those with less experience. "We brought shepherds into the ensemble. In that sense choreography in the early days was closer to the tradition. In those days the performers were really the best authentic carriers of the tradition, whereas today you have students who have studied in rather artificial conditions and cannot or do not show that feeling for the tradition that the older performers could." The color had been bled from the tradition, and its soul emptied; arrangements, choreographies, and beautiful costumes could not cover the loss.

The story of schooled musicians and dancers was thus not unlike the story of music in the Varimezov family and the story of life in Bulgaria in general during the Communist era: there were successes and improvements, failure and decline. The state generated its own world of struggle, antithesis, and synthesis. As much as the cultural establishment tried, however, to keep the state hermetically sealed from outside influences, this proved impossible. Although the government tried to control the emigration of bodies and the immigration of currency and goods, the airwaves carried dangerous new ideas, and, in spite of occasional jamming of political propaganda, Bulgaria's borders proved permeable to music and musical ideas from its neighbors and the rest of the world. These ideas, abetted by changing economic conditions, challenged the regulated growth and willy-nilly decay set in motion by the ideological and social demands of the state.

Reflections on Musical Change

I began this part by arguing that both ethnomusicological and Marxist theory predicted that when culture or the economic base changes, then music will change. What these theories fail to predict are the dynamics of that change in particular cases: what in music changes and what is preserved? and how are the changes achieved?

If we begin by asking what in music changed and what was preserved with the coming to power of the Communists in Bulgaria, the general, somewhat simplified answer is that the underlying *musical elements* (meters, rhythms, modes, ornamentation, and vocal timbres), *forms* (songs, tunes, suites), *genres* (linked to the ritual cycle), and *material resources* (instruments) were preserved, while *context, style, technique, social organization,* and *meaning* changed. Is this a generalizable pattern? Are certain aspects of music practice more malleable or more resistant to change by their very nature or "essence" than others? The history of African-American music in the United States, for example, suggests the opposite of the Bulgarian experience: that many aspects of African style, technique, and social organization (raspy timbre, improvisation, call-and-response) were preserved, while details of tunes, meters, and genres disappeared.

In both the Bulgarian and African-American cases we find ideology operating to force musical change along certain paths. In the latter case, white slave-owners forbade the performances of African genres and instruments as a method of social control and religious conversion. What they couldn't suppress was "cultural style," which reasserted itself in a rich succession of newly created genres, forms, and instruments. In Bulgaria, a nationalist ideology valued musical forms, genres, instruments, and styles as symbols of the nation's heritage, while a socialist ideology demanded the presentation of these preserved forms in styles and contexts suitable to the construction of a new society. Whereas European-Americans destroyed African musical forms to sever their slaves' ties with the homeland, Bulgarians preserved musical forms to maintain links with their past. In both cases

ruling ideologies attached powerful symbolic and psychological meanings to formal elements of musical structure. If one of the things
people operating in culture do is assign meanings to the products and
practices they encounter, then we can conclude that every aspect of
music and its performance is potentially connected to culture and may
therefore change as culture changes.[11]

Having established that, in principle, anything in music can change
as culture changes, as well as the general character of what changed in
Bulgaria, we can ask how and why particular elements were changed
or preserved.

Genre and context before the war in Bulgaria were virtually identical as songs and tunes with distinguishing formal properties were
attached to specific occasions: the harvest, winter dances, leading out
the bride, and so forth. With Communism, genre and context were
pulled apart for a combination of economic and ideological reasons:
genre was preserved and context changed. Some traditional contexts
associated with the agricultural cycle disappeared, first because peasants no longer had an economic interest in ensuring the fertility of
land and animals they no longer owned, and second because the "progressive" ideology of the period forbade their practice as backward
superstition. As genres, however, harvest songs and Easter dance tunes
were maintained in new contexts such as concerts, festivals, competitions, and radio and television broadcasts, first because the latter were
arenas for the newly professionalized, proletarianized, urbanized,
wage-earning village musicians and an intelligentsia of classically
trained composers to make money, and, second, because they preserved acted-out reminiscences and highly edited distillations of a valued national heritage jeopardized by other economic and ideological
projects. It is probably not an exaggeration to say that, in Bulgaria,
economics and ideology, working together at the systemic level, generated the split between genre and context in the course of creating the
new contexts themselves.

Many of the formal elements of Bulgarian folk music, particularly
meters, modes, tune structures, and ornamentation remained largely
intact under the Communists; these, after all, defined the national
style. But certain elements of performance style and technique were
altered as aesthetic ideology conspired with political ideology. From a
political point of view, the prewar folk music tradition was too closely
tied to a supposedly dim, benighted, feudal past believed to be on the
verge of transforming itself into hated capitalism. A peasant had to be
made a "new man" capable of full participation in the Communist vision of the future. Since the precise details of the mechanisms of that

transformation were not spelled out, this left room for an aesthetic intelligentsia to apply its standards to all art, including those of the working classes. In fact, one of the most important actions of these aesthetic ideologues was to resurrect music as art, since, as social practice linked to traditional economic practice, it had been squashed by the state. They decreed that literacy and refined appreciation of great art would help create this new man, and the classicization of the folk tradition was a step on that path.

Thus the style and technique of music changed as part of an ideological plan for the betterment of man. Specifically, instrumental music was 'better organized' [obrabotvan] into regular four- and eight-measure phrases, classical harmonies and counterpoints were added, and notions of absolute pitch and tempered intervals were introduced. Perhaps it could be argued that ideology operated closer to the surface and had a more direct impact on musical style than did economic factors. But we should not forget the economic interest of the composers, conductors, and directors who made substantial livings off the state's commitment to preserving folklore as a nationalistic and educational medium. While economics and ideology didn't operate exactly in concert as they did for context and genre, they interlocked in complex ways to produce the changes, and the conditions for change, in musical style and technique that we observed in this part.

The structure and composition of musical instruments, while partly determined by ideational considerations, were clearly tied, as physical objects, to the ecological and economic conditions necessary to produce them. In Bulgaria before the war, village instruments, even those made by master craftsmen, were limited to materials such as wood, skin, and metal wire that were part of the store of materials available to villagers. When the Communists introduced industrialized manufacture, musical instruments retained most of the traditional materials and forms—even introducing these forms to nontraditional instruments such as bass and cello—as representatives of the national heritage, but produced new, engineered parts, such as metal-and-plastic tuning pegs, to "improve" the functioning of the instruments where they could. Economic conditions also created a new cadre of wage-earning village musicians and thus a market for manufactured instruments. While economic practice opened up the possibilities of change in instruments, an ideology which valued progress and created a need for these musicians influenced the economics of instrument manufacture.

When we consider genre and context, elements and style, and musical instruments, we can talk about preservation of certain features and change of others. The social organization of music changed completely, however, as the social organization of work changed. Just as workers were alienated from their land, specialized musicians were alienated from the audience of which they used to be a part. Just as large collectives of workers subordinated their individual needs to the demands of a centralized economic structure, large, fixed ensembles under the direction of a conductor and artistic director replaced loosely organized and constantly shifting assemblies of family members and neighbors as the locus of music making. What had been somewhat free, improvised, soloistic, individual, and reciprocal in work and music became rigidly formal, manufactured by a disciplined work force of trained musicians performing in the tightest possible coordination under the direction of a conductor. The way musicians organized themselves into groups and how those groups related to audiences was clearly a part of both social organization and economic production. This may be one of the easiest areas for us to find predictable or demonstrable relationships between musical and cultural change.

Finally, the meaning of music, its value to individuals and society, changed substantially after the war for both economic and ideological reasons. As it changed from a pastime into an occupation, it also changed from a matter of strictly local interest to one of national importance. Instead of expressing the tensions and joys of gender relations, it embodied the state's need for discipline, order, cleanliness, and beauty. Rather than marking and commenting on the alternately frosty, muddy, dewy, scorched earth in the cycle of seasons, it symbolized the goals of the state for its citizens in the future, when beauty and cleanliness would reign in place of the drab and difficult life they faced in the present.

This summary of what, why, and how Bulgarian music changed when the Communists took power after World War II suggests the ways music, and therefore musical change, is embedded in economic and ideological systems. The discussion suggests that neither system can be regarded as primary, but that both interlock dialectically to generate musical change. Since music as practiced partakes of both, however, it cannot be regarded as a passive reflection of these larger systems. When people take jobs as musicians, manufacture musical instruments, record old tunes and create new ones, go to concerts and compete in festivals, and assign values and meanings to what they see and hear, their decisions and actions constitute and regenerate the economic and ideological systems themselves.

This summary may overemphasize the systemic nature of musical change, since we learned about internal conflicts between individuals, particularly in the area of value and meaning. Musicians, in particular, as representatives and bearers of the valued past, the ones who could reproduce its meters, tunes, timbres, ornaments, who had experienced its genres and forms *in situ* and who could play its instruments, did not simply abandon their values with respect to style, technique, context, and meaning—although they were happy to give up their opposition to the role of professional musician. Their struggle to maintain the integrity of elements of their tradition was an interesting and psychologically dynamic one, crucial to an understanding of musical experience, even when we focus on systemic change. In part 5, as we learn how Kostadin, Todora, their family, and other Bulgarians continued, advanced, or challenged the changed tradition in succeeding years, individual experience becomes even more important as a key to understanding how and why music changes and does or does not "fill your soul."

Part Five
Continuing the Tradition

That 70-year-old Kostadin Varmezov **is** the Ornette Coleman of
the bagpipe.

Richard Gehr, Village Voice, 1988

NINE

Challenging the Tradition

My personal experience of Bulgaria and its music began in 1969, long after the transformations described in the previous chapter had taken place. But during the twenty years I visited the country, the changes continued, and were particularly striking in the late 1980s during what might be called the Gorbachev era of East European politics and culture. In 1969 I arrived in Bulgaria overland by car from Yugoslavia. At certain points the road through the mountainous terrain was washed out, and we drove through open pastures on our way to an as yet unseen and surely exotic, Shangra-La-like destination. In the 1980s I jetted from major Western European cities into a Sofia of many friends and acquaintances. Obviously Bulgaria had integrated itself more into the modern world in those twenty years, mirroring its move in my consciousness from the exotic to the familiar. In 1969 Bulgaria seemed to my inexperienced and naive eye pristinely beautiful—and perhaps it was. The chauvinistic, yet self-mocking, paean to the local landmarks near Sofia—"There is no mountain higher than Vitosha, no river deeper than the Iskŭr, no plain broader than Sofia's"—possessed a certain poetic verity for me. The water, from spring-fed sources on Mount Vitosha, and the tomatoes, vine-ripened, were the best I had ever tasted. In villages, the roadsides and medians of highways blossomed with flowers, obviously inspired by a latter-day Potemkin, but nonetheless signifying a nation on the move, proud of itself, keeping up appearances. In Sofia, teams of women swept the streets clean by hand, a sign of underemployment but also of the government's vigor, organization, leadership, and sense of purpose.

In 1972 and 1973, Ann, Colin, and I experienced the difficulties of daily life in Bulgaria more vividly and directly, as we lived for more than a year on the local economy. The water, no longer tasty, was piped in from other, less pure, sources, since Vitosha's springs were no longer adequate for Sofia's growing population. Underemployment also meant hopeless inefficiency and long lines for consumers. Although Bulgaria's industrializing economy possessed some first-world trappings, trivial products like safety pins were unknown. Except in intimate work, family, or social circles, workers treated each other and us with an unpleasant combination of suspicion, indifference, and rudeness. Bulgaria's pretty façade hid a society at war with itself, its marvelous instincts and traditions of hospitality, expressive singing and dancing, and hard work frustrated by a political and economic system that rewarded none of those qualities.

Life in the late 1980s was vastly different on the surface from what it had been in the early seventies. Glasnost ['openness'] was on television and the Sheraton Hotel dominated Sofia's central square. Private cars outnumbered state-owned vehicles, and traffic jams and parking problems added to the frustrations of urban life. Uncollected garbage, grit, and dust littered the streets of once-immaculate Sofia, and the countryside had been defiled. The joke was, "There is no river dirtier than the Iskŭr." A green valley in the foothills of the Strandzha Mountains near Rosenovo was scarred by an ugly factory. High-rise apartment complexes and new double-lane highways with overpasses ringed the central city, whose skyline was often obscured by smog as thick as that of Los Angeles. In the twenty years since I had been coming, there had been an obvious decline in both the ability of the state to keep up appearances and in the quality of the environment in which people lived. The Communist government was ruining the country, and, astonishingly, people were now talking openly about it.

While these problems affected all Bulgarians, Muslims living in Bulgaria (ethnic Turks; an estimated 75 percent of Gypsies; and Pomaks, that is, Bulgarian speakers converted to Islam during the Ottoman period) suffered even more profoundly when, in late 1984, the government instituted a repressive program against Bulgaria's ethnic Turks that continued until 10 November 1989, when Todor Zhivkov was removed from office. Apparently concerned that the planned 1985 census would reveal an unacceptably large population of ethnic Turks—an estimated 900,000, or nearly 10 percent of all Bulgarians—the government decreed that all Muslim names would be changed to Christian or acceptably Bulgarian ones, and ceased to recognize Turks as a "national minority," claiming that they were "Islamicized Bulgarians."

Beginning in August 1984, around the town of Stambolovo near Haskovo and eventually spreading to Turkish areas around Razgrad in the north and Kŭrdzhali in the eastern Rhodopes, the government outlawed the most visible and audible expressions of Turkish and Muslim culture in public places, such as wearing *shalvari* (Muslim women's baggy trousers), speaking Turkish, circumcising male children, and playing "Oriental" musical styles and instruments at weddings, family celebrations, and festivals.[1] A newspaper article in November, 1984, condemned these practices and the continuing religious attitudes of Muslims in the face of state atheism as "the extreme aggressiveness of the ideological enemy."[2] Although the government claimed that this forced assimilation was accepted "spontaneously," it was achieved under threat of loss of jobs, internal exile, imprisonment, and even execution. When the Turks staged mass protests in many towns and villages, the army repelled them with force, causing many deaths. This unfortunate turn in Bulgarian policy toward the Turks cast a pall over the country in the late 1980s, and is credited by some as a leading cause of Zhivkov's fall from power.[3]

Life in Bulgaria in 1988 and 1989 seemed headed simultaneously in three directions. First, Communists were still trying to lead, control, and improve the country; some things were getting better: the supply of money and material goods, glasnost, and economic cooperation with American and Japanese firms. Second, in spite of their efforts, things were getting worse. The environment was suffering, food and other basic goods were scarce, and the government's grip on reality, as evidenced by its Turkish policies, was loosening. Third, people were increasingly dissatisfied with the Party's leadership and the decline in quality of life. Individuals and organizations were challenging the state's hegemony, through private enterprise and political opposition.

Not surprisingly, the musical life of the country in the late 1980s was going in the same three directions. The Communists' efforts to "improve" music continued unabated. In spite of improving conditions for a growing segment of the work force—the professional folk artist, whether dancer, singer, musician, director, or choreographer—things were getting worse. Performances and the style itself seemed either stale and little changed since the 1950s and '60s, or even further from people's taste, bedeviled by increasingly dissonant and experimental arrangements. Audiences, always critical, were less and less interested in consuming this product of the state.[4]

By the mid-1980s a third direction, outside the state's direct control, challenged the simultaneous growth and decay fostered by Party policies and practice. People increasingly listened to and admired foreign radio broadcasts from neighboring countries, and paid large sums for Gypsy musicians and others who integrated into their playing those countries' music, modern American styles like jazz and rock, and the musical styles of Gypsy and Turkish minorities. With the increase of personal wealth in the form of savings, the wedding—and other family celebrations such as engagements and the sending off of young men to military service—became ever more important occasions for the economic patronage of musicians, and the economic resources in this music market competed powerfully with state patronage for the loyalty of musicians and influence over the aesthetics of music. Musicians, directly if implicitly, used their music making outside the state's control to agitate for musical change, while intellectuals and ordinary citizens argued for economic and social change. To understand the world in which Kostadin, Todora, and their family made music in the late 1980s, we need to examine in more detail how the increasingly audible wedding music tradition challenged the state's version of tradition and its domination of musical taste.

The Rise of Wedding Music

The state's hegemony in matters of music production and presentation went largely uncontested from the early 1950s to the early 1980s, including the twenty-five years Kostadin worked at Radio Sofia. Although weddings and family gatherings played important roles in people's musical lives during this period, they were made inaudible and invisible at the national level by the state's control of the media of reproduction. When village singers or wedding musicians recorded and broadcasted, the intellectuals of the music establishment always intervened to shape the product into an image appropriate for educating the masses. They transformed whatever was improvisational, rough-edged, and responsive to an expanding aural experience—influences from foreign radio and the increased popularity of Gypsy dance forms such a *kyuchek*—into their idealized image of what 'authentically' represented both the past at the instant it was frozen in the 1950s and the state's image of itself in the present.

Wedding music was a dynamic arena for innovation and change in music, where many players of Western instruments such as clarinet and accordion made their living because folk ensembles insisted on using a purified set of supposedly traditional instruments. Wedding bands, which, since at least the days of the Bistrishka Chetvorka in the 1930s, sometimes included a mix of traditional and Western instruments, were recorded until the late 1980s as either a distinctly traditional or a modern ensemble. When Kostadin's Strandzhanskata Grupa played weddings, they always took an accordion player along, but they never recorded with one.[5]

Similar contrasts existed between the formal organization of state-controlled recordings and live performances at weddings. I remember particularly vividly a wedding in 1969 in which the Gypsy soloists alternately cut into each others solos, the intruder holding a long-held note in the middle of someone's solo, effectively preempting and shutting it off. When someone started a tune the others knew, they jumped in to play it in the middle of the phrase, as soon as they recognized it. The tempos varied in response to the mood and energy of the dancers (CD #39). But the helter-skelter, dynamic quality of these wedding performances never made it out of the recording studio: long-held notes were sometimes used to separate solos in different keys, but never overlapped with another solo; the ensemble tunes were carefully planned and arranged; solos took on the character of memorized tunes, fit into regular four- and eight-measure *kolena;* and tempos were slowed so that everyone could play beautiful, error-free music together for an audience of listeners (CD #40). If Kostadin's problems with the state-created tradition hinged on an invidious comparison between its life in the village in the past and its contemporary manner of presentation, ordinary people surely heard the difference between the exciting music at a wedding and the dry imitation of it on radio and records. Under the system of Communist control of the economy and its attendant institutions, however, there was very little chance for an alternate vision or sound to compete for attention with those created by the state. Predictably, a change in economic practice provided the base for a change in the relative audibility of other musical voices in Bulgaria.

Bulgaria, like the other Eastern European socialist states, was never able fully to proletarianize its population. Spaces were left where individuals, in addition to their state labor, could sell personal services, handmade items, and the products of part-time work. Villagers supplemented their income by raising and selling fruits and vegetables grown in "personal garden plots" or on land rented from collective farms. Intellectuals wrote books and gave lessons in foreign languages, and composers arranged folk songs. As a result of economic reforms begun in the early 1970s, this second economy of petty commodity production and personal services grew to compete with the centrally planned state-socialist sector to form a mixed economy.[6]

Among the occupational groups with the most to gain from this flourishing second economy were musicians, who, throughout the socialist period, were allowed to sell their services to other private indi-

viduals. As the state relaxed controls on this petty form of private enterprise in the 1980s, more and more money flowed into this second
economy, enriching the people who engaged in it in comparison with
those who worked only in the socialist economy. Since the state economy couldn't supply adequate goods for purchase to a society of disciplined savers, people turned more and more to the second economy
as the place to spend their money, and wedding musicians, squarely
positioned there, were among the main beneficiaries.[7]

What kind of music system did this flourishing second economy create? In simplest terms, it generated a music system responsive to economic demands. The best wedding musicians were paid enormous
sums of money in an ostentatious display of wealth by families, many
of them Gypsies, who had made their fortune in the second economy.
The potential for princely patronage from private individuals created
enormous competition among musicians, and the results played themselves out in both the material and structural domains of music. The
increasing amounts of money in the second economy generated an
effective aesthetic challenge to the state's control of music, which had
marginalized and made nearly inaudible a practice close to the hearts
of the people. The important differences between wedding music and
the state's version of *narodna muzika* included (1) new musical instruments, (2) new recording technology, (3) expanded repertoire, (4)
growth in technique and virtuosity, (5) more modern techniques from
jazz and popular music, and (6) more freedom to improvise.

Wedding musicians competed for attention with the musical instruments they bought. Wedding music in the 1980s came to feature the
finest instruments money could buy and international technology provide: French clarinets and saxophones, Italian accordions, American
electric guitars, Japanese synthesizers, and, above all, sound systems.
The best musicians had the best sound systems, undoubtedly a direct,
aural projection and icon of their economic power. One musician told
me, "If you don't have a good, loud sound system, it doesn't matter
what or how you play." In a socialist state whose isolated economy
made it difficult to purchase first-rate equipment from the West, success at acquiring a good sound system also carried with it mildly sub-
versive economic and political implications as well.

The excess money in the second economy, converted on the black
market into hard currency, also bought a new technology on the world
market, the amateur audiocassette recorder. This new device, controlled by individuals rather than the state, recorded what people were
actually hearing at weddings, not what the state wanted them to hear
in the highly produced Balkanton recordings. The second economy

thus provided the means for the circulation of an aesthetic practice
that eventually challenged the state's hegemony in musical ideology
as well.

The repertoire wedding musicians played was dictated by their patrons, the hosts and guests, not the state, and included the folk music
of other ethnic groups in the country such as Gypsies and Turks, and
popular and folk music heard on the radio from Serbia, Macedonia,
Greece, Romania, and Turkey.[8] This mixing of repertoires undercut
the "purity" of folk music presentation on the radio, which served to
defend Bulgarian culture against the feared encroachment of other
cultures.

Competition among musicians for the money in the second economy also led to an enormous growth in playing technique as each musician tried to set himself apart from his peers and thus attract more
and wealthier patrons. The competition and the new technology for
its dissemination then created "stars" who attracted the largest
amounts of money to themselves and conferred the most prestige on
the families who hired them. In the 1980s, the greatest star to emerge
among these wedding musicians was the Gypsy clarinetist, Ibryam Hapazov, who was forced to change his name to Ivo Papazov when the
Bulgarian government ordered Muslims to change their names. An
astonishing musician, Ivo raised the technical level of Bulgarian folk
music to previously unknown heights of virtuosity. Based on a kind of
jazz-folk fusion, he played faster, higher, and more daringly—with
freer improvisation, more modulations, chromaticisms, arpeggios, and
syncopations—than anyone before him. Huge crowds of fans followed
him from wedding to wedding, and every self-respecting clarinetist,
saxophonist, and accordionist in the country tried to imitate his vast
technique and innovative musical ideas.[9] He might not have emerged
as a "star," however, without the freedom, money and attention the
second economy provided him.

The striking new formal elements Ivo and other wedding musicians
introduced into Bulgarian music were the musical equivalent of being
able to buy Western products either on the black market or in
government-run hard-currency stores (CD #41). Both the Western
products and the foreign musical elements carried enormous prestige
in a stagnant economy and political system that generated forty years
of controlled, conservative music. These foreign formal elements were
the new, exciting coin of the second economy's music, for Bulgarians
raised on a steady diet of state-controlled music.

This highly energized musical, aesthetic, and economic system, outside the state's control and led by the stigmatized Gypsy minority, si-

multaneously exercised a powerful attraction on many younger musicians in the music establishment and repelled many of the composers and intellectuals who controlled it. Before we examine those reactions in more detail, however, I describe in the next section three weddings I attended in 1988 to illustrate some of the dynamics at work in actual wedding events.

Wedding Music in 1988

Many of the best wedding musicians and groups lived in or near Plovdiv, Bulgaria's second largest city and, located in Western Thrace, in many ways the geographic symbol of the tension between the previously marginal wedding tradition and Sofia's centralized, state-run music traditions. On one weekend in September 1988, I tagged along with some of the most famous Plovdiv musicians to three weddings, spanning the huge socioeconomic gap between urban Party officials, ordinary villagers, and Gypsies. All the bands contained a mixture of Bulgarian and Gypsy musicians. I describe each event briefly to give some idea of the sound and context of a type of Bulgarian music that developed largely outside the control of the state.

A Bulgarian Village Wedding

For the first wedding, Bulgarian villagers living near Plovdiv hired a band called Trakiitsi [Thracians], led by perhaps the most respected accordionist of the wedding music tradition, Petŭr Ralchev, and a well-known and often-recorded clarinetist, Delcho Mitev. Both had benefited from conservatory training in classical music and brought an enormous technical mastery of their instruments to bear on their performances of wedding music. Both were master improvisors with a more sophisticated chord sense than many wedding musicians. Their style, which included classically influenced tone production, near perfect unison between them, and improvisations with clear melodic shapes within fairly regular phrase structures, placed them fairly close to the state's aesthetic for recorded *narodna muzika*. Yet their technical brilliance and improvisational skills made them respected performers of wedding music.

Communist-era weddings, because of the increased demands on worker productivity, typically lasted little more than a day, starting with a banquet in a restaurant Saturday evening. The banquet I attended was held in a building built especially for weddings called Komsomolska Svatba [Communist-Youth-Organization Wedding], the building an indicator that money was to be made from weddings and that Communists were ready to make it. A special foyer for greeting guests led into a large square room with a dais on one side for the musicians. A raised platform, lined with tables for twelve, ringed the room's other three sides. Long tables lined the main floor, leaving just enough room between them and the raised platforms to dance a quiet *horo* without too much exuberant hopping, stamping, or moving in and out.

The space obviously constrained the movements of the dancers, who this evening danced quietly anyway, perhaps exhausted from a long day's work. Audience requests determined much of what the band played, which included *shlageri* (older pop songs), Serbian, and Macedonian songs. Clearly, Bulgarian folk music did not exhaust the interest of the "folk," and in this context they felt comfortable requesting songs rarely heard on Bulgarian radio. The tips for responding to song requests, instead of going directly to the musicians, went to an emcee acting on behalf of the family to help them pay the tremendous sums the best musicians demanded. As they played, the announcer acknowledged the donors by shouting their names over a microphone along with the request and their greeting to the bride and groom. This patronage of the musicians was so important that it became part of the structure of the performance itself, another line in the texture, often the dominant one. If money talks in many situations, it "sang" in this one. The musicians were not pleased by it, however, and afterward commented on how the distraction prevented them from letting loose in their solos. They stood on the stage for five hours without a break, one *pravo horo* lasting well over an hour.

The most striking feature of the wedding music was not the brilliance of the musicians or the sweetness of the songs, but its loudness. Two soundmen, together with their equipment, came along with the band, their amplifiers turned up to ear-splitting levels. A line in one of Todora's wedding songs speaks of the healing effects of noise at a wedding, but I doubt the elderly villagers had this in mind. They sat in numbed, even sullen, silence as the music blared. Loudness had become an index of modernity, the power of the musicians, and the wealth of their hosts, and not simply a sign of the joy of the wedding celebration.

A Bulgarian Urban Wedding

The second wedding, an urban wedding for a wealthy Party functionary held in the fanciest hotel in Plovdiv, featured Kanarite [The Canaries], one of the best-known wedding bands with a number of influential recordings. Its Gypsy clarinet player, Nesho Neshev, was a young

cousin of Ivo's, but the band's recordings, and this wedding performance, were constrained by the demands and taste of an urban elite.
As the guests assembled for the banquet following the marriage ceremony on Sunday morning, the musicians kept the volume down to a
respectable level and behaved with great discipline, in keeping with
the uptown tone of the event. The leader of the band, Atanas Stoev,
insisted that his musicians arrive sober and on time, clean-shaven and
dressed in white dinner jackets. He didn't allow them to smoke on
stage or drink on the job, two of the musicians' traditional pleasures.
The music was so reserved, so like their recordings in fact, that Nesho
told me, "You won't hear anything today. It's as if you were listening
to classical music. You have to come to a job where I lead. Then you'll
hear something." Although Nesho at one point duplicated Ivo's famous routine of taking one piece at a time off his instrument, first
playing with just one hand on the upper section of the instrument and
eventually playing just the mouthpiece with his hand cupped over the
end, the playing could only be described as competent and sedate.

During the banquet, the band played *shlageri* rather than folk songs,
in a sedate manner that sounded like nothing if not polite, bourgeois
salon music. The music and atmosphere livened up a bit when the
guests started to dance, but the first *horo,* led by the godfather [*kum*],
created a comic air. Although he imitated the style of the dance perfectly and enthusiastically, he neither stepped on the beat nor observed
the simple, three-measure pattern of the dance—a good example of
the tendency, mentioned in chapter 4, to learn style before (and in this
case rather than) structure. Fortunately his wife, the *kuma,* was next to
him in the line and danced well, so the other dancers, after some con-
fusion, smiled indulgently and followed her.

While wedding music functions in the popular imagination as a symbolic alternative to the state's control, this particular wedding illustrated how the state's aesthetic, absorbed by many urbanites and Party
officials, effectively corraled the wilder impulses of gifted Gypsy musicians. This aesthetic was filtered through the economics of patronage.
The musicians knew who was paying their fees, what their tastes were,
and they modified their playing accordingly.

A Village Gypsy Wedding

Later that Sunday afternoon, I attended a Gypsy wedding in a village
outside Plovdiv where I had a chance to observe Gypsy style within the
context of obedience to government regulations concerning its expression. The houses in the Gypsy neighborhood were well kept and new.
Families were bundling up recently harvested crops for market, and

their large brick houses signaled their prosperity. The wedding took place under a ragged tent—set up to protect people from the sun and approximate the ambiance of a town restaurant—with another outstanding band including Yashko Argirov on clarinet and Trifon Trifonov on saxophone, two of the finest soloists on their instruments in the country. They played more aggressively—with more staccato tonguing and freer exploration of the instruments' ranges—than the previous two bands.

Although it was a Gypsy wedding, they obeyed the injunction against Gypsy music current at the time. Instead of the typically solo Gypsy *kyuchek,* a belly-dance-like form in duple meter, the band played and the guests danced *rŭchenitsas,* the Bulgarian solo dance form in seven. Argirov explained that they were forbidden to play "oriental stuff." Later in the evening they played *kyuchek*s, but during the day, when police might be around, the guests danced a Bulgarian repertoire, as prescribed by cultural officials. While the free improvisation of wedding music in some sense stood as a symbol of freedom from government control, the three weddings briefly described illustrate some of the ways that freedom was constrained as musicians tried to please particular audiences in particular circumstances.

The Interpretation and Control of Wedding Music

The extraordinary financial and aesthetic success of wedding musicians in the 1980s, coupled with a cultural policy that suppressed expression by the Gypsy and Turkish Muslim minorities, created a need, felt by some in the cultural establishment, to attempt to control wedding musicians through auditions and registration. At least four issues interlocked in complex ways: nationalism, ethnicity, money, and freedom.

First, Bulgarian *narodna muzika,* as controlled and supported by the state, existed to exemplify, confirm, and celebrate Bulgarian national identity.[10] Wedding musicians challenged that constructed identity by playing what Bulgarians wanted to hear, which included music from all over the Balkans, especially Turkey, Greece, Yugoslavia, and Romania.[11]

Second, under the state's control, Gypsy and Turkish musicians were required to record 'pure' Bulgarian music and suppress both style and repertoire expressive of their ethnicity. At Turkish and Gypsy weddings, however, they expressed that ethnicity, challenging the state's monocultural ideology.

Third, before the 1980s, the state was able to force musicians to hew to the party line on folk music by co-opting them with money. Whereas after the war state-supported music became a better alternative than wedding music as a source of income, by the 1980s wedding musicians made more than state- supported musicians; the private music market challenged the state as the sole patron of music and arbiter of taste.

Fourth, wedding musicians, free of the state's control, acted as a thorn in the side of an establishment that thrived on control.[12] In fact, from the state's aesthetic point of view, wedding musicians' playing style—with the clarinet's high pitch and the undanceable tempos— must haved seemed a parody of *narodna muzika* as presented by the state.

During the late 1980s, wedding music became a primary domain where issues of ethnicity and freedom of expression intersected and could be contested. The performance style and repertoire contrasted in every conceivable way from the standard practices of recorded folk music. Semiotically, this contrast sets up the possibility of meaning and of variable interpretations. At one level, the Gypsies' daring improvisations and refusal to adhere to the constraints of *narodna muzika,* whether in form or nationalistic content, could be read as simply good Gypsy music. They played as they said, 'with gusto' [*s hŭs,* from a Turkish word, *hız,* meaning 'speed, velocity, rush, impetus, dash, elan' (Redhouse 1968)]. At another level, especially given the tense political climate in the country over the issue of Muslim rights and expression, their playing could also be read as a political statement: the improvisations iconically representing personal freedom from government control; the staccato style expressing an aggressive hostility to the state and its 'sweet' music; and the choice of repertoire proclaiming their existence as identifiable minorities at a time when the government was trying to deny their existence.

One musician, a Bulgarian who played accordion in both the state-run and wedding spheres, confirmed part of this reading. He told me, "Music is, in essence, freedom." In fact, it matters little what Gypsy musicians consciously intended or could verify verbally; their interpretation is only part of the story. Government authorities and ordinary listeners constructed their own readings. Many Bulgarian musicians interpreted the wildest Gypsy playing as 'empty' [*prazno*]; lacking the 'sweet' tunes, ornaments, and slower tempos of Bulgarian music, it was incapable of "filling their souls." These aesthetic judgments may also have masked envy and condescending attitudes towards Gypsies.

Government officials explicitly constructed a political interpretation of Gypsy performances in a series of regulations and in festivals designed to assert control even over musical freedom. They seem to have heard in wedding musicians' performances of Bulgarian music unacceptable parodies of the state's versions of folk music and to have interpreted the playing of Gypsy tunes in Turkish-influenced styles as a refusal to acquiesce in the state's nationalist, anti-Muslim policies. In an environment oppressive toward Muslim minorities in the 1980s, it didn't behoove anyone, even the controllers, to talk openly about the world this expressive, aggressive playing referenced. But music made its point in its own, seemingly innocuous way. Under the circumstances, it was easy to read wedding music as an inarticulate, nonverbal, musically stylized, iconic cry for the freedom to live in some kind of acceptable accommodation with a sluggish bureaucracy that stifled both economic initiative and the ethnic identity of Gypsies and Turks.

The wedding musicians' challenge to the state's hegemony in matters of musical performance, taste, and representation of ethnicity resulted in an ill-conceived and ultimately fruitless attempt to control and tax wedding musicians, instituted in the mid-1980s. An intellectual in the music establishment explained the state's position to me: "Hiring the best orchestra is now a matter of prestige, and the tips are enormous. These are gifted musicians. But in 1987 they tried to control these musicians, by asking them to submit a list of all the songs and pieces they play. Ordinary people are enraptured by their [Gypsy] music, and Serbian, Greek, Romanian, and Turkish music is popular. This music replaces Bulgarian music, and so asking them for lists may cause them to learn more Bulgarian repertoire."

Wedding musicians were required to appear before a panel of auditioners and demonstrate that they could play local Bulgarian repertoire competently. If they were poor musicians by the state's standards, or if they only knew Turkish or Gypsy repertoire, they were not licensed and, thus, technically forbidden to play weddings. The intellectual continued, "Of course, I have no illusions. Those who are forbidden to play continue to do so parasitically. But they don't have a right to play. We want them to refuse to play Turkish music, but they do it anyway." His comments illustrated that ethnicity's challenge to Bulgarian nationality was one of the main irritants. He continued, "Ivo Papazov, for example, has the status of a rock star. These Gypsies are rich, but they don't have a stable moral basis. This music cannot be valued. It is a contemporary modification of folklore and exists in the customs of the people. It is not serious art with high presentational demands."

Once again, as in earlier justifications of arranged folklore, urban intellectuals imposed an aesthetic argument—the concept of art—on village tradition in order to justify policies rooted in nationalism, ethnic prejudice, economics, and the need to control. They also clearly believed that folklore as serious art was more valuable than folklore as "customs of people."

In addition to trying to identify, weed out, and scare musicians who did not play Bulgarian music the right way, the auditions and the new practice of monitoring wedding musicians were blatant attempts to get in on the action, as the local "concert direction," an organization that sponsored concerts, taxed players on their income at weddings. At the audition, a jury classified each band as first, second, or third category. According to this classification, band members were paid either 60, 55, or 50 *leva*, respectively, for six hours at a wedding, absurdly small sums given that the best musicians made hundreds of *leva*, and an insignificant difference for all the effort and administration that went into the classification process. It was clearly an effort, not at consumer protection, as the intellectual claimed, but at control and taxation. The district "concert direction" collected 25 percent of the fee, and the jury was paid for its time, and probably bribed as well. A folklorist told me, "Some people have the illusion that they can control things, and at the same time they profit from the act of controlling."

Kostadin's nephew Ivan, himself a gaidar with his own wedding band, complained, "Why should they tax me? They don't get the job. They don't pay my gas. They don't provide the repertoire." He thought he had the answer: "They [the concert direction in each province] need the money. There is a director, an assistant director, a musicologist, an assistant musicologist, a 'helper' for the local village ensembles, two accountants, two cashiers—maybe thirty people." And he was referring to just one province. Each province had a similar apparatus of control, an illustration of how the state bureaucracy and its needs became the raison d'être for its own continuance, obliterating whatever goals for society it might have had.

While the attempt at taxation and control was mildly amusing for outside observers and slightly annoying for musicians, its application in other sectors of the economy, such as manufacturing and agriculture, was disastrous.

Stambolovo: A Festival of Control

As the state thrust its tentacles into every local wedding, it also sought to exercise control at the national level in a tried-and-true way, by means of the competitive festival.[13] State functionaries co-opted what apparently had begun as a local festival of Thracian wedding musicians and changed it into a national festival with a series of regional eliminations, each level judged by a panel of judges to ensure authenticity, quality, and adherence to centralized standards. I attended the third such festival [*sŭbor*] on 16–18 September 1988. There I had the opportunity to observe directly the conflict of values and the various interpretations surrounding wedding music: the state's values versus people's values; the state's notion of 'pure,' regionally differentiated folk style versus a wedding-music style whose popularity might eliminate those differences; the political connotations of the music; and how these conflicts were expressed in musical style.

According to the local organizers, the festival was originally the idea of the local cultural committee in the town of Haskovo, which sought to celebrate the growing popularity of wedding music, many of whose best performers were from nearby towns. One member of the local 'committee for spiritual growth' told me, "This is an area which is a center for [wedding] music. We wanted to provide people with something that would interest them," namely good local Thracian wedding music. The committee chose the nearby village of Stambolovo as the site, and held the first festival in 1984. The festival proved so successful that by 1988 it had been "nationalized," controlled by the central "concert direction" in Sofia, and augmented by preliminary regional festivals all over the country. By taking control of the festival and its aesthetics, the state apparatus tried to alter, defuse, and diminish the anti-establishment challenge of wedding music.

The control and the attempt to alter the meaning of the music began with its name, "The Third National Meeting of Instrumental Groups of Bulgarian Folk Music" [*Tretata natsionalna sreshta na instrumentalni grupi na bŭlgarska narodna muzika*]. In fact, although it was billed as a "meeting of instrumental groups" and of "folk music," these were wedding bands, each group including at least one singer, as wedding bands must. By erasing any mention of wedding music and substituting *narodna muzika*, the national organizers tried to defuse the oppositional character of wedding music, eliminating its name and merging it with the state-controlled category.

The presence of a jury of well-known musicians, scholars, and organizers within the musical establishment helped to ensure presentations that fit the state's aesthetic requirements and notions of folk music. On Friday, the first evening of the festival, the jury was introduced to the audience. Headed by Manol Todorov, musicologist and professor at the Sofia Conservatory and the leader of the program to control wedding music, it included Todor Dzhidzhev, another musicologist from Sofia, and Petko Radev, the famous folk and classical clarinetist. When the jury's names were read to the crowd, only the latter's was recognized and drew enthusiastic applause from the audience of tens of thousands that had gathered in a huge, amphitheater-shaped field outside Stambolovo.

Under the jury's influence, what had begun as a celebration of the efflorescence of Thracian wedding music became a national display of regional styles, the integrity of which was part of the establishment's view of 'pure' folklore. In this view, one of the indexes of its purity was its differentiation by region: Thrace, *Shop*, Rhodope, Dobrudzha, Pirin, and North Bulgaria. Town music, popular music, and wedding music tended to elide regional differences and thus were indexes of modernization and the death of folk music, and had to be resisted. By nationalizing the festival as a display of regional difference, the organizers symbolically reversed the homogenizing effect of wedding music.

Regional competitions were held to select the best two groups to perform at Stambolovo (a pattern used for Koprivshtitsa, the national festival of village folklore groups sponsored by 'artistic amateurism'). Each band was required to play their own local dance tunes and songs, rather than Thracian repertoire, and they were specifically forbidden to play foreign tunes popular at weddings all over the country. The improvisations so characteristic of wedding music were allowed only after the band had demonstrated its knowledge of local tunes.

This insistence on regional content made the festival concerts colorful and varied, but diminished the overall effect of the wedding music challenge, which was encoded in the sonic icon of virtuosic improvisation in the manner of Ivo. The hallmarks of regional style included the use by a group from the Rhodopes of a *kaba* [low-pitched] gaida;[14] a brass band from Northwest Bulgaria; Romanian-style fiddling from North Bulgaria; Macedonian and *Shop* songs. A number of Thracian groups, such as the well-known Kazarevska Grupa, combined gaida, kaval, and clarinet and accordion to good effect. Since the strongest players in the new wedding band tradition came from Thrace, many in the audience complained that weaker groups had been invited simply because they were the best from their region, and consequently many deserving Thracian groups were absent. But that didn't trouble the organizers. They had transformed the festival from a display of the anarchic virtuosity of wedding bands into a representation of national cultural heritage in all of its 'authentic' regional variety.

The two competing aesthetic positions, patronized respectively by the state and by the second economy, were clearly audible at Stambolovo—sometimes in different groups, sometimes within the same group.

In the government-sanctioned category the groups played with

Western-style tone quality, moderate volume, tight rhythmic and melodic unison, moderate tempos, all conspiring to create a relatively
'sweet' sound. The tunes and improvisations, while including some
modern, wedding-music elements such as chromaticisms and arpeggi-
ations, were generally restricted to four- and eight-bar phrases. The
playing displayed self-control and self-discipline, precisely the qualities
the state wanted in its workers. Although the musicians regarded their
music as technically advanced over the playing of older musicians like
Kostadin, aesthetically it was a slightly modernized version of the style
he learned, perfected, and recorded at Radio Sofia.

The "non-sweet" sound of the anti-hegemonic style displayed more
staccato articulation, louder and harsher tone qualities (the latter
achieved by, for example, putting the microphone in the bell of the
clarinet rather than near one of the holes along its length), and unfettered improvisation ranging wildly over the whole range of the instrument; breaking the bounds of conventional four- and eight-bar phrase
structures; and changing keys frequently and unpredictably.

A typical performance lasted about twenty minutes and began with
a 'sweet' local song or two, played at danceable tempos, followed by a
series of instrumental dance tunes typical of the region, and ending
with improvisations that broke the mold of recorded arrangements
and moved into the domain of wedding music proper. However, some
groups, particularly those that played for Gypsy and Turkish weddings, dispensed with the sweet aesthetic all together and played with
hŭs, from the beginning of their performances to the end.

While the two styles in evidence could be viewed simply as competing aesthetic takes on tradition, one from the Bulgarian, the other
from a Gypsy, point of view, the judgments of the jury suggested that
the performances were being interpreted politically as well. The jury
clearly wanted to control the anti-hegemonic style by juxtaposing it
with the Radio aesthetic and reducing its overall proportion in the
festival. One of the groups at the festival, Trakiitsi, featuring the widely
respected Delcho Mitev and Petŭr Ralchev, was received rather coldly
by the audience. Classically trained, they produced some of the most
complex, sophisticated music at the festival, but their precise, clean-
toned style wasn't as popular with the audience as the freer, harsher
playing of other groups. When the audience, made up of many Turks
and Gypsies as well as ethnic Bulgarians, reserved their loudest applause for the wildest improvisations, it became obvious that a gap existed between their aesthetics and that of the government-controlled
jury. A musicologist told me, "[the jury's] ideal is the radio style, while
most people want to hear something new." But in order to be selected

for the national festival, the bands had to perform their acquiescence to the state's control; they did this in order to add to their renown and eventually their fees as well.

Even within the confines of the festival, a number of bands performed with enough *hŭs* to inflame the jury, and the metaphor they used to describe it revealed the style's political connotation for them. On more than one occasion the jurors complained that the playing of the groups best-loved by the audience was 'aggressive' [*agresivno*], implying a challenge to prevailing aesthetic, cultural, and political rule, and it made them very angry. One of the best groups that day was from the town of Shumen, an area heavily populated by Turks. They played the most wildly, with a very loud, staccato, metallic sound (CD #42), creating the very antithesis of a 'sweet,' controlled, Radio sound. One member of the jury told me that this group was actually cut at the regional level because of its aggressive playing, but was reinstated when it was argued that they were simply too good, and it would be a scandal if they were rejected.

Although I wasn't present at any of the regional competitions, the rejection of good groups for their failure to conform was probably not an isolated occurrence. One musicologist who attended many of them felt that the best groups often did not make it to Stambolovo. The jury, when it acted to ban aggressive groups or failed to give them prizes, made a connection between the ethnic tensions in the region and the frenetic playing style of these Turkish Gypsy musicians. In hermeneutic terms, they interpreted the music as referencing the world of ethnic unrest in the country, and they used the same metaphor, 'aggressive,' to describe both musical and Muslim religious and cultural practices.

The highlight of the festival was supposed to be Saturday evening, when the winners of the previous festival—Ivo Papazov, the god of the clarinet, and Ivan Milev, a wild-looking, bearded accordion player—performed.[15] To my surprise, they did not seem to be much better than the rest of the musicians, many of whom had caught up to Ivo's innovations, spurred by the competition for high-paying wedding gigs. Even more interesting was that, while everyone awaited Ivo's performance in almost excruciating anticipation, he was not particularly well received. Ivo was fascinated by a blend of folk and jazz elements that Bulgarians called "folk jazz."[16] Some of his and his band's tunes and improvisations strayed very far from Bulgarian models, and that did not please the audience, who whistled their disapproval through much of his performance. Ivo opened his set with bebop-like tunes, and some of the soloists abandoned the Bulgarian model entirely. What the crowd clearly responded to best were virtuosic solos in a style that combined Bulgarian, Turkish, and Gypsy elements; they had not caught up to Ivo's latest jazz-oriented innovations yet. But Ivo was undeterred and determined to continue to lead Bulgarian music down challenging new paths of experimentation.

After the festival, Manol Todorov appeared on television for a brief interview about Stambolovo. Estimating the size of the crowd at 100,000, he cited the number of young people at the Festival as evidence of its success, and said that the main contribution of these wedding orchestras was to preserve authentic folk tunes in a manner attractive to young people. (Of course, young people didn't care about "preserving authentic folk tunes." They responded to the aggressive adventuresomeness of the playing style, which expressed freedom from government control, and not to the content.) The other goal of the festival, Todorov said frankly, was "to eliminate foreign elements from our neighbors in the music, and we have completely succeeded"—at least at the festivals. A musicologist told me about one musician who was incensed by his rejection at a regional competition. He complained to the jury while Ivo was standing within earshot: "'Why did you reject me? I play Ivo's repertoire as well as he does.' Ivo interjected, 'Yes, but I know when to play it.'"

As Ivo understood perfectly, this public festival, where government minions tried to present an approved picture of Bulgarian musical culture, was not the time to play Gypsy and Turkish music. At local, private events, like weddings, people could do more or less what they wanted; try as it might, the government simply could not control everything. At this festival, the enthusiastic, enraptured response of the crowd to the solo improvisations made it clear that the differences between wedding-music style and state-sponsored folk music, especially the former's improvisational freedom and aggressive, staccato loudness, were interpreted as icons of the freedom that everyone sought and the hostility they felt toward the government and its bankrupt policies. Because music, as opposed to song texts, has no obvious content, but is mainly style, it couldn't be objected to on openly political grounds. Its political meaning was expressed in the aesthetics of performance and then opposed aesthetically in the metaphors of judgment. But some of these metaphors, especially the adjective 'aggressive,' helped to reconnect the domains of politics and music. The music's stylistic and improvisational freedom was understood by many in the audience as an expression of freedom from control and thus functioned as a political statement. Manol Todorov and his juries certainly understood it that way as well, and that was partly why they tried to control it.

The State's Response to the Challenge

In addition to using festivals and juries to control wedding music, the state's institutions of music—the ensembles, radio and television programming, and Balkanton, the recording company—also responded by translating and co-opting some elements of wedding music into their own playing style and productions. They knew they were fighting a losing battle with public opinion and reception if they didn't begin to change in some ways. Significantly, the state's own trained musicians found themselves unavoidably drawn to the domain of wedding music as a source of new ideas.

The Ensemble Response

Ensemble music, as the archetypal purveyor of the state's aesthetic position, was extremely conservative. What began to happen in the 1980s, however, was that younger arrangers and composers, influenced by the popularity of Gypsy music, occasionally inserted Gypsy elements into their melodies, producing in the process music Gypsy musicians had been punished for. This angered older musicians, who interpreted these efforts not as an attempt to make folk-orchestra music more palatable for the fans of Gypsy music but as yet another failure on composers' parts to understand deeply the essence of 'pure' Bulgarian music.

At a rehearsal of the Radio Sofia folk orchestra in 1988, I sat next to Stoyan Velichkov as they rehearsed a piece called *Cherkeska* by a "new composer." Stoyan was openly hostile to it, and when I asked him what the piece was, he answered derisively that it was a *kyuchek,* the Gypsy solo dance. By giving *kyuchek* a different name, composers, protected by government sponsorship, were able to broadcast a type of music that, because of its association with Gypsy culture, was banned for a time in most public settings. Ivo, the story goes, was even imprisoned for playing it. Stoyan was also contemptuous of the arrangement. The tunes were pedestrian and he said, "There is nothing inside. A folk musician would never do something like this. This is why people don't like to listen to the radio."

Referring to a particular melody with long notes uncharacteristic of Bulgarian music, Stoyan said, "Istanbul! Pure Turkish. My *Cherkeska* is more Bulgarian."[17] He found it ironic and worthy of comment that the Turkishisms forbidden to clarinet players were allowed when played on traditional instruments. In his view, either this was hypocritical or the composers simply didn't know better. Thus, the radio ensemble, using sanctioned, trained composers who gave the tunes Bulgarian genre-names and surrounded them with the harmonic trappings of Western music, began to present a style that earned many Gypsy musicians the anger and reprisals of authorities.

Although widespread dissatisfaction with arranged folklore characterized even its earliest days, by 1988 whatever vitality it once possessed seemed to have been largely drained away—save, ironically, for the revivification it received through the popularity of the *Le Mystère des voix bulgares* recordings. One director at the radio tried to rationalize its lack of appeal in practical terms. "The problem today is that we have quantity but not quality. Today there are maybe twenty-two professional folklore ensembles. The first two or three conquered their audiences. The performances were good and people were proud to see their folklore so beautifully presented on stage. But now there are a tremendous number of performers for a small number of composers and their works, and that has destroyed the genre."

While overuse and imaginative stagnation were undoubtedly contributing factors to its decline in popularity, they don't account completely for the alienation many people felt toward this style of music making. The music had been constructed to stand symbolically for the state, and people's dissatisfaction with the state was expressed, among other ways, by their distaste for this kind of music. But the other side of the coin was that, since the Communists partly succeeded in turning rural peasants into urban proletarians, the "folk" no longer wanted to work the land or listen to folk music in any form. Its oldest forms seemed too primitive and the new ones were too closely allied with the state and its inadequacies. The new industrialized class of Bulgarians preferred modern music, particularly jazz and rock but also the music of other, supposedly freer countries, to the music sponsored and produced by their own state.

The Radio Response

Radio programmers faced the challenge of the popularity of foreign and Gypsy music every day. In the countryside, I constantly heard radios tuned to Serbian, Macedonian, Greek, or Turkish stations that broadcast their own modernized versions of folk and folk-derived music, which were less controlled by the state and certainly less influenced by a Western classical music aesthetic.[18] The tuning out of Bulgarian radio in favor of foreign stations was a political as well as a musical act. In doing so, people not only failed to attend to an icon of Bulgarian national identity, they missed the news and other forms of political propaganda interspersed between music programs.

Whether popular or not, the radio had little choice but to continue to present arranged folklore, because it represented the official image of Bulgarian nationality developed during the early years of the Communist period. Grozdan Hristozov, the head of folk music at Radio Sofia, said, the Radio is "an educational institution." It couldn't abandon its standards and political message even if people no longer wanted to hear them. He recognized the problem they had attracting youth to listen to arranged folk music, and the competition provided by foreign music coming in over the airwaves, but acknowledged that it was impossible to make borders impermeable to that kind of infiltration.

The Balkanton Response

The state record company, Balkanton, also felt pressure from a public increasingly interested in alternatives to decades of similar productions. They, however, believed themselves better able to respond to "market demand" and less restricted by an educational mandate. Originally an outgrowth of Radio Sofia called *Radioprom* [short for 'radio productions'], the company later changed its name to Balkanton, but the connection to the Radio, its performers, composers, and conductors, and its aesthetics remained strong.[19] Rumyana Tsintsarska, a director of folk music at Radio Sofia, made a distinction between the radio and recording company based on educational versus commercial goals. According to her, the radio had a greater responsibility both to the state and the people because the listener had no choice. The radio broadcast what the state wanted people to hear, whereas Balkanton "is a commercial enterprise. Fans can choose to buy or not to buy." This distinction based on choice overlooked the fact that both enterprises made decisions partly influenced by a commonly shared aesthetic of what was appropriate for people to hear.

To keep up with changing tastes, Balkanton began in the 1980s to change its approach. To appeal to youth, they released records of younger musicians after years of recording only established performers like Kostadin: Ivan and Tsvetanka Varimezovi (Kostadin's nephew and niece); the sisters Biseri; Lyubomir Vladimirov, a tambura player; and two young male singers, Todor Kozhuharov and Krasimir Stanev. To reach a more youthful audience, Balkanton released a record in 1989 called *Folklorna Diskoteka*, folk music arranged in a pop style using synthesized accompaniments by the composer Dimitŭr Penev, who began his career arranging for the radio orchestra of folk instruments. The modern trappings, including funky bass and drum machine, couldn't hide the 'sweet,' 'arranged' character of the production (CD #43). It was unlikely to attract the audience that "died" for wedding music, although it may have interested briefly a young, urban audience. Balkanton also released 'recital albums,' a telling classicization, by the stars of wedding music, including Ivo, Petŭr Ralchev, Kanarite, and others. But the aesthetics of the Radio dominated, and the musicians were forced to perform at slow tempos, sometimes with the addition of string parts, in a sweet style bearing little resemblance to the way they played at weddings.

Balkanton also tried to increase its impact by improving its distribution system, which worked mainly through the orders of regional bookstore managers from an organization called Creative Economic Combine. Lili Hristozova, Balkanton's folk music editor and the wife of Radio Sofia's folk music director, explained, "Four times a year we meet with them and play for them our suggestions. They decide what number of records they want. In that firm there are some who know quite a lot, but others are not very objective." Thus production was tied not to public demand but to the sales estimates of store managers who were necessarily conservative. And when records sold well and ran out, there was no mechanism for reissuing or reordering them, no market surveys, and Balkanton had very little leeway to estimate its own markets and control its own production. To solve this problem Balkanton created and ran two 'company stores' in Sofia, but, as Hristozova said, "we want one in each province. Then we will have a bit of independence. We know what is wanted in each region." She hoped this new system "probably will have an effect on what is made, for example, perhaps more wedding groups will be recorded."

Hristozova had some difficulty reconciling the competing dictates of good taste—as defined by composers who controlled the recording industry—and commercial success, reflected in record sales. "For many people who weren't interested in folklore, we hope they will be drawn to [folk disco] music. Youth already is drawn to this music by wedding music." Thus she tacitly acknowledged that the music of classical composers, with its supposedly high artistic standards, had largely alienated a mass audience, and recourse to popular forms might be necessary to save the nationalist agenda and rescue folk music from its classically minded purveyors.

Perhaps most significantly, Hristozova was not willing to argue that wedding music or folk disco lacked artistic quality. Like many who join this argument in the West, she tried to justify popular music forms by arguing that they contain the same properties classical and classicized folk music have always claimed for itself, namely, artistic value: "The basic goal is the artistic value of the material. We cannot separate ourselves from the educational goals of the Radio. But we can't believe that the mass of Bulgarian people has no taste. I believe that if people like it, then it has some value." This seemed to be the beginning of an attempt to separate herself and the record company from too close an adherence to the views of composers and intellectuals who controlled culture for so long and who believed that the masses lacked taste and that it must be developed. But by 1988 there was a growing recognition that the composers' work had not increased either villagers' or urbanites' respect for or interest in folk music on this higher artistic plane. The people possessed taste in folk music, they knew good performers and good performances when they heard them, and what they got on radio and on record for the most part didn't correspond to that taste. One musician, who played both in the Radio Sofia orchestra and in a restaurant band that performed requests for Gypsy and foreign tunes, told me with a smile, "The people don't like people's music" [*naroda ne obicha narodna muzika*]. It was ironic that in a 'people's republic' [*narodna republika*] it should take so long for the people to assert themselves, but, on the other hand, the control of folk music was part of the centralization of authority characteristic of the entire political and economic system during the Communist era.

In this chapter I described how wedding music challenged the way the Communists reproduced and represented Kostadin's and other village traditions and how state institutions responded to that challenge. In the next chapter, I turn to individual responses to both the Communist construction and the wedding-music deconstruction of tradition. I examine the processes of growth, decay, and agitation for change in music that I identified in this chapter as they were experienced by a number of individuals—Kostadin, Todora, their family and friends, and a new generation of gaidari—trying to make music in a meaningful way in the summer of 1988.[20]

TEN

Gaidari: The Next Generation

Although individual musicians and listeners operate within force-fields created by the tug of politics, economics, aesthetics, and tradition, those forces determine neither musical practice, interpretations of musical meaning, nor emotional responses to music. Rather, individuals create, interpret, and give meaning to musical practice and its products as they weave music into "webs of significance" that join music to the fabric of everyday life.[1] The interpretations, practices, and emotions individuals generate are not unconstrained, however. To be taken seriously, that is, to be interpreted socially, they must resonate in a truthful way either with conditions as they exist or with an imagined life that responds meaningfully to current conditions. In this chapter, from among all posible musical experiences in Bulgaria in the late 1980s, I examine those with a direct link to Kostadin: in this case, the next generation of gaidari, including Kostadin's nephew, Ivan Varimezov.

Advancing the Tradition

The younger generation of professional gaidari, those in their thirties in the 1980s, grew up under the influence of Kostadin, their teachers at the music schools, and the state's musical aesthetics. In the 1980s, they were also buffeted by the economic and aesthetic power of wedding music. As they responded to the latest musical developments in both arranged folklore and wedding music, they projected a strong, positive belief that the Bulgarian music tradition in general and gaida playing in particular were progressing and advancing.

As the artistic linchpin of a segment of these advances, Ivo Papazov's music tempted a whole generation of younger musicians, including those who played traditional instruments, to follow him into an unprecedented fire of innovation and technical virtuosity. Many older musicians like Stoyan Velichkov hated to see young musicians imitate Ivo because of the distance he put between himself and tradition. Stoyan told me, "Young musicians are very good, all things considered. There are many fine players. But they lack a strong foundation in the old way. They don't want to play like their grandfathers or even their fathers. They follow a single person—Ivo Papazov. We musicians say, 'A Gypsy has mixed up Bulgarian folk music completely.'"

Stoyan's complaint invokes the Bulgarian patriarchal ideology of the 1930s at a time when contemporary economics and Ivo's artistry fueled a challenge to patriarchally enforced and patrilineally transmitted tradition.

Wedding music's widespread dissemination by means of privately made cassettes and the almost legendary status of its main star, Ivo Papazov, enabled it to compete with arranged or authentic folklore for the attention and allegiance of young gaidari and other musicians training in the state's folk music high schools and Institute. With increasing amounts of money flowing into wedding music and the growing public demand for free-wheeling improvisation and displays of technique, the abstract claims for the authenticity and artistic value of 'pure' Bulgarian music by the state's folklore advocates increasingly fell on deaf ears. The realities of the market, where wedding musicians became richer than state-supported musicians in folk ensembles, drowned out the grumbling of teachers and critics who, at least in the early 1980s, labeled wedding music 'cheap'—the irony of the label presumably lost on them—and dismissed it as 'kitsch.' The best and most famous wedding musicians commanded huge sums of money, naturally tempting many young players of traditional instruments to join them.

While the folk music schools' purpose was to foster the preservation of Bulgarian folklore as understood by academics and the "culture establishment" and defend it against both external and internal challenges, the students at these schools heeded the siren call of wedding music and found ways to imitate Ivo and other famous wedding musicians. Instructors and directors at the Kotel school fought a holding action—as the director told me, "We try to preserve the border between folk and classical instruments"—but their students gobbled up the latest cassette recordings of live wedding performances. While studying traditional technique on the gaida, the more advanced players imitated Papazov's chromatic runs and arpeggios, transposed sections of tunes that outran the range of the gaida to fit its range of a ninth, and played in keys and modes previously foreign to the gaida. Some students abandoned everything but a pretense of studying their traditional instrument and practiced outside of class on a Western instrument with more potential in the wedding market. A musician friend from Plovdiv told me that, although he majored in kaval at Kotel, he spent most of his time at school practicing accordion. After graduation he played accordion professionally for ensemble dance rehearsals and weddings, and never played kaval. Two students in Kotel's graduating class of 1988, educated in the state's version of folklore but attracted to the new developments, criticized both: "The old way is too colorless," but the playing of Ivo "lacks musical content. It is mainly for show." They hoped to integrate the excesses of Ivo into the aesthetics of the folk tradition as they had learned it. Young musicians sought ways to accommodate and synthesize the competing aesthetic and economic claims of these two competing traditions.

Although the purpose of the schools was to train cadre for the folk music establishment, many students rejected jobs with ensembles upon graduation. Because of the new economic power of the second economy, musicians made more money playing at weddings or in folkloric shows for tourists in major cities and the Black Sea resorts than in professional ensembles. Lili Tabakova explained, "The problem today is that many musicians don't want to work with ensembles because in the restaurants they pay more and the musicians only have to know five dances. In the ensembles they have to know 30 or 40 pieces by memory." She also alluded to the often superior technical ability of wedding musicians compared to ensemble musicians and attributed it to demands of repertoire: "[A wedding musician may have only] 10 or 15 pieces on which he improvises and becomes a virtuoso. Musicians outside the ensembles can play only what they want to and what shows their technique to good effect."

While this is an interesting justification and rationalization of the supposed artistic superiority of ensemble music, wedding musicians, in fact, had to know a large repertoire of locally popular songs and be able to respond to a continuous series of requests. If they played outside the local area, they needed to know an even greater variety of regional dance tunes plus a non-Bulgarian repertoire—Greek, Turkish, Gypsy, Macedonian, Serbian—another thorn in the side of the traditionalists.

In order to understand in a more detailed way the maneuvering of younger musicians caught in the musical, economic, political and aesthetic web of the 1980s, I interviewed and recorded three young professional gaidari: Dimitŭr Todorov, Kostadin's student with the Kutev ensemble; Maria Stoyanova, the first professional female gaidar, who acknowledged the impact of Kostadin's recordings on her playing style; and Encho Pashov, who learned Kostadin's recorded repertoire and style almost of necessity, then rejected it in favor of his own synthesized style. Their stories illustrate the interplay between musical style and practice and economic and institutional life.

Dimitŭr Todorov

Dimitŭr Todorov, Kostadin's student with the Kutev ensemble, played at weddings and adapted his technique to keep pace with new developments in wedding music. Although Kostadin taught him initially, his development as a musician continued, and he acknowledged the influence of other players: "I wasn't satisfied with the simple way. That is my talent, besides the soul [in my playing]. I take material from all musicians in the end." Here he was referring to clarinet and accordion players in the wedding music tradition. "But everything I play on the gaida, its style and ornamentation, I play with Varimezov's ornaments. I couldn't have learned better [from anyone else]. One does not play from education," a reference to his lack of schooling at Kotel. "One plays from the fingers and the heart"—an illustration of the use of body metaphors discussed in chapter 5.

Todorov explained that he and other younger players tried to play in every key on the gaidanitsa, following the model of the clarinet. Some of these keys rested on pitches that barely sound on the gaida. When I asked whether he could play in d♯'/e♭', a traditionally nonexistent pitch between the two lowest holes of the chanter, he was undaunted. "I can play the note by squeezing the bag [*meh*, lit. 'soft'], but it won't be very clear." Even the gaida's limited range and its consequent inability to play wide-ranging clarinet and accordion tunes posed no problem for him: "I play tunes of more than an octave by transposing them. The gaida is a skin saxophone. There is no ceiling on this instrument."

In calling the gaida a skin saxophone, Dimitŭr acknowledged the powerful attraction, growing aesthetic hegemony, and supposed technical superiority of modern Western instruments over 'pure,' 'authentic,' 'traditional' Bulgarian instruments. Whereas the state had elevated traditional instruments and instrumentalists to positions of high prestige as symbols of the nation's past and present, the younger players of these instruments stood in awe of the economic and expressive power of manufactured instruments from the West and the musicians who had conquered them. Players of Western instruments had advanced Bulgarian music to new heights, and young gaidari and players of traditional instruments felt they needed to change their playing style and repertoire to include techniques from wedding music. They consequently regarded their playing as more advanced than Kostadin's, and apparently Kostadin, at some level, accepted these advances. Dimitŭr said Kostadin once told him, "There is nothing happier for a teacher than to have a student match and surpass him."

To demonstrate some of the new possibilities on the instrument, Dimitŭr played a *rŭchenitsa* 'in complex scales' [*v slozhni gami*] that modulated through a number of keys, many neither typical nor easy to play on the gaida (ex. 10.1; CD #44). Frequent modulation, often by whole steps, is a feature of Balkan Gypsy music that contravenes the Bulgarian practice of a sustained tonal center, often expressed as a drone. As a consequence of its tonal complexity, he had to play it 'a little slowly' and without a drone.

The first tune, in E minor, covers a one-octave range beginning with an arpeggio on the tonic chord, a feature borrowed from clarinet and accordion tradition. The tune chromatically alters b♮′/b♭′ and f♮′/f♯′. While some of Kostadin's tunes included one such alternation within a pentachord, the expanded range of the modern tunes allows for a second chromatic alternation in another pentachord. Tune 3 modulates down a whole step to D major, a key never used by Kostadin because the d′ on the instrument cannot be articulated by a lower note. Beginning with a full octave arpeggio, the melody contains the sharp fourth degree, g♯′, a scale degree Kostadin never used. Tune 4 continues the downward descent by whole step in a variant of the previous one on d′. This provides an antic touch since c′ doesn't exist on the instrument, and so the melody cadences an octave higher on c″, a feature antithetical to Kostadin's tradition. Tune 5 modulates down a fifth to a tonic on f♮′, a chromatic note played by uncovering the *mormorka* while fingering e′. The notion that this rather tenuous-sounding note could be the tonic of a tune and not just a fleeting chromaticism contributes to the tonal craziness of the piece and stretches this "skin saxophone" to its limits.

The scale of tune 5 is not one heard in Kostadin's repertoire; it contains an augmented second, a♭′/b♮′, between the third and fourth degrees of the scale rather than between the second and third degrees. Tune 6 continues to insist on f′ natural as tonic, changing the mode to F major. Tune 7 modulates back to d′ and another unusual mode containing augmented seconds in both upper tetrachord and lower pentachord: d′ e′ f′ g♯′ a′ b♭′ c♯″ d″. After a brief return to some previ-

Example 10.1. *Rŭchenitsa* in Complex Scales

Example 10.1. *continued*

ous material on d', the modulatory pattern continues through more
usual keys and tune types on G major, A hijaz, B minor, and A hijaz
before returning to the opening tunes in E minor. This *rŭchenitsa,* an
exhausting aural (for the listener) and physical (for the player) journey
of key changes, chromaticism, arpeggiation, and unusual modes and
keys, illustrates how gaidari try to keep up with developments in wedding music and apotheosize it as a 'skin saxophone.'

If the wide-ranging, arpeggiated tunes and frequent key changes of
this *rŭchenitsa* seem far from Kostadin's stepwise, pentachordal tunes
on a', the playing style also changed. As Dimitŭr said, "There is a new
trend. [Gaidari] use clarinet style. They run from folk music. They
play more staccato, like an automatic rifle"—a fairly 'aggressive' metaphor. In effect, younger gaidari seem to mix the staccato *Shop* style into
the legato Thracian style in order to create the "gusto" of Gypsy wedding music. A set of tunes for *pravo horo* played by many younger musicians illustrates the new ornamental style (ex. 10.2). The tunes are
in E major, a new, difficult key for gaidari because of its use of g♯'. Instead of using the upper neighbor to separate repeated notes, these
tunes consistently use the lower neighbor, creating a more staccato effect in what is already an unusually syncopated tune. Since g♯' is
played by opening the *mormorka,* which normally produces the upper-
neighbor ornament, that upper ornament becomes impossible to produce and the lower neighbor is used instead. In effect, the emphasis
on new, chromatic notes outside the normally diatonic scope of the

Example 10.2. Syncopated, Staccato *Pravo horo* Tunes

gaidanitsa dictated an altered approach to ornamentation that matched the wedding-music aesthetic of a less sweet, more aggressive style.

Even as Dimitŭr played these new melodies and explored the limits of the gaida's technical possibilities, he continued to value the old village style. "A musician today has to be universal, but you can't forget the sweet village style. The new style is harder. In the new style there is still some of Varimezov's style, maybe 20 percent. The melody is the basic stuff of the stew. The salt and pepper is put in by the cook. From the simplest tune, the sweetest things can happen." Critical of younger musicians who ignore the older style, he said, "They don't play in a human, village way. They can't imitate different regional styles. They have lost the old stuff. You can't follow only the current style. You have to know the basis." When I asked about the criticism that might be leveled at Kostadin, that his playing isn't the most virtuosic, he responded, "This is professional jealousy. He gave the basis [on which new developments were built]." As for Dimitŭr's own aspirations, he expressed the disciplined deference to elders characteristic of village ideology: "I still have much to learn. I still bow to [the older players]. As long as they can make recordings, let them. There is still time for me." Thus Dimitŭr balanced his evaluation of Kostadin's influence, arguing that he and a few other players of his generation built the foundation on which the gaida tradition rests, at the same time acknowledging that the tradition had advanced in the hands of younger players.

Maria Stoyanova, the First Female Gaidar

While wedding music was the source of most recent innovations in the Bulgarian folk music tradition outside the work of Kutev and his followers, the school at Kotel could take credit for at least one remarkable new development: women playing traditional musical instruments professionally, including that most symbolically male of instruments, the gaida.[2] Maria Stoyanova, born in 1953, grew up in Seliminovo near Sliven, a village with a lively music tradition that produced perhaps Bulgaria's most famous male singer, Iofcho Karaivanov. Her father played gaida and kaval in a small band for weddings, engagements, and the village amateur dance ensemble, but, as she told me, "it was unexpected that I would play gaida. When I showed an interest in the gaida, my parents argued with me. They forbade me to play. I waited for them to go out. The neighbors were amazed that I tried to play." She had managed to learn a few simple songs on the instrument in seven or eight months of stolen moments when she heard an announcement about a new school for folk music opening in Kotel.

At fourteen Maria auditioned in 1967 for Kotel's first class. However, she encountered some resistance to this breach of tradition from the admissions jury: "It was interesting for the commission that I wanted to play the gaida. In the beginning they didn't want to admit me. They wanted me to play tambura or gŭdulka. Before that, there had never been a woman gaida player—at least in Bulgaria." Lyuben Botusharov, the musicologist and ensemble conductor invited to conduct the Pazardzhik operetta, was on the jury and remembered the controversy her candidacy caused: Should a woman be allowed to play in what had been a male instrumental tradition, particularly if the goal of the school was to preserve tradition? Wasn't the fact that women did not play wind instruments part of that tradition? Some jury members even interpreted the gaida's blowpipe and the kaval as phalluses being put in the mouth, although for some reason this meaning was apparent to them only when a woman played it.[3] Furthermore, as Maria put it, "The gaida is a strong, leading instrument. With one gaida you can make a wedding." In a band of instruments the gaida, by sheer volume, leads. These defenders of tradition were asking, Is this an appropriate role for a woman playing with men? The controversy is a good example of how musical performance can be read as referencing both the real world, where women didn't play instruments, and an imagined world, where in the future they might. For the jury, nothing less than the moral order of the world was at stake in the decision to admit or reject Maria.

In the end, the new Marxist sentiment favoring equality of the sexes and a new approach to tradition won out. Although by her own account a rank beginner, she displayed some musicianship in the tests, and they admitted her to study gaida. Over the years many girls, originally admitted to study voice, minored in instruments, particularly tambura and gŭdulka, but occasionally kaval and gaida. While still somewhat unusual, I saw a few of them performing in folk ensembles and wedding bands.

Maria remembered that, for the first two years, the school had no gaida teacher in residence. Her main teacher was a fellow student named Dimitŭr Georgiev who came with an already well-developed technique modeled after Kostadin's recordings. Together they continued to learn Kostadin's repertoire and technique from a distance, and, like so many of her generation, Maria pointed to him as her first and most important model.[4] After graduating from Kotel, and later from the newly formed post-secondary Institute in Plovdiv, Maria directed the choir and orchestra of an ensemble in Haskovo for five years, until she was invited to join the faculty of the Institute in Plovdiv as their gaida instructor. The first professional female gaidar in the history of the tradition came to occupy the most central position in the education of future generations of gaidari, and Kostadin's style, technique, and repertoire crucially influenced her development. From that position, she also inspired a number of young women to take up the gaida.

While her playing style struck me as relatively conservative, she made extra money playing with wedding bands like Kanarite, with whom she has recorded—in one case using a tune from Kostadin's *Dzhinovsko hort se* (ex. 8.2; CD #45). Wedding bands around Plovdiv invited her to join them occasionally, because a woman playing gaida still created a stir, and because the gaida still symbolized the wedding tradition. In the Plovdiv area, where modern instruments had long ago replaced traditional instruments for weddings, Maria played Kostadin's nonmetrical wedding tunes. But no one, not even she, had any idea of their reference to the traditions of Gergebunar.

Among the techniques she learned from wedding bands, one 6/8 *pravo horo* tune illustrates a new rhythmic approach to the 3 + 3 subdivision of the beats. She subdivided the first two measures as 2 + 2 + 2, a hemiola not used by traditional players but a kind of syncopation that is part of the clarinet-accordion tradition (ex. 10.3). Echoing Dimitŭr's notion of progress she said, "There is a definite growth of gaida technique in Bulgaria, and I can't get behind. I have to be in step with new developments."

One of Maria's students at the Institute, Bozhidar Georgiev, born in 1964, from the town of Silistra in Dobrudzha, played a *pravo horo* into which he inserted a brief, nontraditional descending chromatic run into a traditional tune in the formerly diatonic gaida tradition (ex. 10.4, notated at the beginning of the second ending of the second tune). Maria worked collegially with her students to produce exercises

Example 10.3. Syncopation (Hemiola) in *Pravo horo* Tune

Example 10.4. Chromatic Run in Traditional Tune

and tunes for them and younger students that were eventually included in methods books and collections for Kotel and other local folk music schools around the country.[5]

Encho Pashov

While Dimitŭr and Maria respected Kostadin as a good teacher and an important source for the "old," "simple" way of playing, some younger gaidars rejected his influence, even where they felt it, and emphasized their search for a personal style. One such musician, Encho Pashov, born in 1951 in Sinapovo near Yambol, played gaida in the resident orchestra of folk instruments at the Institute for Music in Plovdiv. A professional ensemble, it trained the Institute's conductors, rehearsed the composers' pieces, and performed in concerts representing the Institute. Encho's position complemented Maria's instructional work, and, while both received full-time pay, neither worked long hours, their division of labor reflecting serious problems with underemployment in the economy as a whole. A thin, intense, articulate man of 37 when I met him, Encho occasionally affected the rough demeanor and conversational style of an older villager, although he lived in an elegantly furnished new apartment in Plovdiv with his sophisticated wife Violeta and their two children. He claimed to be closely linked to many older musicians, and I interpreted his behavior as an outward symbol of that connection.

In fact, Encho first learned gaida from a very old man, his great-grandfather, who was surprised that Encho wanted to play gaida since both his son and grandson (Encho's father) played violin in wedding bands. While Encho was essentially self-taught, his great-grandfather encouraged him to hear all the best gaidars of the older generation, and often invited them to his home to drink and play after concerts. Encho listed *Bai* Stoyan Dobrev, Kostadin, and two Muslim Gypsy gaidari, Shahpaz Aliev and Mehmed Aliev, as his main early influences. After winning prizes at festivals and playing in wedding bands from the age of 15 into his twenties, he was admitted to the Institute in Plovdiv, where he completed a remedial course in music theory before joining his more advanced classmates, who had attended the high school at Kotel.

Encho professed the highest standards for himself and others in his three passions: playing gaida, arranging music, and making reeds and gaidanitsas. Like many young gaidari, he was engaged in the search for the "perfect" gaidanitsa, one that would play a tempered scale in tune with the accordion. Since he eventually wanted to create a gaida to compare favorably with a clarinet or oboe—a more classical, orchestral ideal than Dimitŭr's skin saxophone—he believed the gaida should be made, as the classical woodwinds are, from ebony rather than from the traditional, but increasingly difficult-to-find dogwood.[6] In the same vein, since good cane for reeds was both hard to find and imperfectly variable in diameter, he made his reeds in two pieces: the body from "perfect" plastic tubing and the tongue from reshaped clarinet reeds. These three modifications of the gaidanitsa—tuning, material, and reed construction—produced a thin, hard sound that he liked, and which sounded good in an ensemble context, but, in the solo, outdoor performances I heard, lacked the full, rich timbre of the older instruments.

Encho's future goal was to create a gaidanitsa with a dynamic range "from pianissimo to forte," and he tried to manipulate loudness when he played. Someday he may succeed in turning the gaida into a skin oboe. His approach to the instrument represented just one way he and some other young players distanced themselves from Kostadin, who was content to live with the imperfections of the older instruments precisely because they sounded like a 'real gaida' to him.

Encho displayed the same zeal for perfection when he talked about arrangements. While Kostadin and many older musicians railed against arrangements generally, Encho and other young musicians embraced them critically but with enthusiasm. It was, after all, the primary way they had experienced modern Bulgarian *narodna muzika*, and they had been trained not only to play them but to create them as well. Unlike older musicians, Encho wasn't opposed to arrangements; he just wanted good, sensitive ones. He loved music that came "from the source" [*ot izvora*] and was "clean." He felt that composers who were insensitive to the source "dirtied it," while those, like himself, who understood it made it cleaner. In other words, pure gets purer through arrangement. By this rationalization, he reconciled his love of tradition with his training in the new aesthetics. His favorite arranger, like that of so many others, was Kosta Kolev.

Encho's own arrangements, which he played for me on his home stereo, were quite complex, involving two or three contrapuntal lines, "but these follow a picture I have of the song and what it requires." To illustrate, he cited a few lines of text. "I don't just follow the rules of harmony. I have to have a picture in my head before I write and then I don't need a piano. I just write it out." Although he didn't say so precisely, Encho—and his ideas were echoed by a number of other young musicians I talked to—was in effect claiming that he arranged "from the heart," not from the notes and rules of classical composers. He was at pains to place himself close to the "source" and distance himself from the excesses of those arrangers with classical training but little direct experience of the playing tradition.

Although Encho acknowledged listening to and learning Kostadin's repertoire, he claimed that he had created his own personal style out of a blend of the best musicians he heard as a youth, in particular, Shahpaz Aliev, who, he said, played slow songs really well. He disliked the way Kostadin played slow songs, particularly the high 'knocking' of the thumb to separate d″ with e″. He preferred what he thought was Shahpaz's subtler technique of a turn around d″, using both e″ and c♯″, sliding the thumb off to produce the e″. "This is the way singers sing. You have to take the best from the singers. The way Varimezov plays, there is no such singing." Shahpaz's playing, Encho said, was "smoother, more moving. He would play legato, then staccato." To demonstrate, he played for me, emphasizing glissandi into each note and the quarter-tone vibrato on held notes. "On each tone [Shahpaz] wanted to give soul, life."

Example 10.5. Thracian (Old?) vs. *Shop* (Modern?) Style

When playing dance music, Encho advocated a 'hardened' [*zatvŭrdeno*] style that created *hŭs*. Technical means of hardening a phrase included changing the playing style from legato to staccato and replacing scalar passages with repeated notes. Encho demonstrated with a common *rŭchenitsa* phrase (ex. 10.5). (While Encho, raised in Thrace, sees this as a new, modern style of playing not used by Kostadin, it is one Kostadin associated with the *Shop* style and, in fact, used when he played a *Shop rŭchenitsa*.)

Encho sought a wider expressive range—a range that moved from the expressive slow playing of Gypsy gaidari to the fast, staccato energy of *Shop* dance tunes—than he heard in Kostadin's playing. "I used to play all Varimezov's stuff, but when I came here [to the Institute] I realized I had to create my own style." In the process the stylistic boundaries between regional styles were blurred in favor of an expressivity that addressed the needs of young musicians to progress.

Without a hint of irony or contradiction, Encho claimed to be more closely rooted to the tradition than Maria. Although from his point of view he was "filling" his playing with a variety of expressive devices and ornaments, from my point of view, colored by long association with Kostadin's repertoire and style, something in his playing seemed empty. In his search for perfection, he may have cleaned up the style and sound too much, making it too pure. In any case, Encho provides a good example of the group of younger musicians who embraced and loved both the state aesthetics of arrangement and the 'pure source' [*chist izvor*] of tradition. While composers of his generation, with their background and training as folk musicians, were more sensitive to tradition's essence than many in the older generation of composers, their bleaching of the tradition's color to make it purer still made it even less competitive in contrast with wedding music's vitality in "filling the soul" of other Bulgarians.

Ivan Varimezov Inherits the Tradition

Ivan Varimezov, Kostadin's nephew, represented an exception among younger professional gaidari. Due to his position within the family, which still exercised its patriarchal pull on him, he was forced to continue Kostadin's tradition more completely than most of his friends and colleagues. Also a product of the high-school and post-secondary education in folk music and cognizant of the new developments in wedding music, he was, more than most younger musicians, caught in a bind between tradition and innovation.

After being taught by Kostadin since childhood, Ivan experienced three significant developments at Kotel and Plovdiv: he learned how to arrange folk music and direct ensembles; he befriended a coterie of the finest young musicians of his generation, many of whom he continued to play music with; and he met and married Tsvetanka, a tall, solidly built, handsome singer from Pazardzhik. Examining in detail their musical life together in the 1980s provides an interesting contrast to the way Kostadin and Todora lived the tradition in the 1930s.

Ivan's Style

While Ivan's style and repertoire were obviously indebted to his uncle's influence, he absorbed elements of the more staccato modern style and uses more thumb ornaments than Kostadin does. From Ivan's perspective, the differences between him and his uncle reflect those between vigorous youth and mellow old age. He characterized his own style as more 'youthful,' with more cutting of the tones with lower ornaments. Kostadin, on the other hand, thought Ivan played well but found his playing *sert* ['hard,' 'strong,' or 'peppery'] rather than 'sweet.' When I played a *kopanitsa* Ivan had showed me, Kostadin objected to a lower, cut tone, which created a staccato effect desired by younger players to 'harden' the phrase and create 'gusto.' The articulation didn't fit Kostadin's idea of legato style, and he wanted me to use a raised tone as ornament to create a smoother, more melodic effect. To Kostadin, Ivan's cut version was 'meatless,' another food metaphor, like 'sweet,' for the "tastiness" of the playing. A closely related metaphor he used in describing the new style, with its lowered rather than raised ornament, was 'empty'; modern gaida playing, for Kostadin, was a stew with no meat.[7] Traditional playing, like a meaty stew, was more capable of "filling your soul."[8] By learning to play gaida, I was able to participate in metaphoric discussions at the finest level of detail. I learned that Bulgarian music's ability "to fill one's

soul" lay, in some measure, in choices between barely audible ornaments.

Ivan claimed that 90 percent of his style was indebted to Kostadin's
and that he had added perhaps 10 percent. His father, Stoyan, listened
closely for new intrusions, not wanting him to stray too far from the
tradition. Thus Ivan was caught between the family pressure of tradition and the advances that other musicians were making around him.
Kostadin argued that he should hew to tradition, because soon few
would remember and be able to reproduce it. Ivan realized, however,
that if he didn't keep up with the changes, there soon might be no
interest in his playing.

Ivan and Tsvetanka as Musicians

Tsvetanka possessed a loud, strong voice and sang in the characteristic,
highly ornamented style of the Pazardzhik region. She grew up in the
town, however, and had no direct family line to a village repertoire.
She learned it in the new way typical of secondary urbanization, in
ensembles organized for local youth. At Kotel and Plovdiv she learned
to play tambura, developed a good ear for harmony—she had studied
piano as a child—and could write her own arrangements. Just as Ivan
carried on Kostadin's repertoire and style, Tsvetanka was the one best
equipped to continue Todora's song repertoire. Unlike Todora's
daughter and daughters-in-law, who never grasped how to learn songs
aurally, Tsvetanka knew many of Todora's songs, and she sang them
enthusiastically at family gatherings. Because the folklore establishment demanded adherence to one's own regional style, Tsvetanka
was reluctant to record them, and possibly was even prevented from
doing so. She also was modest about her mastery of the Strandzha
style. I imagine that one day she will record some of Todora's songs,
but, perhaps more importantly, she will continue performances
of large numbers of them for one or even two more generations.
She already had taught her daughter Radka, age seven, two of them
(pl. 14).

Before and after graduation from Plovdiv, Ivan and Tsvetanka performed with Trakiya, one of the four or five best ensembles in the
country. They had great respect for Kiril Dzhenev, its director during
their tenure, and the high artistic level he achieved. While pleased
with their musical lot, the heavy demands of touring the country and
abroad with the ensemble, especially with a young child to look after,
caused them to request a move to Pazardzhik, a sleepy, provincial town
at the western tip of Thrace where the clip-clop of horse-drawn carts
on its ancient, narrow, curving streets remained a part of the sound-

scape. There Tsvetanka's mother looked after Radka while they worked, and they in turn cared for her mother, who was in ill health.

They both took jobs with Pazardzhik's professional ensemble of folk song and dance: Ivan conducted the orchestra and Tsvetanka the choir. But although they occupied important and influential positions, they were shocked by the low level of ability and lack of discipline in the ensemble and unhappy with its effort and potential. Talking about his fellow musicians, Ivan complained, "They play 'officially,' but there is no enthusiasm, no accent. Everything is flat. I argue with them and sometimes they try, but they really are cut off from the tradition."

Musicians like Ivan, and of course Kostadin, felt themselves privileged to have grown up in a village environment where they learned how to play expressively, and they frequently criticized those who grew up learning the tradition in schools and towns. Kostadin called such music 'city playing' [*gradsko svirene*]. Even though the move to Pazardzhik corresponded to their personal needs, Ivan and Tsvetanka were disappointed and frustrated by the prospect of pulling a provincial ensemble up to their own high standards.

Their dissatisfaction led Ivan and Tsvetanka to consider hopefully a move to Sofia, the apex of ensemble artistry in the country. They received invitations to work with various ensembles there—he with the ensemble of the regional council and she with the choir of Radio Sofia. But moving was not a matter of individual desire. They first had to obtain 'citizenship,' that is, the right to live in the city. Sofia was so crowded and such an attractive center that immigration was controlled; in 1988 virtually no one was getting permission to live there, even if they had a job offer. Ivan and Tsvetanka considered trying to obtain citizenship in a village outside Sofia and commuting into the city, but in the end the problems of child care and her mother's ill health prevented them from acting on their ambitions.[9]

Resigned to staying in Pazardzhik, Ivan continued the village tradition of his father and uncle not only by playing but by buying a *dekar* of land outside Pazardzhik in a nearby village. There he constructed a house with the help of master builders and grew watermelons, which require little care, in the yard in order to sell them for a bit of extra money. As Ivan said, "Playing is playing, but we have a lot of free time," and he chose to pass it in building up his own property in the time-honored—and honorable—village tradition.

The Pazardzhik Ensemble in Performance

One of the Pazardzhik ensemble's mandates was to tour the region, entertaining villagers with their colorful, arranged presentations of music, song, and dance. I attended one of their performances at a village fair in Miryantsi, southeast of the city, where I could observe the performance and reception of state-sponsored folklore. Vendors selling candy and trinkets for children lined one block adjacent to the village square, where a sound system had been set up for the musicians and singers. A concert that included the ensemble and a man and woman who sang *shlageri* accompanied by accordion preceded a dance in the village square. During the singers' performance, wind hitting the microphones caused an unpleasant noise, but the singers battled gamely on. The villagers hardly seemed interested, however, and one woman commented, "Why do they send this kind of music? Don't they know we are villagers. Give us folk music."

The ensemble, on the other hand, was reasonably well received, particularly when they acted out a humorous sketch of an old grandfather who goes after the young girls, only to be set upon and beaten by his wife, a man dressed up as an old granny, the cross-dressing reminiscent of the wedding skit described in chapter 2. No matter how many times they had seen this skit—and they had surely seen it a lot—it seemed to evoke heartfelt enjoyment and laughter. Commenting on their success with the crowd, Ivan said, "It's the only entertainment. The symphony is not going to be too popular."

The symbolism or reference of the performance was striking in context. The musicians, singers, and dancers in their colorful costumes emerged from and returned to a building housing the city administration and Party headquarters. The government and the Party appeared to give folklore to the people and then to take it away. In contrast to the colorful, energetic, youthful ensemble, the villagers looked sunburned and exhausted, dressed in their drab gray and blue workclothes. Except for the humorous sketch, they looked on for the most part indifferently and applauded perfunctorily the choral and orchestral arrangements and choreographed dancing. While folklore was something they may have wanted, as the woman's comment suggested, it was not obviously "filling their souls."

Ivan and Tsvetanka Record for Balkanton

The relatively light demands of the ensemble left Ivan and Tsvetanka free to pursue other musical activities, including recording a record for Balkanton and organizing a wedding band that played primarily in the village of Varvara, south of Pazardzhik. The recording project provides some insight into the world of 'connections' that greased the wheels of life in Bulgaria generally and in the recording business in particular.

Kostadin and Ivan had actively concertized for a relocation project in Strandzha: people from all parts of Bulgaria who were without work and willing to start anew were given homesteads in mostly deserted areas of Strandzha. The Varimezovs' connections to local Party organizations led the project's organizers to request an order for a record of Ivan and Tsvetanka from Balkanton, the organization guaranteeing to purchase enough records to pay for the cost of its production. This procedure was not unusual; as Lili Hristozova, Balkanton's folk music editor, explained, Balkantourist, the Education Ministry, and provincial sponsors of folklore ensembles frequently made such orders. Balkanton agreed to put out a record with Ivan's playing and Tsvetanka's singing as part of two series, one on young performers and another featuring family connections: father/daughter, husband/wife and so on.[10]

Also crucial to the success of the project was enlisting the aid of influential composers to arrange their material: Kosta Kolev, Stefan Mutafchiev, and Stefan Kŭnev. Although Ivan and Tsvetanka liked the work of Kosta Kolev—"He's a master," they said—and Stefan Mutafchiev, the composer and artistic director of the Trakiya ensemble who did innovative work with some of the best younger musicians,[11] they secured the help of Stefan Kŭnev, a well-known and respected composer, because he, according to Kostadin, "has influence. It is easier to get the record out if he is involved." Thus, although undoubtedly deserving young artists, Ivan and Tsvetanka's connections to Party organizations and to key figures in the music business were crucial to getting their record produced—a fact that would hardly surprise young musicians in the United States.

As might be expected of a project where the artists relinquished artistic control to a producer or, in this case, composers, the Varimezovs were not entirely happy with the result, and their comments provide another look into the continuing battle between traditional aesthetics and the artistic control of composers.

In contrast with the musicians' desire to produce a recording capable of evoking dancing in the listeners, after the fashion of live music, composers seem mainly concerned with showing off their compositional skills in a product designed for listening. In Ivan and Tsvetanka's recording, slow tempos, the accompaniment's heavy accents in the form of staccato chords, frequent starts and stops, and fast-moving harmonies impede its danceability.

For the songs Tsvetanka provided, Kŭnev composed the 'interludes' [otsviri] between verses, but Kostadin felt they were not 'danceable' [troplivo], that is, lively (CD #46). "He doesn't have a feeling for the tradition. When we [village musicians] make up an *otsvir,* we try to compete with the song, to make something better," by creating a contrast between the slow-moving rhythm of the song and the denser rhythm of the interlude. The dancers would then respond with two different movement intensities, one slow and relaxed and the other energetic and bouncy. Kŭnev's interludes lacked this contrast, and Kostadin complained, "Who can dance to these arrangements?" (Kostadin persisted in trying to interpret the records as useful to villagers who traditionally dance in response to music, while the composers—if they had an audience in mind at all—could only imagine listening as an appropriate response to their music.) Nevertheless, the producers did follow one of Kostadin's suggestions, alternating songs and dances to create an overall musical structure typical of a family gathering, as he had suggested for an earlier record of Dimka Vladimirova and Strandzhanskata Grupa.

Many of Ivan's instrumental tunes on the record were his own creations, but at least one piece, *Trite pŭti,* harked back to Rosenovo (CD #47). Kostadin had never recorded it, but he and Todora still associated all of its tunes with friends and relatives from the village. Even when the tunes were deeply meaningful to them, however, Kostadin still complained about their realization. "*Trite pŭti* should have been recorded with the [high-pitched] gaidanitsa. People in our area don't recognize the [low-pitched] gaidanitsa as a gaida," and since the melodies were local ones, he thought it was especially important to link them to the appropriate, local instrumental sound.

Since most young musicians were trained to do their own arranging, one can imagine a day when they will bypass the composers, with their lack of understanding, and blend the traditional and modern in a way satisfying to themselves. But Ivan and Tsvetanka said they were too young. To succeed, the record had to go through an established composer. In spite of the Varimezovs' complaints, Lili Hristozova said the record was a success. When they played it for bookstore purchasers, they received orders in large quantities, and far more copies of the record sold than the Party organization ordered or than Balkanton had expected to sell.

Ivan and Tsvetanka's Wedding Band

In addition to playing in the ensemble and making records, both activities within the purview of 'arranged folklore,' Ivan and Tsvetanka could not resist the lucrative wedding market. Their band, including musicians they met, and who still live, in Plovdiv, rarely rehearsed, getting together only on weekends to play. It featured traditional instruments—gaida, kaval, and gŭdulka—in place of the usual clarinet and saxophone, accompanied by modern instruments typical of the wedding tradition: accordion, drum set, and an electric organ [*yonika*] on which Tsvetanka played bass and chords as she sang. Thus, despite their employment by a regime that for most of the Communist period controlled the representation of folk music and demanded the separation of traditional and Western instruments, Ivan and Tsvetanka like nearly every other Bulgarian musician, including Kostadin, managed to incorporate both ensemble and wedding music as an aspect of everyday life.

Predictably, the repertoire of the group included genres that the state wanted to keep separate because of what they symbolized: Kostadin and Todora's Strandzha material, Tsvetanka's Pazardzhik songs, the favorite local dance (*krivo horo* in 11/8), popular *horos* and Gypsy *kyucheks* from famous wedding bands like *Kanarite*, and European and American popular dances. Because of the state's suppression of Muslim minorities and attempts to wipe out their expressive forms during the period from 1985 to 1989, the *kyuchek* was a particularly vexed genre for ethnic Bulgarian musicians, who seemed self-conscious each time they played one. Although Ivan and Tsvetanka seemed to enjoy the scene and the music as they played a *kyuchek*, afterwards they professed their displeasure at playing *kyucheks* at weddings. *Kyuchek* in context (as event, as discourse) unproblematically and ostensively referenced the celebratory joy of the wedding and they played it on request; reflecting on *kyuchek* afterwards (as text), they interpreted it in terms of the aesthetic and political position of the state, where it referenced a troubled, contested world of ethnic unrest.[12]

Ivan and Tsvetanka were proudest of their group's traditional emphasis. Ivan said, "That is a trademark of our group. The other groups only play the new stuff," which presented formidable problems for the gaida, not the least of which was the wide range of many tunes. Ivan, unlike Kostadin's student Dimitŭr, lamented the gaida's limits and admitted, "I drop out when the melody goes too high. If only the gaida had three more notes!" An example of the gaida's problems with the clarinet-accordion repertoire is illustrated in example 10.6 (CD #48), a tune his band played from Kanarite's recorded repertoire.

The first tune and its interlude fit within the range of the gaida, although, unlike traditional pentachordal tunes, they use the entire range of the instrument, a ninth. The second group of tunes ascends to a high ♯″ beyond the range of the instrument, so Ivan stopped playing during that four-measure phrase, rejoining the band in the fifth measure. The third group of two tunes begins with a descent two notes

Example 10.6. Ivan's Wide-Range *Pravo horo* from *Kanarite*

below the range of the gaida to c♯' and b, and so Ivan again dropped out until the fifth measure. Ivan could play these tunes only in an ensemble context where a brief pause was covered by the other instruments. These wedding tunes cannot enter the gaida repertoire per se, although they can be played successfully by gŭdulka and kaval, which have the wider ranges necessary to accommodate them.

In championing the old tradition, Ivan recognized that devoting too much time to its fossilized ensemble form limited a musician's development. Acknowledging that most of the new developments in the tradition were occurring among wedding musicians, he said, "Playing in these ensembles limits the growth of a musician. They play a limited repertoire for years in a row. Meanwhile instrumentalists are progressing by playing at weddings," a statement that echoed Kostadin's explanation that being a wedding musician in the 1930s facilitated his greatest development and that contradicted Lili Tabakova's attempt to minimize the artistic demands on wedding musicians. Ivan and Tsvetanka even considered moving back to Plovdiv, the center for wedding musicians, to participate exclusively in the wedding music scene there, but again rejected that idea in order to help her mother. "We were going to move to Plovdiv and not work for the ensemble [Trakiya], but somehow we got involved [in Pazardzhik]. There was no other way."

An Urban-Rural Wedding

I accompanied Ivan and Tsvetanka one Sunday to the village of Varvara for a wedding, like many in the Communist era an urban-rural, modern-traditional affair. The band arrived late, and, since the groom's family was in a hurry to get started and the village sprawled along the road, the groom's mother decided that instead of processing on foot from their house to pick up the godfather we would drive there. The wedding party, including musicians, piled into half-a-dozen cars and motored to within a hundred meters of the house, parked, and processed from there to the *kum's* house as the musicians played Kostadin's 'godfather's tune' [*kumova svirnya*]. The enlarged wedding party then went by car from the village into Pazardzhik to pick up the bride, who lived in a high-rise apartment building.

Ivan, the musicians, and the rest of the groom's party processed up the stairs to the fourth floor playing traditional wedding tunes from Rosenovo. Only Ivan completely understood the world referenced by these tunes, since they were being played in a region far from the one in which they had been nurtured. After a ritual greeting of the groom's family, the united wedding party processed downstairs, and, once outside, danced a *horo*. The band played a Strandzha tune from Kostadin's repertoire rather than a local Pazardzhik tune, but eventually segued into tunes by Kanarite (ex. 10.6). Typical of many urban weddings, at least one key member of the wedding party could not manage to dance even a simple *horo*. In this case it was the hapless bride, who walked in rhythm to the dance, but could not perform its simple, six-beat, repetitive pattern.

After the celebratory dance, the bride and groom went by car to the city hall to register their marriage while the musicians returned to Varvara to prepare their sound equipment for the celebration to follow. The equipment consisted of primitive Eastern European amplifiers and speakers, and the musicians had to tinker with them before they worked. The sound quality was tinny and distorted at normal levels, and, since the tradition required them to play as loudly as possible, the result was harshly distorted. When the bride and groom arrived, she was met by her new parents-in-law, with gifts, and, following tradition, her mother-in-law forced her to sit on a low chair, a sign of her subservient role in her new family. None of the traditional wedding ritual songs were performed that day, and the business of eating, drinking, and dancing began. Although the bride could not dance, she tried gamely, as tradition requires. Other young people in the village danced enthusiastically all day and into night, however, and, in spite of Kostadin's and Todora's frequently expressed concern that no one liked folklore anymore, young people in these provincial areas loved to listen to it and dance at weddings.

The celebration took place under a long tent, set up to protect everyone from the sun. Two rows of long tables with benches lined the tent, and dancing took place in oblong circles around the outside of the tables. The playing started at 1 P.M. and lasted until 11 P.M., the musicians taking only two short breaks for food. At that they felt lucky that the *chorbadzhiya* [patron, lit. 'soupmaker'] had released them so early; they remembered times when they played to 1 A.M. and even later. The staple form of their performances were long suites of dance songs followed by extensive instrumental solos by members of the band, a dance lasting 45 minutes or more. Comparing their playing to that of other groups, they complained that many newer groups emphasized instrumental tunes, whereas proper Bulgarian music used lots of songs. Tsvetanka sang from her large repertoire of Pazardzhik-region songs and a man from Varvara sang village songs. The pattern of line dances was broken by two solo *kyucheks*, the first danced early in the day by a man who so embarrassed everyone with his drunken rendition that no one else joined in, and the second later in the evening when the mood had improved and a large group of young people danced enthusiastically.

The celebratory spirit was slow to get going that day, a circumstance attributed by the musicians to the fact that the bride's family were 'city folk.' Things didn't really warm up until after dinner, when the remaining guests were mainly villagers, the groom's relations and friends. At one point, a local amateur comedian delivered a comic monologue, dedicated to the bride and groom, that everyone enjoyed immensely. Ivan wanted me to play Kostadin's famous *Trite pŭti*, to which the father of the groom danced with great spirit. The rhythm of the band was very strong and I soon lost my self-consciousness and began to relax. Watching the dancer, I felt my own enthusiasm for playing well up and fill my soul, and I understood in an intimate and personal way what Kostadin meant when he said he "received spirit from the dancers." Later in the evening, when everyone was getting tired, what Ivan called the "fourth phase" began, and the band played some tangos, a blues number, and the "Chicken Dance" for a brief spate of couple dancing.

The next day Ivan was critical of, even angry at, some of the band members and their performance at the Varvara wedding. He said, "At one point only about five people were dancing and yet they continued to play their improvisations." He took this as a sign that they didn't know how to play for a dance. Few of his band members had grown up in villages as he had, where the etiquette of the relationship between musician and dancer was ingrained, and so they approached performance as an opportunity to solo and show off technique rather than to serve the needs of the dancers.

One of the most striking results of amplified sound at weddings was that the kaval came into its own as a wedding instrument. The gaida used to be the loudest instrument and was therefore in demand—"a wedding without a gaida is impossible"—but amplification seemed to diminish rather than augment its sound in ensembles. The kaval, on the other hand, cuts through the ensemble texture when amplified, particularly when played in the highest register, as most younger players do, and it has emerged as an important instrument in these wedding ensembles. In addition, the kaval's wide, three-octave range and ability to play a chromatic scale allows it to keep up with the new, wide-ranging tunes and key changes of the accordion-clarinet tradition.

Having entered the cauldron of professional music making, the musical lives of young musicians roiled with the social tensions of the late 1980s. Pulled by the musically and economically dynamic wedding music tradition and restrained by the technical limits of their instruments and the tug of tradition, they struggled to remain responsive to both. The experience of music for them represented a complex mix of memories of older gaidari and family and village musical events, the physical and musical details of responding to new technical demands, the economic and personal problems of everyday life, and a sense of the tradition slipping away from them as the dancers danced less competently, the musicians competed among themselves rather than paying attention to the dancers, and Western instruments came to the fore. Their aesthetic positions strongly supported the traditional, even as they coped with the newest developments. Trained and employed in the state's music system, they continued to espouse many of its values in the face of the challenge from other economic, aesthetic, and musical positions. Ethnic tensions in the political climate remained largely in the background for these musicians, who, with me at least, never spoke about them. Whereas in the late 1980s some in the state apparatus interpreted wedding music as an "aggressive" expression of Muslim identity and freedom from state control, young ethnic Bulgarian musicians read it strictly as an aesthetic choice to be evaluated, often positively, in relation to the aesthetics of the state, which they had appropriated and were promulgating.

ELEVEN

Kostadin and Todora at Home

Since Kostadin's retirement from the Radio orchestra in 1978, his musical life has centered around teaching a new generation of gaidari, occasional concerts as a soloist or in small groups, tours abroad—either as an individual or with Balkana (pl. 15; CD #49)—and gatherings of family and friends, where music continues to bring people together.[1] In these contexts he and Todora constructed a life for themselves that bound them in many ways to their memories of times past in Gergebunar while negotiating a meaningful existence in the present. In this chapter, I describe a number of events I attended in the late summer of 1988 where I observed their musical practice both as a text to be interpreted and as a discourse about social relations.

Life in the Country

Although village musicians had to move to the cities to pursue jobs as professional musicians, those raised in the discipline of village work tried to maintain ties to their former way of life. Kostadin and Todora returned frequently to Grudovo to visit relatives. They saved money to purchase land in a nearby village for a cottage where they built a house, worked the land, and escaped the gray city's grim concrete.

Over the years, Kostadin built two small three-room houses, providing each of his children's families with its own room, and an outbuilding for storage and a bathroom. He painstakingly terraced the sloping hillside of a valley in the Balkan Mountains north of Sofia, converted a spring into a useable water source, and, together with Todora, tended a garden of fruits, vegetables, and flowers. He arose each

287

morning at six, as discipline required, and watered and weeded the garden until noon, the work interrupted only when Todora prepared a light breakfast of bread and cheese. After a hearty noon meal and nap, lighter work, such as making wine, *rakiya*, and gaidas, occupied the afternoon.

Kostadin purchased the wooden pieces of the gaida from a woodworking *maistor* but spent many days making the gaida itself: preparing the bag, which required skinning a goat kid and washing and salting the skin, clipping the hair, and tying it onto the wooden stocks; whittling a reed and matching it to a gaidanitsa for good intonation; and tuning the instrument by whittling open each hole just the right amount. Growing grapes and making wine and *rakiya* from them was another source of joy and pride. On visits to neighbors' houses in the village he advised them of the best way to tend the vines, and at home boasted to his guests of the quality of this year's vintage of wine and *rakiya*. By leaving the city on weekends and during the summer, Kostadin and Todora replicated many features of life in Gergebunar. It was at their country cottage, particularly at family gatherings, that they experienced music truthfully, the way they remembered it, the way it "brought people together."

Music at Family Gatherings

Although Bulgaria had entered an age in which professionalization and "media-ization" characterized the most audible and visible aspects of music making, private, family music making continued to occupy an important place in the Varimezovs' family life, as it probably did for many musicians. They frequently said that music was the glue that held together their extended family: their three children's families and dozens of relatives still living in Burgas and Grudovo, including her sisters, his brothers, and their spouses and children.

In various configurations, the family gathered regularly to socialize and make music together. These gatherings were enormously important to the family's psychological well-being and a central part of their lives, and they spent a good deal of time planning them and then talking about them afterwards. Nearly every weekend, some members of the family joined Kostadin and Todora at their cottage. On major holidays like the 9th of September (the day celebrating Bulgaria's establishment as a communist country), all of their children—and *their* spouses and children—tried to spend some time there, while neighbors, friends, and cousins from Burgas added to the holiday fun. In this way, enduring village values of hospitality and the importance of having guests—and 'going as guests'—continued to support the music and dance tradition in the dislocated urban and suburban environments where most people lived in the Communist era.

If the staged performances of arranged folklore and the enormous popularity of wedding music provide texts with which to contest the nature of Bulgarian national identity, music at family gatherings creates a more intimate discourse where other values—tradition and change, family solidarity, even gender identity—are negotiated. I describe here two family events I attended (a gathering at the cottage and a family reunion) plus a story about a *koleda* luck-visit to illustrate the way music graced contemporary life while referencing and sustaining the village tradition in newly meaningful ways.

A Gathering at the Cottage

On major holidays, the Varimezov family gathered at the cottage north of Sofia, and in 1988 I joined them on the 9th of September. Among those in attendance were Ivan, their oldest son, and his wife Ivanka; Ivan and Keranka, the son and daughter-in-law of Todora's sister, Petrana; Keranka and Yani, the daughter and son-in-law of Kostadin's brother, Stamat, together with their daughter, Stanimirka; Roza, Stanka's daughter; and Neno Ivanov, the gŭdulka player and Kostadin's friend from Strandzhanskata Grupa, with his wife Stefka. Todor and Stanka were visiting their spouses' parents for the holiday.

The men spent part of the morning digging a trench to run telephone cable up from the main road into the area where the cottages were. Each villager was assigned ten meters to dig in a process known as working "on the brigade," that is, as volunteer labor for the state. Because of the shortage of agricultural workers, crops were routinely harvested this way, and much modernizing work, like road building, was also accomplished in this fashion.

After a morning of digging, chatting, and food preparation, we sat down to eat at 2:30, and the party continued until 11 P.M. We began, as at every meal, with salad and *rakiya*, and after a few glasses Ivan went in search of a gaida. Kostadin and Neno played a few pieces, but then the main course was served. Ivan lamented this interruption, "Ah, food really stops the fun." For him a meal was merely a pretext for gathering people together to sing, dance, have fun, and feel closer to friends and relatives. Alcohol helped, but food disrupted.

After eating, the dancing began and included most of the old village dances: *Boninata, Trite pŭti, Velikdensko horo,* and many others. After the dancing, "cousin" Yani instigated a long round of singing with the aid of Todora. He knew a lot of songs and loved to sing, and was much appreciated by the Varimezovs as a good party person. But he depended on Todora to help him with the words after the first verse or so. Born in 1957, he said, "I don't know many songs, not like the old people do. There are [a few] other young people who know as many songs as I do, but it is rare. They are more interested in disco music. I don't know what they understand. I used to listen to that music, but now I prefer folk music. My mother sang and then I married into this family that is full of songs and fun, so I was motivated to continue."

Yani and Todora had a great relationship, he challenging her to provide the texts of songs he started, she laughing at his inability to finish them. In the fashion of many men who sang, he slurred the words, slid into pitches, and accented certain words more than women typically do, behaviors that suggested he was drunk, even when he was not. In many instances men did become drunk and sang and danced in these ways, but there was a dialectical relationship for men between drunkenness and singing that allowed either one to suggest and induce the other. Both contributed to releasing them from the traditional demands for serious, honorable, upright behavior.

Ivanka, Ivan's wife, played an important role in keeping the celebration going. Every time someone stopped participating, she encouraged others to continue. Kostadin and Todora appreciated the people who married into the family for the way they fit into their tradition of fun, song, and dance. At one point Kostadin said to Yani, "Hey, where did we find such a son-in-law," and he said of the whole group of in-laws, after a certain amount of drink had induced a mellow mood, "These are dangerous [*opasni*, i.e., terrific] people." So important was music, song, and dance to them that when someone married into the extended family who was 'silent' and 'closed,' whose soul couldn't be filled with their music and socializing, it became a serious, much discussed problem for them.

While the adults danced and sang enthusiastically, the children kicked a soccer ball around and shyly refused to join the dancing, although they knew the dances. Roza, Stanka's daughter, had danced in a school group but quit because she didn't like the teacher. Later in the evening, as Kostadin played, she danced a beautiful Gypsy *kyuchek*. Although Bulgarians often ridiculed Gypsies and their dances for their implication, to Bulgarians, of sexual promiscuity and lack of discipline, Roza's modest dancing pleased Kostadin.[2] She had also learned two dance songs from her mother with the help of Todora and sang them for us. Roza and Stanimirka, Yani and Keranka's daughter, told me they liked folk music but only in these situations, not as they heard it on the radio, where they preferred popular music.

Todor and his daughter Miglena arrived late in the evening as the family gathered around a fire to roast sausages and sing more songs. "Miglena really led us here," said Todor, another indication that the grandchildren loved the fun generated by the older people. During the evening Todor and Roza dressed up as Arabs and performed a skit on the theme of whether they could, as Muslims, drink brandy. Here they invoked an array of stereotypes that included the belief that Muslims don't drink alcohol and that they are linked, no matter their ethnicity, to Arab culture. They danced another *kyuchek* as the evening drew to a close.

At this intimate family gathering, the Varimezovs' celebration and performance referenced a number of themes and concerns in their life at the time: the maintenance of family ties and the integration of spouses into it; the continuation of a family tradition of fun, hospitality, song, and dance; the differentiation of male and female roles; and a slightly edgy concern for the political turmoil in the country.

Family Reunions in Strandzha

Family gatherings also took place in Strandzha, where Kostadin's brothers and Todora's sisters and their children lived. Visiting there, as they did many times during the year, recharged their spiritual batteries. There they reentered the family circle that originally inspired their music making. Their home-away-from-home in Strandzha was Todora's sister Irinka's home in Grudovo, a large, two-story, semi-detached house which they shared with her husband's brother's family.

Irinka and her husband, Kolyo Cherpenkov, were both school teachers, he the director of a school for 'slowly developing' children. Their yard in the middle of town was a riot of vegetables and rabbit hutches, and they were able to make a little extra money by renting a small parcel of land from the collective farm, where they grew watermelons to sell to friends and neighbors. Kolyo, a hard-working, strong man, loved Kostadin's music. The two families spent many happy evenings around the Cherpenkovs' table singing, talking, and playing music. Kolyo always started the fun by playing a tune on his okarina. He seemed to know only one slow song tune and one *pravo horo*, but he and everyone else enjoyed his playing. Their son Kircho, a strapping young man in his late twenties, lived with them, along with his wife and child; although an educated professional, Kircho delighted in the music and socializing around the table (pl. 16).

One evening Kircho played recordings he had made on a portable cassette recorder of a previous evening and commented on how memorable and pleasant it had been. The performances had an obviously

improvised, homespun quality even when some of the best professional musicians were there. One recording featured Kostadin, Nikola
Ganchev, and Komna Stoyanova in an enthusiastic, free-wheeling ses-
sion. After listening to the recording, an argument ensued about the
relative value of these performances and recordings as compared to
the radio recordings they were all famous for, treating their own performances as texts for interpretation. Kostadin defended the studio
recordings as cleaner and free of mistakes, but everyone else in the
room preferred these homemade recordings. Todora said of the radio
recordings, "That is not music. There is no emotion, no enthusiasm in
it." And Kircho added, "When I hear these recordings it is as if I am
there again in that time and place and relive it." By implication, the
radio recordings failed to evoke for listeners the unfettered, relaxed
joy of a family gathering or the social meaning that music had for Bulgarian villagers when they experienced it in events as musical discourse.

Reliving the past through recordings was an important part of their
value. When Todora heard one of Kostadin's recordings on the radio,
she spontaneously labeled the sources for many of the tunes, evoking
memories of people and places as she went. These memories were one
of the important sources of emotion for listeners who remembered
village life. Of course, for urban intellectuals, including most composers, recordings either evoked none of these associations or only negative ones linked to stereotypes of backward village life.

At least once a year, family socializing expanded into a gathering of
the entire extended family, an event the Varimezovs referred to as the
'Grudovo meeting,' a family reunion that brought relatives together
for a day and night of music-making and partying in their largely symbolic home of Rosenovo. As Todora said, "Everyone waits for [the Grudovo meeting] impatiently." The one I attended in 1988 was convened
in a grassy clearing on the outskirts of the village where fields meet
the forest. They laid out a traditional 'long table' with blankets on the
ground and served salad, grilled meat, cheese, bread, wine, beer, and
rakiya. Kolyo Cherpenkov started the fun with his okarina (pl. 17), and
Kostadin and his nephew Ivan played for dancing as Todor beat the
tŭpan.

The family danced almost the complete set of dances from Gergebunar. Todora led the singing and most of the women joined in. They
'danced to song' [*igraeha horo na pesen*], a form generally considered
extinct by Bulgarian scholars, just as they had before the war. Stoyan,
Kostadin's youngest brother, surveyed the scene and commented,
"Music brings people together." By the evening everyone was tired

and many had left, but the most enthusiastic revelers, including Kostadin and Todora, their children, and a few cousins, gathered around a bonfire and continued to dance, sing, and play into the night. At one point Todora took a paper plate, held it up as if an icon, and danced a parody of the Strandzha firewalking ritual [*nestinarstvo*] to gales of laughter. They began to dance with arms around shoulders rather than at arm's length, a lessening of the social and physical distance between people putting into practice the ideology of bringing people together. Kostadin and Todora eventually returned to Grudovo to sleep, but their children, Stamat, and a few cousins spent the night in Rosenovo reexperiencing memories of a happy youth, reconstructing family ties, and reinventing an emotional style of interaction denied them in daily life.

Afterward, Todor commented on how different his family was from others he knew. "Other families don't have this tradition. For example, Mimi's [his wife's] family, they sit with their drinks, talk politics, and don't move. I can't stand it. At least if you dance, you don't get completely drunk. At a wedding once, they didn't even dance a *rŭchenitsa* for the bride. This is shameful. How is it possible not to greet the bride with a dance. So I grabbed Mimi and we danced a *rŭchenitsa* for the bride. I really dislike the way people from the village seem artificially to stop celebrating in the old village ways, as if it will help them become city dwellers more quickly. For me celebration is a release [*otdushnik*, lit., 'a thing that empties the soul'], a way of getting rid of the dirt. And it helps bring people together. Mimi's cousin waits impatiently to come to our place as a guest because she knows it will be fun."

Todor provided a cogent analysis of how a failure to practice village traditions helped people construct an image of themselves as urbanites. Furthermore, he offered yet another image of music refreshing and filling the soul while pushing out negative feelings and experiences.

Koleda in the City

The Varimezovs' family musical traditions spilled over to friends and neighbors in the city. Todor explained, "In our apartment building [in a Sofia suburb] they wait every New Year for Grandpa Kostadin to come, because after midnight we go up and down the stairs at New Year's and on each floor dance a *horo*. Everybody opens their doors— everyone is from the provinces—and has a wonderful time. They enjoy this sort of thing, but many don't have the opportunity any more." Todor also believed that those holiday visits "bring people together" in an alienating urban environment. "Now I speak to everyone in the building, although people say, 'How can you talk to so-and-so?' You know how there is unpleasantness between neighbors. But I say, 'Why shouldn't I talk to everyone?'"

In Todor's apartment building, music created a village-like ambience among neighbors who shared a memory of a way of life that included music, song, dance, and ritual at its core. They continued to welcome the possibilities that village music possessed for bringing people together.

Concerts and Banquets

In addition to family gatherings, Kostadin performed occasionally in concerts. Two occurred while I was there in 1988: one in Grudovo to honor him on his seventieth birthday, and one to remember World War II veterans in a small provincial town in Thrace. Anniversaries [*yubilei*, 'jubilees'] are a typical pretext for concerts in Bulgaria, particularly for ensembles celebrating the twenty-fifth anniversary of their founding, but also birthday concerts for older musicians and singers.

Kostadin's Seventieth Birthday Tribute

For Kostadin's seventieth birthday, the film company documenting his life and the local *chitalishte* in Grudovo combined to sponsor a celebratory concert. The Varimezovs felt obligated to host a banquet after the concert, continuing a Bulgarian tradition that the one celebrating the occasion, usually a nameday,[3] hosts the party and provides the food for his or her guests. Grudovo, rather than Sofia, was chosen as the site by the film makers, because his son, Ivan, who was the cinematographer, felt that Kostadin played more expressively in Strandzha. The free concert, held in a 500-seat auditorium in the town square, was packed with people standing in the aisles. Many were turned away, while others strained to hear from the foyer. The film director scripted the concert to reconstruct Kostadin's life story, and sat at the side of the stage introducing each person who spoke or performed.

Representatives from the Radio, Balkanton, and the former director of the Kutev ensemble, Mihail Bukureshtliev, were sent from Sofia to present 'diplomas,' and many of the important musicians and singers in his life came to perform with him: Strandzhanskata Grupa (Stoyan Velichkov, Neno Ivanov, Jimmy Vasilev, and a tambura player from the Radio orchestra [pl. 18]), Nikola Ganchev, Ivan and Tsvetanka, and a number of the best Strandzha singers, including Komna Stoyanova. I and another American, Martha Forsyth, who had hosted Kostadin and Todora in the United States, were also included. All of us in one way or another were part of Kostadin's career, and each of us in turn stood up to speak briefly about Kostadin, to recount moments in his career, or to dedicate a song or tune to him (pl. 19).

Predictably, the unscripted moments were the most touching. Kolyo Cherpenkov rushed on the stage at one point to speak, an older woman presented flowers and exchanged a kiss, and finally Todora was invited on stage and encouraged to sing a duet with Tsvetanka, which she did with extraordinary verve and an unusually powerful voice.

After the concert the musicians played for a *horo* in the town square, another lovely moment which evoked memories of times past for everyone present. Then family, close friends, musicians, and guests repaired to a cafeteria where two long banquet tables and a head table had been prepared, and a party—as Neno Ivanov said, "just like a wedding"—ensued. The musicians, some of the greatest stars of Bulgarian folk music, sang or played from their tables or in the middle of the floor as guests danced enthusiastically around them. Stoyan Velichkov loved it, at one point shouting at me from across the room, "Tim, this is the truth," implying that this is the way Bulgarian music should be played, freely and expressively, in the context of celebration, with love for your friends and neighbors, without arrangements.

A Concert for Pensioners

Although Kostadin had long ago stopped playing for weddings, he teamed with Komna Stoyanova and Nikola Ganchev, who still do, for a concert in a small provincial factory town south of Stara Zagora called Gŭlŭbovo. Just getting to the concert made for a long, tiring day. We got up at 5 A.M. to catch the crowded 6:15 train from Sofia. The ride took nearly five hours, and, after an hour's wait, we transferred to a bus, the aisles packed with people, for the hour-long trip to Gŭlŭbovo. A sad, dirty place exemplifying the worst of Bulgarian industrialization, the town had grown from a village with the addition of factories. But in the midst of the dirty air and dusty streets, we found the usual warm Bulgarian welcome.

Our host, Zhelyo Sokerov, was a thin, wiry, energetic 72-year-old and a great fan of the kaval and of Nikola Ganchev. Just as Kolyo Cherpenkov started family celebrations, Zhelyo, an amateur musician, had no compunction about playing in front of two of the most famous professional musicians in the country, and the professionals in turn welcomed and encouraged his playing, which was rather delightful, in a rough-and-ready village style far removed from Ganchev's smooth professionalism. Ganchev joked that he had recorded hours of material for Zhelyo to listen to but Zhelyo had never learned any of it. The inherent equality of older men and the importance of fun, camaraderie, and companionship over undisciplined, shameful displays of self were again made clear in practice. Zhelyo's wife and daughter served lunch and sat with us as we ate, drank, talked, and played from 1 P.M. to about 5 P.M.—another enormously long meal. These old folks found their own company more invigorating than a nap; there always seemed to be time for talk and fun and maintaining connections.

At 5 P.M. we went to the 'cultural home' where Zhelyo had taken on the responsibility of organizing a 'club for retired people,' and this was their first meeting, honoring World War II veterans. After some speeches, Kostadin and Ganchev each played an extended solo, Komna sang three songs including a slow, sad one about soldiers and their heroic deeds, and Kostadin and I played a duet. After the concert we went to the restaurant in the town square where a banquet had been set out for the pensioners. Ganchev and Kostadin played for dancing, the two instruments in nearly perfect unison, just as Kostadin and his brother Stamat might have played 50 years ago in Gergebunar.

Many people got up to dance, and when the men stopped playing at one point, the women—members of a group of 'artistic amateurs'—began to dance to the accompaniment of their own singing. Kostadin got so excited, he jumped up and joined in the dancing, crying, "They do this just like we do in our village!" So traditional forms like the "dance to song" continued, thanks partly to the support of the state; when they cropped up in contexts like parties and banquets, rather than on stage, they evoked strong emotions. Kostadin was especially pleased with the mood of the evening. "They danced with spirit. We received spirit from them."

Both these formal concerts were designed to honor sincerely those who had served society well. The traditional values of hospitality, however, necessitated the hosting of a less formal banquet at which the participants broke down the barriers between musicians and nonmusicians, strangers and friends, and used music to bring people together. If music at the concerts sometimes seemed at odds with the truth of modern life, at these celebrations musical practice generated real emotions and genuine social relationships unsupervised by the leaders and organizers of the Party.

As I observed both family gatherings and concert banquets, I was also struck by how important quantity was to aesthetic evaluation in Bulgaria. Loudness and knowing many songs were part of this but also how much ornamentation was applied, how many people danced the *horo*, and therefore how long it was, how long it lasted ("In Sliven we played the bride's dance for three hours"), how much we drank, how late we stayed up. The quality of the experience was evaluated largely in terms of its quantities.

New Contexts for Singing

Todora continued to sing at family gatherings, but these must have seemed meagre substitutes for the variety of seasonal contexts in the village. Her singing, freed from the rhythmical experience of passing seasons and appropriate songs, occurred randomly as a particular event evoked a reminiscence of times past. Todora remarked, "We lit a fire the other day [on the 9th of September at the cottage] and I thought immediately of 'Rada Lit a *Sedyanka*'" (ex. 6.10; CD #23). A beautiful sunset one evening caused her to begin the harvest song, "Set, Sun, Set." None of the songs was ever sung completely through, but she sang the opening lines, as we might recite a passage from Shakespeare or the Bible when something stimulated it. Often she remembered a song when she was confronted with the sometimes distasteful conditions of modern life.

Before the war the good life in the cities contrasted with the poverty and illiteracy of the villages, which it was the goal of the Communists to eradicate. Todora and Neno Ivanov both commented on how easy life was under the Communists compared to the hard work and 'that misery' of the past in the village. But while some things may have gotten better, other things had clearly worsened. Comparing the past and present, Todora said, "Then there weren't many problems with drink. Now there are. Then the drunks were in the tavern. Now they're at home. Nearly everyone makes their own wine. They buy grapes. They drink at holidays and weddings. There weren't drunks among the young in the old days. They felt shame in front of older people. Now more young people are drunks, because they have money. They don't have anything else and think they can show they have money in that way. They eat and drink." Her thoughts led her to recall a song dealing with problems of drink, and she began to sing it.

During the filming of the documentary film about Kostadin, they traveled periodically to different locations with a film crew of a dozen or so young men. Todora said, "The other day we were at the Black Sea and some naked women were sunbathing there. We got together that evening with the film crew. I said, 'Boys, boys, how cheap [the nude sunbathers] are. We have a song that tells how valuable girls were at one time.' I said, 'One girl for a thousand [gold coins], 300 boys for a bale of hay.' And now, I said, 'One boy for a thousand, and 300 women for a bale of hay.' They killed themselves laughing" [*laughs*]. In this sporadic way Todora used her songs to reference and illuminate her life experiences in the present; sometimes she even altered them to make them fit an occasion.

Todora recalled making up a new song at the party celebrating Ivan's engagement to Ivanka in the 1960s. The original was about an Ivan who became engaged to eight women in his village, all of whom died. Finally he left the village to seek a bride far away and returned to the village three years later with a beautiful bride and a male child. She felt that the sad words of the text were not appropriate for the happy occasion, and so she made up new words, as she had been doing since childhood. "My mother sang it a lot, but I didn't like it because it was so sad. But she said, 'Listen to it. Later you will find it interesting.' I made up words by myself, especially when I was weaving, because I didn't like the text. Weaving was when I sang the most. I sang all day, and who knows what stupidities I put into the songs." In Todora's new song Ivan became engaged to the best girl, beautiful Ivanka, who worried that she was poor and his large, rich family wouldn't like her. But he reassured her that he didn't want a rich girl, he wanted a beautiful bride like her, echoing a common theme in many village songs.

Zgodil se Ivan zgodil se	Ivan became engaged
za bash momata v seloto,	to the best girl in the village,
v seloto i v mahalata,	in the village and in the neighborhood,
ubava byala Ivanka.	to beautiful white Ivanka.
Ivanka duma Ivana:	Ivanka said to Ivan:
—Lyube Ivane, Ivane,	"My love, Ivan, Ivan,
ya sŭm si mnogo ubava	I am very beautiful
ala sŭm mnogo siromashka	but I am very poor
i nyamam dari ubavi	and I don't have beautiful gifts
da ti daruvam svatove	to give to the in-laws,
svatove oshte kumove.	to the in-laws and to the godparents.
Ie imash roda golyama,	But you have a large family,
golyama roda bolyarska,	a large rich family,
ie ke olŭn razsŭrdat	and they will become angry
che nyamash bulka bogata.	because you don't have a rich bride.
A vzemash mene, siromashka.	But take me, a poor girl."
Ivan Ivanki dumashe:	Ivan said to Ivanka:
—Lyube Ivanko, Ivanko,	"My love, Ivanka, Ivanka,
ya ne shta moma bogata.	I do not want a rich girl.
No iskam bulka ubava.	I want a beautiful bride.

Ti mi si, Ivanko, likata   You are pleasing to me, Ivanka,
likata i prilikata.   pleasing to me and you suit me.

"I made this up at the moment we sat down at the table. I liked the
glas ['voice,' 'melody'] and it spoke about Ivan, but there wasn't an
Ivanka, so I made it up right at that moment. I didn't write it down.
My voice was very rich then and a very good recording was made. It
really pleased him. He [Ivan] said, 'Mother! This song?' I said, 'This
song is for you. I sang it this evening for the first time.'" Thus Todora
continued to compose songs in the city as she had in the village in the
1930s, stimulated by new events. With rare exceptions they died as
quickly as they were created.

Todora was not alone in finding contemporary relevance for her
village songs; her son Ivan did as well. A highly respected cinematographer, he worked on a film about Petŭr Beron, a nineteenth-century
Bulgarian émigré separated from his homeland and family for years.
Ivan proposed to the director that, as Beron lay dying in exile, he
hear his mother's singing on the soundtrack as symbolic of childhood
memories. Ivan also thought a nonprofessional singer would evoke a
more realistic maternal image than a professional one would. He listened to the tapes I had made of Todora in Toronto and chose *Oi
slŭntse slŭntse* [Oh Sun, Sun]. Todora said, "In the film he was remembering his homeland and I sang this song." It had a striking, well-
received effect and so Ivan used his mother's singing in yet another
film. As Todora tells it, "In another film someone from the Burgas
villages went somewhere else to live. He sold everything. He became a
merchant, but was unsuccessful and had to return to the village. When
he arrives, they are harvesting and I sing the song, *Stoyan, Stoyan, mladi
postadzhio* [Stoyan, Stoyan, Young Harvester (ex. 6.9; CD #22)]. My
niece heard it and called my sister, 'Auntie is singing on a film.' She
knew the song and recognized my voice."

In these fragmented and isolated moments of modern life—working
at home, at family gatherings, at concerts and the banquets afterwards,
and in chance intersections of the present with memories of the past—
Kostadin, Todora, and their children continued the tradition as they
searched for ways to make their lives richer and more meaningful
through music, song, and dance (pl. 20).

Reflections on Individual Musical Experience

If by individual behavior we mean unique behavior, then any attempt
to theorize or generalize about it would be doomed. However, individ-

ual actions and the meanings assigned to them are historically, culturally, and socially constituted and constrained. The necessity to create
not just any action but socially meaningful action reduces the possibilities for individual variation in behavior to the point at which some generalizations can be made. Here, I present five consequences that flow
from the dialectic between individual musical behavior and the world
in which those behaviors are created, experienced, and interpreted.

1. When individual experience is made the locus of investigation,
the notion that music reflects culture largely disappears. In its place
we find individuals acting on or through music, acting musically, as
it were, to constitute themselves socially and assign meaning to their
experience. Gypsies resisted subjugation to central authority by playing freely, 'with gusto.' The Party's minions, charged to "lead and
guide," understood their playing as a challenge to their authority, and
tried, where they could, to control and suppress it.

Kostadin chose to teach and did his best to pass on his knowledge
of the tradition to future generations, an act that placed him in the
ranks of the socially disciplined builders of communism. At the same
time, he resisted the Westernizing excesses of composers and sought
ways to keep his recordings true to the village tradition as he understood it. His children and grandchildren rejected the public performance and recreation of village music as inconsistent with their new
urban social life, but used its private enjoyment as a way to define and
keep the family together. Todora made her experience of contemporary life meaningful by recalling, and occasionally reshaping, the song
texts of her youth, while radio and record producers truncated the
same texts to hold the attention of listeners who found them meaningless or irrelevant.

Young gaidari expressed their youth and individuality by manipu-
lating and enriching the instrument's ornamental style, in the process
distancing themselves from what they learned from Kostadin. On the
other hand, they evaluated and enjoyed a performance in terms of
how it matched their notion of tradition. In these simple, multiplex,
and contradictory ways, individuals created themselves and their culture in music.

2. While theories of experience need to leave room for individual
choice and variation, those choices and variations will exhibit a culturally shared and appropriate style or will play with that style in ways
that can be interpreted as meaningfully related to it. Musicians, in particular, use shared notions of musical and cultural style as mediums of
expression. Ivo Papazov might veer unpredictably between Bulgarian,
Gypsy, Turkish, and jazz styles, but when he wanted to fit in to the

demands of a festival or Balkanton-produced recording, he used something very close to the 'sweet' Bulgarian style. Young gaidari may chafe at the strictures of tradition and their instruments, but as they sought to push back the limits of tradition, they did so in a disciplined, thoughtful manner that included respect for their elders and hard work, traditional features of Bulgarian culture. If we can't explain why one urban child embraced the gaida while most of his friends teased him mercilessly as they rejected it, we can explain the economic, aesthetic, and ideological factors that influenced their choices.

3. Individual musical experience is mediated by a history and a memory of previous experience. In that sense, musical experience is historically constructed. For Kostadin and Todora, each new performance of a song or tune called forth a lifetime of memories of people, places, and events. For friends at their country cottage, the tunes provided the medium for fun; they allowed them to share each other's company and, even though the tunes were Thracian rather than *Shop*, to dance together.

For young wedding musicians in Ivan Varimezov's band, the tunes, replete with memories for the Varimezovs, were simply "traditional," to be played before continuing with the more with-it tunes of popular wedding bands. For an urban bride, they provided the beat for a little-understood dance to be endured for the sake of in-laws from a village. Although the examples could be multiplied a hundredfold, crucial to understanding the experience of music is an analysis of the musical, intellectual, aesthetic, social, and ideological background an individual brings to the transaction.

4. Although experience is predicated on inevitably unique personal histories, some elements of those histories are shared by people in the same social formation. Furthermore, people use music to give meaning and life to their group. For example, in Bulgaria in 1988 at least three groups were arguing over the future of Bulgarian music. One group, older musicians and folklorists, favored preserving principles and practices from the past. They turned their vested interest into an argument that what is old is valuable, and they interpreted each new performance in that light. Another group, the intellectuals and composers, acted as if what was old was a remnant of an undesirable feudal past, and attained "artistic" and "social" value in modern times only when dressed up in the accoutrements of European musical "civilization." Again their aesthetic arguments matched their economic interests.

A third group, outsiders to both the village past and the ideology that controlled the present, included Muslim minorities and young people searching for a way to make music meaningfully in a changing society. In the process of absorbing what was known of the tradition and moving it forward, they claimed they performed better than those who had gone before them. By 1988, they were the dynamic force in the tradition, because they were the only ones with an aesthetic and economic interest in progressing. In order to make themselves more attractive on the open market of wedding music, they played with ever more virtuosity.

For members of all three groups, economic interest and social position informed aesthetic perspective and experience. The grinding of their aesthetic axes provided some insight into their experience of music. Village musicians and folklorists complained about the 'mutilation' and 'profanation' of the tradition by both composers and wedding musicians who didn't understand it. The composers felt that village music was too decrepit to broadcast or put on the stage without make-up, and claimed that wedding musicians' playing lacked taste and was often based on composers' innovations anyway. Younger musicians found older playing colorless and drab and most composers' music too stilted, artificial, and confining.

Musical practice and aesthetics, far from an Olympian domain for lofty reflection and formal manipulation, was an arena where economic, political, and ethnic forces battled. Music provides individuals with a feelingful way to experience themselves linked to others in social groups that share common practices and values.

5. The power of music in human experience, its emotional source and force, lies not in some loose conjunction of historical construction and social maintenance, but in their coincidence and union at a particular instant in time. Stoyan Velichkov was enraptured, not by the virtuosity of younger players or the skill of composers, but by a freewheeling, improvisational confluence of good playing and friends that matched a rich life of previous such experiences. Music on the radio failed to move listeners in part because it was connected mainly to memories of previous mediated performances and to a discredited central government and was disconnected from experiences of music at weddings and private celebrations. A song touched Todora when it unified her experiences of *sedyankas* past with family gatherings present. Her children, intimately aware of the tradition through their mother's singing, were moved by an old song she made relevant for an engagement party. Somewhere in that confluence and association of memory with immediate sensory and social experience is the source of music's power to fill your soul.

Part Six
Interpreting the Tradition

One of the things that taste judges is whether a work of art has soul or whether it is soulless.

Hans-Georg Gadamer, *Truth and Method*

TWELVE

Truth and Music

The notion that I would conclude this study of a family's musical tradition with a disquisition on truth and music did not occur to me when I began writing it. And yet as I became conscious of my position in the flow of tradition, as one intellectual and musical interpreter of it, I found myself engaged with other individuals who cared deeply about the tradition and about what they called variously a true [*verno*], truthful [*istinsko*], authentic [*avtentichno*], correct [*pravilno*], pure [*chist*] rendition of it.

Postmodern scholars delight in deconstructing and critiquing claims to truth, showing how each is a self-interested, socially positioned construction—often hegemonically imposed through the exercise of power—when viewed from some higher plane of objective observation where the "real truth," the "real meaning," or the "real function" of music, or other symbolic behaviors, can be analyzed and demonstrated by the researcher. Having chosen hermeneutics over absolute truth, however, I find myself taking everyone's truth claims—and claims for authenticity are one form of those claims—very seriously. When people make claims for truth and authenticity, they are not erring in the face of our refined histories; they are telling us that music is most deeply moving, most expressive, most fulfilling precisely when it is appropriated and understood as true.[1]

The truth that music embodies and symbolically represents is not a propositional, logical truth, verifiable by the niceties of epistemological reflection and explanation, but an existential, ontological truth that sensation, memory, and imagination coalesce into a memorable experience. The analysis and deconstruction of the truth and authenticity claims people make about music denies to it the most crucial aspect of its power to move us. No matter how situated, contexted, and constructed our multiple understandings of music are, each claim is crucial to music's power. Only when we experience music as true does it fill our souls.

In the context of trying to recapture the truth of experience as a locus for research in the human sciences, Hans-Georg Gadamer, in *Truth and Method* (1986), is especially critical of the "historicist hermeneutics" of Dilthey, who sought to interpret a text or a work in terms of the intentions or the life of its author—a tactic basic to anthropology and ethnomusicology. To investigate the background of a work "is to move out of the actual experience" of it (105). Since much musicology does precisely that, music in the process is lost to us as immediate aesthetic experience. Furthermore, Gadamer believes that the historicist attempt "to reproduce in the understanding the original purpose of a work" merely leads to "the recovery of a dead meaning" (148–49). Quoting Hegel, he says, "To place [works of art] in their historical [or cultural] context does not give one a living relationship with them but rather one of mere imaginative representation" (149).

Rather than worry about the historical or cultural placement of a work, Gadamer prefers to analyze that moment when past and present are united in experience. The interpreter's claim to meaning and truth is then as great as the author's: "The artist who creates something is not the ideal interpreter of it. As an interpreter he has no automatic priority as an authority over the man who is simply receiving his work" (170). "Every age has to understand a transmitted text in its own way" and its meaning "does not depend on the contingencies of the author and whom he originally wrote for" (263).

Perhaps Gadamer's most powerful statement of the consequences of understanding a tradition or text primarily in historical or ethnographic terms concerns the loss of its claim to "truth."

> The text that is understood historically is forced to abandon its claim that it is uttering something true. We think we understand when we . . . place ourselves in the historical situation and seek to reconstruct the historical horizon. In fact, however, we have given up the claim to find, in the past, any truth valid and intelligible to ourselves. Thus this acknowledgement of the otherness of the other, which makes him the object of objective knowledge, involves the fundamental suppression of his claim to truth. (270)

This book's subtitle, "Experiencing Bulgarian Music," came originally from a sense that much academic writing about music fails to engage music as experience, thereby giving up whatever claim it may have on our interest. We may be trapped in a "linguocentric predicament," as Charles Seeger would have it, but our problems are exacerbated when we fall victim to the objectifying strategies of the physical sciences. By simultaneously turning music and music making into an object and then making ourselves disappear as observers, we transform the infinitely rich, emotionally intense, everchanging experience of music that caused us to want to think more about it in the first place into studies that lie flat on the page with little hope of resuscitation.

Gadamer shows rather convincingly in *Truth and Method* that the hope for objectivity is doomed in the human sciences because "we can never have the same experience twice." Every experience contributes a new layer of "fore-knowledge" to the next experience. Bias, prejudice, and previous experience are not negative traits that can be eradicated by the power of reason, but are inescapable: "The interpreter does not know that he is bringing himself and his own concepts into the interpretation" (364). Traditions, performances, texts, and the possibilities for interpretation and insight "are inexhaustible. It is the progress of events that brings out new aspects of meaning in historical material" (336). I conceived this study with experience at its core in the hope that I could keep alive that sense of wonder, or at least engagement, that our interaction with music provides us.

Gadamer's problem with historicist interpretations of literary texts cannot be transferred unproblematically to the domain of ethnographic interpretations of sociomusical actions in "other" traditions. Paul Ricoeur and Clifford Geertz have done the main work in rehabilitating Gadamer's hermeneutics for cultural analysis. The obvious problem with respect to this study is that ethnomusicologists are rightly concerned with the intentional meanings of others, particularly in the context of events of musical discourse, and argue, quite to the contrary, that a musical performance cannot be understood until we recover the context, function, and meaning it has for the people who performed it.

Gadamer acknowledges this tension between the historical/ethnographic perspective and his literary/critical approach, but claims that while the former has dominated the latter until recently, historical and ethnographic work actually partake of the same limitations as critical commentary: "in the human sciences the interest in tradition is motivated in a special way by the present and its interests" (253). The result is a radical contextualization of research and interpretation in the historically situated discourse or dialogue between the researcher and the tradition studied, with claims to "truth" never settled and always subject to continuous reinterpretation.

To return to the work at hand, the notion of "experiencing the tradition" had two focuses: my own experience and that of the actors I chose to include in my story. The notion of reporting on one's own experience is sometimes criticized as irrelevant to an understanding of another tradition. However, I would argue that personal experience is neither free nor individual; it is constrained by interaction with the tradition. If I discover something "true" in the experience, it is not because of a virtuosic subjectivity but because I have questioned the tradition and, in the process, opened myself to it.

In this book key moments of insight based on such openness to the tradition included the progress I made in learning to play the gaida, my interpretation of the song texts as women's texts, my appreciation of the transformative power of dancing indoors in a circle, and my sense of musical style as an important arena for defining my and others' relation not only to Bulgaria's past but also to its present. These were insights afforded in the first instance by an active engagement with the music itself, both as would-be producer and aesthetic consumer of it. The truths discovered in these experiences are neither unique and therefore personal to me nor do they claim to exclude other insights. Rather, they emerged in and were constrained by social and musical relationships with others in the tradition and with the musical tradition itself.

Since I believed in advance of the study that experience might be the core of a musical study, I sought to characterize how a selection of Bulgarians experienced the tradition in the hope that such an approach would keep alive that sense of dynamic engagement I feel with respect to music. While the characterization of another's experience might be belittled by Gadamer as mere historicism or psychologism in relation to literary texts, it must remain an important goal of historical and ethnographic research. From that point of view we can reexamine the chronological order of the book as a peeling back of the layers of experience of various individuals.

In the late 1980s the tradition was being appropriated by musicians with many minds about the world their music making referenced. Some thought that music should be modern and contemporary, and therefore they made tradition meaningful by assimilating it to the tastes and experience of popular music, especially rock and jazz. Ethnic minorities thought that Bulgarian tradition should not exclude the possibility of their own expression and therefore sought to appropriate Turkish, Macedonian, and Gypsy traditions as well. At the same time, professional composers and choreographers and their students continued to experience the tradition as both in need of sprucing up with the modernizing, civilizing techniques of Western music and ballet and a source of good tunes for their arrangements and story lines for their choreographies of ritual.

Children and a large segment of the urban population found it increasingly difficult to associate any meaning or truths at all with folk music, except perhaps negative ones about the Party's unfulfilled promises for a glorious future under communism. And older people, like Kostadin and Todora, stripped away the accoutrements of modernization, the instruments howling around them, and the schizophonic (Schafer 1977) radio-listening experience for the "truth" as they understood it: music for friends and neighbors, played for personal satisfaction, and sung with texts that captured something that "must have really happened." Another way to read their descriptions of the past, then, is for the "fore-knowledge" they provide for each new experience of the tradition in the present.

These texts—the music, dances, and songs and the commentary on them—were produced in the present as symbols that referenced many worlds: the past, as preserved differently in a variety of individual memories; the present, with its patterns of political control and oppression, cooperation and resistance; and a number of productively imagined worlds, whether a beautiful, Westernized, industrial utopia or a convivial place where interpersonal distance was dissolved.[2]

As I listened to this music, these songs, and these commentaries, my soul was filled not just with fascinating rhythms, catchy tunes, and vigorous dances, but with a world of ancestors who suffered at the hands of the Turks, of girls mistreated by boys, of fear and loneliness in fields and pastures far from the village, of the terror of building a new society, of the joys of long evenings with good friends and good music, of the excitement and satisfaction of creating something new for modern tastes, of the frustration and anger at having to play someone else's tradition and being prevented from playing your own. In addition to my attempt to understand the meanings that Bulgarians gave to their music, however, my experience of them and their music has widened my horizons, and their truths have deepened and enriched my experience not only of their tradition but of my world as well.

Glossary

aftorsko pravo 'author's rights'; copyright.

baba grandma.

bai term of respect used for older male, from the Turkish *bey*.

banitsa a common dish made from dough rolled into thin sheets that are then buttered, layered, and filled with a mixture of *sirene* [feta cheese], eggs, and milk.

bavna pesen nonmetrical slow song.

bitov traditional.

blaga rakiya sweet brandy, a sweet liquor made from brandy and carmelized sugar, considered a women's drink, also denotes the women's portion of the wedding celebration after the marriage has been consummated. See **zhenska svatba**.

Boninata a line dance in 7/8 time (2 + 2 + 3) that has symmetrical movement with four steps to the right, then three sets of three quick steps and back again.

buchimish a dance type in a brisk 15/8 meter, subdivided 2 + 2 + 2 + 2 + 3 + 2 + 2.

buenek Thracian women's dance step and dance melody type in brisk 2/4.

bŭklitsa a small, decorated wooden cask for wine or spirits used especially for weddings.

bulchenska svirnya bride's tune, slow unmetered instrumental piece played for the bride during the wedding procession (see **svirnya**).

bulka bride.

chest honor, an important value for Bulgarian conduct, found throughout Mediterranean cultures, maintained in social situations through positive behavior and by the desire to avoid incurring social shame, or *sram*.

chetvorno a *Shop* dance type in a brisk 7/8 meter, subdivided 3 + 2 + 2.

chist clean, pure, an adjective used to designate perceived folk or rural roots in Bulgarian folk musical practice.

chitalishte 'reading room,' learning room, small school or cultural center in a village.

chorbadzhiya 'soupmaker,' formerly a rank in the Ottoman army and a wealthy Bulgarian during the Ottoman period; frequently used by musicians to refer to their patron at a wedding or celebration.

daichovo 9/8 meter dance type subdivided 2 + 2 + 2 + 3.

davul Turkish cylindrical, double-headed bass drum played with large stick and thin wand, predecessor of the Bulgarian tŭpan.

dever best man in the wedding; if possible, the groom's brother.

distsiplina 'discipline,' the Bulgarian value of honor reflected in hard work.

drobezhi fast, pulsatile variations that follow song tunes. Musicians also call these sections *sitnezhi* ['tiny, fine things'].

drushki friendship pair, particularly refers to female singing partners.

dŭlga trapeza traditional long feast table.

dushevno razvitie 'spiritual development,' a Socialist ideological concept that stressed the cultural and educational development for all levels of society.

dyado grandpa.

firuglitsa wedding banner, made by tying a handkerchief, together with an apple and flowers, to a newly cut branch of the *shipka* tree.

folklorna diskoteka 'folk discoteque,' folk music arranged in a pop style using synthesized accompaniments.

gaida bagpipe with goatskin air reservoir, one melody chanter, a blowpipe, and a dronepipe.

gaidanitsa melody pipe or chanter of the gaida.

gaidar bagpiper [pl., *gaidari*].

gaidarski prŭsti 'gaida player's fingers,' that is, the ability to play the ornamentation on the gaida correctly.

gama scale or key.

gimnaziya high school.

glas 'voice,' vocal melody.

godezh engagement party.

gostopriemlivi 'guest-receiving'; hospitable.

gŭdulka pear-shaped bowed lute with wooden soundboard, three melody strings and eight or so sympathetically resonating strings.

gyurultiya joyous noise, a raucous cacophony of unmatched song, instrumental tune, and the shouts of wedding guests that creates an uncoordinated polyphony typical of the wedding and denotes a desirable aesthetic and social effect at a wedding or dance.

haiduks men who went into the forest to wage guerilla warfare against the Turks during the time of Ottoman occupation, viewed as national folk heros.

hijaz a *makam* commonly used in Turkish and Arabic modal systems; among contemporary Bulgarian musicians is used to refer to a pentachord with an augmented second between the second and third degrees of the scale.

horishte dance place in the village's central square.

horo generic name for a line dance.

horo na pesen 'dance to song,' a dance form in which the steps are accompanied by singing.

hŭs from Turkish *hız*, meaning brash, brazen; in Bulgarian gusto, intensity. An adjective used by musicians to designate the staccato, "aggressive" performance style typical of contemporary wedding music.

igra game, often a dance-like game accompanied by singing.

igriva lively.

izvivki ornaments, specifically vocal ornaments.

izvor 'spring,' 'source'; denotes rural source of folklore.

kaba gaida the low-pitched gaida from the Rhodope Mountains.

kaka 'older sister'; a term of respect for a slightly older female nonrelative.

kaval end-blown, bevel-edged flute.

koleda an animal fertility ritual involving the return or "birth" of the sun, a Christmas caroling ritual.

koledari caroling boys who go from house to house during **koleda,** imitating animals, singing songs, and bringing good fortune and fertility to the household.

kolyano 'knee,' 'joint'; denotes a typically four-measure musical phrase that is then repeated.

kopanitsa 11/8 meter dance type, subdivided 2 + 2 + 3 + 2 + 2.

krivo horo 'crooked dance'; dance type in 11/8 meter, subdivided 2 + 2 + 3 + 2 + 2, characteristic of the Pazardzhik region.

krŭstnitsi 'christeners'; godparents.

kukeri mummers who dress in animal skins on **kukerovden** and process from house to house to insure the fertility of the season's crops.

kukerovden Mummer's Day or Carnival, an agricultural fertility ritual around planting time, coincides with the beginning of Lent.

kumova svirnya 'godfather's tune'; slow, unmetered instrumental piece played for the godfather during the wedding procession.

kŭrma a half-holing technique on the gaida used to play chromatic pitches in the instrument's lower pentachord.

kyuchek a Gypsy solo belly-dance-like form in duple meter and in 9/8 time.

lev Bulgarian monetary unit [pl. *leva*].

maistor 'master,' used to denote a master craftsman, such as an instrument maker; also a term of respect.

makam general term for Turkish mode.

makamliya 'with *makam*'; used to describe a singer with good melodic sense.

mane from Turkish musical practice, an improvised, nonmetrical solo instrumental piece that introduces the **makam**.

medzhiya female working bee where communal work was done.

megdan village square where dances were held.

meh bagpipe bag.

melodiya melody.

merak enthusiasm, desire.

mominska chest 'maiden's honor'; female virginity.

mormorka 'flea hole'; a tiny hole at the top of the bagpipe chanter covered by the first finger of the upper hand. It helps to produce a chromatic scale on what otherwise would be a diatonic instrument.

na filek song games with rhythmic motion played by boys and girls during Lent, a period in which dancing was forbidden.

na moabet 'in conversation'; a Turkish term denoting a gathering of men marked by eating, drinking, conversation, singing, and playing music.

nadpyavane 'singing competition,' especially a genre of short songs sung at **sedyankas** in which boys' and girls' names were paired in a teasing manner.

narodna muzika usually translated as folk music in English, its meanings are multiple in Bulgarian and other Slavic languages: folk, popular, mass, people's, national.

nestinarstvo a firewalking ritual honoring Saints Constantine and Elena and practiced in the villages of Kosti and Bŭlgari in Strandzha.

obraboten folklor arranged, improved folklore.

obrabotki musical arrangements.

okarina clay whistle flute with eight fingerholes and two thumbholes.

otsvir instrumental interlude between verses of a song.

ovcharska svirka 'shepherd's flute'; an end-blown flute with beveled edge, six fingerholes, and one thumbhole.

paidushko 5/8 meter dance type subdivided 2 + 3.

panayir village fair associated with a saint's day.

peperuda 'butterfly'; a summer rain-begging ritual.

persenk musical motives or instrumental "licks" used by instrumentalists to build improvisations.

pesen song.

pesen na trapeza 'table song'; slow, unmetered song that was traditionally sung at feast tables.

pesnopoets a person who sang and sold songsheets or chapbooks.

pesnopoiki songsheets or booklets of printed ballads.

pishtalka double-reed pipe with six fingerholes made of straw.

pogach ritual bread, especially for Easter and weddings.

Pomaks Bulgarians who converted to Islam during the Ottoman period and speak Bulgarian, not Turkish.

pravo horo 'straight dance'; the most common Bulgarian line dance in 2/4 or 6/8 meter.

pripev instrumental interlude between vocal verses.

rakiya strong grape brandywine.

razsvirvane stylized instrumental flourish performed by bagpipe players when warming up.

rŭchenitsa dance step and melody in a meter of 7, subdivided 2 + 2 + 3, commonly performed at weddings.

sedyanka 'sitting bee'; a female working bee at which each girl or woman sews, knits, spins, or embroiders her own work.

shaferki groups of four girls who sing and participate in ritual gift exchanges during the wedding ritual.

Shop a person from the central-western region of Bulgaria around the capital city of Sofia; the *Shop* region.

shlageri from German *schlag* ['cream'], popular songs, particularly from before World War II.

sirene a type of soft, white, fresh cheese found throughout the Balkans; called feta in Greece.

sitnezhi 'tiny, fine things'; a performance style in which long notes are subdivided and a more pulsating, motoric rhythmic effect is created. Also called *drobezhi*.

sofra small round table with three legs.

sram shame; the negative component of not comporting one's self honorably or with *distsiplina* ['discipline'].

sŭbor 'gathering'; village fair, before World War II associated with a Saint's day celebration, after the war with state-sponsored competitions and festivals.

sŭvet 'council'; an administrative body.

svirach 'player'; instrumental musician.

svirnya 'played tune'; slow, nonmetrical tune consisting of collections of slow song motives and phrases that the musicians improvise during long periods of playing.

tambura long-necked, fretted, plucked lute with four double courses of strings.

testemelichka 'handkerchief dance'; an old name for **rŭchenitsa.**

trite pŭti 'the three times,' a dance step and melody type in brisk 2/4 meter subdivided 4 + 4.

tropliva stampable, danceable.

trudolyubivi 'work-loving'; an adjective Bulgarians use to characterize themselves.

tsigani Gypsies.

tulum from Turkish, the bagpipe's bag.

tŭninika humming; a style of vocal performance of instrumental and song tunes without words; resembles "scat" singing in jazz.

tŭpan cylindrical, double-headed bass drum played with large stick and thin wand.

vecherni hora evening dances.

Velikden 'Great day'; Easter.

veselba fun, especially that created by music, song, and dance.

vodena rŭchenitsa 'led *rŭchenitsa*'; a dance in which the leader takes the line in a serpentine pattern as the dancers run in rhythm.

vŭrtenata a line dance in which two dancers at the beginning and end of the line curl in the ends of the line.

yubilei 'jubilee,' or anniversary. A typical pretext for concerts in Bulgaria, particularly for ensembles and groups celebrating the twenty-fifth anniversary of their founding but also birthday concerts for older musicians and singers.

zamesarka 'the one who begins to mix [the dough],' the leader of the *shaferki*, the girls who sing and perform other ritual acts at a wedding.

zhenska svatba 'women's wedding,' held on Monday after the marriage has been consummated and the bride's virginity established; also called *blaga rakiya*.

zhŭtvarski pesni 'harvest songs,' which are nonmetrical and distinguished textually in most cases from other songs by reference to field work and harvesting.

zurna oboe-type aerophone, usually accompanied by tŭpan, originally from Turkey and played by Gypsies.

Notes

1. Dancing in the Scholar's World

1. Charles Seeger was one of the first musicologists to suggest using these approaches and one of the few musicologists to examine the gap between language and musical experience, which he called the "linguocentric predicament" and the "musicological juncture," in detail. In a series of brilliant articles (edited and collected in Seeger 1977), he outlined a set of dichotomies that seem to divide music and musical experience irrevocably from speech and musicology (music + *logos*/'word'):

Speech	*Music*
reasoned mode	affective mode
fact	value
intellection of reality	feeling of reality
social values	inner experience
speech knowledge	music knowledge

Seeger (1977:18) concluded, "The affective mode pits a belief in nonspeech and the knowledge of inner experience against speech knowledge and social values; the reasoned mode, speech knowledge and social values against belief in nonspeech inner experience."

Seeger's dilemma might seem to leave scholars with a choice between: (1) abandoning musicology because it is prevented epistemologically from elucidating precisely what seems most important about music; or (2) continuing to describe and analyze musical structures, performances, contexts, and cultures for the intellectual rewards such activity provides while postponing indefinitely an approach to what interested us about music in the first place. Seeger rejected these unhappy alternatives and cast about for ways to mediate between the dichotomies he had identified. He examined the possibilities for homologies between music logic and speech logic ("On the Moods of a Music Logic," 1977:64–

101); he thought of both music and speech as semiotic subspecies of communication ("Speech, Music, and Speech about Music," 1977:16–30); and he tried to imagine what music thinking, as opposed to thinking in language about music, might be like ("The Musicological Juncture: Music as Fact," 1977:45–50).

2. Works on insider verbal categories using the techniques of cognitive anthropology include Zemp 1978, 1979 on the 'Are'Are; Rice 1980a on Bulgarian village music; Powers 1980 on the Oglala Sioux; Feld 1981 on the Kaluli; and Sakata 1983 on Afghanistan. Works on homologies between musical and other modes of production include Kaeppler 1978 and Keil 1979. The seminal works on iconicity of musical style were written by Alton Becker 1979; Judith Becker 1979; and Judith and Alton Becker 1981 on Javanese music and culture. Feld 1988a provides a richly textured study of the Kaluli along these lines.

3. The hermeneutical trail includes Heidegger (1962) in *Being and Time,* first published in 1927; Gadamer (1986) in *Truth and Method,* first published in 1960; and Ricoeur in a long list of publications, but especially a series of essays mostly written in the 1970s and translated and collected in *Hermeneutics and the Human Sciences* (1981).

4. Gadamer (1986:273) uses the concept of a "fusion of horizons" to capture the notion of a changing self, inescapably building on, reacting to, and altering its historically conditioned prejudices and thus expanding the horizons of the world of symbols into which it was thrown.

5. A two-record set of various Bulgarian choirs with the title, *Le Mystère des voix bulgares,* was produced and released in Europe by Marcel Cellier and later reissued in the United States on Nonesuch 79165, 79201. A third volume with the same title was released in 1990 on Polygram/Fortuna 846 626.

6. In the 1960s and '70s, for example, there was some tension between the performance-oriented ethnomusicology programs at UCLA and Wesleyan, which attracted, in addition to some excellent scholars, performing musicians interested primarily in the how-to of non-Western musical traditions, and more anthropologically focused and self-consciously non-performance-oriented programs at Indiana and Illinois. During this period, some effort was expended to explain that performance of non-Western music was not ethnomusicology.

7. A growing number of articles treat critically the appropriation of "world music," among them Meintjes 1990 and Feld 1988b. Meintjes emphasizes the negative connotations of appropriation by placing it in a series of power-inflected terms: "a process of appropriation, exploitation, and domination" (47). While appropriation of third-world cultural material by first-world scholars and musicians is fraught with ethical questions due to the imbalance of political, economic, and racial power, ethnomusicologists cannot escape these problems. We are, from a hermeneutical perspective, as implicated in acts of appropriation as are musicians and dancers. Since appropriation is a useful philosophical concept to describe how our socially and historically positioned selves understand other worlds, we may want to use terms such as misappropriation or expropriation for the most ethically vexing instances.

8. Although interpretive approaches and self-reflexivity in research are in-

creasingly taken-for-granted aspects of ethnomusicological discourse, Jeff Titon's book, *Powerhouse for God* (1988), is the only other work in ethnomusicology I know of to delve into the philosophical roots of these positions: "Hermeneutic phenomenology, then, seems to me to be the best available framework, as today's folklorist contemplates the affective performance of folklore within a community within memory and history" (13). As Titon points out, the means by which understanding occurs is the dialogue between the researcher and the "folk." "This is the world, the intersubjective reality, that the field worker comes to know; and this is the only world one can truly reconstruct in one's interpretive writings—if one comes to any understanding at all" (ibid.)

9. Victor Turner, in an article in a collection of essays entitled, *The Anthropology of Experience* (Turner and Bruner 1986:35), follows Dilthey in distinguishing between "mere" experience ("the passive endurance and acceptance of events") and "an" experience, one that is "formative and transformative." Gadamer writes extensively on the history of the concept experience, captured in the German word *Erlebnis*, a word that became common only in the 1870s. It develops from the older verb *erleben* ['to live, see, experience'], which contains elements of "both the immediacy, which precedes all interpretation, treatment, or communication" and the "yield or a residue that acquires permanence, weight and significance from out of the transience of experiencing" (1986:55–63). "What we emphatically call an experience thus means something unforgettable and irreplaceable that is inexhaustible in terms of the understanding and determination of its meaning" (60).

10. Ricoeur (1981:193) writes of the inevitability of competing interpretations: "It is because absolute knowledge is impossible that the conflict of interpretations is insurmountable and inescapable. Between absolute knowledge and hermeneutics, it is necessary to choose."

11. In an earlier article (Rice 1987), I offered these questions as a possible "model of" how existing research in ethnomusicology might be related and organized, and as a "model for" how to think interpretatively when doing research in the future. This well-known of/for distinction is borrowed from Geertz, who also stimulated the set of questions with his observation that "symbolic systems . . . are historically constructed, socially maintained, and individually applied" (1973:363–64). In this book, I use these questions not as a model of or for ethnomusicology but simply as tools for orienting the narrative.

12. See their articles in the collection *Writing Culture: The Poetics and Politics of Ethnography* (Clifford and Marcus 1986), and also James Clifford (1988), "On Ethnographic Authority," in *The Predicament of Culture: Twentieth-Century Ethnography, Literature, and Art*.

13. Ricoeur (1981:138–42) presents the most elegant analysis of the distinction between discourse as event, which references ostensibly or directly the world implicated in the dialogue between sender and receiver, and a text, which, by being fixed in some way, usually in writing, can be decontextualized and recontextualized. In this sense, recordings of music are just such texts. In a subsequent chapter, he shows how the notion of text, originally dependent on the idea of fixation by writing, but also generalizable to other "monuments," can be

taken as a model for "meaningful action." It is this enlarged sense of text as meaningful action to which I apply notions of understanding and interpretation.

14. Stephen A. Tyler (1986) is among the earliest and most enthusiastic advocates of a postmodern ethnographic style. The phrase, *local knowledge,* is taken from Geertz's 1983 book with that title.

15. Hobsbawn (1983:4) advocates the study of such reappropriated, "invented traditions" as symptomatic indicators of changes in modern society, "when a rapid transformation of society weakens or destroys the social patterns for which 'old' tradition had been designed," as in Bulgaria after 1944.

16. Pierre Bourdieu's *Outline of a Theory of Practice* (1977) claims that many practices, traditions as it were, are "embodied" and never brought to consciousness: "The child imitates not [cognitive, verbalized] 'models' but other people's actions," which "pass from practice to practice without going through discourse or consciousness" (87). He finds "a whole cosmology, an ethic, a metaphysic, a political philosophy" implicit in "injunctions as insignificant as 'stand up straight' and 'don't hold your knife in your left hand'" (94).

2. First Impressions

1. Ethnomusicologists usually label the poles between older and newer expressive forms "tradition and change" or "tradition and innovation." However, many studies have shown that so-called tradition was not unchanging (for example, Erlmann 1983) and that changing forms are often reinterpretations of traditional ones. Thus I substitute "modernity," in the sense used by Giddens (1990), for change. For Giddens, modern social orders, whether capitalist or socialist, are distinguished from traditional ones by the pace and scope of change, the nature of modern institutions (including capitalism/socialism, industrialism, and the nation-state's nearly complete control of information and military power), and an altered epistemology involving self-reflexivity and the substitution of a sense of fate with calculations of trust and risk.

2. The suspicion we were under as Americans working in a communist country during a period of great tension between the superpowers, before detente and glasnost, came to a head when a friend of ours was called in for questioning by the secret police, or *militsia,* of the Ministry of Internal Affairs (MVR) toward the end of my 15-month, dissertation research period in 1972–73. The MVR asked him to inform them what the "real purpose" of my stay in Bulgaria was, since they assumed I was a spy and my other activities were only a cover. He remembered them telling him, "Not only is he a spy, he is one of America's best spies! He brought with him his wife and child. He is interested in music, which is harmless. He has a very sincere smile. And we have been following him for over a year, and we haven't seen him do anything wrong!"

3. At church weddings in the late 1960s and early 1970s, the clash of religious tradition with communism sometimes took a comic turn. At one church ceremony I attended, the priest proffered his ring to the important members of the wedding party for them to kiss. The bride and groom dutifully obeyed, but when

it came the godfather's turn, he leaned back and refused, loudly proclaiming, "I am a Communist!" The priest and the assembled guests dissolved in laughter.

4. This continuous appropriation of lived experience results, in Ricoeur's terms, in an evolving self. As Émile Durkheim put it, "in each of us, in varying proportions, there is part of yesterday's man who inevitably predominates in us, since the present amounts to little compared with the long past in the course of which we were formed and from which we result. Yet we do not sense this man of the past, because he is inveterate in us; he makes up the unconscious part of ourselves" (quoted in Bourdieu 1977:79). Ricoeur (1991:2) states, "the common feature of human existence . . . is its *temporal character.*"

5. Stamov 1972 contains a good English-language account, with pictures, of the history of Bulgarian architecture.

6. I call Bulgaria's history "condensed" because most the developments in Europe since the Medieval period—the Renaissance, Reformation, Enlightenment, Industrial Revolution—were introduced to Bulgaria after its mid-nineteenth-century emancipation from the "Turkish Yoke." For a summary of that history, see Crampton 1987.

7. Czekanowska (1972) and Kaufman (1968) have developed comparative perspectives on common features of Slavic music, presumably due to shared heritage.

8. This name for the Ottoman period was made an evocative literary metaphor in the novel by Ivan Vazov, *Under the Yoke* [*Pod Igoto*], written in 1894. The novel is a good example of how a text and its title give to its readers (in this case, Bulgarians who have read it or heard about it) a deeply felt way to understand and experience their history. Rather than cold fact, Bulgarians continue to experience anger at the supposed degradation of the Ottoman period through metaphors that awaken negative associations: 'under the Turkish yoke' and 'under Turkish slavery.' From this metaphorically charged oppressive environment, Bulgarians needed not just to gain a kind of neutral 'independence,' as Americans say of their national formation, but a more emotionally charged 'liberation.' The Communists then self-servingly reconstituted the metaphor for emotional effect by speaking of their coming to power as a 'liberation' from the 'Fascist yoke' of the pre-Communist period. The images of yoke and slavery seemed to evoke in many Bulgarians an immediately felt sadness; in effect, they experienced their history in the present as a source of great sadness. Kostadin's and Todora's son, Ivan, at one point asked me, "Don't you find Bulgarians to be a sad people?"

The metaphors also contain the word "Turkish," which refers to a modern ethnic group within Bulgaria and a nation formed out of the Ottoman Empire after Bulgaria's independence. The continuing, self-conscious use of "Turkish" in the present, rather than referring to what some historians call the Ottoman period, suggests that these metaphors not only create emotions in the present, but have the effect of directing those emotions—sadness, bitterness, and anger—toward present-day Turkey and Turks, about a million of whom still live in Bulgaria, rather than to the historically distant Ottoman Empire. Conversely, those historians who refer to an Ottoman period, perhaps without intending to, defuse the emotional force and relevance of the past for the present, distancing it through a labeling whose historical "truth" denies the emotional "truth" of the metaphors.

9. The phrase "capacities and habits" comes from E. B. Tylor's (1871:1) famous definition of culture as "that complex whole which includes knowledge, belief, art, morals, law, custom, and any other capacities or habits acquired by man as a member of society."

10. In Bulgaria, agriculture fell from 65 percent of net material product in 1939 to 11 percent in 1980, while industry rose from 15 to 57 percent. The industrial labor force and its management more than doubled in size in the nine-year period from 1948 to 1957. The urban share of the population, which increased only 3 percent from 1900 to 1940, rose from 23 percent in 1940 to 65 percent in 1983 (Lampe 1986:144–45, 160).

11. The most widely available records that purport to represent "village music" include many musicians and singers who were professionals at the time of the recordings. They are, nonetheless, important aural sources for understanding Bulgarian music and should be consulted: Lloyd 1959, 1964; Bhattacharya 1968; Koenig and Raim 1970a, b. See discography for complete citations.

12. Martha Forsyth's published recordings of nonprofessional village singers include *Traditional Song in Southwestern Bulgaria* (1981), and *Two Girls Started to Sing: Bulgarian Village Singing* (1983).

13. One of the more ironic segments of the JVC Video Anthology of World Music (Japan Victor Co., 1990) includes Bulgarian field workers happily singing as they harvest grapes, an evocation of a traditional practice, but almost unimaginable in the present, except in a propaganda film.

14. I tried, in fact, to study village music making during my second trip to Bulgaria for fifteen months of fieldwork in 1972–73 and concentrated on one particularly archaic and intractable part of the tradition, the drone-based polyphonic singing from the villages of southwestern Bulgaria (Rice 1977, 1980a, 1988). Using the techniques of cognitive anthropology, I elicited the villagers' musical terminology, talked to them about how singing groups were formed, and tried to understand better how they experienced their tradition. But it soon became clear that my interest in these ancient forms of music-making was not matched by a similar interest in the country itself. The women I recorded were invariably old and complained that young girls could no longer learn the harmonic style, with its squashed, "ringing" intervals, even if they wanted to, because their aural experience was shaped by listening to popular and classical music on the radio. A part of the tradition that had awakened my curiosity was dying in the country itself. Compare Nahoma Sachs's 1975 dissertation on village musical life in the then Yugoslav portion of Macedonia.

15. Filip Kutev's choral arrangements for his choir of singers recruited from villages can be heard on *Music of Bulgaria* (1955).

16. Buchanan (1991) provides a list of the professional ensembles designated as 'national ensembles' and points out that there was a well-recognized hierarchy

of ensembles, based partly on commercial and partly on artistic success. At the top of the list was "*the* national ensemble," founded by Kutev in Sofia, with the Pirin Ensemble from Blagoevgrad close behind, mainly because of its flashy performances and success in organizing frequent tours abroad. The Trakiya Ensemble from Plovdiv had a certain prestige, especially among younger musicians and choreographers, because they had trained in it and had great respect for the innovative work of its past and present directors, Kiril Dzhenev and Stefan Mutafchiev. The Rodopa Ensemble from Smolyan, founded in 1960, had seniority over more recently established ensembles. Further down the list were a bevy of ten local ensembles, sponsored by the town or district süvet, that had been honored with the title 'national ensemble' for their artistic achievements. At the bottom of the hierarchy was the Pazardzhik Ensemble, merely a 'professional ensemble' without the honorific 'national' designation. Somewhat outside this hierarchy was the Ensemble for Folk Songs of the Bulgarian Radio, which contained some of the best and most famous singers and musicians, but lacked a dance group— for obvious reasons.

17. Boris Schwarz (1972) provides a good history of Communist doctrine and its application to music in the early years of the Russian revolution. Significantly, his story is less about the support of folk music than the attempt to bring classical music out of the Bolshoi Theater to people who had not previously experienced it: to soldiers, workers' clubs, and factories.

18. Silverman (1986:52) worked among Bulgarian Gypsies who referred to themselves with five different designations: (1) *Erliya* (a "dialect designation" presumably of Romani, the Gypsy language); (2) *Horahane* or *Turski Tsigani* (Turkish-speaking or Muslim Gypsies); (3) *Bŭlgarski Tsigani* (Bulgarian-speaking or Christian); (4) *Kalaidzhii* (coppersmiths); (5) *Kopanari* or *Vlashki Tsigani* (Romanian-speaking). "All these groups, with the exception of the *Kopanari,* speak *Romani* and refer to themselves as *Rom.*" Her categories, which are based on different criteria, reflect the difficulty of pinning down Gypsy self-groupings. Marushiakova 1992 contains a more detailed account and points out that there are eight different ways in which Gypsies name themselves: by way of life, religion, idea of a common group origin and so forth.

19. Poulton (1991:105–72) reviews the situation of minorities in Bulgaria, especially in a chapter entitled, "Bulgaria's Ethnic Turks—Forced Assimilation from 1984 to 1989."

20. Clarinetists and accordionists are the main figures in the wedding tradition, and their recordings can be heard on Balkanton, Bulgaria's national record company, and on a number of releases intended for the "international folk dance" scene. The most famous and important of the current wedding musicians, the clarinetist Ivo Papazov, recorded two CDs on Hannibal Records: *Ivo Papazov and his Bulgarian Wedding Band: Orpheus Ascending* (1989); and *Ivo Papazov and his Orchestra: Balkanology* (1990).

21. As Nahoma Sachs (1975:91) pointed out in her study of a Macedonian village, the family is the locus of celebration and as such is an important place for music making, singing and dancing. In Bulgaria, this is true of both pre- and

postwar periods, although the number of families who 'create fun' with musical performance may have decreased in the latter period.

22. Robert LeVine (1984:68), in his essay, "Properties of Culture: An Ethnographic View," provides one summary of the anthropological notion of shared culture: "A recurrent experience of ethnographers is that they are dealing with shared, supraindividual phenomena, that culture represents a consensus on a wide variety of meanings among members of an interacting community approximating that of the consensus on language among members of a speech-community. . . . Members of a community can vary greatly in thoughts, feelings, and behavior, yet hold in common understandings of the symbols and representations through which they communicate. Indeed, without such common understandings (of symbolic forms such as gestures, dress, . . . relationships), what kind of social communication, of community, would be possible?"

23. The problem with the notion of a unitary culture applied to modern societies, a problem partly responsible for my attempt to define different types of individuals in Bulgarian culture, is also examined by Rosaldo (1989:217): "A renewed concept of culture thus refers less to a unified entity ('a culture') than to the mundane practices of everyday life. . . . Ethnographers look less for homogeneous communities than for the border zones within and between them. . . . In the present postcolonial world, the notion of an authentic culture as an autonomous internally coherent universe no longer seems tenable, except perhaps as a 'useful fiction' or a revealing distortion. . . . All of us inhabit an interdependent late-twentieth-century world marked by borrowing and lending across porous national and cultural boundaries that are saturated with inequality, power, and domination."

24. Few ethnomusicological works use the individual as more than a token for more general cultural processes. Two of the important ones that place an individual or individuals at the center of the enquiry are Judith Vander's (1988) study of five Shoshone women of different ages, *Songprints,* and the autobiography of Frank Mitchell (1978), a Navajo singer, edited by David McAllester and Charlotte Frisbie. The chapters of the textbook, *Worlds of Music,* edited by Jeff Todd Titon (1984), highlight individuals in various ways, and Nettl (1983:278–89) reviews some of the issues involved in the study of individuals.

25. Even Bulgarian musicologists felt restricted in working with Gypsies. Although they were prominent on the musical scene, as Carol Silverman (1986:52) points out, "In the 1970s there began a silence in print. . . . In the early 1970s the internal passport designation 'Gypsy' was abolished, and Gypsies with Muslim names were given new Slavic names. Gypsies were legislated out of existence and therefore the "Gypsy problem," i.e., their low status, was solved." In 1988, one musicologist joked with me, "It would be interesting to work on the music of Gypsies, if there were any!" Silverman, working in the late 1970s and 1980s, managed to overcome some of these limitations (see Silverman 1983, 1986, 1988).

26. Marcia Herndon and Norma McLeod (1980:149) touched, in an amusing way, on how one's own interests affect research. Taking a tack rather opposite to

mine, they wrote, "The authors' study of bagpipes in Malta will probably always be a poor one, since neither one understands bagpipes well."

3. Social Processes of Music Learning

1. The generous conditions of the Treaty of San Stefano were drastically modified a few months later by the Treaty of Berlin on 13 July 1878, and "the modern Bulgarian state was born" (Crampton 1987:20). See Crampton 1983 for details on the drawing of national boundaries at that time.

2. The Turkish davul-zurna tradition is discussed in Picken 1975 and Reiche 1970. Loutzakis 1984 provides a dance ethnography of Greek immigrants from Bulgarian Thrace now living in Greek Macedonia.

3. The links to the original Turkish expression, which might have been *var, vermez* ['there is,' 'he doesn't have'] are somewhat blurred. I am grateful to Dr. Ilhami Gökçen of Toronto for the etymology of this name. Most family names are patronymics: Ivanov, of Ivan; Stoyanov, of Stoyan; and so on. Nicknames, such as Varimezov, are less common and usually point to a trade (Terziev, of the tailor; Popov, of the priest), a favorite activity (Kavaldzhiev, of the kaval player), or a prominent physical feature (Mustakov, of the mustachioed one).

4. See the collection of essays, subtitled "The Wesleyan Symposium on the Perspectives of Social Anthropology on the Teaching and Learning of Music," dealing with the social processes of music learning (Music Educators National Conference 1985).

5. See, for example, Merriam 1967 on the Flathead as composers; Blacking 1967, 1974, on the Venda as fulfilling their humanity in music making.

6. Kingsbury (1988) has critiqued effectively the concept of talent in the West and demonstrated its social construction.

7. There may be a cross-cultural correlation between specialization of labor and the degree to which musicians and singers are singled out as a special group with a separate achieved or ascribed status. John Blacking (1974) argued that culture limits our musical horizons; musicality is a basic human quality; and music making is a crucial aspect of being human. If the Venda illustrate reasonably well this egalitarian stance, the unequal distribution of musical talent and performance in the West represents an artificial truncation of human possibilities. Ethnomusicologists influenced by Marx have been especially vehement in blaming advanced capitalism for a specialization of labor that may deprive people of one of the sources of their humanity, namely music making. For related arguments, see, for example, Keil 1982 and Shepherd et al. 1977.

8. While men were almost exclusively instrumentalists, there were a few exceptions, including Pena Grozeva, who accompanied her singing on tambura; she can be heard on *Songs and Dances from Bulgaria* (Bhattacharya 1968). Katsarova (1952:44) reports that the few women who played instruments were given unflattering nicknames such as 'manly Maria.' Although men sang at family gatherings and in taverns, folksong collectors have, since the earliest publications, regarded women as their best sources. The Miladinovi Brothers' important

collection of Bulgarian folksongs, published in 1861, begins with the sentence, "Nearly all these songs were heard from women" (Miladinovi 1861:iii). There also was an important category of male singers [*pesnopoitsi*] who traveled to village fairs singing and selling chapbooks (Roth and Roth 1982–83). The relationship between men's and women's singing will be dealt with in more detail in chapter 5.

9. The words girl/boy and man/woman, as I use them here, are part of a set of Bulgarian gender-differentiated, age-graded, and marital-status-defining social categories. Before marriage, a female was called girl [*moma*] or maiden [*devoika*]; after marriage, bride [*bulka*] and woman [*zhena*]; and in old age, grandma [*baba*]. Before marriage, a male was called boy [*momak*] or bachelor [*ergen*]; after marriage, man [*mŭzh*]; and in old age, grandpa [*dyado*].

10. There are important exceptions, of course, to this generalization about male singers. Iovcho Karaivanov and Boris Mashalov are two important, famous, and often-recorded male singers, and there are others. Stoyan Velichkov, the well-known kaval player with Radio Sofia, told me that he originally wanted to be a singer, because his father had been such a good one. But the large ratio of famous female singers to male singers is perhaps a function of the distribution of singing skill between men and women in the village population as a whole.

11. I am using function here in the careful sense spelled out by Merriam (1964:209–27), where he contrasted function with use. While I don't completely subscribe to the structural-functionalist paradigm, the notion that singing functions within a larger system of social relations and activities remains a useful one.

12. Bakalov 1988 and Ognyanova and Bukureshtliev 1981 contain interviews with many singers and musicians, many of whom tell a variant of the story of how songs were first learned within the family circle.

13. Atanassov 1983 lists and provides photographs of the varieties of Bulgarian flutes and pipes and their terminology.

14. See, for example, Hopkin 1984 on Jamaican children's songs.

15. The record, *Bulgaria* (Lloyd 1959) contains a picture and recording (*Trakiiska Rachenitsa,* B20) of *Bai* Stoyan Dobrev. *Bai* is an honorific used in conjunction with the first name of an older male who is not a relative; it is possibly related to a similar Turkish honorific, *bey,* which follows the name (for example, Ilhami *Bey*). The Redhouse Turkish-English Dictionary (1968) defines *bey* as, "(1) gentleman, Sir; after name Mr., Mister. (2) prince, ruler, chieftain; chief, head, master. (3) notable country gentleman." Redhouse also includes *bay* as a neologism meaning 'Mr.,' 'Mister,' or 'Sir.'

16. While these recollections come from my interviews with Kostadin, this detail, that his grandfather put up half the money for his first gaida, comes from Ognyanova and Bukureshtliev (1981:78), who published interviews with twelve "popular performers of folk music," including Kostadin.

17. In 1973 at the market in Ohrid, a town in southern Yugoslavia, I observed a group of thirty or so older men surrounding a maker and seller of gaidas. Over the course of several hours virtually everyone of them tried his hand at an instrument, all of them playing rather well.

18. This trill technique is used by the Macedonian gaida player Pece Atanasovski. Hear, for example, *Makedonska Narodna Ora,* Jugoton LPY-50985.

19. Similarly there were no rules about which hand is placed on top or higher on the instrument. Kostadin encouraged his students to play with the left hand on top, because that is standard for classical instruments with keys, such as the clarinet and oboe, and also leaves the right hand free to adjust the drone, which falls away to the right side of the body. On the other hand, Nikola Atanasov, who replaced Kostadin in the Radio orchestra after his retirement, plays with his right hand on top. On keyless woodwinds it doesn't matter; only when keys are added does their position determine which hand must be on top.

20. Roth and Roth (1982–83) have written the most important studies of *pesnopoiki* and of the singers who performed them, a tradition similar to the British broadside ballads.

21. Wrestling matches were a prominent feature of village fairs, and can still be observed in neighboring Turkey and Macedonia. The spectators formed a ring, and a zurna or gaida player joined the contestants in the center, the musician signaling the stages of the match: metric tunes as the wrestlers stalked each other, a nonmetric wail as they fought furiously on the ground.

22. Zheni Iordanova (1989:110) provides a variant of this phrase, collected from a village near Veliko Tŭrnovo in north Bulgaria, that illustrates the antipathy of most villagers to musicians in the 1930s: "A fiddler doesn't feed his mother, a fiddler doesn't keep up his house, a fiddler constantly asks where are the beautiful girls and the hot, strong brandy."

23. I didn't record any metaphors from Todora to describe different voice qualities, but in Rice 1980a I mentioned *Shop* singers who distinguished between "buttery" [*mazhen*] and "reedy" [*piskliv*] voices.

24. The verb 'die' is a common expression of enthusiasm. Bulgarian studies of the size of song repertoires suggest that many village singers knew between 100 and 200 songs. The *Encyclopedia of Bulgarian Musical Culture* (EBMK 1967:51) mentions the following singers (and the number of songs collected from them by the Institute for Music of the Bulgarian Academy of Sciences) who knew an exceptionally large number of songs: Penka Poptodorova from Dryanovo (1,000), Vasila Vŭlcheva from the Silistra area (800); Dyado Pavel Atanasov from Dobrudzha (742); Tina Mutafchieva from Ihtiman (570); Anka Dimitrova from the Pazardzhik area (450); Ivan Rusinov Stoyanov from the Plovdiv area (340); and Ana Pankova from the Sofia area (540). Studies of an individual singer's repertoire include Madzharov and Bukureshtliev 1983 and Keremidchiev 1954.

25. In its General Report of 1952, the International Folk Music Council (IFMC 1953) discussed "definitions and general principles" of folk music and, although they failed "to define folk music to the satisfaction of all scholars, accept[ed] the following provisional declaration: Folk music is music that has been submitted to the process of oral transmission. It is the product of evolution and is dependent on the circumstances of continuity, variation and selection" (12). In the discussion of "selection of material," the assembled scholars were mainly concerned with how "repertory are constantly subject to the verdict of the com-

munity," and remained somewhat suspicious of the individual, whose "accretions and modifications . . . do not outlive him unless they meet with the approval of his fellows" (13). Such definitions disregard the psychological force of individual experience in favor of some imagined community process; tellingly, most of their discussion focused on how individual scholars, rather than communities, select valuable material and save society from "individuals who are busy catering for the public amusement" (13).

26. I use this locution, "we were not able to find a vocabulary," quite consciously to indicate the dialogic nature of field research. Descriptions of musical structure, even academic talk about music, are highly metaphoric, a fact we often deny by regarding them as descriptive or objective. Where the ethnomusicologist's "conventional metaphors"—high/low, descending/ascending—are not used by informants, it may be that they use "new metaphors," at least to the researcher. A number of studies provide examples of metaphoric language new to the researcher that has descriptive validity, for example, Zemp 1978, Feld 1981, and recently Vander 1988. It is at least imaginable that Todora had such a metaphoric vocabulary, which I did not manage to understand, and so I say that we did find a way to talk metaphorically about musical structure, not that she lacked such a vocabulary. The distinction between conventional and new metaphor is taken from Lakoff and Johnson, *Metaphors We Live By* (1980).

27. At a *sedyanka*, here translated as sitting bee, girls did individual work: spinning yarn, sewing, knitting and embroidering the clothing, bedding and other material they would need for wedding gifts and their trousseaux. At a *medzhiya*, here translated as corn-shucking bee, girls helped the host family with tedious work, such as shucking corn, that went more quickly and pleasantly with communal labor and music making.

4. Cognitive Processes in Music Learning

1. Dimitŭr Grivnin's playing and part of his repertoire are discussed in Rice 1971 and in a Ph.D. dissertation on Rhodope bagpiping by Mark Levy (1985).

2. Levy (1985:251–53) provides short case studies of six Rhodope gaidari, one of whom tells a story very similar to Kostadin's. His father objected to buying him a gaida, and he remembers being laughed at when he first began to play, probably because he was, like *Bai* Dimitŭr's grandson, noodling nonsensically. Rather than learning from notation, Levy quotes him as saying, "We got our notes from the liquor bottle."

3. According to Jean Piaget's influential theory of cognitive development, a child passes through four stages of cognitive development: "the sensorimotor stage (0–2 years), the preconcrete operational or intuitive stage (2–7) years, the concrete operational stage (7–12 years), and the formal operational stage (12–15 years)" (Kitchener 1986:17). The latter two stages include "true logical operations of symbolic thought" (19). The ability to generalize rules of melodic formation from songs to instrumental music is probably a formal (that is, logical) rather than a concrete (that is, applicable to concrete manipulable objects) operation, but this would have to be demonstrated.

4. Carterette and Kendall (1989) find the notion of schemas a useful heuristic device and trace the idea to Sir Frederic Bartlett's 1932 work, *Remembering*.

5. I am grateful to Roger Kendall, a systematic musicologist at UCLA who studies music perception and psychoacoustics experimentally, for this suggestion and for a lengthy discussion of the issues raised in this section.

6. Donna Buchanan (1991:369–71) provides a third interpretation of the meaning of *persenk*, equating it more or less with a term for instrumental melody or phrase, *kolyano* ['knee,' or, in music theory, 'phrase'], which Bulgarian composers and musicians applied to instrumental performances of folk music in the postwar period.

7. *Testemelichka* is a dance name based on an archaic or dialect word in Bulgarian for handkerchief, *testemel*, and thus might be translated 'handkerchief dance.' While one Bulgarian dictionary claims the word is from Turkish, I have not found it in either Turkish or Greek dictionaries. It is the name the Varimezovs and the people of Rosenovo used for the 7/8 (2 + 2 + 3) dance, which in the postwar period was commonly called *rŭchenitsa* throughout Bulgaria. (I do not know whether *testemelichka* and *rŭchenitsa* were also used for 9/8 meters in Strandzha in the 1920s, as Stoin does in this example, or whether this is a labeling error.) The latter term comes from the Bulgarian word for hand, *rŭka*, and, like *testemelichka*, might be translated as 'handkerchief dance.' It is probably no accident that officially sanctioned generic dance names like *rŭchenitsa* were clearly Bulgarian in character and erased or obscured the welter of local names, some with possibly non-Bulgarian roots like *testemelichka*, that might have suggested impure contact of Bulgarian culture with other cultures. The issue of the purity of Bulgarian tradition is taken up again in the chapters devoted to the postwar period and is also discussed in Buchanan 1991.

8. In Toronto in the 1970s I met a Balkan folk musician who had yet to move from fragments to melodies. Although the musician was a Serbian accordion player and not a Bulgarian gaidar, the anecdote is relevant because both styles present similar cognitive problems: the traditions are largely learned but not taught, both use fast tempos, and there is a close correspondence in density and character of ornamentation in the two traditions, especially between Serbian and West Bulgarian ornamentation. After hearing him practicing in his room as I walked down my street one afternoon, I asked him if he would play for me when I saw him on his porch a few days later. What amazed me on closer listening was that he repeated one 2-measure fragment of melody. He played it very well, properly ornamented and with a great sense of style, but those two measures represented the extent of his musical development. He apparently had not yet learned a complete melody even though he had more or less mastered the difficult ornamental technique of the instrument. In Kostadin's case, friends and relatives guided him towards learning longer melodies once they realized he had acquired some technique. But this Serbian accordion player in Toronto was cut off from the social support that might have helped his musical development, and so his repertoire and musical ability remained somewhat stunted.

9. It probably was no coincidence that Kostadin remembered learning his first tune from an accordion player. Although accordion playing, like all Bulgarian music and singing, is rich in ornaments, melodies tend to emerge on it more clearly and less obscured by the ornaments than on the gaida. Kostadin may have made the connection between instrumental melody and song melody not by listening to other gaidari, but to an accordion player.

10. In 1969 I met a man in his sixties from the *Shop* region who had just begun to play the gaida four or five months earlier. To my astonishment, he had a very nice technique although a limited repertoire, which he repeated endlessly with great enthusiasm and pride. He claimed that it had taken him only a few weeks to learn to play the instrument. He had, of course, spent a lifetime listening to it, and so it was perhaps simply a matter of finding on the instrument the sounds in his head. Having acquired the ornamental style, he needed to enlarge his repertoire. For me, as an outsider, it was very difficult to organize the style or manner of playing, whereas the tunes were relatively easy to understand, and it took me years, not weeks, to learn to play. The anecdote illustrates, however, that in this aural tradition, which was learned but not taught, ornamentation was acquired together with melody to form an aesthetic unit not bifurcated into structural melody and applied style, as I heard it at the time.

11. Dooling and Hulse (1989:129) write that the study of "the development of music perception in babies and children [is] a topic truly in its infancy"; Carterette and Kendall (1989) summarize findings that imply an increase in cognitive concepts with time. Summarizing the conclusions of Sloboda (1985), they point out that at ages 1–5 imitation increases from melodic fragments to whole songs, the same order I posit for young gaidari. From ages 6–10 ability increases to make subtler, more complex distinctions leading, by the age of 11, to the ability to detect errors in chord sequences. Similarly, Serafine (1988:134) found that young children have the ability to perceive the broad outlines of phrase, but "the capacity to string motives together successively is not generally acquired until age 10 or later." In general, she concludes that (1) many cognitive processes necessary for music cognition are not in place at age 5; (2) there is "a rapid period of growth in musical understanding" from ages 8 to 11; and (3) the ability to organize music is "generally well in place in human cognition by the age of 10 or 11 years" (224). My ethnographic findings seem largely consonant with these psychological findings, but it would be interesting to study music learning in other cultures in a more rigorous way.

12. As we will see in the chapters dealing with the postwar period, professional training, musical notation, and a different kind of self-consciousness about music has given musicians both a greater ability, and new reasons, to talk about musical styles and structures.

13. In the 1960s and '70s some questions were raised about the usefulness and even appropriateness of "bi-musicality," a term introduced by Mantle Hood (1960) to suggest one of the methods of ethnomusicological research: was it possible to achieve it "really"; did it have any scholarly payoff; was it perhaps mainly useful as a means of establishing rapport; was making music a

distraction from more important ethnomusicological research goals? By the 1980s bi-musicality, or at least the attempt to acquire it, was a taken-for-granted research tool that contributes to scholarly enquiry and the answering of important ethnomusicological questions.

14. The choice of note values is somewhat arbitrary. Bulgarian musicologists tend to use sixteenth-note pulses for the fastest dance tempos, eighth-note pulses for medium tempos, and quarter-note pulses for slow tempos, that is, 5/16, 5/8, and 5/4, respectively. For the transcriptions in this book, I use eighth-note values for the pulse regardless of tempo, because it illustrates the grouping of pulses most cleanly and simply.

15. The tonal center and drone pitch of gaidas was not linked to any absolute pitch in the 1930s, the period discussed here. The gaida today is pitched on d″. It became common in the 1950s to play a chanter without drone in orchestras of folk instruments using the pitch a′ as the tonal center. Since it is easier for most other Bulgarian instruments to play on a′ than on d″, I have chosen to use that pitch in the transcriptions for this book.

16. There is an interesting literature on music knowledge as hand knowledge, including Sudnow 1978, Baily 1981, Yung 1984, and Chernoff 1979.

17. That Bulgarians were willing to include me within the horizons of their world became apparent when I attended a village festival where I danced and chatted with people. After eyeing me for quite a while, one man called me over and demanded to know where I was from and what I was doing there. Although I was worried that he was going to accuse me of being a spy, when I answered that I was from America and was there to study Bulgarian music, he responded, "You lie! You speak Bulgarian and you dance Bulgarian dances. Therefore, you are a Bulgarian!"

18. Sonia Tamar Seeman, a graduate student at UCLA who spent a number of years in Skopje, Macedonia, during the 1980s studying with Gypsy clarinetists, reports (pers. comm., 1993) that "Macedonian Gypsy musicians refer to this technique not only as a 'Turkishism' but as sweetening the sound, making it *blago* [sweet]."

5. Perspectives on Musical Experience

1. One of the ironies of the history of Bulgarian folk music is that, in this stage of economic development, social organization of labor in Bulgarian villages in the 1930s resembled that envisaged for the utopian future communist society. To quote Marx and Engels (1972:43), "nobody has one exclusive sphere of activity but each can become accomplished in any branch he wishes; society . . . makes it possible for me to do one thing today and another tomorrow, to hunt in the morning, fish in the afternoon, rear cattle in the evening, criticize after dinner . . . without ever becoming hunter, fisherman, shepherd or critic."

2. This discussion of the problems with terminology and its application illustrates how the past is appropriated and understood through a filter of new concepts and experience, and provides a good example of the temporal character of the self, whose continuing development and use of new concepts, terms, and

metaphors provide new means for experiencing the world. When the researcher's task is an imaginative reconstruction of the past, as here, the methodological
problems of changing selves and filtered understanding through new categories
becomes particularly acute.

3. The Bulgarians' stolid, unrelenting approach to work in comparison to
their supposedly more temperamental, relaxed, Mediterranean neighbors has
earned them the epithet, "the Prussians of the Balkans."

4. Bulgarian musicologists and folklorists sometimes write as if the patriarchal
family was a thing of the past, but many of its features, such as patrilocal residence, the father's on-going sense of responsibility to his sons, and a son's deference to his parents' wishes even into adulthood, continue to describe accurately
the family relations I observed in the 1970s and '80s.

5. Early studies of "native music theory" purported to speak about "'Are'are
musical theory" or "Bulgarian musical thought," the article titles implying a unified view of the topic even when we learned that 'Are'are theory was elicited
from and known primarily by one particular instrument maker (Zemp 1979)
and Bulgarian thought was constructed from the isolated comments of a few
individuals (Rice 1980a). These arguments, by implication, construct a typical,
average listener or "musical thinker" within a culture or else focus only on musicians or theorists and present their thought as if it represented the culture's
view of music. In both cases the analyst creates an imaginary composite thinker,
listener, or theorist—the Bulgarian, the 'Are'are—and speaks monolithically of,
for example, "Bulgarian musical thought." As a corrective to this tendency to
overgeneralize, a few studies, such as Koskoff 1982, deal with the range of variation and even the unique features of individual musical classifications and
thought patterns in a given culture. In this approach, each individual is assumed
to have a unique aural experience based on a unique life history, which makes
generalizations about cultural patterns almost impossible. No matter the implicit
approach of the study, we know that musical knowledge and understanding is
rarely, if ever, uniformly distributed in society, and therefore ethnomusicologists
interested in native understanding and experience must ask a set of related questions: What kinds of listeners seem to exist in a tradition? How is musical knowledge distributed? What kinds of music knowledge are there?

6. There were those who, perhaps for social reasons, didn't sing or dance and
whose musical cognition, therefore, could not be observed. Todora recalled, for
example, that some people didn't sing because the family seemed socially a bit
withdrawn. Another important social category of nonperformers included
people in mourning for deceased relatives. Auerbach (1989) discusses this phenomenon among women in a community in northern Greece.

7. My use of rhythm and meter is taken from Kolinski's (1973) rather precise
distinction between meter as the organization of pulsation and rhythm as the
organization of duration.

8. One fascinating issue is whether Turkish *makam* names might have been
used for that purpose at one time by traditional musicians. In the postwar environment, when Turkish influences on Bulgarian culture were beyond discussion,
traditional musicians did not use such terms at least with me. One likely group

that may have used them were Muslim Gypsies. The writers and some of the subjects, none of whom were Gypsies, in the set of musicians' and singers' biographies compiled by Ognianova and Bukureshtliev (1981) use the word *makam* rather frequently to describe not differences in melody but differences in the musicality of singers, describing the best singers with the best melodic sense as *makamliya*, having good *makam,* that is, rich melodies. Although I attempted on numerous occasions to elicit terminology for modes from musically uneducated village musicians, I was never successful. In one case, I interviewed a middle-aged kaval player about his somewhat random alternation of the second degree of the scale from major to minor. Was this conscious I wanted to know? I struggled haplessly to find a way of asking him this question without putting the words in his mouth, and he tried sincerely to understand my question. Suddenly he realized what I was after and shouted happily, "You want to know about modes [*ladove*]!" "How do you know about modes," I asked in amazement. "Oh, my son plays clarinet and studied music at school. He told me about them." So much for the naive informant.

9. I don't have much direct evidence for greater expressivity for men than women in Strandzha singing, but in my study of Rhodope singing (Rice 1971), I noticed, and the transcriptions clearly show, more ornamental turns and twists in men's than in women's singing.

10. In Rice 1974, I described the formation of one of the most famous early groups, the Bistrishka Chetvorka, based on an interview with one of its founders. Kostadin believes that such groups began to flourish in the 1930s because the economic climate provided increasing amounts of money to sustain groups, in addition to individuals, in taverns.

11. Today musicians call such a fixed four-measure phrase played with repeats a *kolyano* [lit., 'knee'; pl., *kolena*], a term Kostadin learned from musicologists during his postwar musical training. In Bulgarian classical music theory, *kolyano* corresponds to the English music-theory terms "phrase" or "sentence," and Bulgarian musicologists call instrumental suites of such tunes "kolyano form" (Kaufman 1984; Buchanan 1991:367–74).

12. Mark Slobin (1992:74–75) calls the phenomenon of a musician's or group's response to various cultural contexts "banding," meaning the way the band interacts with clients to please them. In cases of "banding," whatever desire the musicians have to please themselves musically is constrained by the need to please an audience, which, in the modern world, is often a shifting or different one.

13. Buchanan (1991:414–30), in a section on the impact of musical notation, contrasts playing from the heart, that is, from a deep knowledge of the tradition, with a *notno horo* [notated dance], in which a lack of connection to tradition is made visible, and presumably audible, by the musician's need to refer to notation.

14. Ricoeur (1981:140–42, 146) makes the distinction used here between ostensive, "pointing" reference in discourse versus the more complicated, open reference of a text. Anna Caraveli (1985) has written an excellent article on how the meaning of text is generated in the performance of couplets [*mantinades*]

in a Greek island village, where its ostensive reference to the situation provides layers of meaning not obvious in the text alone.

15. Mark Slobin (1992:51), in his article, "Micromusics of the West: A Comparative Approach," mentions a parallel instance documented in a film about Ukraine. In response to "the horrors of life on a large, successful poultry farm," the women formed "a sisterhood of singers to do Ukrainian folksongs. A spokeswoman says their informal song group keeps them from crying or cursing."

16. Cowan (1990:82) makes a similar point about women in a northern Greek village: "Married women bear a particular burden with respect to both the reality and the public image of family unity. To the extent that a woman's identity is domestically defined, her sense of competence, self-worth, and satisfaction may be strongly tied to how well she carries out her domestic responsibilities." In speaking, a woman often "upholds the dominant ideology because, ironically, it is against her interests (as a wife, mother, ...) to assert her interests (as a woman, an autonomous person)."

17. Jane Sugarman (1988, 1989) describes a similar relaxation around drinking and singing for Albanian men from the Prespa region of Macedonia: "They say that, as they [men] drink, their self-consciousness leaves them and that a state of social intimacy is generated. The goal of a men's gathering is to nurture that quality of intimacy toward an almost ecstatic state in which the men experience a surge of affection for each other" (1989:203).

18. I have transcribed the music and text of Todora's 250 songs and translated the song words and interviews with her in a collection I call "A Sharp-witted Woman: Songs in the Life of a Bulgarian Folk Singer" (manuscript).

6. Music as Seasonal Experience

1. The term *music* in my lists of music, song, and dance refers to instrumental music, which is its primary meaning among Bulgarian villagers. For them, music does not seem to be a cover term that includes song, as it can in English (Rice 1980a). When music appears by itself, however, as in "Bulgarian music is ——," I am using it in its global, English sense to include song and singing.

2. Some musicians I knew jokingly referred to a penis as a *ruchilo* [drone-pipe], and Kostadin said that he playfully put his drone under the skirts of girls at *sedyankas*. When viewed against this background, the end of the drone, which fans out and then narrows, suggests the glans of a penis. Botusharov (1989:45) takes the phallic symbolism of gaidas and kavals for granted—"with its well-known meaning in traditional culture"—but like most Bulgarian folklorists and musicologists is reluctant to discuss it in detail—or even to name it.

3. Raina Katsarova (1957), in her study, "Folk Dances and Games of Strandzha," describes and notates 10 games (nos. 28–37) *na filek,* many of them similar to Todora's, from villages around Strandzha.

4. Todora's rather happy and benign interpretation is apparently only one possibility. Some Bulgarian scholars believe that it was a gesture of mourning and celebration of the dead, as the dancers viewed the ground as the home of

the dead. It is likely that both interpretations are valid: Todora's comes from the memory of a young girl while Bulgarian ethnographers often talk to the elderly, who are more occupied with mourning.

5. It was fashionable in Kostadin's and Todora's day to dance with umbrellas during summer fairs, and they fondly remember that a boy and girl would dance next to each other holding an umbrella, ostensibly to shade them from the sun, but also to signify that they were a couple and to hide them briefly from the gaze of onlookers.

6. The syllable *de*, and in the next line *be*, are expressive syllables without precise denotation that are frequently interspersed in conversations for emphasis.

7. Radost Ivanova (1987:93–96) analyzes the significance of the ritual bread and makes slightly different points about ritual meaning and symbolism, while confirming the relationship between bread-making and human fertility and sexuality: "the sexual differentiation of the ritual personages and objects and actions associate the kneading of the dough and bread-making with coitus and conception. This is unambiguously expressed in the movements performed by the ritual personages in kneading, simulating the fertilizing state of coitus" (95).

8. In the 1970s and '80s these banners typically used the Bulgarian flag rather than a handkerchief and were quite creative and humorous in their phallic symbolism. On one I saw, a cucumber was strategically placed between two apples. Sometimes a live chicken was attached; I assume its death represented the bride's loss of virginity, since its blood may have been used, in the distant past, to prove the bride's honor. On one modern banner I saw, a frozen chicken in a plastic bag, a new product on the market, substituted for a live chicken. Significantly, one of the common names for the wedding banner was *pryapor* or *pryaporets* [priapus *or* phallus]. Ivanova (1987:96–100) interprets the flag pole as symbolizing fertility and male-female union without specifying the phallic character of the pole, which nevertheless should be "hard and straight" and possess "sturdiness, strength and resilience" (96).

9. My wife Ann wanted to learn to roll this dough, the trickiest part of the operation, and in 1973 our hosts in the village directed her to an old woman they considered particularly skillful. That woman agreed to show her the next time she was making some, and on the appointed day Ann arrived, pencil and paper in hand, to observe the technique. As the work proceeded, she turned to Ann and asked, "Why didn't your mother teach you to make *banitsa?*" When Ann responded that Americans don't eat *banitsa*, the woman asked incredulously, "What do you eat?" After more than a year in Bulgaria, Ann couldn't remember.

10. *Ishala* comes from the Turkish (originally Arabic) *Inşallah*, which means "Allah [God] willing" or "if Allah wills." It is uttered in conjunction with a wish, hope, or statement of future plans. *Mashala* comes from the Turkish (originally Arabic) *maşallah*, which means "What wonders Allah has willed." It is offered as congratulations after the fact or after an event. Both expressions acknowledge Allah's fateful power and serve to ward off the evil eye.

7. The New Society and Its Music

1. Music may also change because of supposedly "internal" stylistic pressure, but ethnomusicologists have been less interested in this than in the influence of culture change. One exception is Nazir Jairazbhoy's 1971 *The Rags of North Indian Classical Music: Their Structure and Evolution,* in which he claims that the tritone is an unstable musical element that causes shifts in scale usage.

2. Levin (1979:158) provides a trenchant comparison of the process of directed musical change in Socialist countries and in the "free" world, with its supposed lack of ideological barriers: "Soviet Central Asia, due to ideological opposition, has stayed, but not stopped the absorption of Western cultural influence in the most crucial recent years since the development of radio, television, phonograph, and tape recorder. The result is that the effects of radical Westernization, which in the final analysis might prove more deforming than Soviet style 'nationalization,' have thus far been averted."

3. This quote about changes in the base causing changes in the superstructure is taken from an article by that famous Marxist philosopher Joseph Stalin (1972:80–81).

4. The distinction between base and superstructure and the supposed primacy of the former over the latter have dogged Marxist theorists and their opponents in much the same way that the culture concept has vexed anthropologists. Those who espouse an unalloyed version of Stalin's simple theorem are condemned as "vulgar Marxists" or "vulgar materialists" by those who favor a subtler, dialectic relationship between the two.

5. I take the concept of symbolic capital from Bourdieu 1977:171–83.

6. Danforth 1989 contains the most extensive account of *anestinaria,* as it is called in Greek, as practiced today by immigrants to Greece from these Bulgarian villages.

7. The *Encyclopedia of Bulgarian Musical Culture* (EBMK) contains no reference to this institution, so it may have been considered either unimportant in retrospect, considering future developments, or simply not in line with subsequent musical ideology.

8. A collection of such songs is printed in Stoin and Kachulev 1958.

9. The choreographers sent to the USSR in 1952 included Kiril Dzhenev, K. Haralampiev, H. Tsonev, L. Zarkov, P. Zahariev, and T. Kyuchukov (EBMK 1967:137).

10. The phrase 'perfumed folklore' [*parfyumiran folklor*] was heard in Bulgaria and reported to me by Eran Fraenkel.

11. See Rice 1977, 1980a, 1988; Messner 1980; and Markoff 1975 for descriptions of traditional drone-based singing styles in southwestern Bulgaria.

12. A good sample of Kutev's arrangements can be heard on *Music of Bulgaria,* Nonesuch 72011.

13. In an analogous Soviet case, Slobin (1971:10) describes the "improvement" of Uzbek instruments and their reconstruction in a range of sizes: "It took Petrosian (and his forerunners) roughly twenty years to create the new *dutar* and its piccolo-to-bass look-alikes."

14. That Kostadin could hear a tune once and play it better than the musician he heard it from is reminiscent of Albert Lord's (1960) tales of Yugoslav epic singers, who could hear a song once and sing back a more elaborate version immediately. In both cases the musician and poet are listening for structures— melody and plot—stripped of style and ornamentation and then recreating those structures in their own personal manner. If the style and technique of the listener is richer than the performer's, then the listener will effortlessly produce a more elaborate performance on the spot. Once a folk tradition's style is learned and made inevitably personal, it is no longer attended to in the transmission process. Repertoire is passed from person to person on one hearing as the listener concentrates on the gross elements of structure and recreates the performance in his or her own personal style. This process is at the root of the tremendous variety observed in all aural traditions and the ease with which it is transmitted without the benefit of writing.

15. Buchanan (1991:342) points out that the concept of arranging [*obrabot-vane*] and arrangement [*obrabotka*] comes from a verb meaning 'to cultivate, process, polish, manipulate, treat, or train.' She quotes a Bulgarian ethnomusicologist who told her *obrabotvane* implies "transformation of something for the better."

16. The notion that harmonized arrangements of folk song and music on traditional instruments would bring peasants to a greater appreciation of the European classics is a less radical variant of the changes in Soviet Uzbekistan reported by Slobin (1971). There, much larger orchestras of folk instruments (up to seventy) even more closely emulated a Western orchestra and performed "such seeming monstrosities as a full-length score of the overture to 'Carmen' for Uzbek instruments only" (11). As Levin (1979:154) put it, "Every *gidjak* or *tanbur* player at the [Tashkent] Conservatory, for technical mastery of his instrument, assails not [the Uzbek modes] *rāst* or *segāh*, but the Bach E major violin concerto, or Brahms Hungarian Rhapsodies." While Filip Kutev tried to fuse the folk and classical traditions by composing a Concerto for Kaval with Western orchestra, Bulgarian folk orchestras and their newly trained professional musicians did not regularly play Western music.

17. The unison playing style and a similar uniformity among dancers contrasts strikingly with the agonistic heterophony and dramatic display by male dance-line leaders in Greek music and dance, which themselves are undoubtedly icons of Greek cultural values (see Cowan 1990; Herzfeld 1985).

18. On private cassette recordings given to me by collectors, I have heard Greek Thracian gaidas with drones pitched on A and on c, below what has become the standard Bulgarian gaida drone pitch of d.

19. Levy (1985:65–78) provides a detailed discussion of traditional and modern approaches to intonation on the Rhodope gaida, lower-pitched than the modern Thracian gaida and one that has preserved older intonations, largely because of its isolation from the mainstream of professional ensemble music.

20. Using the Western scale, the hijaz tetrachord includes an augmented second, but in both Turkish and Arabic classical music, the hijaz tetrachord or its equivalent includes an interval slightly smaller than the augmented second,

achieved either by raising the second and/or lowering the third, just as described here.

21. My source for this number of his recordings is a list prepared at my request at Radio Sofia. I am grateful to Rumyana Tsintsarska for arranging to have this list prepared.

22. Kostadin's repertoire will be published in a forthcoming collection from A-R Editions with the working title, *Music for the Bulgarian Bagpipe: The Repertoire of Kostadin Varimezov.*

23. Singers changed as well under the influence of professionalization. When I asked Komna Stoyanova whether Todora had the voice of a professional singer when she arrived in Sofia, she said, "None of us did." Komna said her own singing was higher pitched, with shorter notes and fewer ornaments. Now she sings with more legato, more vibrato, more slides between melodic tones, and uses Western expressive devices like dynamics.

8. Reception and Teaching of the New Tradition

1. Grozdan Hristozov (1974) provides interesting details about reception of arrangements. He begins by acknowledging that Bulgarian folk music plays a large role in radio programming "not only for its place in our national culture," or because it is popular or to be preserved but rather "because of those large duties which the radio and television have as powerful propaganda-educational institutions, as important means of the party for ideological coercion" (141). The radio had a "Center of Sociological Studies" that conducted a survey of 1,167 families in 1968 to determine their musical preferences. While village audiences at that time claimed folk music was their favorite type of music, only 22.4 percent of urban audiences said folk music was their favorite and, in response to the question, "Which of the musical programs of Radio Sofia do you listen to with pleasure?" only 17 percent of intellectuals responded favorably to folk music (143). On the other hand, while "the first attempts at arranging folk music were met disapprovingly by most listeners, similar arrangements today are accepted as completely natural, almost as pure folklore" (145).

2. Todor Prashanov is well-known as a writer of the first methods books and collections of tunes for folk instruments, for example, Prashanov 1968, 1973.

3. This number of recordings by Strandzhanskata Grupa comes, as did the earlier number, from a list supplied by Rumyana Tsintsarska from the files of Radio Sofia.

4. The record is *Dimka Vladimirova i strandzhanskata narodna grupa,* Balkanton BHA 10160.

5. Of course the issue of ownership is not inextricably linked to money. A number of Native American groups have concepts of ownership linked to spiritual, rather than economic, power (see, for example, Merriam 1967 and Witherspoon 1977).

6. In a survey of the history of arrangements, Nikolai Kaufman (1974:199) praised Kolev's treatment of *Lyulka se lyulya* for its "masterful weaving of folk

orchestra" with choral singing, and it is the first piece on a long-playing album of Kosta Kolev's arrangements (Balkanton BHA 10822).

7. Buchanan (1991:302–3) points out that the training of professional musicians to take these newly available positions in ensembles is part of "a Marxist-Leninist view of education that links training closely with employment." In her view, this approach to education reduces creativity and improvisation in favor of "calculable rules" and a technical, scientific approach to "cultural development."

8. During the Communist era, *koleda* was sometimes celebrated on New Year's Eve rather than Christmas Eve, to unlink a "Bulgarian tradition" from its Christian associations.

9. Levy (1985:264–67) contains an account of gaida instruction at the other folk music high school in Shiroka Lŭka, a village in the Rhodopes. There students were required to study both Rhodope and Thracian gaida but, indicative of the economic and aesthetic pull of Thracian ensemble and wedding music, the local instrument "is considered by most teachers and students as inferior, old-fashioned, and primitive, with limited possibilities and a narrow repertoire" (264).

10. In ethnomusicology, Kathleen and Adrian L'Armand (1983) used the concept of secondary urbanization in their study of the history of music in Madras. They called it part of the "Redfield-Singer (1954) model of the cultural role of cities." In the first part of the model, "folk" or "little" traditions move into the city to become "Great traditions."

11. This line of argument is a response, in part, to claims by Lomax (1968) in *Folk Song Style and Culture* that he could find no statistical correlate between certain formal elements in music and social practices; rather he found correlations between musical performance practice and certain social practices. What his approach ignores, and mine (and others) introduces, is the notion of meaning. The assignment of meaning to musical elements and practices may be a local phenomenon resisting global, statistical procedures. But the assignment of shared meanings to music is one of the ways music enters into and affects cultural processes.

9. Challenging the Tradition

1. Silverman (1988, 1989) reported, for example, that the *zurna*, a double-reed oboe typical of Turkey, played by Gypsies, and excluded from the canon of traditional Bulgarian folk instruments, was banned from the 1985 regional folk festival in the Pirin region of southwest Bulgaria.

2. This quote and the bulk of this account of forced assimilation of Turks from 1984 to 1989 is taken from Hugh Poulton's (1991) *Balkans: Minorities and States in Conflict,* 129–71.

3. In the atmosphere of glasnost, three human-rights organizations, formed in 1988 and 1989, took up the Turks' cause. The government expelled some dissidents and gave all Turks the right to leave the country. An apparently unexpected exodus of some 300,000 Turks ensued in the summer of 1989, causing

international embarrassment for Bulgaria. Zhivkov's ouster was led by Petŭr Mladenov, the foreign minister, and others in the foreign ministry who had to defend the anti-Turkish policy abroad. "On 18 January 1990, Todor Zhivkov was arrested and charged with, among other things, 'incitement of ethnic hostility and hatred'" (Poulton 1991:165).

4. The older style of Kutev, with its relatively simple drone-based approach and triadic harmonies can be compared to the more dissonant and modulatory approach of younger arrangers such as Krasimir Kyurkchiiski on *Le Mystère des voix bulgares,* vol. 1, Nonesuch 79165.

5. Levy (1985:113) reports seeing pictures from the period shortly before and after World War II of Rhodope wedding orchestras with gaida and Western instruments together. As he points out, such combinations were rarely if ever seen in the 1970s when he worked there. By 1988, however, a Rhodope wedding band appeared at the Stambolovo festival that included the Rhodope *kaba gaida.*

6. Lampe (1986:210–12) describes profits to be reaped from personal garden plots "which typically adjoined the family house. . . . Special measures to expand the number, activities and market sales of the personal plots did not begin until 1971. . . . From 1974 onwards, peasant households have been permitted to lease additional plots and to have free access to fertilizer, fodder seed and equipment, from the agricultural complex" (210). By 1979 private plots were supplying a significant portion of foodstuffs to the urban market. "The more successful extended-family enterprises earn profits that are large enough to pay for luxuries like second cars or lavish weddings" (212).

7. Many of the terms and ideas in this paragraph, like "proletarianization," "mixed economy," and "second economy," are taken from Ivan Szelenyi's (1988) *Socialist Entrepreneurs.* In studies of industrial Hungary, he and his co-researchers found that workers had a good deal of countervailing power over "bureaucratic despotism" and the source of the power was the "second economy" where workers were making high incomes. The "real source of countervailing popular power is self-employment [and] petty commodity production" (8).

8. Sonia Tamar Seeman pointed out (pers. comm., 1993) that there was considerable mutual influence between Bulgarian and Macedonian Gypsy musicians. Two of the most famous, Bulgaria's Ivo Papazov and Macedonia's Ferus Mustafov, even traded tunes over the phone at a time when Ivo's recordings were prohibited in Bulgaria.

9. See Silverman 1988 for an extensive account of Bulgarian wedding music.

10. Donna Buchanan's 1991 dissertation contains an extended analysis of constructions of Bulgarian national identity (36–125) and the way 'folk orchestras' [*narodni orkestri*] represent them (229–61).

11. Not coincidentally, Ivo Papazov's second recording released in the West on Hannibal Records was entitled *Balkanology* (HNCD 1363) and demonstrated his mastery of many different Balkan styles that he was not allowed to record in Bulgaria for most of the 1980s These include "Mladeshki [youth] Dance" in Turkish style, "Ergenski [bachelors'] Dance" in Macedonian style, "Tsiganska Ballada" [Gypsy ballad] in Romanian Gypsy style, and "Proleten [Spring] Dance" in Greek style. See also the recording notes, written by Carol Silverman.

12. On the Gypsies' ability to operate outside state control, Silverman (1986:60) writes, "Gypsies display an attitude of freedom and daring in cultural and economic spheres which other Bulgarians do not enact. They supplement wage income with free market enterprise, whether legal or not, just as they play and dance their music, whether legal or not."

13. Frank Dubinskas (1983) and Mark Forry (1986) discuss festivals and "festivalization" in Yugoslavia. Competitive festivals as means of ideological and aesthetic control are widespread in Europe, including nontotalitarian countries like Great Britain, Ireland, Norway, and Sweden.

14. See Levy 1985 for an extensive account of the Rhodope version of the Bulgarian gaida.

15. Carol Silverman (1988:3) quotes the musicologist Todor Todorov describing Ivan Milev in 1986 as an "artist who grasps the audience and leads them to react violently to every one of his gestures." His use of "violent" was probably not intended to invoke the political context of violent resistance to forced assimilation of the Turks, and yet, in its similarity to "aggressive," provides insight into how Bulgarian cultural authorities "read" wedding music at that time. I am grateful to Carol Silverman for permission to quote from her unpublished manuscript.

16. Perhaps the first recording of Bulgarian "folk jazz" was released on a record entitled *Folk Dzhaz Bend Plovdiv* [Folk Jazz Band Plovdiv]. It combined a jazz group called "Jazz Line" consisting of keyboards, guitar, bass, and percussion with well-known wedding musicians Petŭr Ralchev, Trifon Trifonov, and Delcho Mitev.

17. The irony Stoyan may have intended here, but which was too delicate to discuss, was that the composer, an ethnic Bulgarian, was less able to construct a pure Bulgarian melody than Stoyan was, the irony proceeding from that fact that he was considered by some musicians to be a Gypsy even though he was able to play Bulgarian music purely. The issue of who is and who is not a Gypsy is difficult because it is, like so many cases of ethnicity, largely a matter of construction by the self and others, and entails matters of appearance, language, kinship, and behavior. While aspects of Stoyan's appearance and family background index him as Gypsy, his behavior, musical style, language, and self-identification are clearly Bulgarian.

18. In Yugoslavia, for example, the folk-derived popular music that was so popular in Bulgaria as heard on Yugoslav radio was called 'newly composed folk music' and is discussed at some length in Rasmussen 1991 and Kos 1971.

19. One of the effects of centralized control was that only a relatively small number of musicians and singers were ever recorded. They tended to be primarily those who worked in the Radio orchestra and chorus and secondarily some singers and musicians with the Kutev ensemble. Many fine musicians from around the country never recorded. When I asked Kosta Kolev why they recorded so few artists and typically those at Radio Sofia, he said, "We don't have the material basis to produce more. I made three records for the Sliven Ensemble, but we had to promise to buy 1,000 copies and the recordings just sit there." So a small market for folk music, or at least a market with no connec-

tion between supply and demand, created part of the problem, but central control and a particular nationalistic, artistic goal were also at work.

20. Things have changed even further since what Bulgarians call 'the events' of November 1989, when Todor Zhivkov, the long-time Communist party chairman, was ousted and the country began a fitful journey toward multiparty democracy.

10. Gaidari: The Next Generation

1. Geertz (1973:5) writes: "Believing, with Max Weber, that man is an animal suspended in webs of significance he himself has spun, I take culture to be those webs, and the analysis of it to be therefore not an experimental science in search of law but an interpretive one in search of meaning."

2. Female Bulgarian musicians are reported in the literature, but rarely. One of them, Pena Grozeva, a Pomak (Bulgarian-speaking Muslim) from North Bulgaria, can be heard singing and playing *tambura* on Bhattacharya's (1968) record. Kachulev (1965:42) reports that researchers discovered the previous year the first female gaidar [*gaidarka*], a woman he called *baba* [grandma] Desha Manafova, aged 68. She grew up herding sheep, preferred wearing a man's jacket and pants, and smoked. As a youth she played at school and at weddings; as she is quoted as saying, "In the village they called me 'manly' Desha, but who listened to them." Kachulev (43) prints a picture of her playing for a dance and points out that her daughter showed no interest in the instrument. Levy (1985:98) also mentions a female gaidar from the Rhodopes in the period before the 1960s, Choka Peevska.

3. Botusharov (1989:45) committed this interpretation to print in a somewhat roundabout way: "And if in the girl who sits modestly behind the music stand of a folk orchestra in the Western model there is nothing strange, this girl, having sunken her teeth into the wedding flute—with its well-known symbolic meaning in traditional culture—would at least have to disconcert us."

4. In her third year, Kotel hired Krŭstyu Velikov to teach gaida. According to Maria, "he is the biggest master of *kŭrma*," the technique of half holing to produce g$\sharp$', a half step below the tonic a'. She also demonstrated his technique, not used by Kostadin, of half holing the e' to produce f$\natural$'. If Kostadin needed that pitch, he covered the top half of the hole with tape or wax before beginning to play.

5. One of her collections is called *Piesi za gaida sŭs sŭprovod na piano* [Pieces for Gaida with Piano Accompaniment], Sofia: Muzika, 1988. Another collection to which she contributed gaida tunes is called *Avtentichni melodii za narodni instrumenti* [Authentic melodies for Folk Instruments] (Stoikov et al. 1988) which, despite its title, includes many of the difficult keys and chromaticisms new to the tradition. Although the need to reference authenticity fits the Institute's ideological goals, authenticity, in this case, certainly doesn't reference older practices.

6. Encho Pashov obtained ebony for his gaidas from friends in the United States, including the fine American gaida player and maker, Hector Bezanis.

7. I am reminded here of a similar metaphor used by the Shona of Zimbabwe

who say, "Mbira music without singing is like sadza without muriwo" (grain porridge without vegetables) (Berliner 1978:160–61).

8. The stylistic argument is not unique to the gaida. In interviewing Stoyan Velichkov about kaval technique, he complained that younger players use the thumb too much to ornament melodies in the highest range, while he used the first and third fingers. By playing in what he felt was a more subtle way, Stoyan felt that he was better able "to fill your soul" than younger players could.

9. In the less controlled environment after the demise of communism in November 1989, Ivan joined the Kutev ensemble and Tsvetanka the Radio choir, taking the positions of other musicians who left these ensembles in search of more money in the private economy and abroad.

10. Their record is called *Tsvetanka and Ivan Varimezovi* (Balkanton BHA 12180) and was recorded in July, 1987.

11. Stefan Mutafchiev's choral arrangements can be heard on *Le Mystère des voix bulgares*, vol. 3, Fontana 846 626, 1990, and his instrumental arrangements on *The Long Road: Teodosi Spassov, Stefan Moutafchiev*, Balkanton BHA 12215.

12. The distinction between *discourse* as event, with an ostensive reference to the surrounding situation and the various interlocutors present there, and *text* as the meaningful action that remains as a residue of discourse and that is then subjected to interpretation even by those not witness to the original discourse is taken from Ricoeur (1981) particularly the chapter, "The Model of the Text: Meaningful Action Considered as a Text," 197–221.

11. Kostadin and Todora at Home

1. Balkana was the invention of Joe Boyd, an American record producer working out of England, and Rumyana Tsintsarska, a director of folk music programming for Radio Sofia. It included two established small groups from the Radio ensemble: the Trakiiska Troika ['Thracian Trio'] of Stoyan Velichkov, kaval; Mihail Marinov, gŭdulka; and Rumen Sirakov, tambura; and the Trio Bŭlgarka ['Trio Bulgarian woman']. Four individuals rounded out the group: Kostadin Varimezov on gaida, Ognyan ("Jimmy") Vasilev, who played tŭpan for both the Kutev and Radio ensembles, Georgi Musurliev, Rhodope gaida, and Rumen Rodopski, Rhodope singer. Boyd and Tsintsarska recorded the group in 1987 for a CD on Hannibal (*Balkana: The Music of Bulgaria*, HNCD 1335); they have since toured (minus the Rhodope musicians) Europe, the United States, Japan, and Australia.

2. Elsie Dunin (1971, 1973) describes the ritual character of *kyuchek* dancing among Gypsy women in Skopje, where the dance is called *čoček* [pronounced "chochek"]. She contrasts its ritual purpose in sex-segregated circumcision and wedding celebrations with its reputation as entertainment provided by Gypsies to a non-Gypsy audience. The sexual interpretations of the dance movements are manifested primarily in mixed company or when performed for non-Gypsies, and some Gypsy women considered them tasteless displays when performed in those contexts. Among women, the sexual connotations were apparently minimized, and they drew curtains to shut out the male gaze.

3. One's nameday is the day in the church calendar honoring the saint after

whom Bulgarians were traditionally named: Georgi/St. George; Kostadin/St. Constantine; Maria/St. Mary and so forth. Traditionally in Bulgaria namedays were celebrated rather than birthdays.

12. Truth and Music

1. The concern for truth and music and how it is expressed, interpreted, and known is also discussed in, among others, Becker and Becker 1981, Feld 1988a, Turino 1989, and Buchanan 1991. Their focus is variously on iconicity of style and metaphoric mediation in language. My focus has been on a less methodologically refined notion of experience and reference to a world, however expressed and interpreted.

2. Levin (1979:157) has a nicely skeptical attitude toward some of these issues of meaning and reference as they were being argued about in Soviet Uzbekistan: "In the final soup of Socialist Realist art, what truly reflects traditional reality, and what reflects a new, imposed reality, to hoist the theory by its own petards, seems a peculiarly arbitrary matter."

Discography

Balkanton, Bulgaria's national recording company, produced many important LP records and recently CDs, but they are not well-distributed abroad. A few relevant recordings are referenced in the text and CD examples. The following titles are more easily located and provide a good introduction.

Bhattacharya, Deben. 1968. *Songs and Dances from Bulgaria.* Argo ZFB 47.

Boyd, Joe. 1991. *Ivo Papazov and his Orchestra: Balkanology.* HNCD 1363.

Boyd, Joe and Rumyana Tzintzarska. 1987. *Balkana: The Music of Bulgaria.* Hannibal HNCD 1335.

Boyd, Joe and Rumyana Tzintzarska. 1988. *The Trio Bulgarka: The Forest is Crying (Lament for Indje Voivode).* Hannibal HNCD 1342.

Boyd, Joe and Rumyana Tzintzarska. 1989. *Ivo Papazov and his Bulgarian Wedding Band: Orpheus Ascending.* HNCD 1346.

Cellier, Marcel. 1987, 1988. *Le Mystère des voix bulgares,* vols. 1, 2. Nonesuch 79165, 79201.

Cellier, Marcel. 1990. *Le Mystère des voix bulgares,* vol. 3. Polygram/Fortuna 846 626.

Forsyth, Martha. 1981, 1983. *Traditional Song in Southwestern Bulgaria.* Two 60-minute cassettes available from Martha Forsyth, 51 Davis Avenue, West Newton, MA 02165.

Forsyth, Martha. *Two Girls Started to Sing: Bulgarian Village Singing.* Rounder 1055.

Lloyd, A. L. 1959. *Bulgaria,* Columbia KL 5378.

Lloyd, A. L. 1964. *Folk Music of Bulgaria.* Topic 12T 107.

Music of Bulgaria. 1955. Nonesuch 72011.

Raim, Ethel, and Martin Koenig. 1970a. *A Harvest, A Shepherd, A Bride: Village Music of Bulgaria.* Nonesuch 72034.

Raim, Ethel, and Martin Koenig. 1970b. *In the Shadow of the Mountain: Songs and Dances of Pirin-Macedonia.* Nonesuch 72838.

References

Atanassov, Vergilij. 1983. *Die bulgarischen Volksmusikinstrumente: Eine Systematik in Wort, Bild und Ton.* Munich: E. Katzbichler.

Auerbach, Susan. 1989. "From Singing to Lamenting: Women's Musical Role in a Greek Village." Pp. 25–43 in *Women and Music in Cross-Cultural Perspective,* ed. Ellen Koskoff. Urbana: University of Illinois Press.

Baily, John. 1981. "A System of Modes Used in the Urban Music of Afghanistan." *Ethnomusicology* 25(1):1–40.

Bakalov, Todor. 1988. *Maistori na narodnata muzika* [Masters of Folk Music]. Sofia: Muzika.

Bartlett, Sir Frederick. 1932. *Remembering.* Cambridge: Cambridge University Press.

Becker, Alton. 1979. "Text-building, Epistemology, and Aesthetics in Javanese Shadow Theatre." Pp. 211–43 in *The Imagination of Reality,* ed. A. L. Becker and Aram Yengoyan. Norwood, N.J.: Ablex.

Becker, Judith. 1979. "Time and Tune in Java." Pp. 197–210 in *The Imagination of Reality,* ed. A. L. Becker and Aram Yengoyan. Norwood, N.J.: Ablex.

Becker, Judith, and Alton Becker. 1981. "A Musical Icon: Power and Meaning in Javanese Gamelan Music." Pp. 203–15 in *The Sign in Music and Literature,* ed. Wendy Steiner. Austin: University of Texas Press.

Benveniste, Emile. 1971. *Problems in General Linguistics.* Coral Cables, Fla.: University of Miami Press.

Berliner, Paul. 1978. *The Soul of Mbira.* Berkeley: University of California Press. Repr. 1993; Chicago: University of Chicago Press.

Blacking, John. 1967. *Venda Children's Songs: A Study in Ethnomusicological Analysis.* Johannesburg: Witwatersrand University Press.

———. 1974. *How Musical Is Man?* Seattle: University of Washington Press.

Blum, Stephen. 1975. "Towards a Social History of Musicological Technique." *Ethnomusicology* 19(2):207–32.

Botusharov, Lyuben. 1989. "Bŭlgarska narodna muzika ot gledishte na profesio-nalnata traditsiya na Iztoka" [Bulgarian Folk Music from the Point of View of the Professional Traditions of the East]. *Muzikalni Horizonti* 12/13:42–46.

Bourdieu, Pierre. 1977. *Outline of a Theory of Practice.* Cambridge: Cambridge University Press.

Buchanan, Donna. 1991. "The Bulgarian Folk Orchestra: Cultural Performance, Symbol, and the Construction of National Identity in Socialist Bulgaria." Ph.D. diss., University of Texas at Austin.

Caraveli, Anna. 1985. "The Symbolic Village: Community Born in Performance." *Journal of American Folklore* 98 (389):259–286.

Carterette, Edward C., and Roger A. Kendall. 1989. "Human Music Perception." Pp. 131–72 in *The Comparative Psychology of Audition: Perceiving Complex Sounds,* ed. Robert J. Dooling and Stewart H. Hulse. Hillsdale, N.J.: Lawrence Erlbaum Associates.

Cavanagh, Beverley. 1982. *Music of the Netsilik Eskimo: A Study of Stability and Change.* Ottawa: National Museums of Canada.

Chernoff, John Miller. 1979. *African Rhythm and African Sensibility.* Chicago: University of Chicago Press.

Clifford, James. 1988. "On Ethnographic Authority." Pp. 21–54 in his *The Predicament of Culture: Twentieth-Century Ethnography, Literature, and Art.* Cambridge: Harvard University Press.

Clifford, James, and George E. Marcus. 1986. *Writing Culture: The Poetics and Politics of Ethnography.* Berkeley and Los Angeles: University of California Press.

Coplan, David B. 1985. *In Township Tonight! South Africa's Black City Music and Theatre.* London, New York: Longman.

Cowan, Jane. 1990. *Dance and the Body Politic in Northern Greece.* Princeton: Princeton University Press.

Cowdery, James. 1990. *The Melodic Tradition of Ireland.* Kent, Ohio: Kent State University Press.

Crampton, R. J. 1983. *Bulgaria 1878–1918: A History.* Boulder, Colo.: East European Monographs. (Distributed by Columbia University Press.)

———. 1987. *A Short History of Modern Bulgaria.* Cambridge: Cambridge University Press.

Czekanowska, Anna. 1972. *Narrow-range Folk Melodies in Slavic Countries.* Krakow: Polskie Wydawnictwo Muzyczne. In Polish.

Danforth, Loring. 1989. *Firewalking and Religious Healing: The Anastenaria of Greece and the American Firewalking Movement.* Princeton: Princeton University Press.

Dooling, Robert J., and Stewart H. Hulse, eds. 1989. *The Comparative Psychology of Audition: Perceiving Complex Sounds.* Hillsdale, N.J.: Lawrence Erlbaum Associates.

Dubinskas, Frank. 1983. "Performing Slavonian Folklore: The Politics of Reminiscence and Recreating the Past." Ph.D. diss., Stanford University.

Dunin, Elsie. 1971. "Gypsy Wedding: Dance and Customs." *Makedonski Folklor* 4(7/8):317–26.

———. 1973. "Čoček as a Ritual Dance among Gypsy Women." *Makedonski Folklor* 6(12):193–98.

EBMK. 1967. *Entsiklopediya na bŭlgarskata muzikalna kultura* [Encyclopedia of Bulgarian Musical Culture]. Sofia: Bulgarian Academy of Sciences.

Erlmann, Veit. 1983. "Marginal Men, Strangers and Wayfarers: Professional Musicians and Change among the Fulani of Diamare (North Cameroon)." *Ethnomusicology* 27(3):187–226.

Feld, Steven. 1981. "'Flow like a Waterfall': The Metaphors of Kaluli Musical Theory." *Yearbook for Traditional Music* 13:22–47.

———. 1982. *Sound and Sentiment: Birds, Weeping, Poetics, and Song in Kaluli Expression.* Philadelphia: University of Pennsylvania Press.

———. 1988a. "Aesthetics as Iconicity of Style, or 'Lift-up-over Sounding': Getting into the Kaluli Groove." *Yearbook for Traditional Music* 20:74–113.

———. 1988b. "Notes on World Beat." *Public Culture Bulletin* 1(1):31–37.

Forry, Mark. 1986. "The 'Festivalization' of Tradition in Yugoslavia." Paper read at the 31st annual meeting of the Society for Ethnomusicology.

Gadamer, Hans-Georg. 1976. *Philosophical Hermeutics.* trans. and ed. David E. Linge. Berkeley and Los Angeles: University of California Press.

Gadamer, Hans-Georg. 1986. *Truth and Method.* New York: Crossroad.

Geertz, Clifford. 1973. *The Interpretation of Cultures.* New York: Basic Books.

———. 1983. *Local Knowledge.* New York: Basic Books.

Giddens, Anthony. 1990. *The Consequences of Modernity.* Stanford, Calif.: Stanford University Press.

Gourlay, Kenneth. 1978. "Towards a Reassessment of the Ethnomusicologist's Role in Research." *Ethnomusicology* 22(3):1–35.

Heidegger, Martin. 1962. *Being and Time,* trans. John Macquarrie and Edward Robinson. New York: Harper.

Herndon, Marcia, and Norma McLeod. 1980. *Music as Culture.* Norwood, Pa.: Norwood Editions.

Herzfeld, Michael. 1985. *The Poetics of Manhood: Contest and Identity in a Cretan Mountain Village.* Princeton: Princeton University Press.

Hobsbawm, Eric. 1983. "Introduction: Inventing Traditions." Pp. 1–14 in *The Invention of Tradition,* ed. Eric Hobsbawm and Terence Ranger. Cambridge: Cambridge University Press.

Hood, Mantle. 1960. "The Challenge of Bi-Musicality." *Ethnomusicology* 4(1):55–59.

Hopkin, John Barton. 1984. "Jamaican Children's Songs." *Ethnomusicology* 28(1):1–36.

Hristozov, Grozdan. 1974. "Bŭlgarskiyat radioslushatel i televizionen zrital i nashiyat folklor" [The Bulgarian Radio Listener and Television Viewer and our Folklore]." *Izvestiya na Instituta za Muzika* 17:141–48.

IFMC. 1953. "General Report." *Journal of the International Folk Music Council* 5:9–35.

Iordanova, Zheni. 1989. "Plashtane na folklorni izpŭlniteli" [Paying of Folk Performers]." *Muzikalni Horizonti* 12/13:108–18.

Ivanova, Radost. 1987. *Traditional Bulgarian Wedding.* Sofia: Svyat Publishers.

Jairazbhoy, Nazir. 1971. *The Rāgs of North Indian Music: Their Structure and Evolution.* London: Faber and Faber.

Japan Victor Company. 1990. "Europe III: Romania, Yugoslavia, Bulgaria, Albania." *JVC Video Anthology of World Music and Dance,* Tape 22. Distributed by Rounder Records.

Kachulev, Ivan. 1965. "Bŭlgarski duhovi dvuglasni narodni muzikalni instrumenti: Gaidi i dvoyanki" [Bulgarian Wind Two-voiced Folk Musical Instruments: Gaidas and Dvoyankas]. *Izvestiya na instituta za musika* 11:23–78.

Kaeppler, Adrienne. 1978. "Melody, Drone, and Decoration: Underlying Structure and Surface Manifestation in Tongan Art and Society." Pp. 261–74 in *Art in Society,* ed. Michael Greenhalgh and Vincent Megaw. London: Duckworth.

Kolinski, Mieczyslaw. 1973. "A Cross-Cultural Approach to Metro-Rhythmic Patterns." *Ethnomusicology* 17(3):494–506.

Katsarova, Raina. 1952. "Tri pokoleniya narodni pevitsi" [Three Generations of Bulgarian Female Singers]. *Izvestiya na Instituta za Muzika* 1:143–96.

———. 1957. "Narodni hora i igri v Strandzha" [Folk Dances and Games in Strandzha]. Pp. 359–423 in *Kompleksna nauchna strandzhanska ekspeditsiya prez 1955 godina,* ed. Petko Stainov and Lyuben Tonev. Sofia: BAN.

Kaufman, Nikolai. 1968. *Nyakoi obshti cherti mezhdu narodnata pesen na bŭlgarite i iztochnite slavyani* [Some Common Features of the Folk Song of the Bulgarians and the Eastern Slavs]. Sofia: BAN.

———. 1974. "Narodnite horove i ansambli i narodnite pesni, obraboteni ot tyah" [Folk Choirs and Ensembles and the Folk Songs Arranged for Them]. *Izvestiya na Instituta za Muzika* 17:193–202.

———. 1976. *Bŭlgarskata svatbena pesen* [The Bulgarian Wedding Song]. Sofia: Muzika.

———. 1984. "Iztorichesko razvitie na obrabotkite na narodnata ni muzika" [The Historical Development of Arrangements of our Folk Music]. *Bŭlgarska Muzika* 35(2):21–27.

Keil, Charles. 1979. *Tiv Song.* Chicago: University of Chicago Press.

———. 1982. "Applied Ethnomusicology and a Rebirth of Music from the Spirit of Tragedy." *Ethnomusicology* 26(3):407–411.

Keremidchiev, Gencho. 1954. *Narodniyat pevets Dyado Vicho Bonchev.* Sofia: BAN.

Kingsbury, Henry A. 1988. *Music, Talent, and Performance: A Conservatory Cultural System.* Philadelphia: Temple University Press.

Kitchener, Richard F. 1986. *Piaget's Theory of Knowledge: Genetic Epistemology and Scientific Reason.* New Haven: Yale University Press.

Kos, Koraljka. 1971. "New Dimensions in Folk Music: A Contribution to the study of Musical Tastes in Contemporary Yugoslav Society." *Review of the Aesthetics and Sociology of Music* 2(2):61–73.

Koskoff, Ellen. 1982. "The Music-Network: A Model of the Organization of Musical Concepts." *Ethnomusicology* 26(3):353–70.

Kremenliev, Boris. 1952. *Bulgarian-Macedonian Folk Music.* Berkeley and Los Angeles: University of California Press.

Krustev, Venelin. 1978. *Bulgarian Music.* Sofia: Sofia Press.

Lakoff, George, and Mark Johnson. 1980. *Metaphors We Live By.* Chicago: University of Chicago Press.

Lampe, John R. 1986. *The Bulgarian Economy in the Twentieth Century*. London: Croom Helm.

L'Armand, Kathleen, and Adrian L'Armand. 1983. "One Hundred Years of Music in Madras: A Case Study of Secondary Urbanization." *Ethnomusicology* 27(3):411–38.

Levin, Theodore C. 1979. "Music in Modern Uzbekistan: The Convergence of Marxist Aesthetics and Central Asian Tradition." *Asian Music* 12(1):149–58.

LeVine, Robert A. 1984. "Properties of Culture: An Ethnographic View." Pp. 67–87 in *Culture Theory: Essays on Mind, Self, and Emotion*, ed. Richard A. Shweder and Robert A. LeVine. Cambridge: Cambridge University Press.

Levy, Mark. 1985. "The Bagpipe in the Rhodope Mountains of Bulgaria." Ph.D. diss., University of California, Los Angeles.

Lloyd, A. L. 1967. *Folk Song in England*. London: Lawrence and Wishart.

Lomax, Alan. 1968. *Folk Song Style and Culture*. Washington, D.C.: American Association for the Advancement of Science.

Lord, Albert B. 1960. *The Singer of Tales*. Cambridge: Harvard University Press.

Loutzaki, Irene. 1984. "Dance and Society in a Complex Greek Peasant Community." M.A. Thesis, Queen's University, Belfast.

Madzharov, Panaiot, and Mihail Bukureshtliev. 1983. *Strandzhanski narodni pesni* [Strandzha Folk Songs: From the Repertoire of Kera Panaiotova Madzharova]. Sofia: Muzika.

Markoff, Irene. 1975. "Two-part Singing from the Razlog District of Southwestern Bulgaria." *Journal of the International Folk Music Council* 7:134–44.

Marshall, Christopher. 1982. "The Aesthetics of Music in Village Macedonia." Pp. 162–173 in *Cross-cultural Perspectives on Music*, ed. Robert Falck and Timothy Rice. Toronto: University of Toronto Press.

Marushiakova, Elena. 1992. "Ethnic Identity among Gypsy Groups in Bulgaria." *Journal of the Gypsy Lore Society*, Ser. 5, 2(2):95–115.

Marx, Karl, and Friedrich Engels. 1972. "The German Ideology." Pp. 39–47 in *Marxism and Art: Writings in Aesthetics and Criticism*, ed. Berel Lang and Forrest Williams. New York: David McKay Company.

Meintjes, Louise. 1990. "Paul Simon's Graceland, South Africa, and the Mediation of Musical Meaning." *Ethnomusicology* 34(1):37–73.

Merriam, Alan P. 1964. *The Anthropology of Music*. Evanston, Ill.: Northwestern University Press.

————. 1967. *Ethnomusicology of the Flathead Indians*. Chicago: Aldine.

Messner, Gerald Florian. 1980. *Die Schwebungsdiaphonie in Bistrica: Untersuchungen der mehrstimmigen Liedformen eines mittelwestbulgarischen Dorfes*. Tutzing: Schneider.

Miladinovi, Bratya [Brothers]. 1942 [1861]. *Bŭlgarski narodni pesni* [Bulgarian Folk Songs]. 3d Edition, ed. Mihail Arnaudov. Sofia: Dŭrzhavna Pechatnitsa.

Mitchell, Frank. 1978. *Navajo Blessingway Singer: The Autobiography of Frank Mitchell, 1881–1967*, ed. David P. McAllester and Charlotte J. Frisbie. Tucson: University of Arizona Press.

Music Educators National Conference. 1985. *Becoming Human Through Music.* Reston, Va.: Music Educators National Conference.

Nettl, Bruno. 1983. *The Study of Ethnomusicology: Twenty-nine Issues and Concepts.* Urbana: University of Illinois Press.

Neuman, Daniel M. 1980. *The Life of Music in North India: The Organization of an Artistic Tradition.* Detroit: Wayne State University Press.

Ognyanova, Elena, and Mihail Bukureshtliev. 1981. *Populyarni izpŭlniteli na narodna muzika* [Popular Performers of Folk Music]. Sofia: Narodna Prosveta.

Peirce, Charles S. 1931–1966. *Collected Papers.* 8 vols. Ed. C. Hartshorne and P. Weiss. Cambridge: Harvard University Press.

Pelinski, Ramon. 1981. *La musique des Inuit du Caribou: Cinq perspectives méthodologiques.* Montreal: Presses de l'Université de Montréal.

Perris, Arnold. 1985. *Music as Propanda: Art to Persuade and to Control.* Westport, Conn.: Greenwood Press.

Picken, Laurence. 1975. *Folk Musical Instruments of Turkey.* London: Oxford University Press.

Popov, Vesselin. 1993. "The Gypsies and Traditional Bulgarian Culture." *Journal of the Gypsy Lore Society,* Ser. 5, 3(1):21–33.

Poulton, Hugh. 1991. *The Balkans: Minorities and States in Conflict.* London: Minority Rights Publications.

Powers, William K. 1980. "Oglala Song Terminology." *Selected Reports in Ethnomusicology* 3(2):23–41.

Prashanov, Todor. 1968. *Narodni hora i rŭchenitsi za gŭdulka* [Folk Dances and Rŭchenitsas for Gŭdulka]. Sofia: Nauka i Izkustvo.

———. 1973. *Nachalna shkola za gŭdulka* [Beginning Method for Gŭdulka]. Sofia: Nauka i Izkustvo.

Pratt, Mary Louise. 1986. "Fieldwork in Common Places." Pp. 27–50 in *Writing Culture: The Poetics and Politics of Ethnography,* ed. James Clifford and George E. Marcus. Berkeley and Los Angeles: University of California Press.

Rabinow, Paul. 1977. *Reflections on Fieldwork in Morocco.* Berkeley and Los Angeles: University of California Press.

Rasmussen, Ljerka Vidic. 1991. "Gypsy Music in Yugoslavia: Inside the Popular Culture Tradition." *Journal of the Gypsy Lore Society,* Ser. 5, 1(2):127–39.

Redfield, Robert, and Milton Singer. 1954. "The Cultural Role of Cities." *Economic Development and Cultural Change* 3:53–73.

Redhouse. 1968. *Redhouse Yeni Türkçe-İngilizce Sözlük.* Istanbul: Redhouse Yayinevi.

Reiche, J. P. 1970. "Stileelemente südturkischen Davul-Zurna-Stücke." *Jahrbuch für musikalische Volks- und Völkerkunde* 5:5–54.

Rice, Timothy. 1971. "Music of a Rhodope Village in Bulgaria." M.A. thesis, University of Washington, Seattle.

———. 1974. "The Origin of Folk Orchestras in Bulgaria." Pp. 11–13 in *Balkan Arts Traditions,* ed. Martin Koenig. New York: Balkan Arts Center.

———. 1977. "Polyphony in Bulgarian Folk Music." Ph.D. diss., University of Washington, Seattle.

———. 1980a. "Aspects of Bulgarian Musical Thought." *Yearbook of the International Folk Music Council* 12:43–67.

———. 1980b. "A Macedonian Sobor: Anatomy of a Celebration." *Journal of American Folklore* 93(368):113–28.

———. 1985. "Music Learned but not Taught." Pp. 115–22 in *Becoming Human Through Music*. Reston, Va.: Music Educators National Conference.

———. 1987. "Toward the Remodeling of Ethnomusicology." *Ethnomusicology* 31(3):469–488, 515–516.

———. 1988. "Understanding Three-Part Singing in Bulgaria: The Interplay of Concept and Experience." *Selected Reports in Ethnomusicology* 7:43–57.

Ricoeur, Paul. 1981. *Hermeneutics and the Human Sciences.* John B. Thompson, ed. Cambridge: Cambridge University Press.

Ricoeur, Paul. 1991. *From Text to Action: Essays in Hermeneutics, II.* Kathleen Blamey and John B. Thompson, trans. Evanston, Ill.: Northwestern University Press.

Rosaldo, Renato. 1989. *Culture and Truth: The Remaking of Social Analysis.* Boston: Beacon Press.

Roth, Klaus, and Juliana Roth. 1982–83. "'Naj-nova Pesnopojka s Narodni Pesni': Populare Liederbucher und Liederheftchen in Bulgarien." *Jahrbuch für Volksliedforschung* 27/28:242–57.

Sachs, Nahoma. 1975. "Music and Meaning: Musical Meaning in a Macedonian Village." Ph.D. diss., Indiana University, Bloomington.

Sakata, Hiromi Lorraine. 1983. *Music in the Mind: The Concepts of Music and Musician in Afghanistan.* Kent, Ohio: Kent State University Press.

Sanders, Irwin. 1949. *Balkan Village.* Lexington: University of Kentucky Press.

Saussure, Ferdinand de. 1959. *Course in General Linguistics.* New York: The Philosophical Library.

Schafer, R. Murray. 1977. *The Tuning of the World.* New York: Knopf.

Schwarz, Boris. 1972. *Music and Musical Life in the Soviet Union, 1917–1970.* New York: W. W. Norton.

Seeger, Anthony. 1980. "Sing for Your Sister: The Structure and Performance of Suya *Akia.*" Pp. 7–43 in *The Ethnography of Musical Performance,* ed. Norma McLeod and Marcia Herndon. Norwood, Pa.: Norwood Editions.

———. 1987. *Why Suya Sing.* Cambridge: Cambridge University Press.

Seeger, Charles. 1977. *Studies in Musicology, 1935–1975.* Berkeley and Los Angeles: University of California Press.

Serafine, Mary Louise. 1988. *Music as Cognition: The Development of Thought in Sound.* New York: Columbia University Press.

Shepherd, John, Phil Virdon, Graham Vulliamy, and Trevor Wishart. 1977. *Whose Music? A Sociology of Musical Languages.* London: Latimer.

Silverman, Carol. 1983. "The Politics of Folklore in Bulgaria." *Anthropological Quarterly* 56(2):55–61.

———. 1986. "Reconstructing Folklore: Media and Cultural Policy in Eastern Europe." *Communication* 11(2):141–60.

———. 1988. "Contemporary Wedding Music [in Bulgaria]." Manuscript.

———. 1989. "The Historical Shape of Folklore in Bulgaria." Pp. 149–58 in *Folklore and Historical Process.* Zagreb: Institute of Folklore Research.

Singer, Milton B. 1972. *When a Great Tradition Modernizes: An Anthropological Approach to Indian Civilization.* New York: Praeger.

Slobin, Mark. 1971. "Conversations in Tashkent." *Asian Music* 2(2):7–13.

———. 1992. "Micromusics of the West: A Comparative Approach." *Ethnomusicology* 36(1):1–87.

Sloboda, John A. 1985. *The Musical Mind: The Cognitive Psychology of Music.* Oxford: The Clarendon Press.

Stalin, Josef. 1972. "Marxism in Linguistics." Pp. 80–87 in *Marxism and Art: Writings in Aesthetics and Criticism,* ed. Berel Lang and Forrest Williams. New York: David McKay Company.

Stamov, Stefan, ed. 1972. *The Architectural Heritage of Bulgaria.* Sofia: Tehnika.

Stoikov, Nikolai, and Vasilka Spasova. 1989. *Pesni za naroden hor sŭs sŭprovod na naroden orkestŭr* [Songs for Folk Choir with Accompaniment by Folk Orchestra]. Sofia: Muzika.

Stoin, Elena. 1981. *Muzikalno-folklorni dialekti v Bŭlgaria* [Musical-Folklore Dialects in Bulgaria]. Sofia: Muzika.

Stoin, Elena, and Ivan Kachulev. 1958. *Bulgarski sŭvremenni narodi pesni* [Bulgarian Contemporary Folk Songs]. Sofia: Bulgarian Academy of Sciences.

Stoin, Vasil. 1928. *Narodni pesni ot Timok do Vita* [Folk Songs from the Timok to the Vita (Northwest Bulgaria)]. Sofia: Ministry of Public Instruction.

———. 1939. *Bŭlgarski narodni pesni ot iztochna i zapadna Trakiya* [Bulgarian Folk Songs from Eastern and Western Thrace]. Sofia: Institute of Thracian Culture.

Stoikov, Nikolai, et al. 1988. *Avtentichni Melodii za Narodni Instrumenti* [Authentic Melodies for Folk Instruments]. Sofia: Muzika.

Stone, Ruth M., and Verlon L. Stone. 1981. "Event, Feedback and Analysis: Research Media in the Study of Music Events." *Ethnomusicology* 25(2):215–25.

Stoyanova, Maria. 1988. *Piesi za gaida sus sŭprovod na piano* [Pieces of Gaida with Piano Accompaniment]. Sofia: Muzika.

Sudnow, David. 1978. *Ways of the Hand: The Organization of Improvised Conduct.* Cambridge: Harvard University Press.

Sugarman, Jane. 1988. "Making Muabet: The Social Basis of Singing among Prespa Albanian Men." *Selected Reports in Ethnomusicology* 7:1–42.

———. 1989. "The Nightingale and the Partridge: Singing and Gender among Prespa Albanians." *Ethnomusicology* 33(2):191–215.

Svitova, K. G. 1966. *Narodnye pesni Brianskoi oblasti* [Folk Songs from the Briansk Region]. Moscow: Muzyka.

Szelenyi, Ivan. 1988. *Socialist Entrepreneurs: Embourgeoisement in Rural Hungary.* Cambridge: Polity Press.

Titon, Jeff Todd. 1988. *Powerhouse for God: Speech, Chant, and Song in an Appalachian Baptist Church.* Austin: University of Texas Press.

Titon, Jeff Todd, ed. 1984. *Worlds of Music: An Introduction to the Music of the World's Peoples.* New York: Schirmer.

Todorov, Todor. 1978. *Sŭvremennost i narodna pesen* [Modern Times and Folk Song]. Sofia: Muzika.

Turino, Thomas. 1989. "The Coherence of Social Style and Musical Creation among the Aymara in Southern Peru." *Ethnomusicology* 33(1):1–30.

Turner, Victor W. 1969. *The Ritual Process: Structure and Anti-structure.* London: Routledge and Kegan Paul.

Turner, Victor, and Edward M. Bruner. 1986. *The Anthropology of Experience*. Urbana: University of Illinois Press.

Tyler, Stephen A. 1986. "Post-Modern Ethnography: From Document of the Occult to Occult Document." Pp. 122–40 in *Writing Culture: The Poetics and Politics of Ethnography*, ed. James Clifford and George E. Marcus. Berkeley and Los Angeles: University of California Press.

Tylor, E. B. 1871. *Primitive Culture*. London: J. Murray.

Vander, Judith. 1988. *Songprints: The Musical Experience of Five Shoshone Women*. Urbana: University of Illinois Press.

Vazov, Ivan. 1976 [1894]. *Under the Yoke: A Novel*. Sofia: Sofia Press.

Wade, Bonnie. 1985. *Khyal: Creativity within North India's Classical Music Tradition*. New York: Cambridge University Press.

Wallis, Richard, and Krister Malm. 1984. *Big Sounds from Small Peoples: The Music Industry in Small Countries*. New York: Pendragon Press.

Witherspoon, Gary. 1977. *Language and Art in the Navajo Universe*. Ann Arbor: University of Michigan Press.

Yung, Bell. 1984. "Choreographic and Kinesthetic Elements in Performances on the Chinese Seven-String Zither." *Ethnomusicology* 28(3):505–17.

Zaharieva, Svetla. 1987. *Svirachŭt vŭv folklornata kultura* [The Player in Folk Culture]. Sofia: Bulgarian Academy of Sciences.

Zemp, Hugo. 1978. "'Are'are Classification of Musical Types and Instruments." *Ethnomusicology* 22(1):37–67.

———. 1979. "Aspects of 'Are'are Musical Theory." *Ethnomusicology* 23(1):5–48.

Index

ability, differences in, 60–62
accordion: in postwar period, 200, 206,
    220, 224, 240, 252, 254, 263, 264, 272,
    278, 281; in prewar period, 50, 68; role
    of in Kostadin's learning, 332n.9
accordionists, 325n.20
action, meaningful, 300, 322n.13, 345n.12
aesthetics: as bodily experience, 113–15; as
    challenge to the state, 242; of classical
    music, 176–78, 257; of composition, 195,
    201; of composers, 183, 189; conflict of,
    301–2; of fixed repetition, 194; of folk
    ensembles, 256–57; of folk tradition,
    263; of intonation, 192; of the literate,
    205; of noise, 155–56; of ornamentation,
    77–80, 85–86, 192; of performance,
    103–13; postwar, 176, 259; of quantity,
    296–97; of singing style, 116, 176; of
    song selection, 58–60; state's, 246, 248;
    of state vs. second economy, 252–54; of
    villagers, 206
age, hierarchies of, 96–97, 139
agent. *See* individual
aggression. *See under* metaphors
agriculture, Bulgarian, 324n.10
akŭl (mind), 113–15
Albania, singing style in, 336n.17
alienation, 232
amateurism, artistic, 215–17, 224, 252, 296
anestinaria. See firewalking
anniversaries, 294
anthropology, cognitive, 320n.2, 324n14

antiphony, 141, 153
appropriation: of Bulgarian music by
    Americans, 5, 103; definition of, 6; non-
    verbal, 7; by individuals, 32; of lived ex-
    perience, 20, 320n.7; as losing the self,
    73; performative, 7, 114; for scholarly
    purposes, 5; of tradition, 14, 15, 72; as
    truth, 305; of village music by the state,
    180–83; of world music, 323n.4
Argirov, Yashko, 247
arrangements: choral, 177–78, 205, 207,
    213, 215–16, 278, 324n.15, 338n.12,
    345n.11; history of, 340n.6, 342n.4; as
    improvement, 181, 339n.15; by musi-
    cians, 272–73; truth of, 295; reception
    of, 203; state's goals for, 183–84; in So-
    viet Union, 339n.16. *See also* folklore, ar-
    ranged
art, socialist, decorative function of,
    182–83
articulation. *See under gaida*
Atanasov, Nikola, 219
Atanasov, Pece, 329n.18
atheism, 239

bagpipe, in Malta, 327n.26. See also *gaida*
bai, 328n.15
Balkana, 287, 345n.1
Balkanology, 342n.11
Balkanton: aesthetics of, 242, 301; fees
    paid by, 213; Ivan Varimezov's re-
    cordings for, 278–80; Kostadin's re-